THE COMPLETE home IMPROVEMENT BOOK

English Style
Details

Better Homes and Gardens®

THE COMPLETE home IMPROVEMENT BOOK

MURDOCH BOOKS®
Sydney • London • Vancouver • New York

Contents

Planning 7

• Look at what you have 8 • What you hope to achieve 10
• Special considerations 12 • Renovation ideas 16
• Making a plan 21 • Turning the plan into reality 25

The Framework 31

• Walls 32 • Ceilings 53 • Floors 65 • Stairs 87

Doors and Windows 91

• Doors 92 • Windows 112

Wet Areas 135

• Kitchens 136 • Bathrooms 157
• Laundries 199

Paint, Painting and Wallpaper 213

• How colour works 214 • Take the pain out of painting 216
• Preparation and painting 219 • Pointers for painters 224
• Applying paint 227 • Paint finishes 231
• Wallpaper 235

Storage and Furniture 239

• Storage 240 • Furniture 266

Practical Matters 285

• The workroom 286 • Workroom essentials 288
• Some simple how tos 292 • The dangers of renovating 299
• 'Green' renovating 300

Index 301

Planning

In planning any home improvements the first step should be to assess what you have. Look at the whole house and consider how renovating a part of it will affect the older area. Living in an unrenovated house for at least a year, through all the seasons, is the best way to get to know its shortcomings. Your lifestyle and the number of people occupying the house are other important factors to take into account.

Good planning for your home improvements and renovations is vitally important. Mistakes can be costly as well as depressing to live with. People often begin with a 'wish list', but it is best to consider your budget first. Many grand schemes have had to be pared back after a visit to the bank manager! So, work out what you can afford and, if you have to borrow money, decide whether you can afford to pay it back over a specific period.

Planning your renovations should be an exciting and creative process and not something done in a rush; ideas, not to mention fashions, change. Look for inspiration in magazines, brochures and home exhibitions and keep a file of your favourite ideas. Visit houses for sale that are open for inspection in your neighbourhood to see how other people have handled renovating a house similar to yours. This can be a particularly useful method in ascertaining the sorts of changes your local council will allow. Knowing exactly what you want will make briefing the architect, builder and suppliers much easier.

Renovating an older house usually involves opening up the living areas to the outdoors. This combined living and dining room brings in more natural light and gives easy access to the garden through the French doors. By retaining the old fire surround and using polished timber floorboards and beams the look is warm and inviting as well as practical.

Look at what you have

The list of questions to ask yourself in the initial stages of planning may seem endless, but it is important to address them all if you are to achieve the desired result.

Layout

Is the layout of your house logical? How do you use the existing space? Are you making the most of it? Which way does the house face? Do you need to create more privacy? If you have a kitchen you can eat in do you really need a large, formal dining room as well? How often do you have guests to stay? If it's infrequently, a spare bedroom could be more useful as a study or workroom. In an older house, an out-of-date bathroom may have the best view of the backyard and might be better relocated to the inside of the house. The space created could then be used as a living area that opens to the garden in the warmer months. How far are the functional areas such as kitchen, dining room, laundry and bathroom from each other? Does the laundry have easy access to the outdoor clothes line?

If you have a two-storey house with no bathroom upstairs you have several options. You could relocate the main bathroom upstairs and use the new space downstairs for a toilet and hand basin only; convert a smaller upstairs bedroom into an en suite; or, if you have plenty of space and five or six occupants, you may want two full bathrooms. Bear in mind that relocating plumbing can be an expensive exercise.

Urban

Older houses in the inner city have become highly desirable as they

ABOVE: The same tiles for interior and outdoors create unity and spaciousness.

RIGHT: Existing columns support the ceiling beams and align with the island bench.

BELOW: From the kitchen out to the verandah, this kitchen-cum-family room brings the family together every day, and it's all achieved by removing the wall between the two rooms and installing a partition wall to create a cosy corner for the dining table.

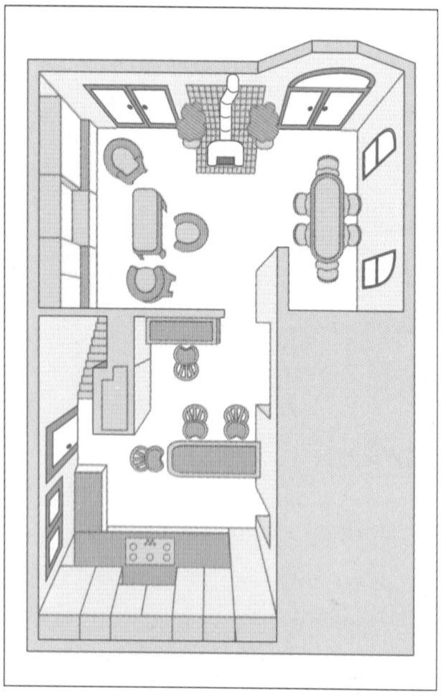

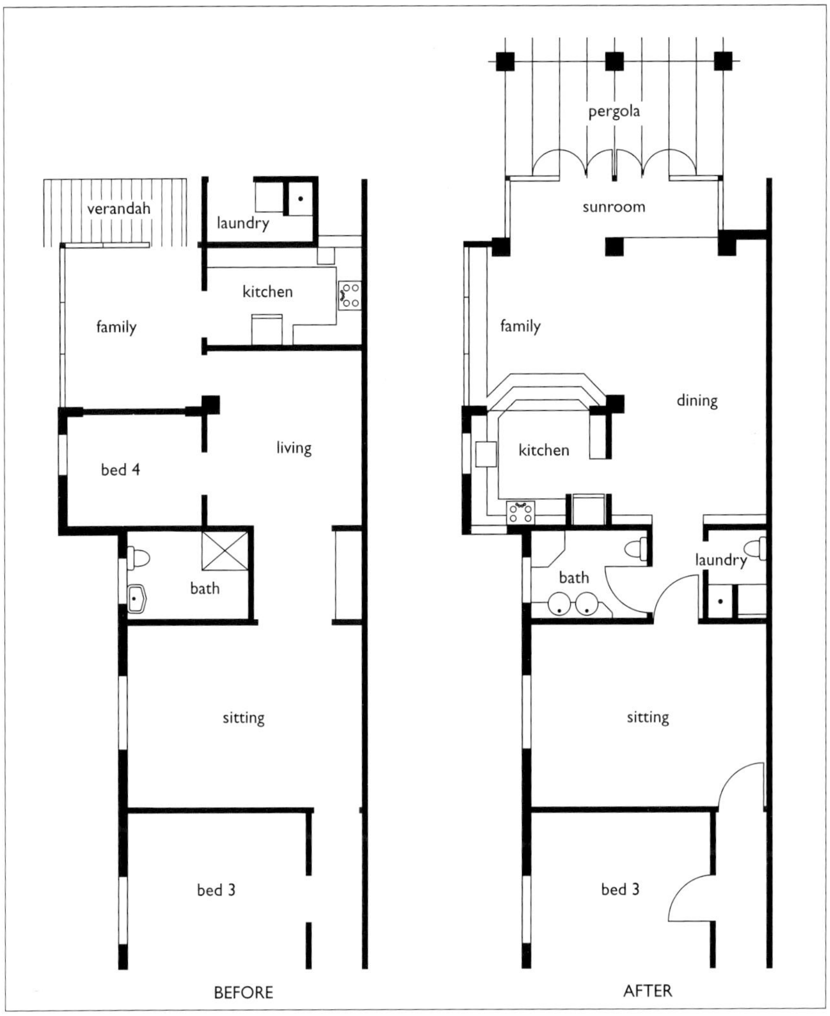

LEFT: Before renovation, the rear section of this turn-of-the-century semi was a good example of space that hadn't been used to the best advantage. For example, the kitchen was in the middle of the house's back section, leaving only small rooms either side of it. The laundry was makeshift and had the best garden view of any room in the house. The bathroom's position was fine but the room needed refurbishing. The family room was too small. The fourth bedroom was tiny and, therefore, dispensable.

BELOW: This spacious, airy bedroom makes use of waste space under the eaves for wardrobes. A bed can also be placed in a slope where there isn't quite enough height to stand up straight, thus using all available space.

are close to the CBD for workers in the city and are generally affordable for first-home buyers wishing to renovate. Victorian terraces and semi-detached houses vary in size from tiny, one-bedroom workers' cottages to three- or four-level mansions, but they were not designed for today's lifestyle or to take advantage of the outdoors. A well-planned renovation that is sometimes only a reconfiguration of the existing space can make them attractive and functional for modern living. In many areas councils stipulate that the facade must be retained, but an open-plan, smooth-flowing living space can easily be achieved behind that facade. If the house is large and two-storeyed it is often the downstairs living area that requires the most thought as the bedrooms will generally be retained upstairs. A worker's cottage or single-storey semi presents more of a challenge, especially if the land area is small and you cannot extend the house area.

Suburban and rural

The advantage of living in the outer suburbs is that land space is not so restricted, so renovating can involve extending the house on one or two levels or adding a granny flat. You may want to add a garage and workshop that adjoins the house so that you can enter the house under cover. Rural areas, of course, do not have the space limitations of the city, but gaining access to builders and a range of materials and fittings can be more difficult.

What you hope to achieve

Once you are familiar with all aspects of your house you can more easily define what you hope to achieve. List your priorities in order. Think first about what you want, then consider how to achieve it. How much disruption will the renovations cause to your normal routine? In what order should the work be done? If you are planning major renovations it may be less disruptive to have the work done in stages, although builders generally prefer to get the job over in one stage.

Your ideal house

Your list of priorities should be closely related to your lifestyle. Do you want large indoor entertaining areas? How many people live in the house? Do you want to create one large living room out of two smaller rooms? Add an extra bedroom or bathroom? This is a good point at which to summarise the key features of your ideal home. It's not always possible to be specific at this stage but you should have some general goals, such as the need for a spare bedroom or separate laundry or workroom. This way your list will develop from your 'ideals' to 'how to go about achieving them'.

ABOVE: Efficient heating and storage are essential.

BELOW: Paint is an inexpensive way to make a change.

CENTRE RIGHT: Before — The setting here allows plenty of scope for extensions.

ABOVE: After — Adding another storey is a tidy option that doesn't encroach on the garden space.

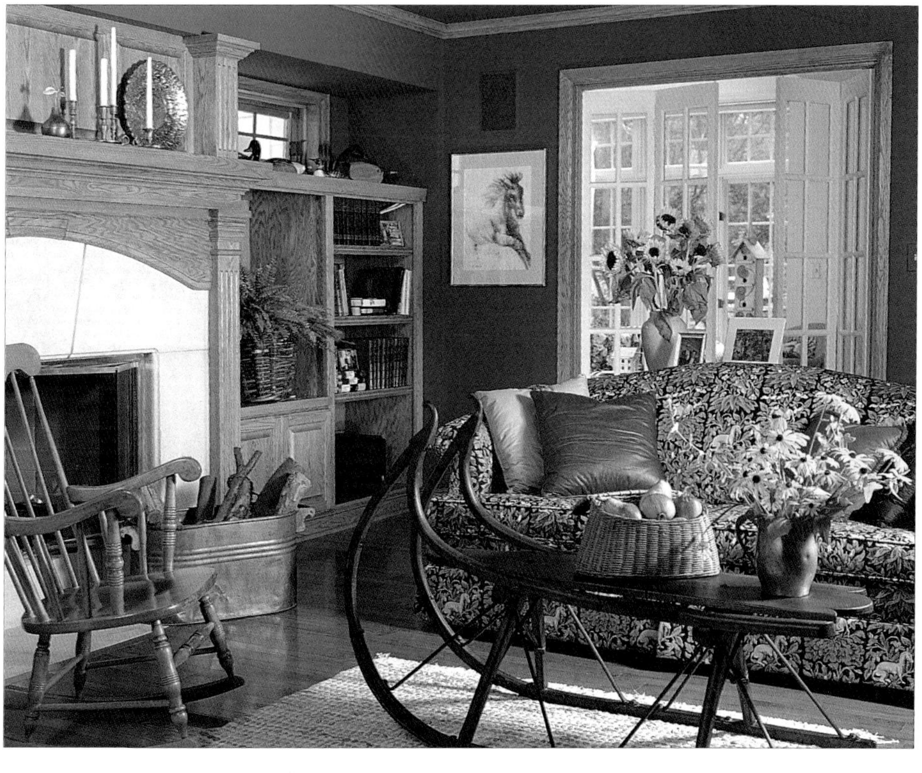

RIGHT: Interior French doors prevent this green from being too sombre.

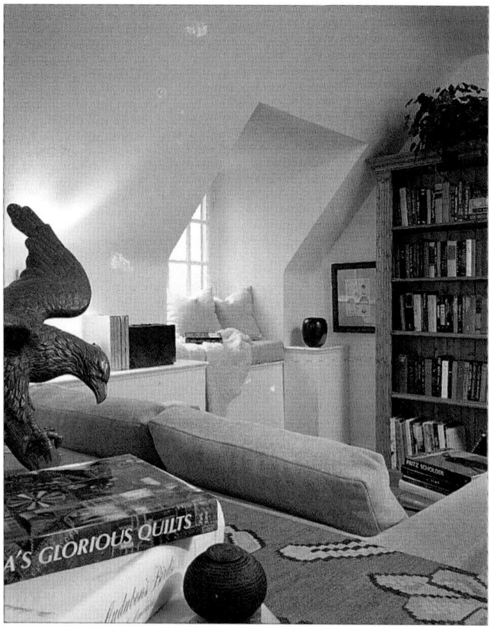

Special considerations

Although every household has its own special needs to consider when renovating a house, common aspects include the amount of space available and the number of people to accommodate and their lifestyle. By solving storage, light and room-size problems you will automatically make your house more attractive.

Limited space

Space may not be a problem if you have a large house on a suburban or rural block, but inner-city residents often find a bit of lateral thinking is in order to make the most of the available space.

Too few rooms?

If there are no longer enough rooms to go around now that everyone requires a room of their own and you need a study as well as a second casual sitting room, there are several solutions. Re-allocating the existing space may be the most obvious. This may mean merely changing the functions of some rooms which, therefore, requires mainly cosmetic changes such as painting and installation or demolition of built-in furniture. You may consider converting the small laundry at the back of the house into a study and stacking the washing machine and clothes dryer in a niche in the bathroom.

ABOVE: This library in a loft would serve equally well as a home office or parents' retreat. The wide window sill provides additional seating and the neutral colour scheme makes it an inviting space for work or reading and relaxation.

RIGHT: You may be lucky enough to find you have sufficient space under your existing roof without having to change the roofline. This is the cheapest form of attic conversion and, with a few minor structural changes to allow for windows, you can have your own secluded space such as in this charming retreat.

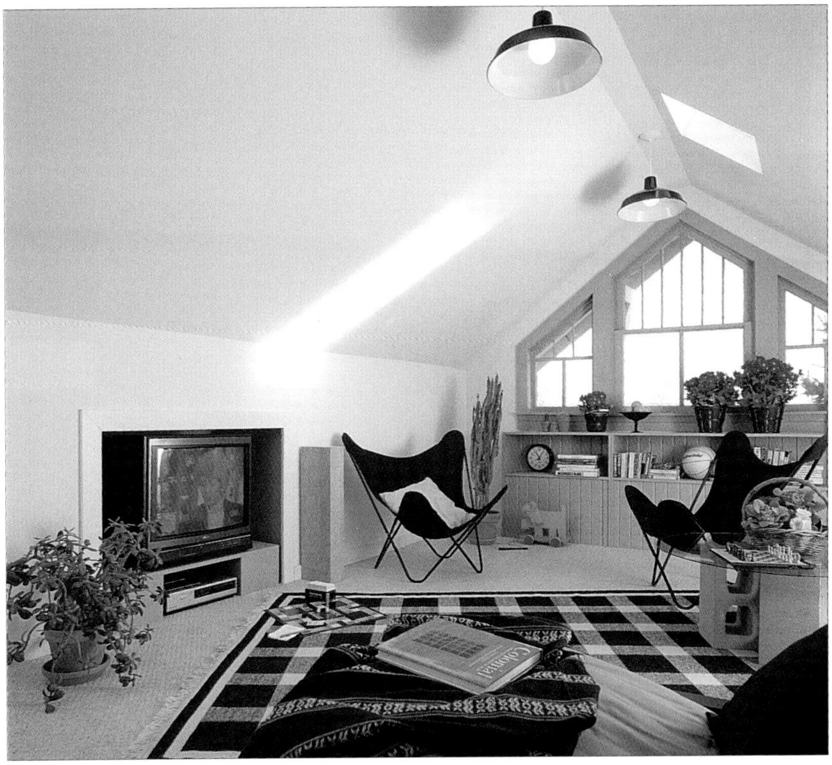

LEFT: Move your family room upstairs and leave downstairs free from the bustle. Keep the furnishings simple and uncluttered and carpet the floor to help deaden the noise of thumping teenage music and loud laughter. Children will appreciate their new-found freedom.

BELOW: This light casual living space is enhanced by polished timber floorboards.

Laundry facilities can now legally be located within the kitchen, so stacking the washing machine and dryer behind louvre doors in this area can be an option that doesn't infringe on the existing space.

Living space too cramped?

Many older houses and some modern bungalows have a series of small rooms that were neither designed to take advantage of the light nor for today's lifestyle. A small formal sitting room at the front of the house can be opened up to the adjacent room to create a feeling of spaciousness by knocking out the wall in between. Space must be allowed to flow around the walls of partitions. If the walls stop short at the top the ceiling line will be maintained and there will be an illusion of more space beyond. Some ordinary doorways can be expanded into larger openings for a flow-through effect. Opening up rooms this way with a timber beam across the opening may be all that is needed to create an alcove off a sitting room. To create a study area consider using such an alcove,

RIGHT AND BELOW: Storage can be located where you previously thought not possible: in the middle of a wall of glass or right where the bedhead is positioned, for example. In fact, the more difficult the problem, the more eye-catching the solution. Around the bed, your shelving will result in a central recess; in an expanse of windows it is an effective interruption which becomes a room's focus.

especially if a separate dining room or a formal sitting room is under-utilised. Space reflected in mirrors does give the illusion of a greater area. This is not a new idea and may seem obvious but it does in fact 'double' the room.

Not enough storage?

Are you making the best use of the cupboards you have? One solution is to intensify your main storage areas so that you can leave other parts of the house uncluttered. This applies to books as well as clothes or kitchenware. Alternatively, storage can be grouped. For example, placing the television, sound system, CDs and all your books together on one wall or in one corner will look better than if the different elements are scattered around the room. Streamline things to achieve storage order. Where possible always use a whole wall, lining up the different elements with continuous shelves or benches to create order. Exploit every opportunity. Spaces that can't be used for anything else can be used for storage.

Privacy

In country and suburban areas this is not usually an issue, but in high-density city areas where the houses are either very close together or joined in a row, privacy is an important aspect to consider when planning any renovation. If you are adding an additional storey adjacent to the neighbour's balcony you will want to ensure that they cannot see directly into your rooms. While you don't want to be overlooked by neighbours, you also don't want to be heard (or to hear them), so good wall insulation is essential to reduce noise as well as to retain a comfortable room temperature. Calculate just what the degree of exposure will be. Sometimes you can have uncovered floor-to-ceiling windows in the most unexpected places, simply by having them look into private outdoor spaces. Check the sight lines and decide whether you need

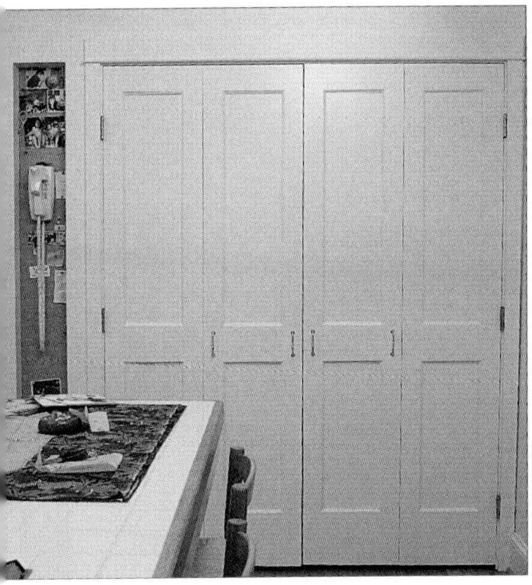

a screen at the window or at the boundary of your property.

Too plain?

An ordinary house with no special architectural features can be enhanced by knocking out a small window and replacing it with a larger one. Installing a shallow bump-out-style window will give a square room an extra dimension, and a window seat underneath it can be used for additional storage space. A small window over the kitchen sink can be replaced with a bump-out-style window with a large sill which creates extra bench space or an ideal position for potted herbs. By following the line of the roof with glazing the traditional window over the kitchen sink can become a wonderful conservatory, and a change in ceiling height will make the room seem less oppressive. Existing windows can be built in with pelmets with lighting above them, shelving between and a shallow sill-height cupboard. Shutters added to the windows remove the plain look and light is diffused. The entrance to the house can also be transformed with a new floor finish such as tiles so that it appears separate from the house and makes a pleasing impact. It can be further separated from the interior by the addition of a pair of internal French doors. In older houses the architraves are often in need of repair and, with the enormous range of mouldings now available, a completely fresh look can be achieved by changing architraves, cornices or skirting.

Not enough light?

Dark rooms that require the lights to be on during the day can have a gloomy feel. The addition of windows on the northerly aspect will make an excellent summer room that will also be comfortable in the winter sun. Glass bricks are another ideal solution because even where privacy is a concern the room can still be flooded with natural light. Skylights, especially on a room with a long easterly aspect and a narrow southerly one, are a good idea. In such situations by the time the sun reaches its summer midday intensity the room is in semi-shade.

ABOVE AND RIGHT: A work centre enables a usually untidy activity to fit harmoniously into any room in the house. And that is what making your home work for you is all about. Sewing, paper work or even children's hobbies can be hidden behind closed bi-folding doors. Effectively you get an extra room without losing the space.

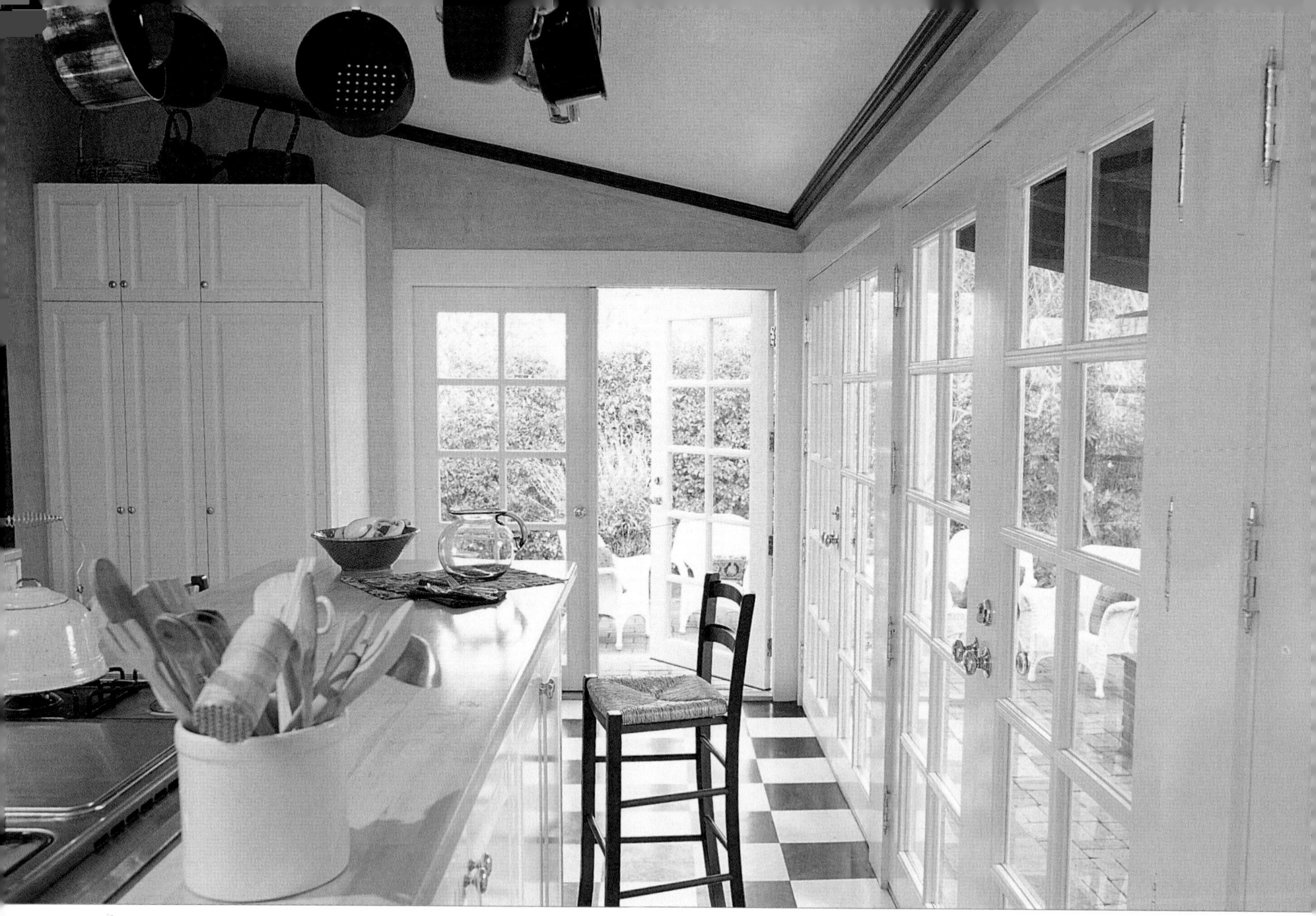

Renovation ideas

Whether you are opening up a room with French doors, creating additional storage, putting in a staircase to the attic or rearranging the functions and layout of your house, the possibilities are endless. The key is to make the most of the improvement opportunities your house offers; this need not mean that you need unlimited funds—an unlimited imagination is more helpful.

ABOVE: The path at the side of a house is often an under-used resource. Even if it's up against a paling fence, it's still an opportunity for a continuous line-up of French doors. These allow the cook to be included in backyard activities.

Have you thought of this?

If you feel your home is too small or it no longer meets your family's needs, the time has come for you to consider renovating by adding on or simply updating what you have. After all, who needs the trauma of a major house move and everything associated with it? Our interesting ideas may inspire you to action on the home front. Once you've survived the renovations, you will have a special place that you'll never want to leave.

Opening up

If you need more space without an extension, knocking down walls to create larger rooms could be the answer. The number of rooms you need depends on the make-up of your household. For families with teenagers, the emphasis is on privacy—everybody needs their own space. But what happens when the children leave home or if your house was designed for a larger family than yours? Homeowners often complain that their house isn't

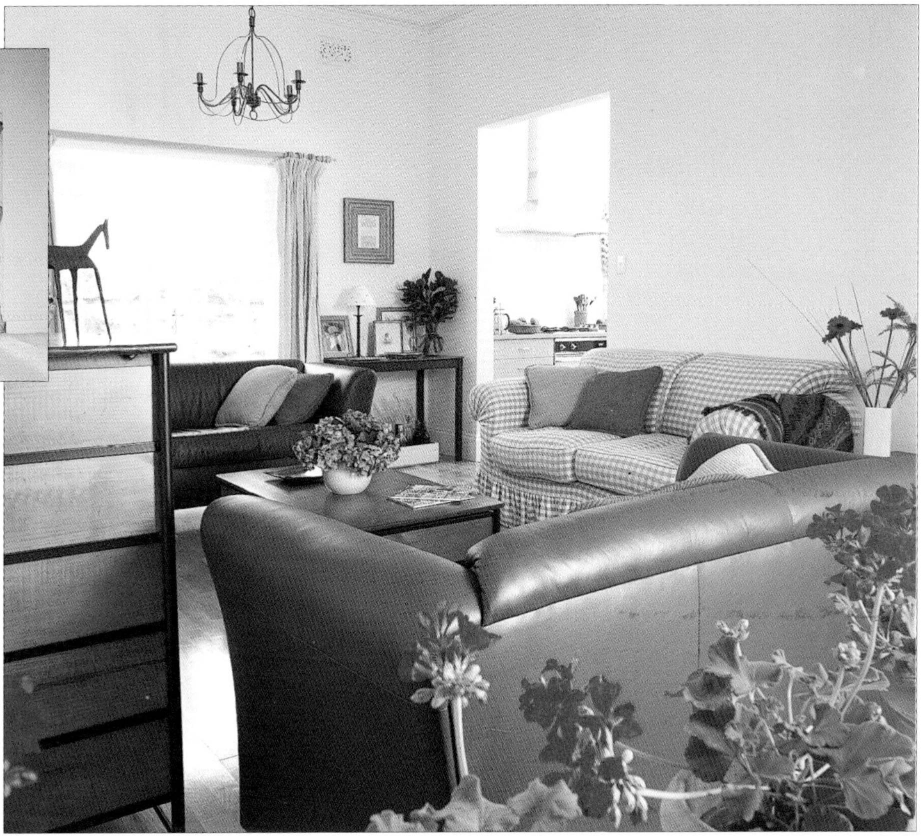

ABOVE: Knocking out a wall will make one well-proportioned living room.

RIGHT: A larger window brings more light to the new room.

LEFT: The living area flows into the kitchen/dining space.

BELOW: Before the transformation.

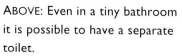

ABOVE: Even in a tiny bathroom it is possible to have a separate toilet.

LEFT: A small, well-designed and well-ventilated bathroom.

BELOW: Before—The drawing room of this Victorian terrace had been restored but because it was small, it was seldom used. The small room on the other side of the wall was in a similar situation.

RIGHT: After—By opening up the dividing wall and trimming the arch with plaster mouldings in keeping with the Victorian character, the entertainment potential of these two small rooms has been fully realised.

LEFT: Classical columns used in a large room make a grand division between dining and living areas. These are made of fibreglass and are purely decorative. The overhead steel beam, concealed in the plaster bulkhead, spans the full 3.75 m.

BELOW: French doors are a quick and effective way to give any room an extra dimension. As well as creating light, they provide easy access to the outdoors.

spacious enough but, at the same time, they often have one or even two rooms that are hardly used. The solution seems obvious — if you want larger spaces, you need fewer rooms. When a house needs more useable space, 'opening up' or knocking down walls between rooms and installing archways is one of the most common methods. Walls, however, don't just separate rooms; they also hold up the roof and the floors above. Therefore, knocking out walls is a job for a professional, particularly if they are made of masonry and require the installation of a beam (or lintel).

But before anybody starts knocking down walls, make sure you've thought about the new room you're creating. Will the shape of this enlarged room suit your needs? Will removing the wall deprive you of privacy or make the placement of furniture difficult? How will the new room affect the heating and lighting? While a professional builder will handle the structural detail, it will be up to you to ensure that the alteration will maintain the house's character. You must make sure that the archway is trimmed to match the other doorways. Architrave profiles will vary according to the period in which your house was built, so they must be matched. For very contemporary interiors, plain square-set corners are the most suitable.

Look up!

Many older single-storey houses have vast attic space and a lot of local councils are now more lenient about both height limitations and floor-to-site area ratios. In fact, there is no requirement for a building permit if you want to use this area for storage only. If the attic area is opened up for storage with the use of a drop-down ladder, you will have the ease of access without the problem of putting in a staircase. If you want to convert the area to living space, either for a

bedroom or a study, then the usual building and planning permits are necessary, and it is important to remember that the requirements vary at each local council.

If you are thinking of adding a top floor, using a series of metal railings to 'close off' the staircase will maximise the feeling of spaciousness by letting light and visual space flow. The same principle applies to the ceiling treatment—leave the pitched roofline plastered and the rafters exposed. The bolts and hardware now become functional and decorative features. Windows high on the wall above the staircase will not only throw light upstairs but will also filter it down to the floor below. Plan ahead to make the most of all your building options.

ABOVE: A generous opening (3.5 m) allows the dining room to spill out into the hallway when necessary.

LEFT: Where an extension is added, the old and new spaces usually have to be opened up into one another. This three-sided kitchen bench sits right on the boundary between the two. Because the new opening is so generous, however, the two spaces merge.

Making a plan

Having organised your priorities, the next step, and probably the hardest, is to develop your plan. It is very important to take your time and make sure you are completely satisfied with it.

Measure up the existing area to be renovated and do some rough sketches. These can be used to show the local council, who will tell you what is permitted before you go to the expense of engaging an architect or draftsperson. Your final plans will have to be submitted for approval by the council. Many councils have strict by-laws about tree removal so it is worthwhile checking these as well if you are extending your house and a tree is in the way. Once you have ascertained what is allowable and decided exactly what you want then you can have a plan drawn up to submit for council approval. Most councils take an average of six weeks to approve plans and copies will be sent to your immediate neighbours so that they may submit any objections. When making your plans, think of your future as well as your present requirements. If you are middle-aged, how many years do you intend living in your present house? Traipsing up and down stairs may not be so easy as you become less agile. With plenty of land space a granny flat or separate accommodation for teenagers is an option that can add value to the home. If you add a granny flat it must be easily accessible for the

ABOVE: The dining area is defined by its distinctive floor tiles.

occupant. However, another point to remember with teenagers is the time in the future when they leave home. You then may find you have spare bedrooms that are hardly used and could be turned into a study, workroom or TV room.

A new angle on design

Keep the 45° option in mind when you're making any changes to your home — not every corner has to be a right angle. Whether you are changing walls, doorways or kitchen and bathroom layouts, you should consider incorporating 45° angles into the design. Use this technique to solve some of your planning problems.

Family room + kitchen + garden = highly desirable neighbours

Work on perfecting this relationship if you are undertaking renovating projects. The best houses have the kitchen adjacent to both the outdoor living area and the family room. There's a very good reason for that. When you encourage these three functions to keep company with one another, you immediately create a home nerve centre which becomes the focus of family life. When planning renovations or additions, think how you can best achieve this harmonious household triangle. Here we show you five successful solutions.

BELOW: Opening up the interior allows you to reallocate space. Without actually building on, this house was made more generous by the removal of walls leaving a network of posts and beams. A disproportionately large laundry was then incorporated into the new open plan. The kitchen and informal sitting room are of similar size.

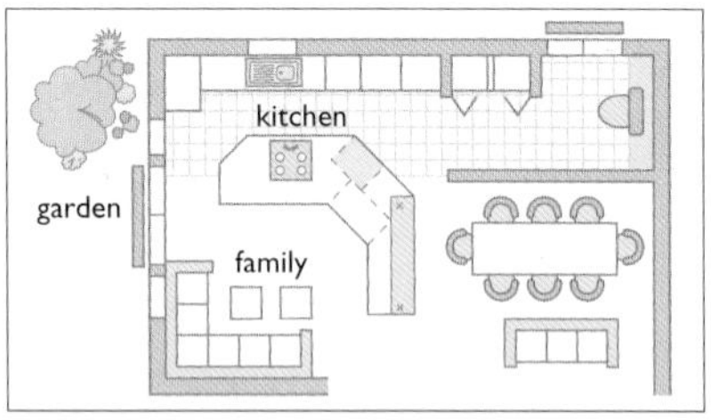

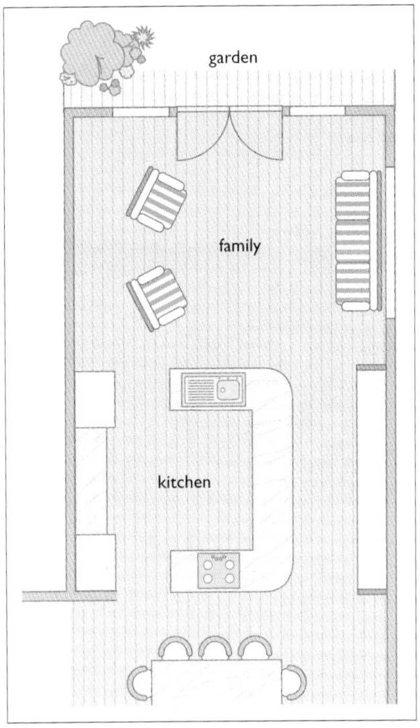

ABOVE AND RIGHT: Relocating the kitchen and family room in a new first floor addition allowed both view and aspect to be taken in. The outdoor living space takes the form of deck platforms which connect to the garden via external stairs. The result is a light and airy high-activity kitchen/family area.

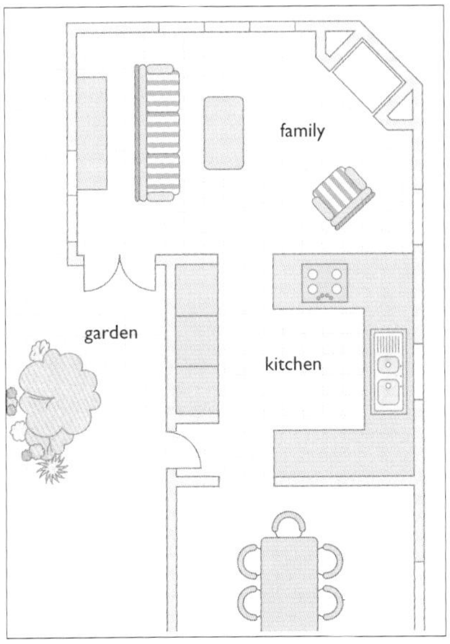

LEFT AND ABOVE: Adding on a family room made the existing kitchen internal rather than overlooking the backyard. So instead of looking like a tacked on after-thought it was thrust into the heart of the home, surrounded by the existing structure (with its formal dining room), the new room and the garden.

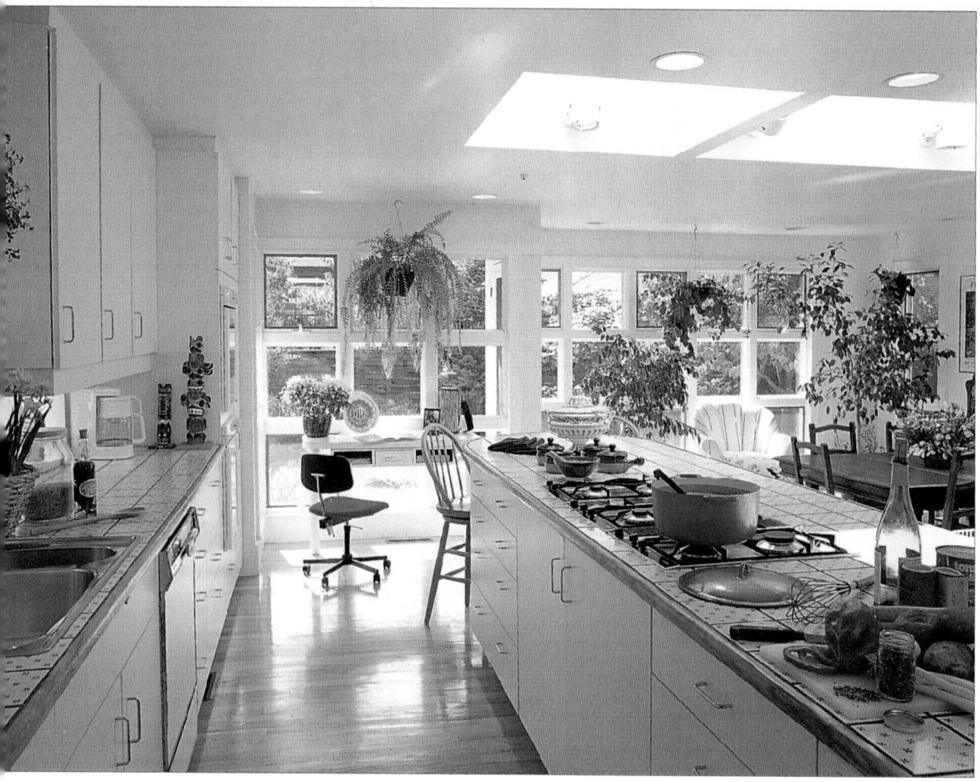

ABOVE: Knocking out a wall may be all that's necessary to make a space workable. This kitchen was already in place but it was behind closed doors. By replacing a wall with a steel joist, the food preparation area was drawn out into the new, open space. It still remains in its own separate alcove but with a new island that cadges just a bit of space from the adjoining room.

ABOVE LEFT: Tightening up the plan a little may set up a chain reaction. This kitchen used to spill out to where the table is now. The breakfast table used to be where the sunny sitting corner has been positioned. Cane chairs are a compact family room solution and the table can always be moved away from the wall when it has to perform its full function.

LEFT: Here a galley kitchen is practical and doesn't encroach on living and dining space.

Turning the plan into reality

BELOW: A modern room with a traditional look.

Now is the time to decide how you want the renovations or additions to be undertaken. You can do the work yourself or hire a licensed builder to do the job for you. Whichever approach you decide on, there is much preparation to do before the work is begun.

Surviving renovations

Renovating a house means mess, disruption to routine and sometimes, where major structural changes are involved, it may be necessary to move out for the duration. The prospect of finding temporary accommodation for family and pets is daunting, but it usually means that the work will be carried out more efficiently and quickly if the builder has unrestricted access to the premises. If you are not well prepared, turning your house into your dream home can be a nightmare. It's a good idea to talk to your local council before you begin; sometimes what you have in mind may not be permissible.

If you are clear about what the council will allow you can proceed with the plan. Once you have decided exactly what you want and you have a plan drawn up, you should obtain several quotes. The draftsperson or architect you use will supply multiple copies of the plan so that you can distribute

them simultaneously to several builders to quote from. It is very important to establish as accurate an idea of the costs as possible in order to avoid blowing the budget.

The disruption that results from renovating will be easier to handle if you remove as much clutter as possible from the house. Clear the working area to make the job easier and safer. If the rest of the house is clutter-free, it will be much easier to cope with the mess of the actual building.

Vacate the area being worked on. For example, if the kitchen is under construction, consider cooking in a microwave and a frying pan in the laundry.

Simplify your lifestyle during this time to avoid any added stress. Now is not the time for guests. Keep your children's routine as simple and uninterrupted as possible during this time. Don't be surprised if they react badly to the changes and inconveniences of renovating.

Doing the work yourself

Do the most difficult or time-consuming aspects first, so the remaining portion will not be as overwhelming if you run out of energy. Find ways to restrict the interruptions. If necessary, engage a baby-sitter to look after the children away from the house and take the phone off the hook.

If you lack motivation, write a list of all the benefits of having the job completed (e.g. room for the children to play, storage space for hobbies, etc.). Pin the list up on a wall on site. Keep reminding yourself that the reason for the renovations is to make life easier

BELOW: Keeping the result uppermost in your mind will help you survive renovations. Painting and adding the finishing touches yourself can be particularly satisfying after the builder's mess has been cleaned up. Yellow is an uplifting colour, and in this room it works well on the walls with the stencilled border adding an interesting detail.

BELOW: Before — This weatherboard cottage is typical of older unrenovated houses with utility rooms such as the bathroom and laundry overlooking an uninspiring backyard.

LEFT: After — Renovation has transformed this cottage with a large open plan living area opening onto a newly landscaped back garden.

and more enjoyable. Try to keep your mental image of the end result uppermost in your mind.

If a project seems overwhelming, write a list of all the jobs that have to be done in smaller, more manageable portions, in the correct order. Cross them off as you do them.

Set yourself some long- and short-term goals, along with realistic completion dates, and try hard to stick to them. Tell friends or family about your plans to renovate so that meeting their expectations will serve as an added incentive.

Don't allow yourself to be put off starting when you only have a short time to spend on the task. Doing a little at a time is better than none at all.

Complete one task before starting another. Having several incomplete assignments will be too disheartening. Promise yourself a treat or reward when you have finished the job.

Employing someone to do the job

Before employing someone to do the work, know exactly what you want done. Having a vague idea of what you want the builder to do is not enough. Unless you are in need of suggestions, you should have all the details of the work to be accomplished and the materials to be used ready to give to the prospective builder in order to obtain a fixed price. Changing your mind halfway through can be costly. If you do change your mind, obtain a written quote from the builder before proceeding. Recommendations for contractors can come from other tradespeople, local real estate agents, friends and acquaintances, local timber and hardware suppliers, or draftspeople and architects.

Always get three written quotes. Look for a professionally presented quote containing lots of detail. All quotes need to relate to the same brands and quality of materials. When the quote has been accepted it is time to look at the fine print of the contract. Sample contracts which can be adapted to your specific needs can be obtained from the Master Builders Association or appropriate local body.

While it is desirable to stay within your budget it is usually impossible to budget down to the last cent. Major renovations that come in under budget are rare. Those that go over by 20 per cent are very common, despite the best intentions of all concerned.

Use only licensed contractors. It is a requirement in all states for builders engaged in residential

Only sign a contract after:

- the types and quality of materials are agreed upon;
- a fixed price has been agreed upon;
- a time span has been agreed upon, including compensation for delayed completion;
- both parties understand what is to be done with old materials and appliances;
- the clean-up procedures have been agreed upon. Unless written into the contract, you could be left with a large amount of builder's rubbish to dispose of;
- agreeing that the final 10 per cent of the cost will be paid 30 days after completion, to allow time for building inspector's approval;
- all blank spaces have been filled in. Don't sign a contract that can be filled in later. Don't be pressured into signing a deal that only applies for that day. Give yourself plenty of time to read the contract, and make sure you read and understand the fine print! If you don't understand the jargon, ask advice.

construction to have a licence. If your builder has a gold licence it means he or she is experienced and has passed the appropriate building standard tests. If you have any doubts at all, you should contact your local licensing authority.

Consult your lawyer on matters regarding the contractor's legal obligations concerning personal liability, workers' compensation and property damage. He or she may wish to look at the contractor's insurance certificates. Most states also have compulsory insurance coverage for residential work linked with the builder's licence, so don't be tempted to use an unlicensed builder.

If you are working directly with a builder and not through an architect, give the builder a sketched plan as reference. Also include detailed notes clearly outlining your requirements for surface materials for floors, walls and ceilings, bathroom and kitchen fixtures and appliances as well as dimensions. You should also stipulate whether or not you wish to be consulted at every stage of the building process; if you don't consider this necessary you should still meet with the builder on a regular basis to discuss progress and any problems. Things do change as major works proceed and sometimes it is not possible to have something originally agreed to, so communication and flexibility are the keys to a successful builder–client relationship.

Don't accept verbal promises — every detail should be clearly spelt out in writing. Don't accept materials or fittings inferior to those you have requested. The builder should check availability of all these things at the time of quoting. As the renovation progresses, keep a close

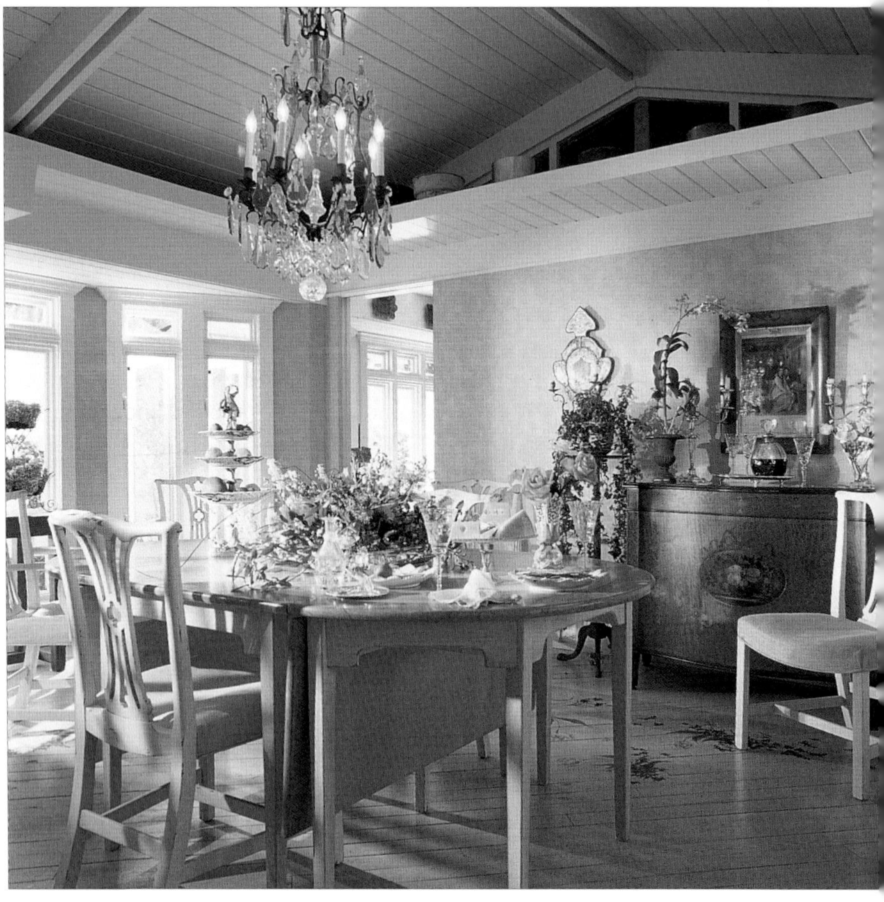

RIGHT: The wall's painted finish adds to this classic look.

LEFT: Warm colour and polished floorboards improve an older room.

check on every detail. If you are not happy with something, speak to the contractor immediately. Any delays can make mistakes more difficult to rectify.

Finding a good tradesperson

Ask anyone about his or her last attempt to get a tradesperson in and you'll probably get an earful. But it needn't be like that. Shop around. The best advice is: get a recommendation! Ask friends for the names of tradespeople they are happy with. Ask for references and inspect previous work. For a big job, it is worth getting three or four quotes.

Solving disputes

Discuss any complaints with your tradesperson first. But when disputes can't be solved easily, there are other, more formal remedies, including:

- mediation, through your state licensing authority or relevant trade associations;
- arbitration, through either statutory or trade bodies. Be careful of contracts which tie you to industry arbiters;
- consumer courts or tribunals. These provide cheap, accessible justice. Check the dollar claim limits for big jobs;
- court. This is expensive, time consuming and exhausting, but sometimes the last resort.

Tips

- Get recommendations and testimonials, and check references. Ask trade associations for advice.
- Check licenses and qualifications. Plumbers and electricians must be licensed in all states and territories, but requirements for builders and contractors vary. Check with your state licensing or registration body, asking especially about the contractor's insurance cover.
- Get itemised quotes and compare them.
- Once you've given the go-ahead, keep an eye on the work. Make sure the final bill is fully itemised, too. And check it!

The Framework

Walls, ceilings, floors and stairs are the framework of your house and you should ensure that this framework is solid before you even begin renovating. Whether you are creating additional space by knocking out walls, erecting new walls, installing a staircase or merely making cosmetic changes such as repainting walls and sanding floors, the framework will be affected to some extent.

It is important, especially in older houses, to check for any rising damp which can affect floors, walls and ceilings. This is often identified in pre-sale building inspections and can usually be treated quite easily. If you are painting damp-affected areas preparation is especially important; use an anti-mould wash before applying the final coat of paint, or an anti-mould paint, or both.

Erecting new walls and ceilings in older houses provides the opportunity to install effective insulation. In all terrace and semi-detached houses insulation serves not only to retain heat or cold but also to minimise noise.

There are many different types of staircase available in easy-to-assemble kit form. The one you decide on will be dictated by the amount of space you have available. In some cases a drop-down attic ladder is a good space-saving option. These ladders are also available ready made.

Knocking out walls, replacing floorboards, erecting new ceilings and installing staircases are all major structural changes that generally require expert help but, with a little know-how, you will be amazed at how much you can achieve yourself.

The ceiling is an important part of the framework but it is not often a decorative feature. In this house the unusual beams on a high ceiling are emphasised even though the whole room is monochromatic. The polished timber floorboards and dark framed doors contrast warmly with the coolness of the white.

Walls

A new finish can make a big difference to an old wall. But before you begin any improvements involving walls you should be aware of any potential problems or pitfalls.

Interior walls

Unless you take on a major remodelling project, you may never have occasion to break into an interior wall. Often, though, you need to know what's inside—and where—before you can perfom such simple tasks as hanging a heavy picture.

All wood-framed walls begin with a bottom plate nailed to the subfloor. The plate supports vertical studs, which in turn are nailed to a top plate.

Around any opening the studs are 'doubled up' for extra rigidity and topped off with a head, usually a 100 x 50 mm or 150 x 150 mm piece of timber installed on edge. Some walls also include horizontal nogging, usually at the 1.2 m level.

Finally comes the wall's surface, the only element you actually see. This might be plasterboard, fibrous plaster or panelling.

How to identify a bearing wall

Carpenters say all walls divide into two structural categories: bearing walls, which help support the entire house; and non-bearing walls, which support only themselves. If you remove or make a big opening in a bearing wall you could literally bring down the house.

To determine whether a wall is bearing or not, you'll have to do some sleuthing in the basement or attic—wherever there are exposed

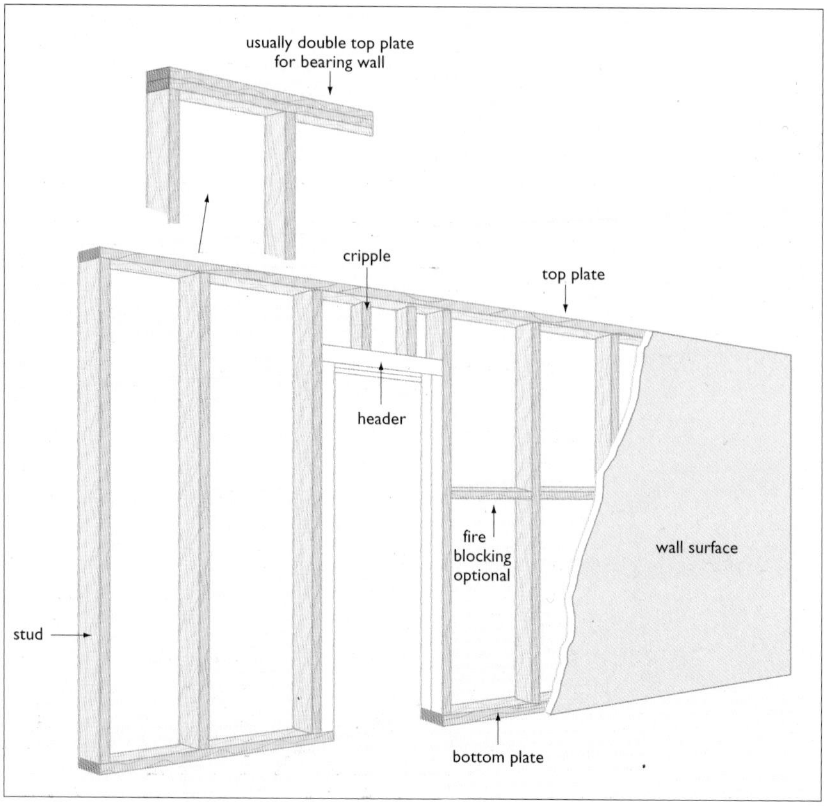

ABOVE: A section of the wall has been knocked out so that this small work area is partially open to the hallway beyond it and easily accessible to the rest of the kitchen.

RIGHT: Anatomy of a plasterboard partition.

The wall guide

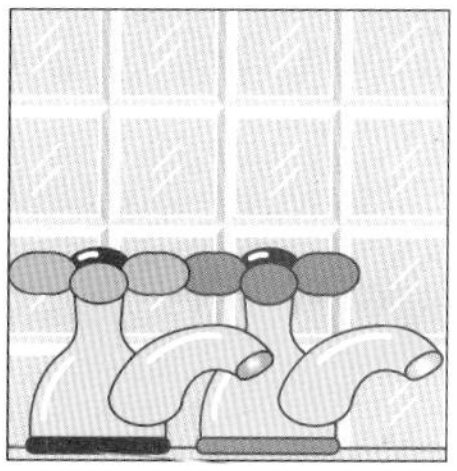
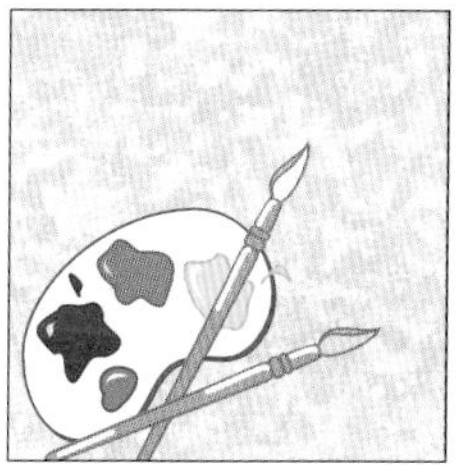

	Brick	Ceramic tile	Decorative paint	Fabric
Rooms	All. Seal in wet areas.	Ideal in wet areas. Can use with other finishes.	All.	Most. Avoid wet areas.
Durability	Excellent.	Excellent if properly installed.	Shows less wear and marks because of pattern.	Fair. Depends on fabric.
DIY	Easy to seal or paint, more complex to bag, lime or plaster.	Requires skill. Walls must be dry, smooth and stable.	More time consuming than difficult.	Quite easy: staple to wall-mounted battens or hang.
Cleaning	Easy to clean: simply dust or wash.	Easy. Damp sponge and commercial cleaners.	As for paintwork.	Hard. Dust and vacuum. Test before using liquids.
Comments	Natural, clear seal, paint, plaster, bagged or lime-wash finish.	Loads of patterns, colours, sizes and styles. Machine or handmade.	Stencilling, ragging, marbling, combing, murals and more.	Many decorative fabrics. A good cover for bad walls.

	Paint	Textured plaster	Timber	Wallpaper
Rooms	All.	All.	All.	All. Water/steam proof in wet areas.
Durability	Quality acrylics: 8 – 10 years. Oil-based: 6 years.	Good.	Very durable, easy to maintain.	Heavyweight vinyls are harder wearing.
DIY	Painting is easy. Preparation is the hard part.	Skill required for hard plaster. Textured panels easier to install.	Can be attached to battens or used as primary facing.	Not too hard. Follow instructions carefully. Heavier papers are normally easier to handle.
Cleaning	Depends on type. Wash and wear easy, some others hard to clean without marking.	Dust, damp sponge.	Depends on the type of finish, usually easy. Natural timber can be polished.	Easy-to-clean vinyls, thin matt papers more difficult. Try using a gum eraser.
Comments	Gloss, flat/matt, low sheen, semi-gloss.	Paint or mix in coloured oxides to hard plaster. Panel finishes vary.	Warm, natural look. Can be limed, stained or painted.	Vast range of colours and styles. Helps hide bad walls.

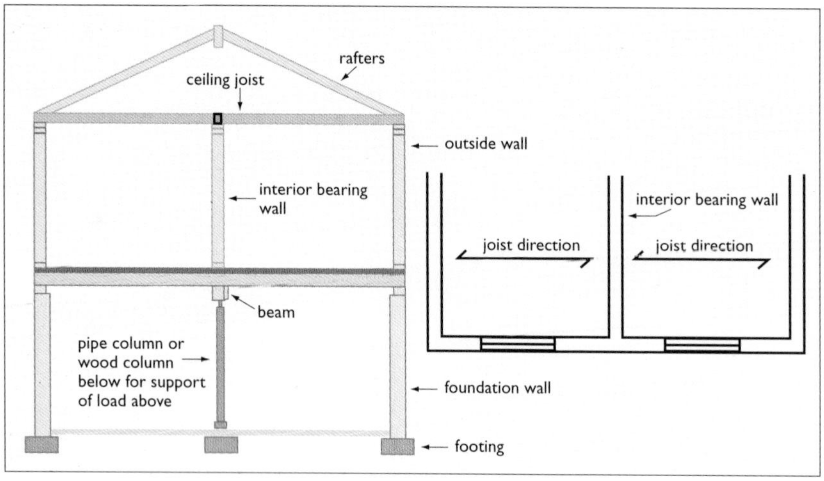

BELOW: Light through the skylight combined with a warm wall colour and polished floorboards are practical in a heavy-traffic area such as this hallway.

LEFT: How to identify a bearing wall.

joists or rafters. If these run parallel to the wall in question, you can be sure it's not a bearing type. If, however, they're perpendicular to the wall, you can be fairly sure it is bearing a load.

How to find studs

Almost anything you attach to a wall will be more secure if you can fasten it to one or more of the studs underneath. How, though, can you locate them without ripping open the plasterboard or plaster?

No one technique works for every situation, but all are based on the same principle—that most of the studs in a wall are spaced at regular intervals. This means that after you've found one or two, you generally can plot the others with a few measurements.

When looking for studs, begin your search towards the wall's centre, not at the ends, where spacing might be irregular. Also, ignore the studs on either side of a door or window opening.

There are four common ways to find that first stud:

1 Usually you can 'sound out' a wall by rapping along it with your knuckles. A solid thunk indicates you've found a stud.
2 If rapping doesn't tell you anything, look along the skirting board for any nails. They're usually driven in at stud intervals.
3 You can use a special magnetic finding device that homes in on nails or screws holding the wall surface to the studs.
4 Take the face plate off a receptacle located somewhere along the wall. Power points almost always are nailed to a stud.

Once you've pinpointed a stud, measure 450 mm—the most common spacing—in one direction or the other. If you can't find a second stud there, try 600 mm, a spacing now being used in most newer houses.

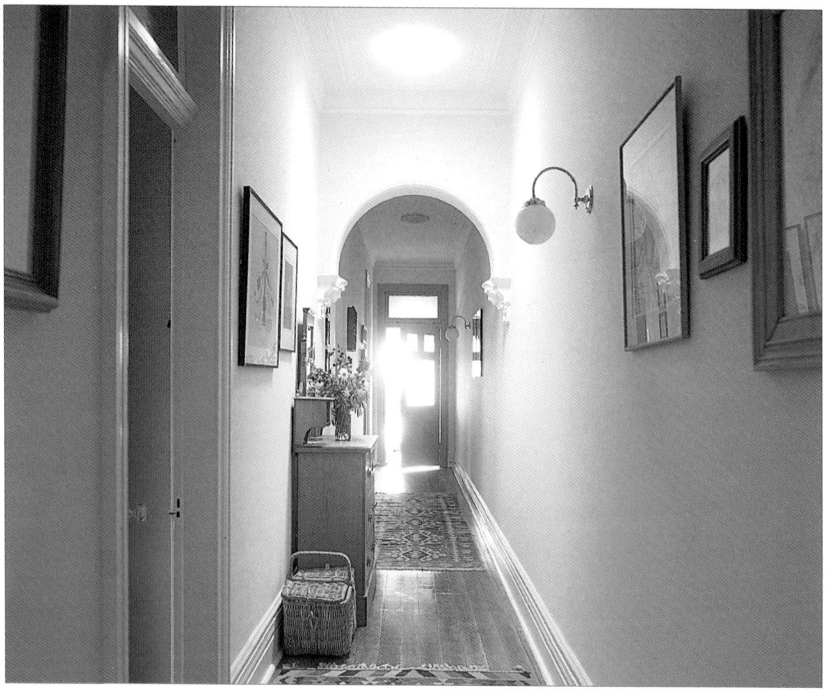

BELOW: A wall with windows on an upper storey brings in the light and the view.

Solving wall problems

Dealing with damp

Your home may be your castle but, if it's afflicted with damp, it feels more like a dank, dripping dungeon. Wet patches on walls and floors are unsightly, unsafe and can peel thousands from the value of the property. Moisture, which could be coming from the ground, through the walls or even from inside the house, is the culprit; you'll have to work out the source before you can tackle the problem.

Rising damp

As the name suggests, rising damp is ground water which is sucked up through the foundations into the walls of the house. It should be stopped at ground level by the building's damp-proof course — a waterproof layer of lead, plastic or slate. However, if this is cracked or defective, the water will get through, leaving brownish 'high-tide' marks and whitish deposits. These stains mostly occur about a metre above ground level; if they are any higher, they probably are not due to rising damp but to problems with the roof or flashing around windows or doors. If unchecked, rising damp will result in bubbling paint work, mouldy wallpaper and rotten plasterwork. It's a particularly common problem in older buildings, which typically have poor ventilation and/or inadequate drainage.

There are several treatments for rising damp, including electro-osmosis, plugging the wall with porous tubes and 'cosmetic' treatments such as rendering the affected wall.

However, there are really only two effective remedies: increasing evaporation by improving ventilation and drainage, or replacing the damp-proof course. The latter can be done by replacing the faulty barrier (with plastic, not metal sheeting, which can react with salt) or by chemical injection (or flooding). Chemical injection involves drilling the wall and inserting poly-oxy-aluminium-stearate or silicone-based materials to create a chemical barrier against damp. This should be done by professionals for the best results.

Lateral damp

Most noticeable after rain, this type of damp is caused by water penetrating through the sides of walls. It can result in white powdery deposits on the wall or clearly defined stains which may strike at any level. Penetrating damp can be a particular problem in old homes with solid (single-skin) walls, but even cavity brick walls aren't immune, as problems can arise if a 'bridge'—mortar, brickbats, roof debris, even a dead rat or bird—allows moisture to cross the gap between the two skins.

Check and repair any damage, such as defective brickwork or cracked rendering, to the external wall. Look for other sources of moisture, such as windowsills with blocked or damaged drip channels, or broken gutters or downpipes. Allow the wall to dry thoroughly, then seal the exterior with a silicone water repellent. If the wall is porous and constantly exposed to bad weather, consider cladding it with weatherboard, tiles or rendering.

Clearing cavity 'bridges' is a difficult job and you may be better off with professional help. If, however, you're a die-hard do-it-yourselfer, you'll have to climb up on the roof and remove a few tiles to get a bird's-eye view of the problem. It may be possible to dislodge the offending material with a long batten poked down the cavity. If it's too tightly wedged to move, you'll have to shift operations to the exterior wall: chop out the joints of the brick closest to the obstruction, remove the brick, remove the obstruction, then re-lay the brick.

Condensation

Condensation is caused by moisture from within the house. It can leave 'sweaty' patches on walls and fog up windows.

To treat it you must stop the steam! Always open a window or turn on ventilation fans when you're creating water vapour, whether in the kitchen or bathroom. See that your shower is properly enclosed, and run cold water before adding hot when filling the bath (it reduces steam and it's safer, too). Keep bathroom

Stopping damp where it starts

Roof. Inspect regularly—broken tiles may be allowing water through, particularly if damp appears in rooms on the top floor. Check for faulty chimney stacks, and leaking valleys and flashing.

Gutters. Blocked gutters overflow and contribute to damp problems, so clean them out a couple of times a year. Mend cracked gutters by cleaning the inside well with a wire brush, then sealing by binding the crack and its surrounds with waterproof tape. Repair leaking joints by removing the old seal with kerosene or petrol and replacing it with a new rubber seal or waterproof tape, wound in overlapping layers around the pipe.

Downpipes. These can be blocked by birds' nests, leaves and so on, and will back up, causing gutters to overflow. Inspect regularly and clear blockages with a long batten or long-handled broom. This is relatively easy on single-storey properties; longer, multi-storey downpipes will probably need professional attention. If downpipes are repeatedly blocked (by leaves dropping from an adjacent tree, for example), try fitting a wire cage over the top of the pipe.

Foundations. Clear away any dirt and debris that is over the damp-proof course.

Air vents. These should also be kept clear of vegetation, dirt and debris.

Redecorating. Once you've found and fixed the fault, allow walls to dry out, then seal the exterior with a silicone water repellent. Remove peeling or damaged wallpaper and paint, then seal internal walls before re-papering or painting.

and kitchen doors closed, and cover cooking pots with lids. Use the clothes dryer as little as possible and avoid gas cylinder and kerosene heaters; slow, steady heaters generate less moisture than those which produce a sudden burst of warm air.

Wet rot

Wet rot results from fungal spores infesting wood which is regularly exposed to moisture. It typically strikes basement floors or unpainted or poorly maintained window or door frames. The affected wood feels soft and spongy when wet, crumbly when dry. Tell-tale visual signs include dark thin strands of fungus, cracks along the grain of the wood and flaking paintwork.

Locate the source of the moisture, fix and allow surround to dry out, then replace the affected wood completely.

ABOVE: This kitchen has large opening windows that allow steam and cooking odours to escape easily and prevent any build-up of damp. Good ventilation, light and damp-proofing is especially important in wet areas.

Repairs

Knocking out a wall

A little-used small room becomes a household asset when it flows into a bigger space.

If your internal walls are masonry the actual removal of the wall is a job for a professional builder. Even for lightweight timber partitions you should get professional advice on the building code.

A masonry lintel is used in the demonstration here. It is a terracotta pipe which contains steel reinforcement and is filled with concrete. It is the same dimension as one course of bricks (110 mm thick and 75 mm high). The span is 2100 mm and we cut the lintel to size.

Consider the advantages of having a wall knocked out and have a go at doing the trimming yourself. You'll be surprised at the immediate improvement it will make.

1

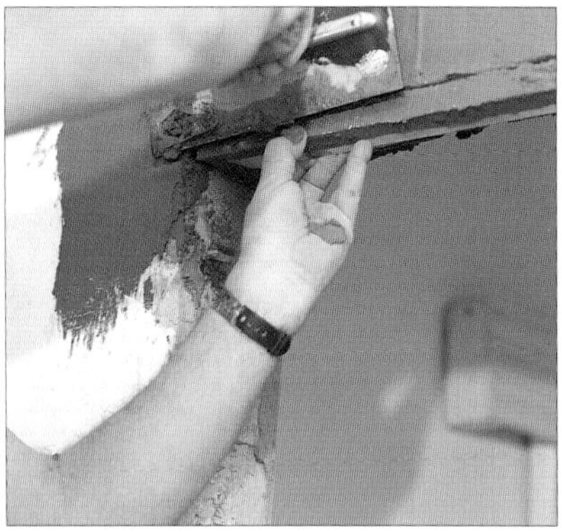

2

3

4

1 In this old house where the floor joists were actually resting on the ground, subsidence on one side of the wall meant that the two floor levels had to be evened up after the wall was removed. Chock up joist bearers and floorboards to the same level and fill the space left by the wall with boards or sheet flooring material.

2 Use a steel float and sand and cement to render over the new lintel. Hold a piece of timber against the edge to achieve a sharp corner as you proceed.

3 Similarly, fill any gaps at the bottom of the wall render that may have resulted with changing floor levels. They might harbour vermin.

4 Clean up your archway as much as possible before you begin fitting it out. Remove any rough chunks of masonry and check that the opening is as near to square as can be.

5 Use 19-mm-thick timber to line the arch. Glue and nail the two top joints using three 75-mm-long jolt-head nails at each corner. Allow the top horizontal to run the full width of the opening to brace the inverted U shape. Step the verticals in 10 mm increments and use scrap timber to chock behind them, establishing perfect verticality using a spirit level.

6 Drill 6 mm holes to the verticals in pairs and at four points down their length. Drill through the timbers and well into the masonry. These holes are to take 6 mm dowel pegs, not nails.

7 Hammer 90 mm lengths of 6 mm dowel into the holes and then drive 90 mm nails into the dowels. The timber will expand when the nails are inserted, giving an extra-solid fixing to the lining of the archway.

8 Position the architraves. Choose a moulding that matches the others in your house. Mitre the top horizontal with inside dimensions to match those of the wall opening span. Pin the architrave in place using a 45-mm-long fine-gauge jolt-head nail. Do not drive the nails in all the way at first.

5

6

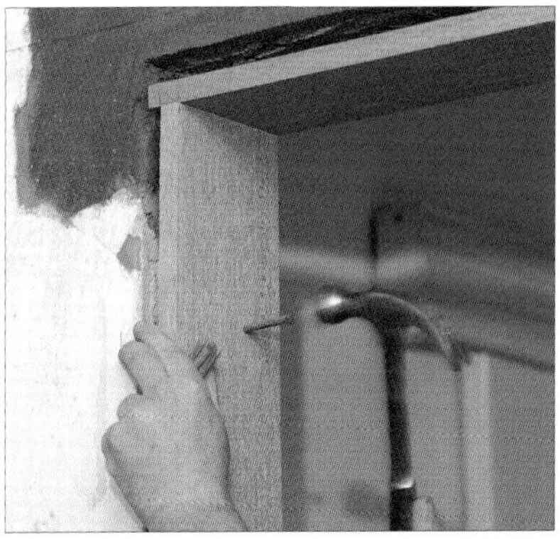

7

8

9

10

9 Now fit the side vertical architraves, checking that the corner joint is as good as possible before you punch the nails below the timber surface using a nail punch. Don't forget, however, that you can always fill the joints before painting.

10 Nail down through the mitres to entirely secure the corner joints. Fill all the nail holes and sand the job before sealing both the timber and the new cement render prior to applying your top coats. You will need a few coats of paint to blend in the new wall render.

RIGHT: The end result, space and light.

ABOVE: Living and dining flow easily into one another.

LEFT: A soft colour with a moulded cornice for interest.

Making openings in plasterboard

Measure carefully and transfer dimensions to the panel's face. For receptacles, trace an outline around a spare electrical box.

Then bore holes at each corner, or simply try poking the pointed end of a keyhole or plasterboard saw through the plasterboard. Most saws slice through plasterboard like a knife through bread. Protect your floors; plasterboard dust is difficult to clean up.

Fitting around pipes

Rather than going to the trouble of disconnecting a plumbing fixture, plasterboard just to the middle of the studs flanking the pipes.

Next, cut a piece to fit the opening, measure and mark the locations of the pipes, bore holes and connect them with the cuts.

Finally, piece your puzzle back together and nail to the studs. Cement small pieces in place with joint compound.

Laminating plasterboard

To beef up a wall's sound and fire resistance, glue one layer of 13 mm or 10 mm plasterboard to another, or use this same technique to bond a new surface to an existing wall. For either job, you'll need wall-board adhesive and joint compound, plus some 40 mm flat-head nails to tack the top layer until the adhesive sets.

First, find all wall studs and mark their locations on the floor and ceiling. Apply cement to the wall surface according to the directions on the tube, or use dabs of joint compound spaced 200 mm apart.

Fit the panel then, with a hammer and scrap of timber, go over its surface, firmly tapping to embed it in the adhesive or compound.

Partially drive a few nails through the top layer into each stud to temporarily hold panels in place. Then, after the adhesive has set, pull them out. Alternatively, countersink nails and cover the heads with compound when you tape the joints.

Plan to stagger the panel joints so one never falls atop another. At the outside corners, laminate layers.

At inside corners, nail only the overlapping board of the first layer.

Taping plasterboard

The trickiest part of a plasterboarding project comes when you finish off the joints and nailheads. For this multi-step process you'll need about 15 L of pre-mixed joint compound and 75 m of paper 'tape' for each 45 sq m of surface.

BELOW: A dramatic effect is created here by distressed treatment of the wall colours.

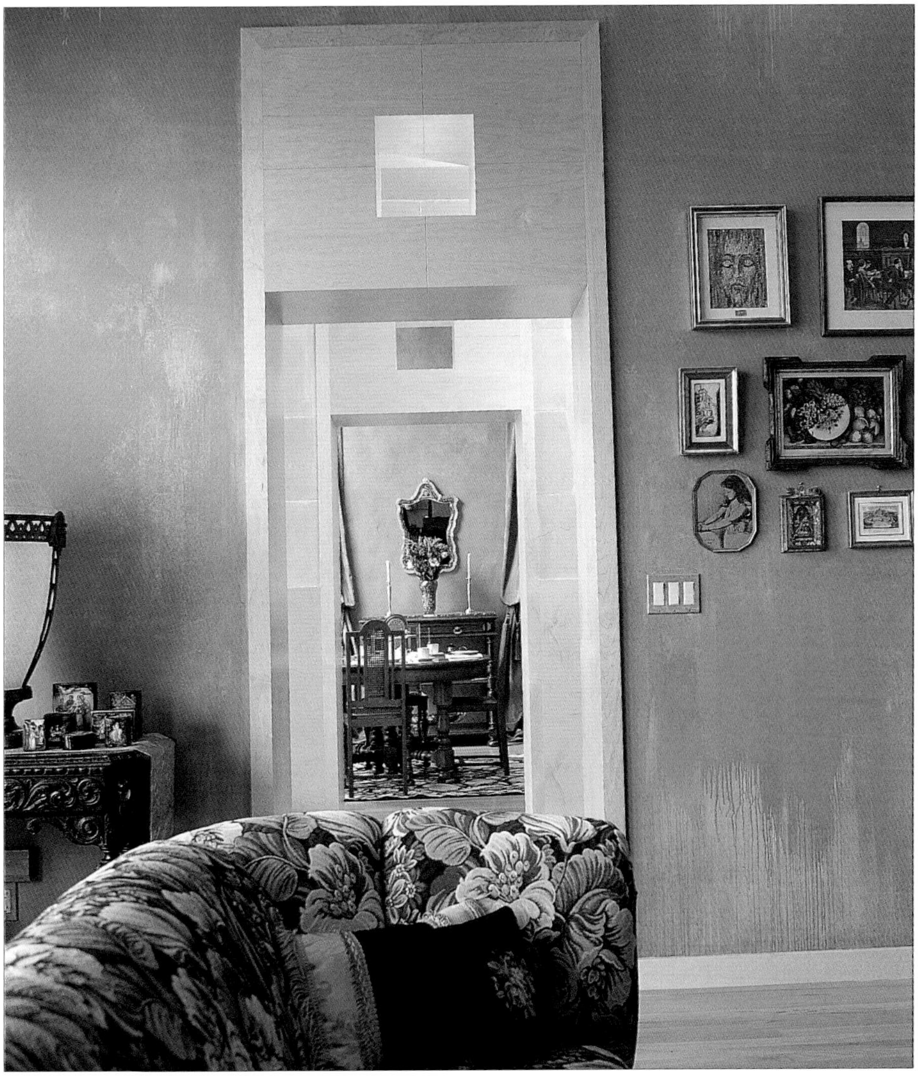

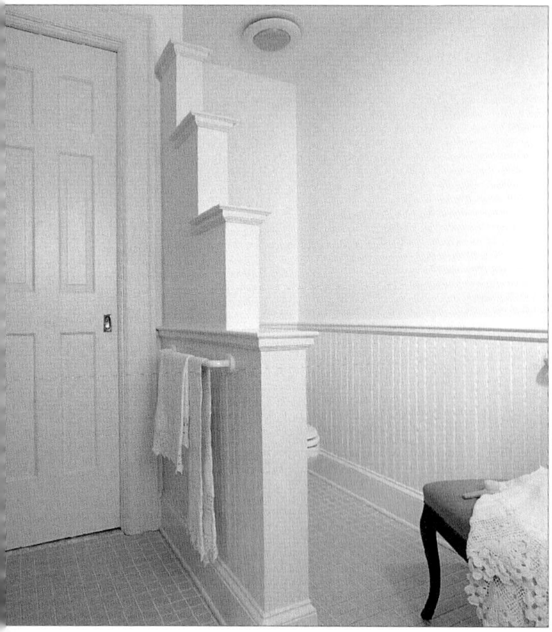

Invest, too, in a pair of 100 mm and 250 mm broad knives. Allow plenty of time for the first coat and get the tape up smoothly.

Starting with the 100 mm knife, apply a full, uniform swath of compound to the tapered trough between the two panels. Immediately begin to unroll the tape, using the knife to embed it in the compound. Saturate the tape; smooth out wrinkles.

Fill nail dimples and other imperfections at this time, too. Pack in a dab of compound, then level with the surface.

Give your 'bedding' coat about 24 hours to dry, then apply compound again, feathering out the edges about 150 mm.

After it's dry, smooth the second coat by lightly sanding or wiping with a damp sponge. Don't sand the paper surface.

Finally, apply a skim coat with the 250 mm knife or a trowel, spreading edges to about 300 mm. Sand or sponge if needed.

Taping corners

Inside and outside corners call for slightly different taping techniques. Reinforce outside corners with strips of lightweight perforated metal angle.

Install a metal 'corner bead' by nailing through the plasterboard to the framing every 130 mm. Be careful not to dent the metal.

Apply two or three coats of compound as explained above. Feather it out about 100 mm on each wall surface.

Use ordinary joint tape for inside corners, but cut it to length first, then crease it vertically down the middle before applying.

For the inside corners, spread compound down both walls, cut the tape and fold it down the middle before embedding it.

Apply later coats with an inside-corner tool or use a filling knife on one wall, let the compound dry, then do the other.

Mending cracks and bubbled tape

You can repair minor cracks simply by filling the voids with compound. But if the joint tape curls up from the plasterboard surface, first use a utility knife to remove all loose tape. Be careful you don't remove the sound-fitting tape.

Cut a piece of joint tape to fit. Apply a bed of joint compound to the wall or ceiling, press the tape in place and apply another coat of compound. Let dry, then add another layer of compound, then another if necessary. Feather each coat into the surrounding surface to help hide the seam.

Patching small holes

Filling nail-sized holes is by far the easiest plasterboard repair you can make. Use a putty knife to fill the hole with spackling compound, allowing some excess to 'mound' above the surface. When the compound dries, lightly sand away the excess to leave a smooth surface.

An even easier procedure, although it is somewhat unorthodox, is to dispense with the spackling compound and the sanding, and simply fill small holes with white toothpaste. Believe it or not, it really works.

Patching medium-sized holes

To mend medium-sized holes you must provide backing to which the joint compound can adhere. Fashion this backing from a scrap of perforated hardboard cut slightly larger than the hole, but small enough that it can be manoeuvred through the wall. To hold the scrap firmly against the back side of the wall, run a length of thin wire through a couple of the perforations. Now, using joint compound, butter the perimeter of the backing with a spatula.

Insert the hardboard backing into the hole and centre it behind the opening. When dry, the joint

ABOVE: Panelling to dado height is a classic look.

RIGHT: Rag-rolled walls soften the blue and white colour scheme.

BELOW: A twisted cord attached to the timber border at dado height is an attractive definition between the two wall surfaces.

compound will help the backing cling to the back of the plasterboard. To hold the backing in place during the interim, bridge the opening with a pencil and twist the wire ends together until the wire is taut. When the compound dries, clip the wire and remove it.

Now it's simply a matter of filling the recess with joint compound. Because the compound shrinks as it dries, you'll have to apply several coats to achieve a satisfactory result. Let each coat dry before adding the next. Once you've completely filled in the void and don't see any hairline cracks in the compound, sand the patch lightly and re-texture its surface.

If you don't have any perforated hardboard around the house, try this alternative which uses a scrap of 6 mm or 12 mm plywood. Cut the plywood backing as you would the hardboard. Drill two holes in the centre of the piece to run the wire through. Now follow through with the remaining steps as they are described above.

Patching large holes

After squaring off the area to be repaired, cut and remove the damaged plasterboard. Use a keyhole saw to make the horizontal cuts between the studs and a sharp utility knife guided by a straightedge for the vertical cuts along the stud centres.

Cut a plasterboard patch the size of the hole from scrap plasterboard. Then cut two lengths of 50 x 50 mm timber to serve as backing supports for the top and bottom edges of the patch. Skew nail the 50 x 50 mm battens in place, making sure they're flush with the edge of the studs. (Make this installation easier by first drilling angled starter holes for the nails.) Now fit the plasterboard patch into the opening and secure it with 40 mm plasterboard nails spaced at least 10 mm in from the edges. 'Dimple' each nailhead.

Lay down a bed coat of joint compound around the perimeter of the patch with a 100 mm filling knife held at a 45° angle to the wall. Avoid creating too much of a mound. Immediately centre an appropriate length of plasterboard tape over each seam, using your hands to press it in place. Then, with the filling knife, embed the tape further into the bed coat, holding one end of the tape secure with your other hand. Follow this with one or more coats of compound, feathering each coat into the surrounding surface and letting it dry thoroughly before applying the next. When the last coat has dried, finish and re-texture the patch.

Finishing and re-texturing the surface

With enough care and patience, you can finish your plasterboard repairs so they'll be all but invisible.

Begin by smoothing the surface of the repair with either 80 or 100 grit sandpaper or a dampened sponge. (If you use sandpaper and the repair requires a lot of sanding, be sure you wear a painter's mask to avoid inhaling too much dust. Also be careful not to sand all the way through the compound and into the tape. After sanding the area, wipe the dust off the surface with a cloth.)

Most plasterboard surfaces are not glassy smooth. Instead, they have a texture designed to conceal seams, nails and minor defects in the plasterboard surface. You can closely duplicate most textures, each in a slightly different way. (It is a good idea to practise on a piece of scrap plasterboard before attempting to re-texture the actual patch.)

You can approximate an 'orange peel' texture by watering down some pre-mixed joint compound and dabbing it over your repair with a sponge.

If you want to blend a patch into a sand-textured surface, roll on some texture paint with a paint roller. To match an existing texture, apply a layer of plasterboard compound. Then, using a whisk broom or other stiff-bristled brush, replicate the existing pattern. If you're dealing with a travertine finish, apply one layer of compound and let it set up slightly. Then, flick more compound onto the surface using a paintbrush and knock off the high spots by lightly trowelling the surface.

Beaded polystyrene and vermiculite textures on ceilings are hard to match. Although you can rent texturing equipment, your best solution may be to call in professional help to identify the type of finish you have and to duplicate its coarseness.

Repairing cracks and holes in plaster

Professional plasterers are scarce these days, but, fortunately, with a little practice, you can handle most common plaster repairs yourself.

Choose pre-mixed spackling compound for small repairs such as hairline cracks and nail holes. For larger cracks and holes, mix powdered patching plaster with water — it's stronger than spackling compound and less prone to shrink.

Make plaster patching a regular part of your preparatory work whenever you repaint. And be sure to correct any moisture leaks that might be responsible for your problems.

1 To prepare hairline cracks for patching, widen the fissures to about 3 mm with a screwdriver, then blow out any dust and debris that remain.

  A hammer and cold chisel make short work of removing loose plaster from holes. To ensure a successful repair, work out in all directions until you reach sound plaster. Also, knock the plaster from between the laths and undercut the edges as shown to help lock in the patching material.

2 If moisture has rotted the laths behind the loose plaster, cut the plaster back to at least the centre of the studs adjacent to the damaged area. Remove the laths (if using a circular saw, adjust the blade to the proper depth) and nail up new wood or metal mesh-type laths.

3 To prevent the water in the plaster patching material from being drawn into surrounding surfaces and thereby weakening the patch, moisten the area shortly before making repairs. You can do this with either a spray bottle or a damp sponge.

4 Fill in the hairline cracks by forcing spackling compound into the void with a putty knife. Let the compound dry, then apply another coat, if necessary, to bring the filler material flush with the surrounding surface.

  When dealing with larger repairs, mix a batch of patching plaster according to the manufacturer's directions on the packet. Starting at the edges and using a 150 mm-wide filling knife, work the plaster into the undercuts, then fill in the centre. (Make sure you apply enough pressure to the patch material so that some of it fills the spaces between the laths. This is known as keying, or tying, the plaster to its backing.)

  Because patching plaster shrinks as it dries, be prepared to lay on two or more coats of material. Let each coat dry completely before applying the next. To achieve the best possible bond between coats, wet the surface of each base coat before laying on more plaster.

5 After the top coat of plaster has had sufficient drying time (at least 24 hours), it is ready for sanding. Using a medium-grade sandpaper (80 or 100 grit) wrapped around a sanding block, sand the surface with light circular strokes. Focus a portable work light on the repair

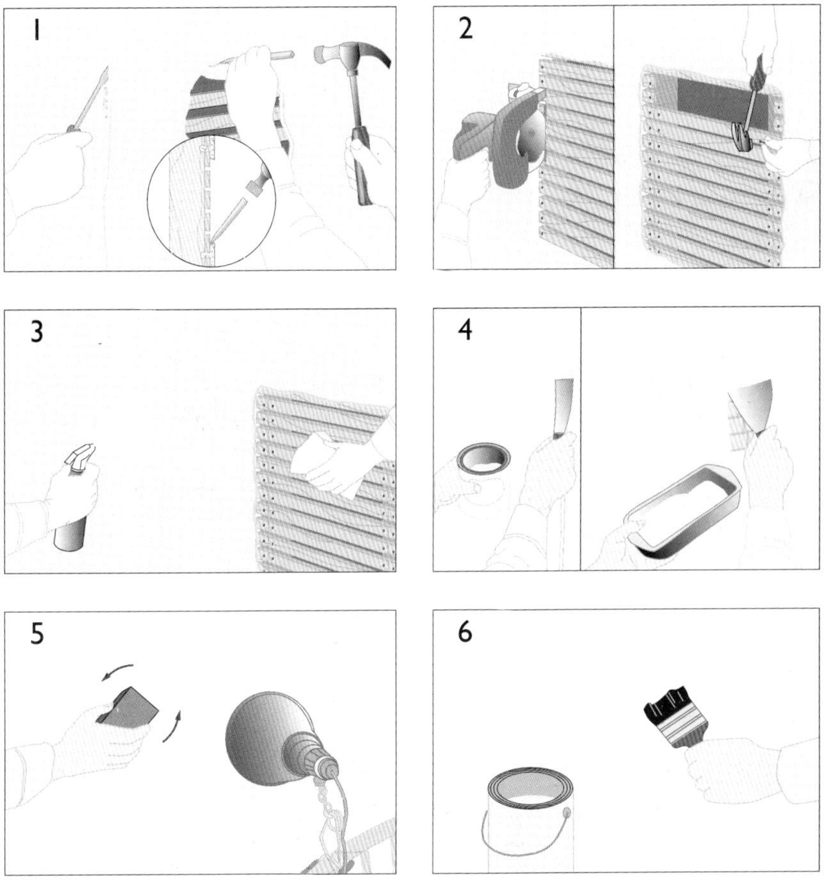

LEFT: Modern wallpaper is easy to apply and can transform a room.

area to help detect slight surface irregularities you might otherwise overlook.

6 Never try to paint a plaster repair without first priming it. If you do, the new plaster will absorb paint more readily than the surrounding surface and your patch will show through. Before you begin priming, however, make sure your new plaster has had sufficient time to cure and set up. To be safe, wait another 24 hours after you finish sanding.

Installing battens

How flat are your walls? To find out, select a long and straight 100 x 50 mm piece of timber and hold the edge against the surface you want to cover. Move it around, trying out horizontal, vertical and diagonal positions. If you can see hollows under the length of timber, or if it rocks at points, you will need to even up the wall with battens before applying panelling or plasterboard.

Also plan to batten out any masonry wall. In a basement, you may prefer to build a 100 x 50 mm stud framework instead. This makes more space for pipes, insulation and electrical outlets. Make sure, too, that your foundation walls have been properly sealed against moisture.

For battening materials, choose inexpensive 50 x 25 mm or 75 x 25 mm battens. You'll also need several tubes of panel adhesive and some wood shingles for shimming (or packing out) the strips.

When putting up battens, be sure to use standard 450 mm centre-to-centre spacing. This lets you put up standard, 1800-mm-long materials without a lot of trimming.

Begin putting up battens by gluing up a strip at one corner. With all verticals, leave a 12 mm space at the bottom to facilitate installation.

Set the first panel in place, plumb it and check the fit at the corner. Trim if necessary, then mark for the first joint. Take all future measurements from that joint line, not from the corner. Remember to maintain the correct centre-to-centre spacing.

BELOW RIGHT: Cutting an architrave into the wall allowed these two rooms to become one large area for entertaining. The glass doors can be closed for everyday living and warmth.

BELOW: Open plan living is common in most new and renovated houses. Ease of access between kitchen and dining and living areas is practical and can be achieved simply by knocking out part of a wall.

Now lay wavy beads of adhesive along the lines, press strips against them, remove the strips and re-apply after 10 minutes.

Plumb each batten carefully before you permanently fix it to the wall. Be sure to double check the 450 mm spacings, too.

If the wall was even to begin with, just glue up short horizontals top and bottom and your battening job is complete.

For uneven walls, use 75 x 50 mm, 100 x 50 mm or 600 mm centres for vertical support. If you plan to insulate the wall, do it now.

Next, nail either 50 x 75 mm or 75 x 25 mm battens across the verticals. Inset shims behind these horizontals wherever you need to pack them out.

Then fill in the spaces between the horizontals with short lengths of batten. Shim low spots here, as well, if necessary.

Framing a partition

'Roughing in' the studs for a new wall calls for a different carpentry orientation than you may be used to. With framing, appearances don't count much. What does matter is that you keep everything plumb, square and structurally sound.

Start by working out how you are going to tie a new partition into your home's structure. How do the ceiling joists run in relation to your proposed wall? In a basement with an exposed ceiling, that's easy to determine.

If the new wall will cross the joists, simply pinpoint exactly where you want the wall and nail the top plate to the joists at those points. If, however, it will run parallel to the joists, you may have to shift the wall's location a few centimetres so you can nail directly to a joist or install an intermediate joist.

Next, check out the walls you'll be attaching to. Fasten to masonry with expansion bolts. In a hollow-wall situation, you may be lucky enough to find a stud behind it. If not, secure the new wall's first and last studs with toggle bolts.

After you know exactly where everything is, mark chalk lines for the top and bottom plates. If you're not proficient with a plumb bob, tape your spirit level to a straight 100 x 50 mm length of timber and use it to take vertical readings.

Two different framing techniques are described below. Pre-assembly makes sense for relatively short walls on relatively level floors. Build the entire partition flat on the floor, making it 40 mm shorter than the ceiling height then lift it into place atop a second bottom plate.

Skew nailing studs saves you the timber for that extra plate and better accommodates uneven terrain. But it takes some practice before you can squarely skew nail the studs to the top and bottom plates.

Pre-assembly

Lay out your new wall with chalk lines, as explained above, then level a 100 x 50 mm piece of timber with shingle shims and nail or screw it to the floor.

Next, measure the height of the ceiling at several points. Tailor your partition to fit the shortest floor-to-ceiling dimension.

Cut the top and bottom plates, lay them side by side, and mark off stud spacings. Begin 20 mm from one end and mark at 40 mm intervals.

Then cut the studs, making sure you allow for the plates' thicknesses. Assemble the framework by nailing through the plates.

If your new wall will include a doorway, now add the trimmers. Cut out the opening's bottom plate after positioning the wall.

You'll probably need help to lift the partition into place. Once it's up, plumb carefully, then nail the top and bottom plates.

Skew nailing studs

Installing the top and bottom plates first, then custom cutting the studs one at a time assures you of a tight-fitting wall and you needn't bother with shimming anything.

You will encounter two problems, though. The first comes when you attach the top plate—a four-handed job that requires you to hold a heavy length of timber against the ceiling, then nail up through it to the post.

Make this job easier by starting the nails first, then asking a helper to force the plate against the ceiling with another length of timber or hand pressure while you nail. Wear goggles and keep your mouth closed while you hammer; you'll probably create a shower of dust and debris with each blow.

Expect frustration, too, the first time you try to skew nail at an angle through the stud into the plates. With each hammer blow, the stud will move a little. To minimise this, cut each stud about 3 mm longer than necessary and tap it into place for a force fit. Next, make a 450 mm-long block (the space between two studs), lay it against the plate and nail as described below. After you get the knack of hitting the nail, not the stud, you can dispense with the block.

With a helper, secure the top and bottom plates and the partition's end studs. Then skew nail the wall's intermediate studs into place. To skew nail, drive one nail at a 45° angle. Don't be surprised to see the stud move from its mark.

Now drive a second nail from the other side. With practice, you'll be able to knock the stud back into its original position.

Until you get the hang of skew nailing, use a spacer to temporarily brace each stud against the previous one.

Adding finishes to walls

Choosing and buying ceramic tile

Made of clay fired in high-temperature kilns, ceramic tiles are relatively brittle. But once you've cemented them to a solid

ABOVE: A wall in the corner of this room cleverly combines unobtrusive storage for decorative items with the sound system and the television set.

backing and grouted the joints with special mortar, you have an exceptionally sturdy wall.

When shopping you'll discover an enormous range of tile colours, shapes, sizes and textures. Specialty items, especially vivid colours, can cost two or three times as much as standard tiles. You should note, too, that wall tiles are thinner and slicker than floor tiles.

For a smooth installation, you'll need two different types of tiles. Ceramic tiles (100 mm and 150 mm squares are typical sizes) cover most of the surface; trim tiles round off edges and get around corners. Don't get carried away with a low per-square-metre price for ceramic tiles until you've checked out what the trim tiles will cost. Sold by the lineal metre, these can add quite a bit to the final bill.

Smaller mosaic tiles come bonded to pieces of 300 x 300 mm paper or fabric mesh; they go up a little faster, but need more grouting.

Many experts still prefer to 'mud set' ceramic tiles in cement-based mortar — a tricky masonry process. Fortunately, you can now choose from a number of mastic-like adhesives specially developed for amateurs. You can ask your dealer for a recommendation.

Estimating tile needs

To compute how many ceramic tiles you'll need for an entire bathroom or other complex installation, draw each wall on graph paper, count the squares and add about 5 per cent for waste. Or simply calculate the square meterage and let your dealer do the working out; most outlets will give credit for returned tiles.

In a shower, plan to take the tiles to a height of at least 1800 mm above the showerhead; other bathroom walls usually are tiled to the 1200 mm level; kitchen walls to the bottoms of the wall cabinets.

Estimate trim tiles such as bullnoses, caps and coves by the lineal metre; but order mitred corners, angles and other specialty items by the piece.

For adhesive, choose a thin-bed PVA adhesive for most areas, including showers and other wet areas. For walls that may vibrate or for tiling over old adhesive that cannot be removed, use a flexible adhesive. Wall tiling with a 3 mm bed of adhesive requires 2 kg of adhesive per square metre.

Grout comes in 500 g, 1.5 kg and 5 kg packages. Usually, 0.5 kg of grout will cover 1 sq m of 150 x 150 x 5 mm tiles with a 3 mm joint or 300 x 300 x 6 mm tiles with a 5 mm joint. One and a half to 2 kg of grout covers 1 sq m of 150 x 150 mm thicker tiles with a 6 mm joint.

Tools for tile work

Many tile dealers hire out some of the specialised equipment shown below. But since a good job can take a surprising amount of time, plan to first set all the tiles that don't have to be cut, then hire the cutter and nippers you'll need for trimming the edges.

A tile cutter cuts quick, accurate, straight lines. Ask your dealer for a demonstration and expect to ruin a few tiles before you get the hang

Tips

- If you have to tile around an existing pipe, cut the tile in two and clip away a semicircle from each piece using a tile nipper. Leave space for the pipe to expand and contract.
- After wiping away excess grouting and polishing off the tiles, smooth the grouting between the tiles with a piece of thin dowel or an old round chopstick.
- Remember grout dries quickly and when hardened it is almost impossible to remove. Never leave anything but a smear on the tile surface. Wiping across the tile diagonally prevents you from dragging the mixture out of the joints. Wipe again to even the grout surface.

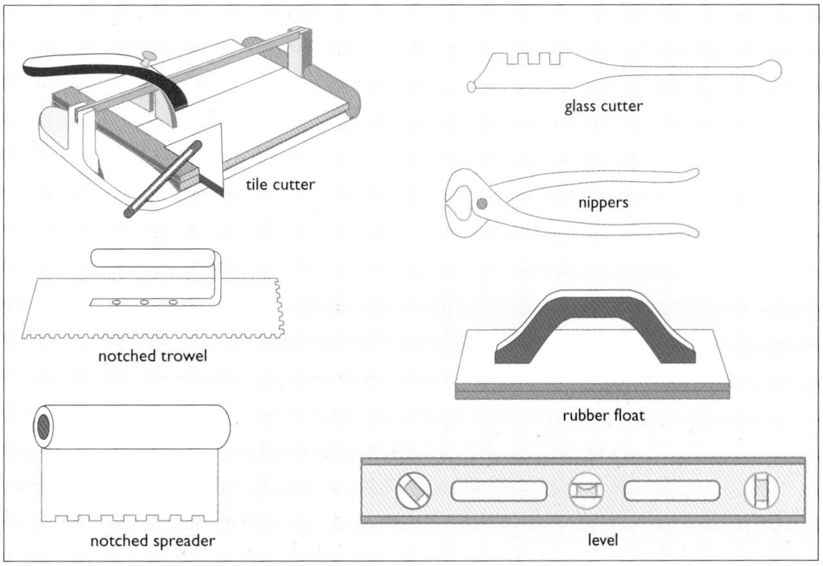

BELOW: Large, square tiles finishing at picture rail height are unusual in a kitchen but the result is effective as well as practical.

of it. You can also trim with a glass cutter, but this is slower. Nippers nibble out curved cuts.

Serrated edges on the notched trowel let you spread adhesive to the right thickness; a notched spreader gets into tight spots.

A rubber float facilitates grouting, but you can also get by with an ordinary window washer's squeegee.

Preparing walls for tiling

You can apply ceramic tiles to any rendered, fibre cement and some plaster surfaces that are smooth, sound and firm. With existing walls, strip off flexible coverings such as wallpaper, and scrape away loose paint. Knock the sheen off glossy finishes with a light sanding.

Don't bother taping and smoothing joints in new plasterboard. Seal it first, though, with a thin coat of adhesive, taking care to pack any openings where pipes come through. In a shower or other high-moisture location, use special water-resistant plasterboard or exterior-grade plywood.

Pay particular attention to the point where tiles will meet the top of a bath or a shower base. Chip away any old material here and leave a 6 mm space.

Now you're ready to begin laying out the job. An installation that starts in the centre of a wall and proceeds towards the edges is best as it gives you equally sized cut tiles at each corner. If that's not important to you, start in a corner. But be sure to check it for plumb first; you'll probably have to trim some tiles to compensate.

To plumb, improvise a layout tool by fastening a spirit level to a board that you know is straight. Then mark off tile widths, including 1.5 mm grouting.

Mark a plumb line at the wall's midpoint. Now use your guide to see what will happen at the edges. Shift the field if necessary.

Finally, find the wall's lowest point. Mark a level line one tile width above it. Begin setting full tiles above this line.

How to tile bathroom walls

Thinking ahead

Before you start, turn off the water supply at the mains and unscrew all taps and the shower rose. This will make your job a lot easier.

When you begin tiling, decide on the most obvious point (such as the top of the bath or the basin) that must line up with a tile course. Count the number of tiles downwards to establish a tile position close to the floor. Lay this bottom full course of tiles first — against a hard edge nailed to the wall. Return to the lower course of cut tiles, adjacent to the floor, last (when the rest are dry and you can remove the hard edge without having all the tiles slide down the wall).

Tiling

After you have marked the tile line above the floor, spread a cement-based tile adhesive with a notched trowel or spreader right up to the drawn line.

Butter the back of the tiles to enable you to control the size of the gap between the tiles and the wall. Insert spacers as you go to keep spaces even.

When the adhesive is dry, remove the spacers, mix the grout and, using diagonal strokes, fill the joints with a squeegee. Remove excess with a damp sponge.

Trimming and cutting

Mark the tap position and nibble out the shape with pliers or tile nippers, working inwards from a corner. Butter the tile and position it, pressing firmly until tile fronts line up evenly.

To cut tiles into a corner, mark the area to be trimmed, allowing a couple of millimetres grace. Score along the mark and cut with a tile cutter. Check and adjust the size before fixing.

Timber panelling

Timber panelling has been used as a wall finish for hundreds of years. It's easy to put up and hard to knock around.

1 Remove window and door trims, skirting boards and any fittings. Tap walls to locate studs and mark centres with a pencil. For vertical panelling apply 42 x 19 mm battens horizontally spaced at around 600 mm centres. Nail the battens to the studs using common 40 mm nails.

2 Cut the boards 10 mm shorter than wall height: when nailing in place leave 5 mm at top and bottom for expansion. Start with the groove edge to the corner. Check for plumb. Pre-drill all nail holes. Sink the nails with a nail punch and fill the holes. Nail remaining boards through the tongue edge.

3 As you install the boards, tap tongue-and-groove boards together lightly with a hammer, using a piece of scrap planking over the tongue as a tapping surface to protect the wood. Leave a few millimetres of space between planks for expansion. If the boards aren't long enough, join ends together over battens, staggering the joins. Mitre the external room corners or butt them together and cover with trim. Butt all internal room corners and trim the width of the last board to fit.

4 Drill and saw openings in the boards for electrical outlets, light switches and other fittings as the boards go up. You will need an electrician to re-wire power points.

1

2

3

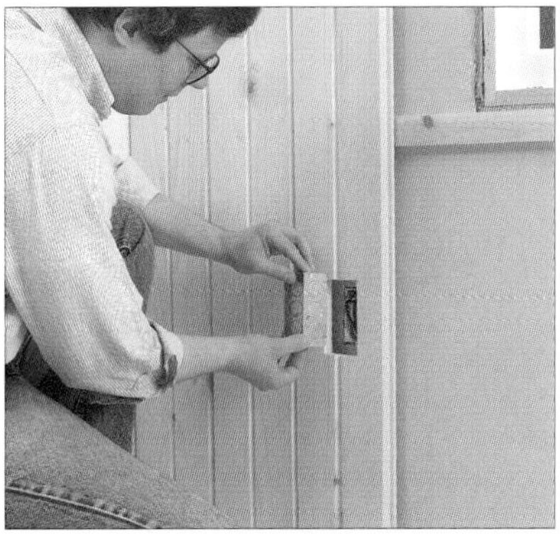

4

5

6

5 After panelling, extend window and door jambs flush with the surface of the panelling with a timber strip of a thickness to match the width of the battens plus panel width. Pre-drill nail holes and use nails that will extend at least 20 mm into the original jamb. The drill bit should be slightly smaller than the nail shank.

6 Apply your finish coats before you replace the casings and cover the holes. Nail the window and door casings in place with the finish nails, making sure the gaps between the jamb extension and panelling are covered up. Replace the original floor and ceiling moulding.

Tip

- Store boards for at least 48 hours in the room where they are to be installed. That way the wood has time to adjust to the room's atmosphere, and warping and buckling are prevented.

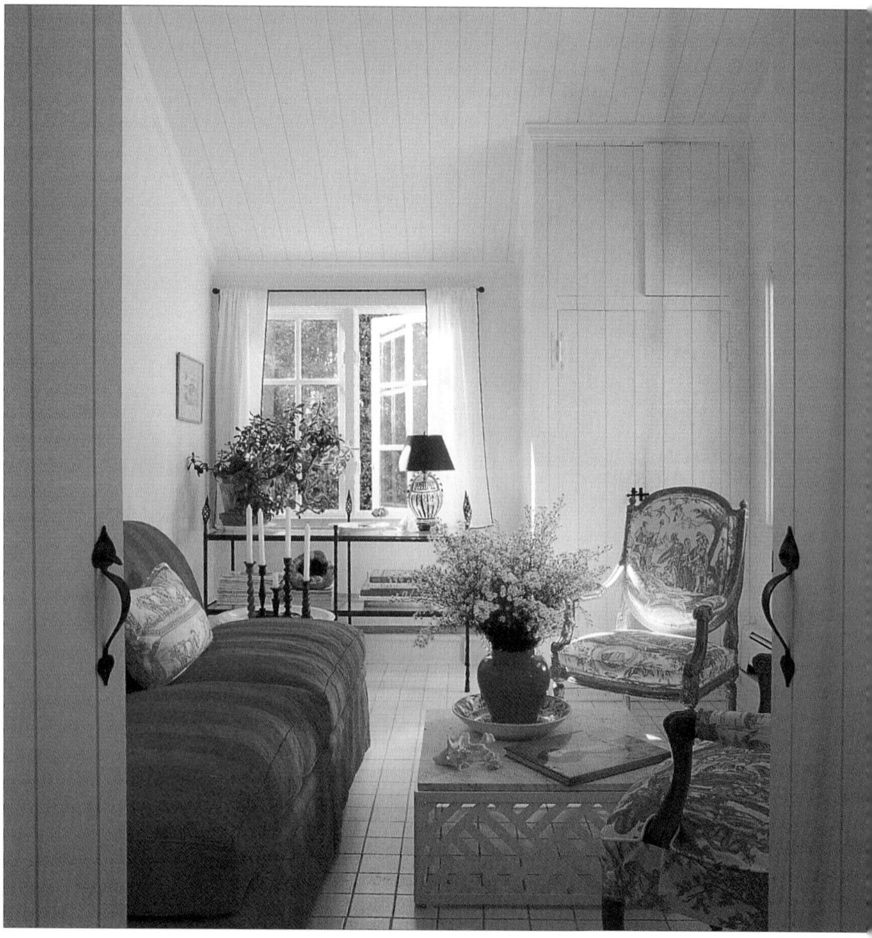

ABOVE: Timber panels in this room have been painted to maintain the original character of the old house.

RIGHT: Timber panelled walls in rich natural tones can be overpowering, unless you use a light coloured timber or lime (whiten) the boards.

Ceilings

Combine the framing of a floor with the covering materials used for walls, and you get the anatomy of a typical home ceiling shown below.

It begins with the same joists that support the subfloor above. Next, the builder may level off the joists' bottom edges with battens or, if the timber is even to begin with, plasterboard or plaster lath may be fastened directly to the joists. Finally, the ceiling is finished with plaster, or joint tape and compound.

You'll find several obvious exceptions to this construction cutaway, though. Sloping top-floor ceilings, for example, usually are attached to the roof framing and, in properly built homes, have insulation above them. You also may encounter lightweight tiles suspended below the joists of an old ceiling. Open-beam ceilings consist of nothing more than the underside of the roof decking above.

Ceiling insulation

Insulation in ceilings places a thick 'blanket' over each room. The cost for an average home is not high and is an investment that could achieve a 30 per cent saving in your heating bills.

If you're handy, agile and sure that the wiring in the roof is safe, and the roof is of high enough pitch, you could insulate the ceilings yourself. Calculate the floor area and get up into the roof to measure the average distance between the ceiling joists. Your insulation supplier will calculate the quantity and size of batts required.

With a lead light and a trimming knife (for cutting the batts to size), begin packing the batts lightly between the joists. Leave no spaces. Take care that you always keep your weight on the joists and not on the ceiling. A short plank will make the procedure more comfortable. Be especially careful around any wiring. For low-pitched roofs, loose-fill material can be sprayed in position.

If you have uncarpeted floors, put batts between the floor joists.

Solving ceiling problems

Repairing large holes

Though plaster and plasterboard ceilings resemble walls in many ways, they're more difficult to patch. First of all, you have to tackle the repair from an uncomfortable position. Second, the patch must cling to the ceiling more securely than is necessary with a wall. That's why you may as well forget about trying to re-plaster a broken-out section yourself. Either hire a professional, or piece in plasterboard.

If you choose to do the plasterboarding, use annular-ring nails or, better yet, self-tapping plasterboard screws (these hold better than nails, are easier to drive into ceilings and make less mess). Protect yourself against dust and debris with goggles, a hard hat and a painter's mask.

For a smooth repair, measure the exact thickness of your ceiling, then either buy plasterboard that size or purchase thinner material and shim it.

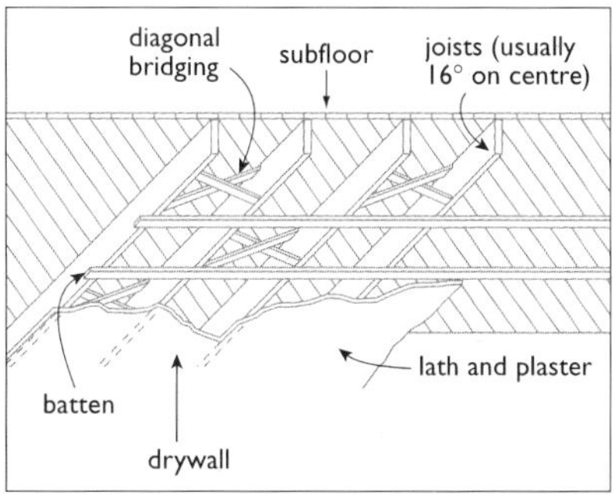

ABOVE: Besides serving the practical purpose of letting in light, skylights can be decorative. Here, a line of fixed skylights in a sloping roof accentuates the upstairs corridor. Fixed skylights are set into a panel of roofing material so that they can be sealed from the weather before they are installed.

BELOW: Anatomy of a ceiling.

Plaster ceilings

Small holes and cracks can be filled with compound, but when the hole is larger, patching is easier. The patching technique works well for repairs when the lath above is in fairly good condition. If the lath is as much of a problem as the ceiling plaster, you'll want to consider redoing the whole thing.

To begin, locate sound plaster around the damaged area, then carefully square off a section and chip it out with a hammer and cold chisel.

Cut a plasterboard patch to size. Butter the edges with joint compound and press in place. Drive nails or screws into the lath above.

Plasterboard ceilings

The technique described above will mend a plasterboard ceiling, too. But because the plasterboard's backing is as regular as its face, you'll get an even smoother repair with the technique illustrated here.

Begin by squaring off around the hole, then bore holes at the corners and cut out the section with a keyhole saw. Then cut a piece of 8 – 12-mm-thick plywood that's about 50 mm longer and 50 mm narrower than the opening. Make sure the plywood will clear the joists on either side, then slip it into place and secure it and the plasterboard patch with screws as shown.

Tape a ceiling repair as you would any plasterboard joint. But when you apply the second and third coats of compound, feather them out more than you would on a wall. To check your progress beam a strong light at the ceiling, stand back and note where you need to do more work. Especially on ceilings, imperfections in taping don't become obvious until you paint.

Raising a sagging ceiling

Look at the diagram shown here and you'll see that a plaster ceiling is keyed into its lath support system. Sometimes humidity, vibration or old age breaks off several of those keys and lets the ceiling down. More rarely, the lath itself begins to pull away from the joists.

If big expanses are descending on you, resign yourself to the arduous task of ripping them out and either piecing in plasterboard or redoing the entire ceiling.

For lesser sags try anchoring the plaster with screws and washers as illustrated here. Make a T-shaped brace about 12 mm taller than your ceiling's height, then wedge it in place to raise the sag. Space the anchors about 10 cm apart, drilling pilot holes first and gouging out shallow depressions for the washers and screw heads. Wherever you encounter a joist, drive several longer screws for additional support.

Replacing a damaged ceiling tile

Completely cut away the damage first so you can get a grip on the tile, then work in a knife and slice the edges free.

Trim the appropriate edges from a new tile, guiding your cuts with a metal straightedge. Lift the tile into position to check for a snug fit.

Clear away any old adhesive or staples from battens and the other tiles, then apply fresh adhesive to them.

Fit one edge first, then press the tile firmly into position and hold it there for a few minutes until the adhesive grabs.

Common ceiling problems		
Problem	**Cause**	**Cure**
Cracks	Settlement and vibrations. These conditions bedevil plaster ceilings especially, but also affect the joints of plasterboard.	Try packing them with spackling or joint compound.
Popped nails	Improperly nailed plasterboard ceilings pulling away from the joists or battens.	Shore up the ceiling, then drive plasterboard screws or annular-ring nails.
Peeling tape	Excessive humidity or improper installation.	In high humidity areas improve the ventilation, then re-tape.

BELOW: Plasterboard ceiling.

BOTTOM: Raising a sagging ceiling.

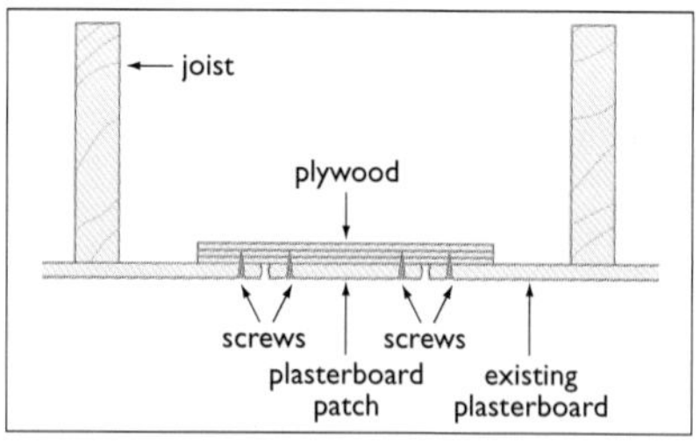

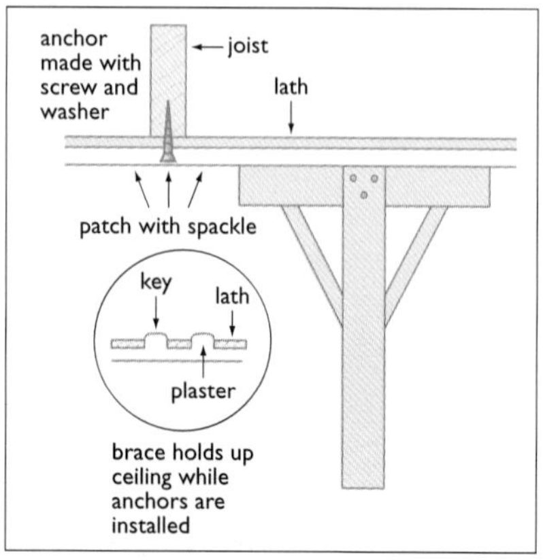

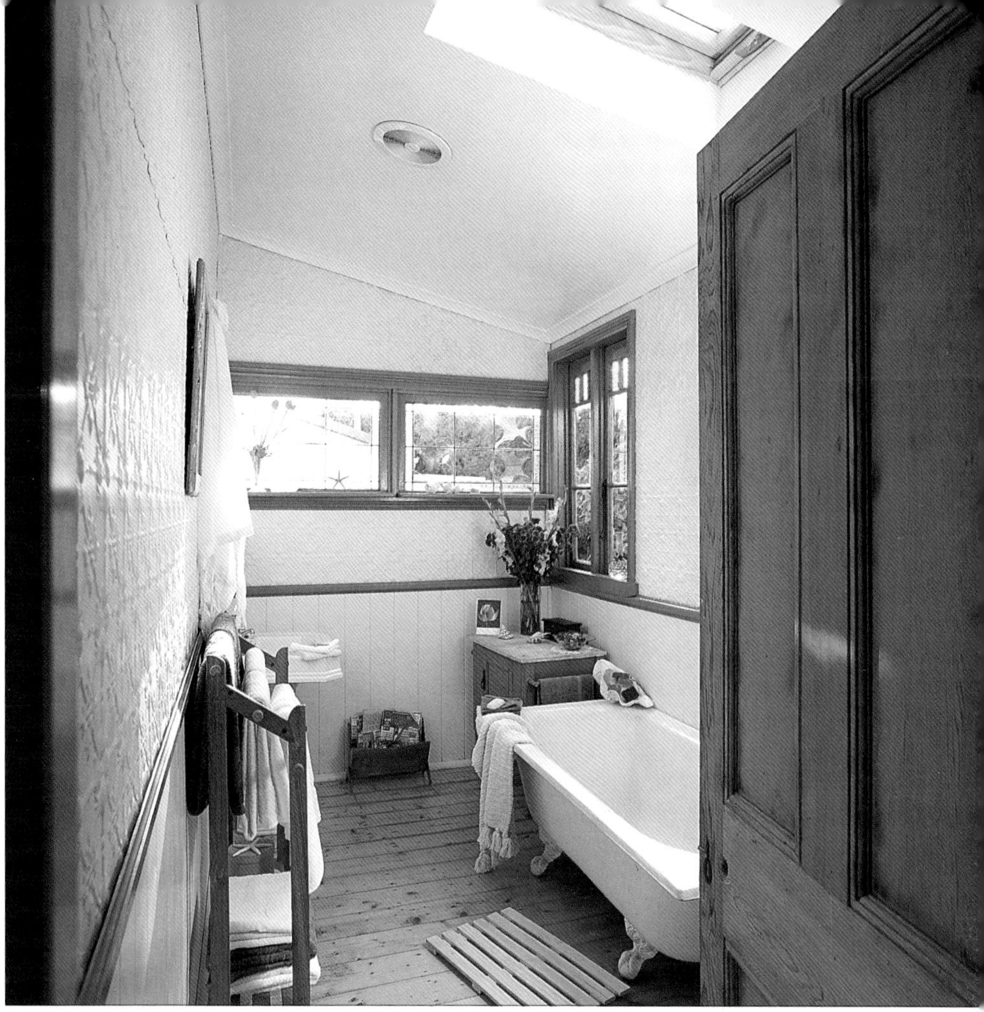

ABOVE: A new ceiling and skylight.

Putting up new ceiling materials

Replacing a ceiling

When a ceiling becomes unsightly, one option is to paint it. If this won't do the trick you may have to replace it. However, it's not always necessary to pull down the old ceiling.

If you have enough headroom (minimum 2400 mm floor to ceiling in a bathroom is the general rule, but there are exceptions) you can simply put new battens on the existing ceiling and Gyprock over these. Battens must be screwed into the existing ceiling joists for solid purchase. At the same time, consider the possibility of putting in a skylight if your room is a little on the dark side.

If you're going to replace the ceiling in the bathroom make sure you use waterproof Gyprock. Conventional Gyprock and water should never meet.

Gyprock sheets come in varying sizes so be sure to measure the dimensions of the ceiling and order so that cutting and waste are kept to a minimum. It's a good idea to give the Gyprock sheets a couple of coats of paint before nailing them to the ceiling. This will save a lot of the difficult painting after they are in place.

You'll need help to lift the sheets into position, as well as a couple of ladders and preferably trestles with long planks between them. Put stud adhesive on 50 x 25 mm radiata pine battens and use Gyprock nails to secure the Gyprock to the battens. Keep going until the whole ceiling is covered. If you need to cut the sheet of Gyprock, the best way is with a Stanley knife. Mark out the section you want to cut and score the surface of one side only. The Gyprock will then snap along this line so you don't have to cut through the whole thickness. Nail on the sheets so that the rebate for the jointing cement faces the floor.

There is a knack to cutting cornices so that the corner join is neat. Buy a mitre box from your plastering supply company or hardware store. Use pre-mixed cornice cement as a fixing agent. Sometimes you'll need to hammer in the occasional tack or nail supporting the bottom edge of the cornice to keep it in place until the cement sets.

The next step is to cover the joints. Start with jointing tape; there is a type specifically made for plastering, which is like a sticky cross-woven cloth. Run this along the joint and cover it with pre-mixed finishing cement. There's a broad knife for the cementing which you can pick up at any hardware store.

When the jointing cement has dried it will need a light sand to smooth the surface for final painting.

Plasterboarding a ceiling

The hardest part of this project comes when you have to wrestle those big plasterboard panels into place. If you have someone to help you, try donning soft hats and supporting each sheet with your heads while fastening it to the joists or battens.

If that proves cumbersome, rig up bracing as shown here. For bigger ceiling jobs you can rent a jack designed for ceiling work.

To determine whether or not you need battens, stretch level, diagonal strings 12 mm below the old ceiling or joists. If the surface rises or falls more than 6 mm, batten it down with 75 x 25 mm battens.

Choosing and buying ceiling tiles

Compared with installing plasterboard, putting up ceiling tiles or panels is a breeze. Instead of handling awkward, 2400 x 1200 mm sheets, you work with lightweight materials and modular installation techniques tailor-made for do-it-yourselfers. And once your new ceiling is up, just wipe off any fingerprints and forget about it — there's no need to mess around with plasterboard joint compound or painting.

Before choosing from among the dazzling array of materials available today, ask yourself a couple of questions. First, how's the headroom? If you have space to drop the new surface a minimum of 75 mm, and especially if you want to cover a network of pipes, wiring and ducts, consider suspending panels from a grid system, as shown on page 58 (see under Installing a suspended ceiling).

If, however, a dropped ceiling would cut the room's overall height to less than 2.4 m, you'll have to apply interlocking tiles to the old ceiling or to a network of battens. You can cement or staple tiles directly to a sound, even ceiling; with uneven surfaces or exposed joists you must put up battens first.

Also ask yourself what you expect the tiles or panels to do. Some, but by no means all, have acoustic properties that help to reduce the noise within a room. But don't expect them to completely muffle sound transmission from one space to another.

Finally, compute your ceiling's square meterage by multiplying the

BELOW: Plasterboarding a ceiling.

1 To locate hidden joists drill a hole, insert a bent wire and rotate. Double check the joist's location by tapping with a hammer.

2 Next, measure carefully to find the ceiling's exact centre, then nail strips across the joists, spaced 400 mm apart.

3 Start plasterboarding at the centre and work towards the edges. Use two braces to hold the panels while you drive nails or screws.

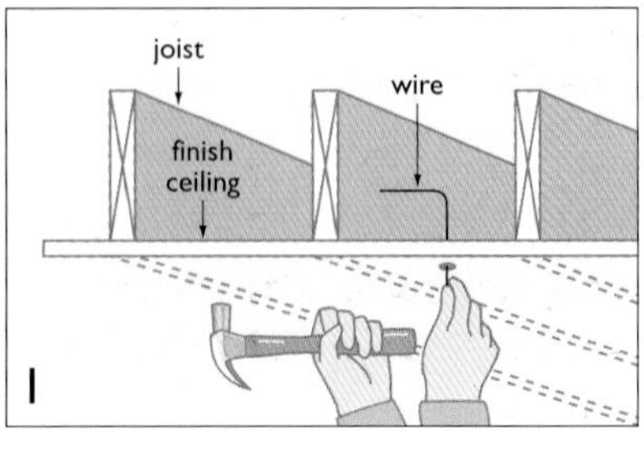

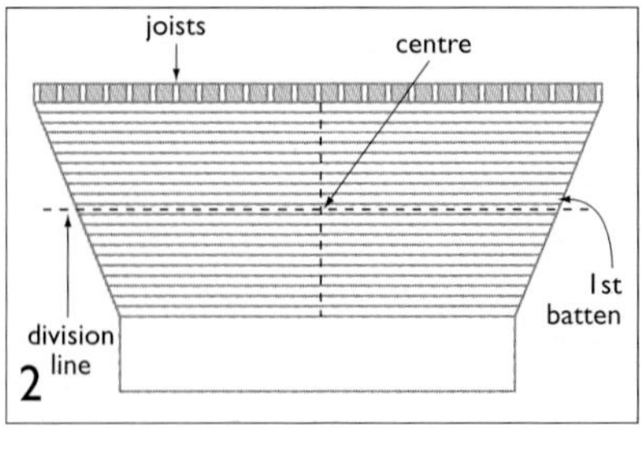

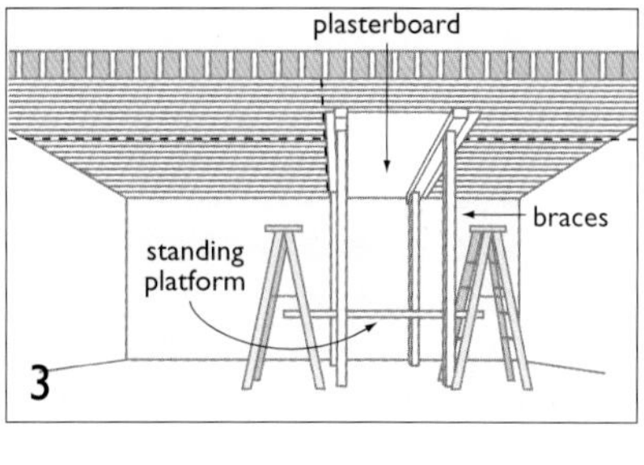

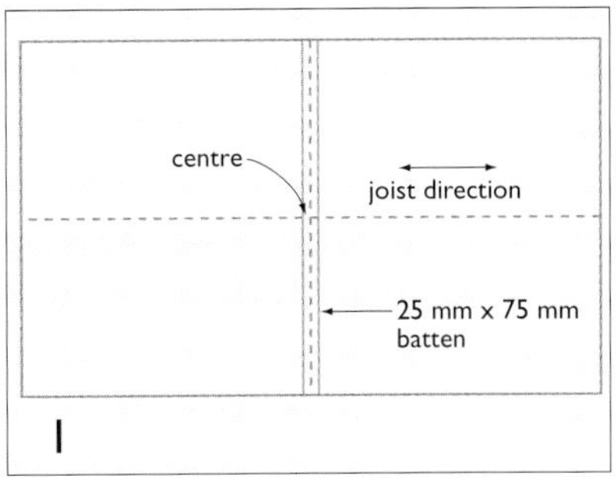

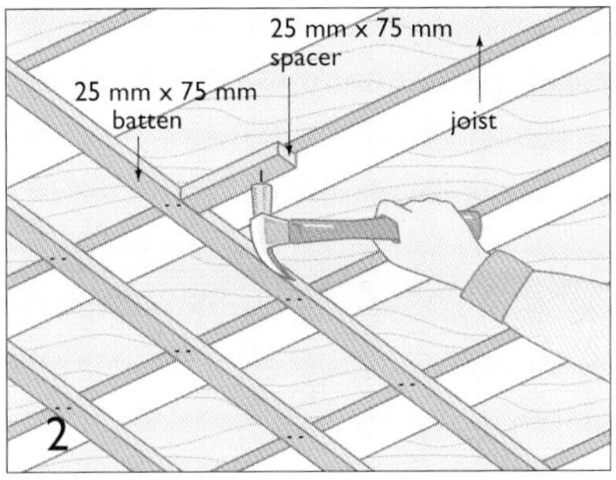

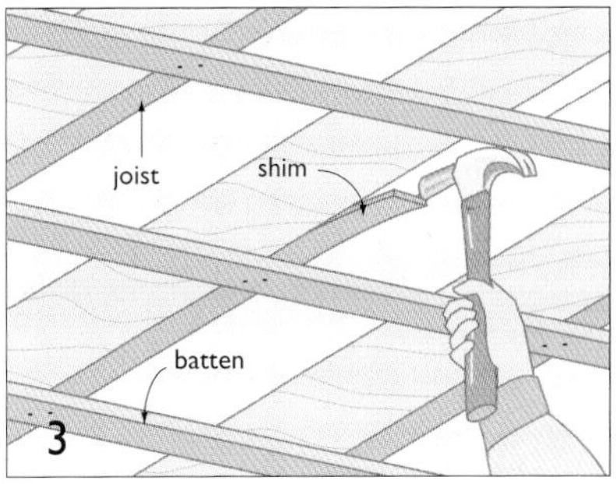

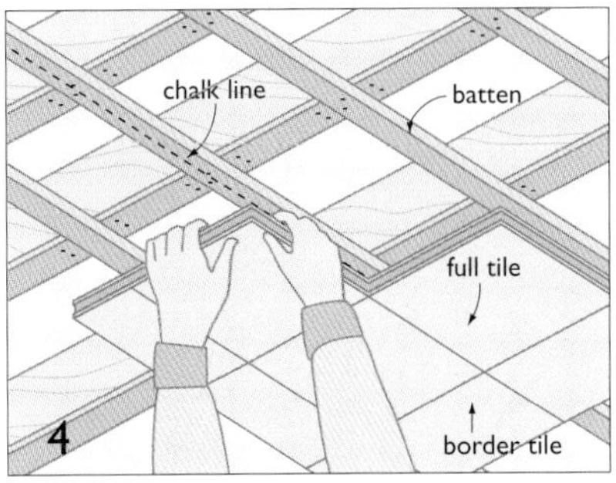

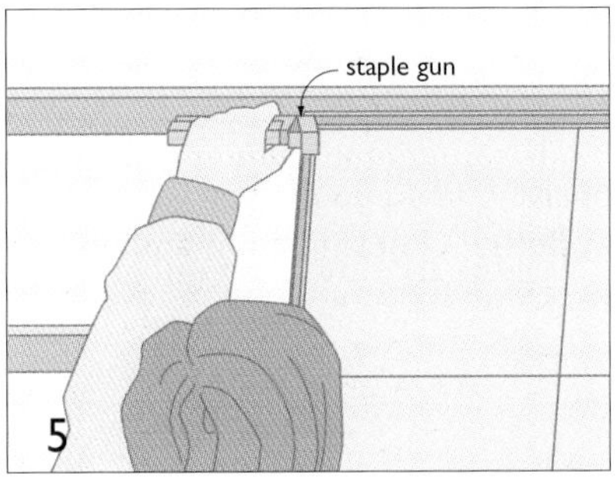

ABOVE: Attaching tiles to battens.

1 Locate the room's exact centre and put up the first batten there. Battens should always run perpendicular to the joists.

2 Space the subsequent strips with centres a tile's width apart, then nail up a spacer wherever two tiles will interlock.

3 Shims level minor irregularities. With a very bumpy ceiling, use the double battens technique shown below.

4 Begin in a corner, cutting the border tiles first. Chalk lines on the battens will help you align the first full tiles.

5 Drive two staples — one atop the other — into each exposed tile corner. The first staple flares the legs of the second.

length of the room by its width. Then add several extra tiles to allow for cutting and waste.

Before making a final decision about tiles, shop around and compare the various types available, their characteristics and relative cost.

Attaching tiles to an old ceiling

Make a drawing to scale of the room, then lay a tracing-paper grid over it. Shift until the partial border tiles are equal.

With a chalk line, transfer measurements from the grid to the ceiling. Mark starter lines and cut the border tiles to fit.

Begin tiling in a corner. Apply tile adhesive according to the manufacturer's directions or staple as illustrated above.

Attaching tiles to battens

Even up an irregular ceiling or exposed joists with wood battens (shimmed) spaced to suit the size of the tiles you've chosen. Some tile companies may offer a metal batten system similar to a suspended-ceiling grid, except that all supporting elements are hidden from view. This method requires a minimum 50 mm drop from the existing ceiling line.

Concealing obstructions

Heating ducts, wiring, beams and plumbing lines usually need hiding when you finish off a room. If the obstruction is small, you may be able to tuck it against the joists and add battens as shown below.

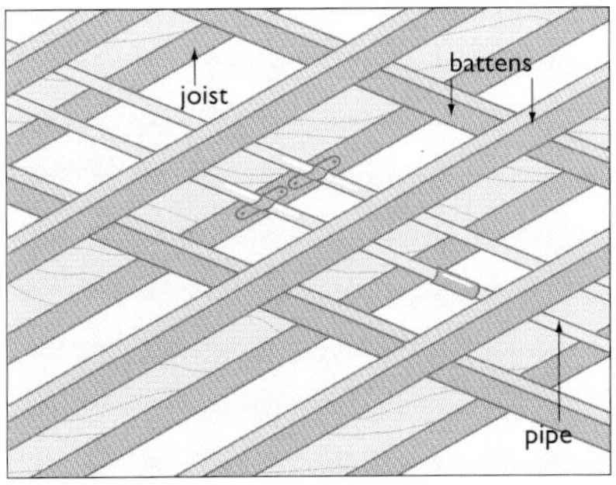

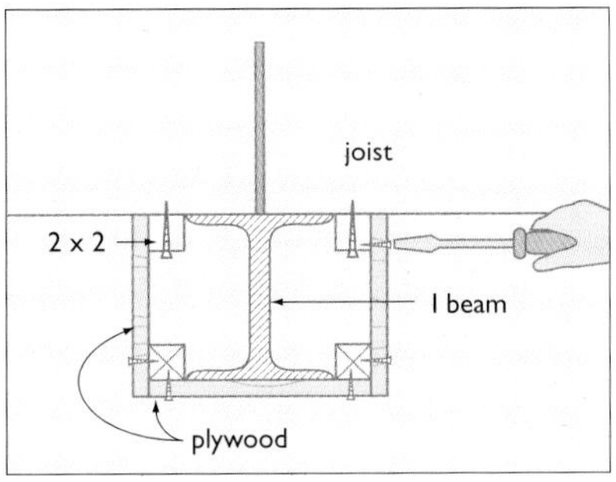

FAR LEFT: Double battens often lower a ceiling line just enough to get below electrical conduit and plumbing supply lines.

LEFT: To cover a support beam, nail up 50 x 50 mm timbers along either side, then build a three-sided plywood box. Attach it as shown.

Chances are, though, you'll need to do some boxing in. If you do, bear in mind that ceilings do only light duty, so you should use light-weight materials — 50 x 25 mm, 75 x 25 mm and 50 x 50 mm for framing, and 12 mm or even 6 mm plywood or hardboard coverings.

Installing a suspended ceiling

Finishing an exposed-joist ceiling isn't the tedious, labour-intensive job it used to be. Today you can crown any room with a suspended ceiling in a day or so without much sweat at all. The secret lies with the components — lightweight steel or aluminium channels that you hang from wires and snap together into a grid, then flesh out by simply setting the ceiling panels into place.

Systems differ somewhat, but you'll need to check that:

- The wall angles extend around the room's edges at finished-ceiling height.
- The main tees run perpendicular to the ceiling joists and are suspended from wires. They come in 3.6 m lengths, which you can cut or splice.
- The cross tees measure 600 or 1200 mm long, depending on the size of your ceiling panels and the direction you want them to run. Clip them to the main tees at each intersection.

One joy of a suspended ceiling installation is that you need to do almost no preparation work. Just mark the locations of any concealed joists and establish a height for your new ceiling.

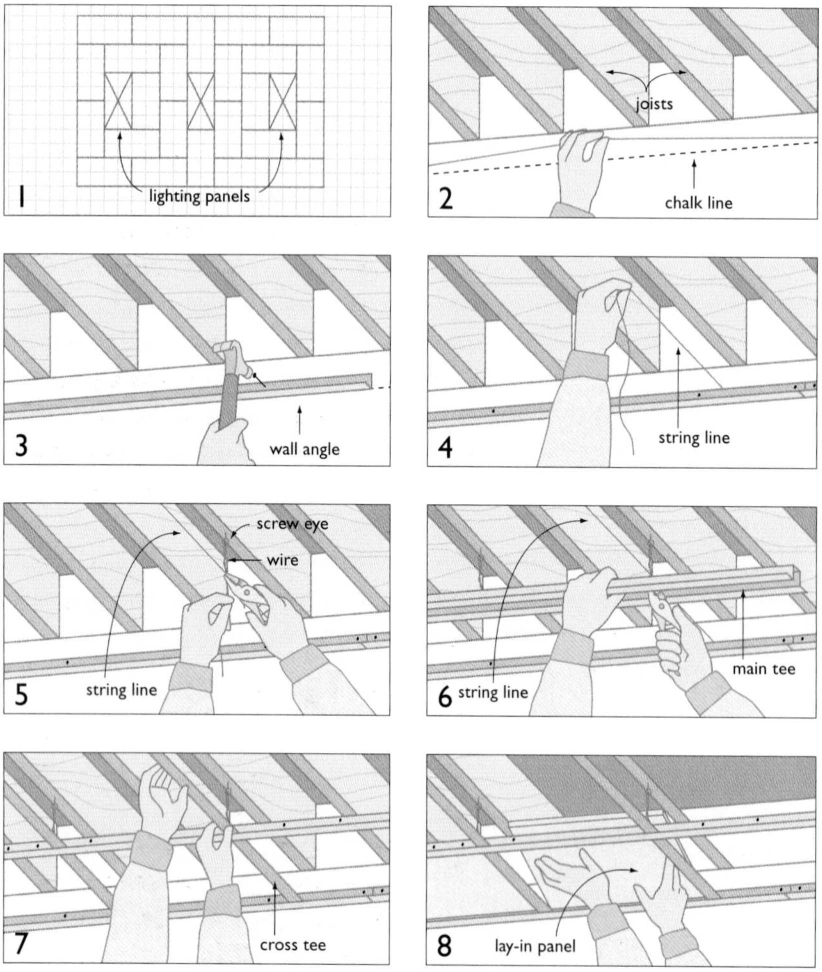

BELOW LEFT: Installing a suspended ceiling.

1 Make careful measurements on a scaled layout to plot sizes for the border tiles and locations of lighting panels.

2 Next, determine the height necessary for clearance above the grid, then snap chalk lines along the walls at this level.

3 Attach the wall angles, aligning their bottom edges with the chalk line. If you're fastening to concrete, use adhesive.

4 To guide you in hanging the main tees, stretch strings across the room at several points. These must be perfectly level.

5 Starting a border tile's distance from the wall, drive screw eyes into every second joist at 1200 mm intervals. Hang and twist wire.

6 Loop the wire through the holes in the main tees, level them, then twist the wire tight. Make minor adjustments with the screw eyes.

7 Install the cross tees now. Cut them to length wherever this is necessary and rest their ends on the main tees.

8 Trim the border panels with a knife and straightedge, set them in place, then fill in the rest of the grid with uncut panels.

Skylights

The building industry has found many ways of introducing light into our homes. These range from whole conservatory-style rooms of only glass and framework to custom-made atrium-style roofing sections to smaller-scale fixed or opening transparent panels fitted into an existing roof.

No matter how much light you want indoors, it is important to know how to go about it. The diagrams and photographs show you most of the skylight options available on the market today. Some of these require relatively inexpensive and small-scale installation, others involve large-scale customised fabrication and design work. It is important to know exactly what sort of skylight you want before it is installed as mistakes are costly and messy.

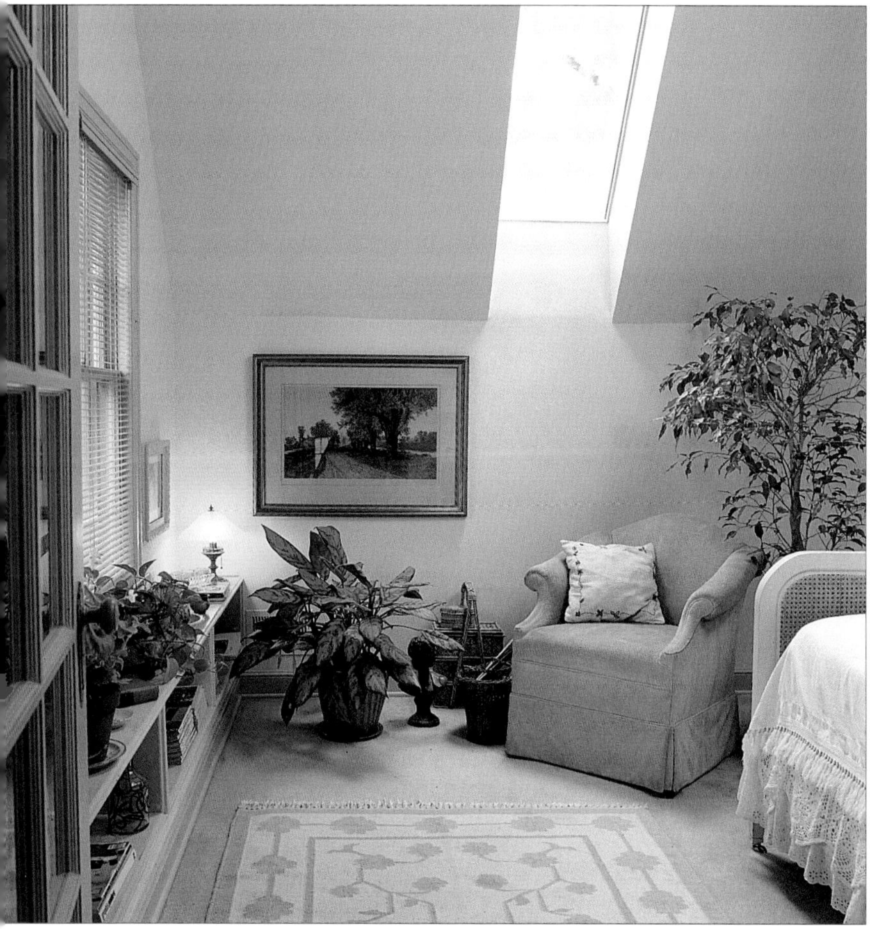

ABOVE. The new room built onto the back of this house is set at garden level and the old part of the house looks down onto it. Roofing the addition was a simple matter of pitching a one-way sloping skillion off the back of the house. The inclusion of several skylights has effectively turned the new roof into a grid running between the rectangles of light.

LEFT: Always think about ceiling geometry when you are considering skylights. Long narrow shapes going all the way down to the line of the eaves create the effect of slots of light internally. When all the surfaces are plaster set, the skylight looks even more pristine.

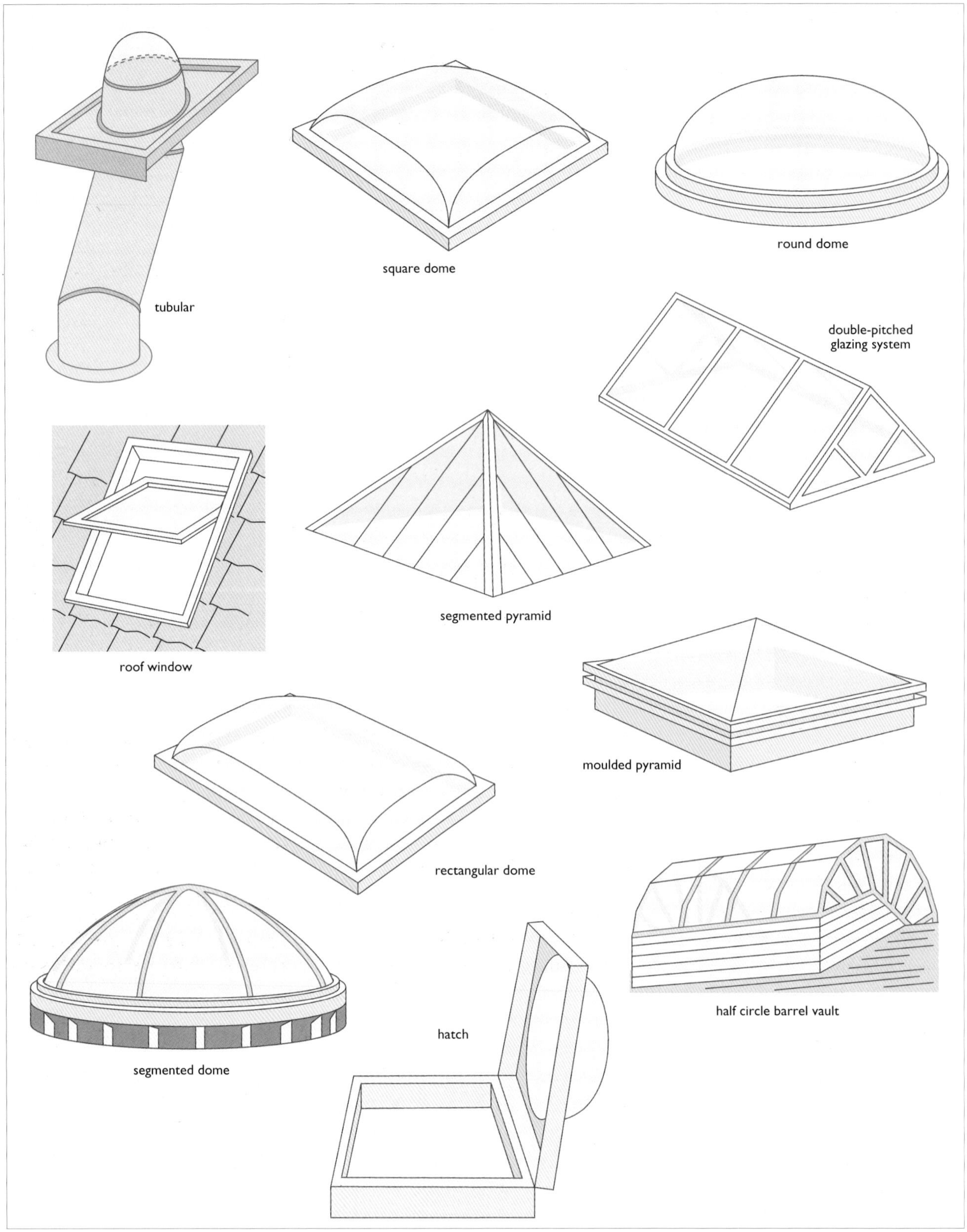

ABOVE: There is a range of options in skylight design. Pictured here are the most commonly used skylights.

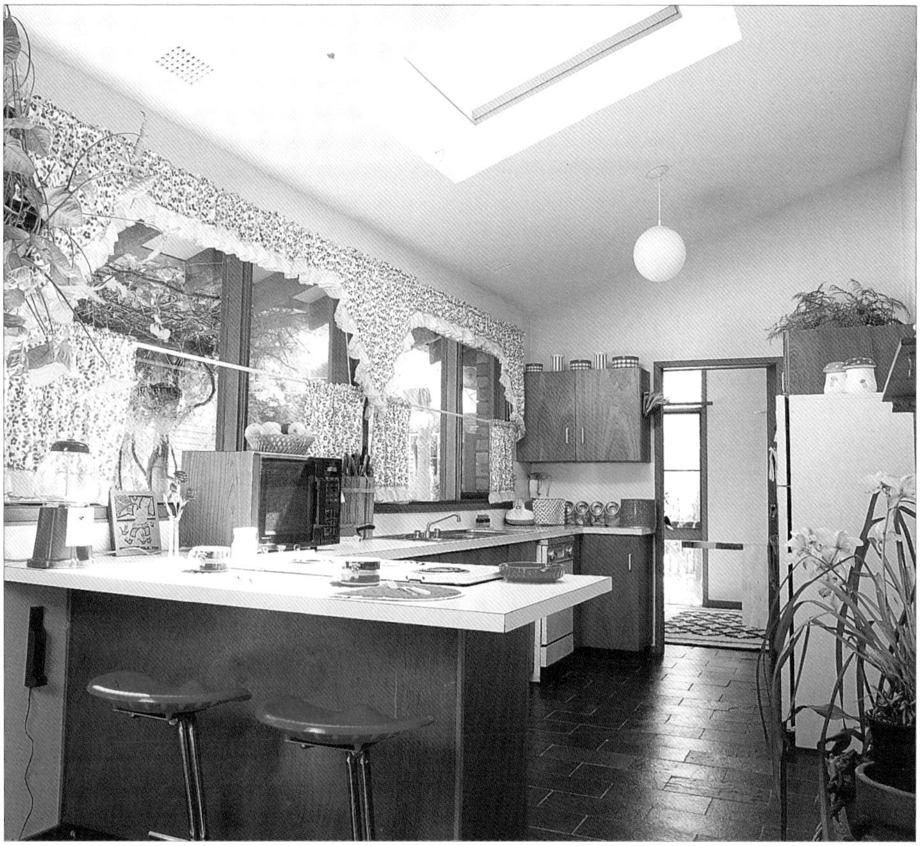

RIGHT: A skylight is an excellent way to let light, heat and air into any room.

BELOW: Installing a skylight.

1 Mark the position of the skylight on the ceiling; make sure that one side of it fits alongside the ceiling joist. Drive a stout nail through its centre.

2 Once tiles are removed and stacked close by, cut the battens. If you don't have a chainsaw (as shown) use a circular saw or handsaw.

3 After cutting the rafters, until they are trimmed keep your weight off them. Frame joints must be well nailed— use a minimum of four 75 mm nails in each.

Installing a skylight

A skylight is a fantastic way to let light and heat into dreary rooms. It is suitable for a roof with a pitch between 15° and 85°. This is a fixed unit, not to be confused with a roof-mounted window which can be opened and closed.

Putting in a skylight, especially if the ceiling follows the slope of the roof, is certainly not beyond the capability of the average do-it-yourselfer.

First, decide how large a skylight you require; two smaller ones might be better than one large one. Discuss your needs with several manufacturers or suppliers. When it's delivered, carefully read the installation

1

2

3

4

5

6

7

8

9

instructions. Keep in mind that you're going to put a hole in your roof, one which could let in the rain if there is a hold up because you don't know exactly how the unit should be fitted or there's a part missing. Get a small tarpaulin and some ropes, in case.

Drive a thick nail into the ceiling where the skylight is to go. Wearing non-slip shoes, get up on the roof. Walk on the noses of the tiles, locate the area and remove the tiles. The skylight must not interfere with a ceiling hanger or a purlin.

Cut the tiling battens. Mark out the frame size that will hold the skylight, cut the rafters and put in trimmers in accordance with the manufacturer's instructions (see photo 3). Watch carefully for wiring.

Cut away the excess plaster with an old saw. Take the skylight from its box; remove flashings, trims and so on.

Stand the frame in the recommended position and fix it to the rafters and trimmers using the brackets provided (photo 7). It must be level across the roof at both ends (photo 8).

Fit the bottom flashing; bend it to follow contours of tiles.

Fit the side flashings, the top flashing (see 11) and so on. Refit the tiles around the skylight. You could use tile cutters or a carborundum wheel fixed in your circular saw for this. (If the latter is used, make sure you wear goggles and long protective clothing.) If you've followed the steps correctly, your kitchen won't be a swimming pool.

Cut and fit the gypsum plaster so it fits into the skylight rebate. Cut and fix the metal angles that strengthen the corners.

Plaster the corners. Sand, dry and paint them.

4 Before sawing the hole in the plasterboard, cut deeply into the sheet from underneath with a trimming knife. This will lessen the likelihood of the paper lining tearing.

5 In this instance, an electric cable is running right across the skylight opening. Don't make any attempt to move it yourself! This is definitely a job for an electrician.

6 If you've made the opening the correct size, the brackets of the sides of the skylight should stand on the framing members. Make sure the sarking fits the opening.

10

11

12

13

14

15

7 Read the manufacturer's instructions carefully, then position the skylight and, after double checking it's correct, temporarily fix it to one of the rafters or trimmers.

8 Use a spirit level to check whether or not the skylight is level. If it is not, pack it up on the low side and then, using screws or nails, fasten it securely in place.

9 The flashings are important; they are there to stop leaks developing between the skylight and the roof covering. They must be installed carefully and without damage.

10 When you are fitting the flashings to the roof tiles, a softwood block can be used for beating the metal gently. Do this until it fits the contours of the tiles exactly.

11 When fitting the side and top flashings, proceed slowly. Double check each step. Imagine the volume of water that runs down the roof in a storm — you don't want a drop inside!

12 The final step outside is to replace the tiles. This will involve cutting. Once the job is done, be sure to clear away all the debris that could block the downpipes.

13 Measure the exposed area between the rebate in the skylight and the ceiling and cut the plasterboard to suit. Then nail the plasterboard in place, using plasterboard nails.

14 Metal angles, fixed over corners, strengthen the join and give a straight line to work to when you are plastering. Cut them with a hacksaw and nail them in place.

15 Using a trowel, apply the jointing cement in three separate layers, each one getting wider and wider. Make sure that you feather each of the joints away to nothing.

1

2

3

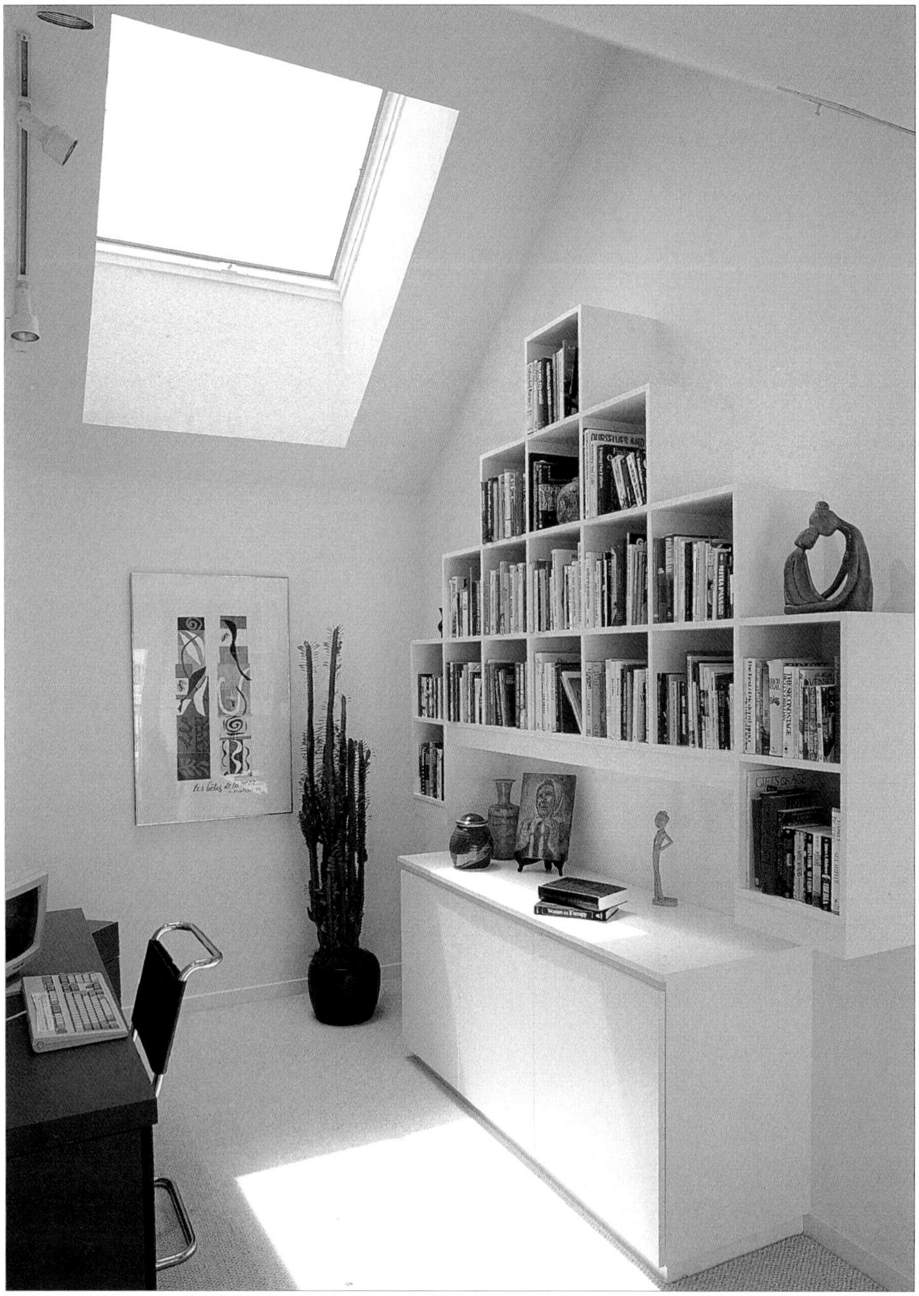

ABOVE: How to cut plasterboard.

1 Measure and mark the shapes required. Make sure the face side (unmarked) faces outwards. With a sharp utility knife, cut deeply along the line.

2 Turn the board over and, holding one edge in your hand, give the sheet a bang with your fist. This should cause the sheet to break, creating a 'V'.

3 Using the utility knife, cut along the 'V' on the back of the sheet. This will ensure that the paper does not get ripped. Alternatively, use an old saw to cut the sheet.

LEFT: Opening roof windows solve all the ventilation and sunlight problems associated with internal rooms. Particularly in the case of attic conversions like this one, where dormer windows are not an option, an opening skylight turns an old roof cavity into a useful space.

Floors

The choice of floor surface is usually determined by the function of the room. This section provides a practical guide to the types of flooring and how to maintain and repair them.

What's afoot?

When you are deciding what to use on your floor, remember that this is one of the largest spaces in your room to decorate. It is the area you are least likely to change and, unless you are using paint, the floor covering is likely to be a sizeable investment. Consider how much traffic each room will receive and allocate your funds accordingly. Try to buy the best quality you can.

Choose carefully, because the type of flooring you select will have a great influence on the mood and style of your room.

ABOVE: Place a beautiful, bright rug over the top of wall-to-wall carpet to give a whole new look. The rug's colours and pattern can then be continued in a wonderful array of plump pillows and scatter cushions. This is specially suitable if the carpet is not to your liking or you are in rented premises.

RIGHT: Link a casual family area with the garden by carrying brick paving right into the family room — it will enlarge the space visually. There's no need to worry about wet feet or placing pot plants on this floor, as it's practically indestructible.

ABOVE: Casual coir matting makes a delightfully natural background for big, comfortable canvas-covered chairs. You can lay it as wall-to-wall carpet or have it finished around the edges and use it as an area rug on timber or tiled floors. If a dressier look is what you're after, a similar design is now available in wool.

LEFT: Quarry tiles can look formal or casual, depending on the roughness or smoothness of their surface and whether they are machine or handmade. Hand-painted feature tiles in this dining alcove act as a decorative space definer.

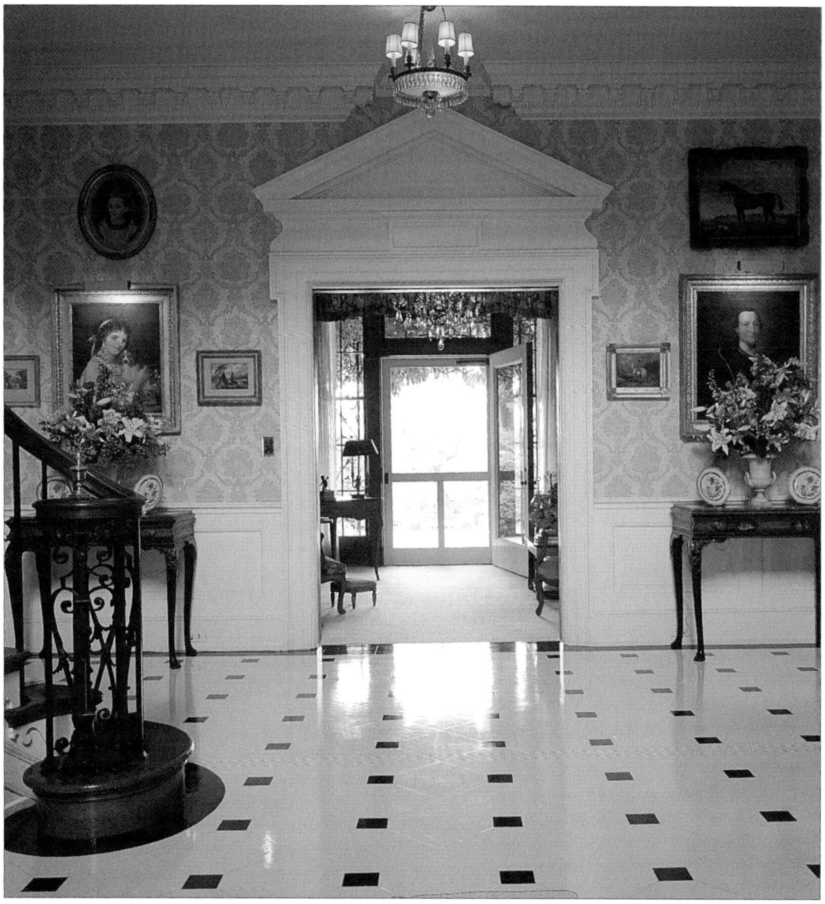

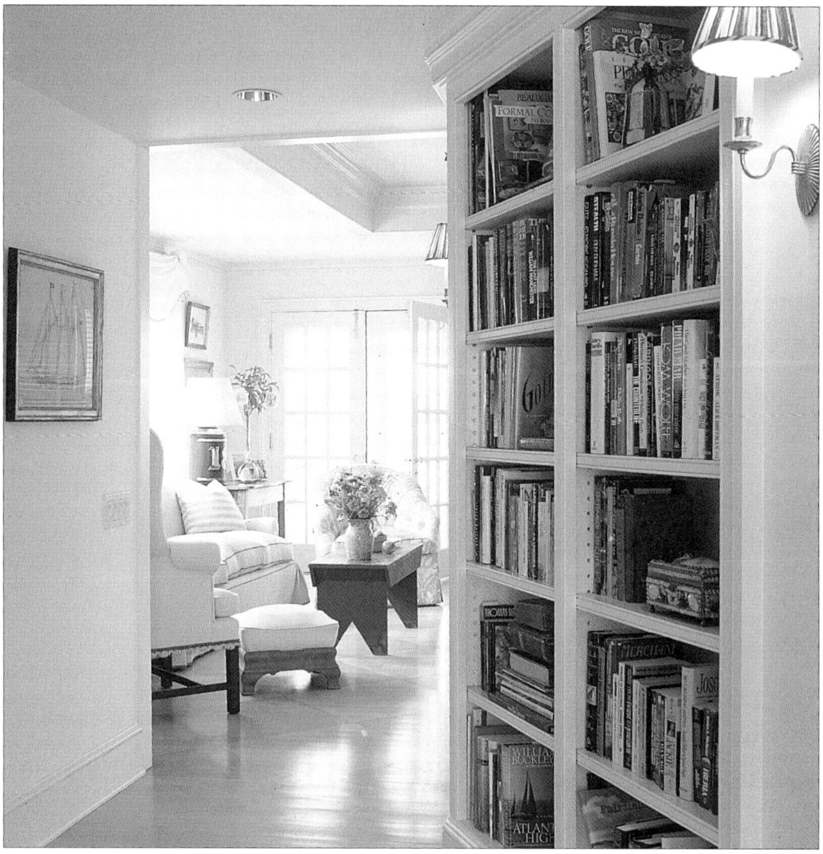

ABOVE: The regular grid pattern of terracotta quarry tiles in this hallway repeats the clean architectural lines of the building and provides a background for richly patterned Persian rugs.

ABOVE RIGHT: Real marble tiles are beautiful but expensive. If they are beyond your budget, there are many excellent vinyl substitutes, which have the advantage of being softer and warmer underfoot. A classic design looks good even in a small space.

RIGHT: After sanding the floor, you could bleach it and stencil on a diamond pattern or other design with thinned paint. The grain of the timber will show through.

The file on flooring

The ground rules for flooring emphasise both appeal and practicality. The floor finish you choose will have a considerable impact on the rest of your decorating scheme. Appearances aren't everything, though, so it is important to bear in mind that the function of a room determines the degree of durability you require. And, because subfloor (and, therefore, building considerations) play their part in the decision making, floors are not solely the domain of the decorator. Here are some flooring options.

Vinyl squares

Subfloor. Any level surface.

DIY. Yes.

Decorative character. Plain, chequerboard or flecked.

Advantages. Cost efficient, serviceable and crisp looking.

Seagrass matting

Subfloor. Any floor surface.

DIY. Yes. Installation instructions included. No underlay necessary.

Decorative character. Casual.

Advantages. Cost efficient. Distinctive natural look. Serviceable.

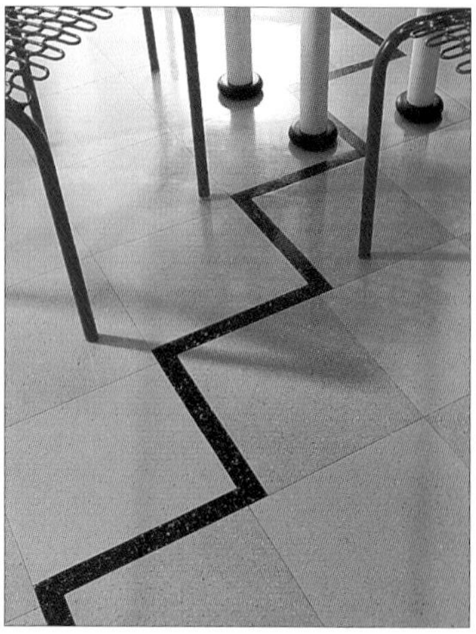

Inlaid vinyl

Subfloor. Any perfectly level surface.

DIY. Not possible because it requires precision cutting. Executed by specialist layers only.

Decorative character. Dramatic and sharp.

Advantages. Allows the floor to make a graphic statement.

Slate

Subfloor. Timber or concrete with rubberised glue.

DIY. Laying yourself requires comprehensive technical advice.

Decorative character. Rocky, natural and organic in many colours and shapes.

Advantages. Absorbs solar heat. Warmth of feel and appearance. Can be resealed for maintenance.

Marble squares

Subfloor. Timber or concrete with rubberised glue.

DIY. Better to employ a tradesperson.

Decorative character. Cool, crisp, severe, elegant.

Advantages. Prestigious, opulent, classical and natural appearance. Light reflective. Available in a wide range of colours.

Ceramic tiles

Subfloor. Timber or concrete with rubberised glue.

DIY. Yes, but should seek expert advice.

Decorative character. Depending on selection — crisp and contemporary or Mediterranean and traditional.

Advantages. Fully glazed and, therefore, extremely serviceable — ideal for wet areas and where interior and exterior floor surfaces merge.

Cork

Subfloor. Perfectly level surface.

DIY. Possible but not recommended.

Decorative character. Rich, warm and textured.

Advantages. Shiny surface but still soft to walk on.

Terrazzo

Subfloor. Concrete slab for concrete terrazzo. New lightweight epoxy requires 6–10 mm of epoxy and can be laid on timber/particle-board floors.

DIY. Professional laying essential.

Decorative character. Hard, flecked surface that can vary in colour and texture depending on its composition.

Advantages. Ideal for indoors and outdoors. Easy to maintain. Distinctive, fashionable appearance.

Sheet vinyl

Subfloor. Concrete, timber or particle board.

DIY. Possible to lay yourself if subfloor is even.

Decorative character. Fresh. A wide range of finished effects depending on colour and texture.

Advantages. 4 m roll width allows seamless floors. Very easy to clean.

Carpet

Subfloor. Concrete, particle board or timber. Rubber underlay.

DIY. Not recommended.

Decorative character. Soft, plush and luxuriant.

Advantages. Warm in winter, absorbs sound, immediately gives a room a furnished feeling.

Paving bricks

Subfloor. Concrete slab.

DIY. Yes

Decorative character. Rustic.

Advantages. Retain heat. Easy maintenance, especially if you use silicon-dipped, pre-sealed variety. Novelty value for interior application. Good for interior/exterior continuity.

Terracotta tiles

Subfloor. Concrete, timber or particle board with rubberised glue.

DIY. Yes. Especially uneven styles that do not require precision.

Decorative character. Warm, earthy, Mediterranean.

Advantages. Either untreated or with wax surface sealer, terracotta has a soft, natural look and distinctive feel.

Particle board

Subfloor. Floor joists at 450 mm or 600 mm centres.

DIY. Simple to lay yourself.

Decorative character. Warm, textural. Similar to cork.

Advantages. Cost efficient. Can be polished and exposed or laid with a covering of your choice.

Rubber

Subfloor. Any surface that is without irregularities. Subfloor preparations can take the form of self-levelling compounds in the case of concrete slabs or masonite sheets for timber floors.

DIY. Possible to lay yourself using the correct epoxy glue.

Decorative character. Contemporary but can be made to suit different styles of rooms depending on colour.

Advantages. Will last forever. Has distinctive hi-tech appearance. Can be sealed later when required.

Carpet tiles

Subfloor. Any level surface. No underlay required.

DIY. Yes. Instructions supplied.

Decorative character. Bold patterns that can be tailored to room shape and size.

Advantages. Tiles can be replaced and rotated to avoid wear. Appear seamless when well installed.

Floorboards

Subfloor. 100 x 50 mm joists at 400 mm centres or concrete slab.

DIY. You can lay your own floors if you hire floor cramps and seek building instruction. Sanding and polishing can also be a DIY job.

Decorative character. Traditional — ideal for floor rugs.

Advantages. Long life because of ease of maintenance and re-finishing. Cost efficient, especially if renovating where floors are already laid.

Coir matting

Subfloor. Any floor surface.

DIY. Professional laying recommended because of tendency to fray when cut.

Decorative character. Natural, textural.

Advantages. The complete cover of carpet but with a less formal character. Very serviceable.

Parquetry

Subfloor. Concrete, particle board or timber.

DIY. Difficult. Professional laying highly recommended.

Decorative character. Formal, rich and traditional.

Advantages. The most prestigious of timber floor finishes which can be laid in a variety of designs and types of timber.

BELOW: Carpet is an ideal floor covering in a bedroom. Besides being warm in winter, it absorbs sound and feels soft and plush underfoot.

Carpet

Many homeowners are confused when it comes to choosing carpet for their house. It's not surprising, given the range of styles, colours, fibres, grades and prices to be considered. But you can make the choice easier by understanding how different types of carpet can suit your needs.

Types of carpet

Carpet comes in several different fibres. The main ones are nylon, wool, wool/synthetic mix and polypropylene. Wool and nylon are both excellent if you buy good quality.

Nylon carpet is the most durable carpet but it does not retain its appearance as well as wool. Wool is generally regarded as having better stain resistance, but improvements in stain treatments to nylon carpets have meant both fibres are excellent when it comes to cleaning and stain resistance. Nylon carpet isn't as resistant to burns as wool. Generally, nylon carpets have a brighter colour range because they're easy to dye.

Wool carpet will look good longer, cleans well, resists burns and wears well. It is softer than synthetic carpet and will age more gracefully than synthetic carpet.

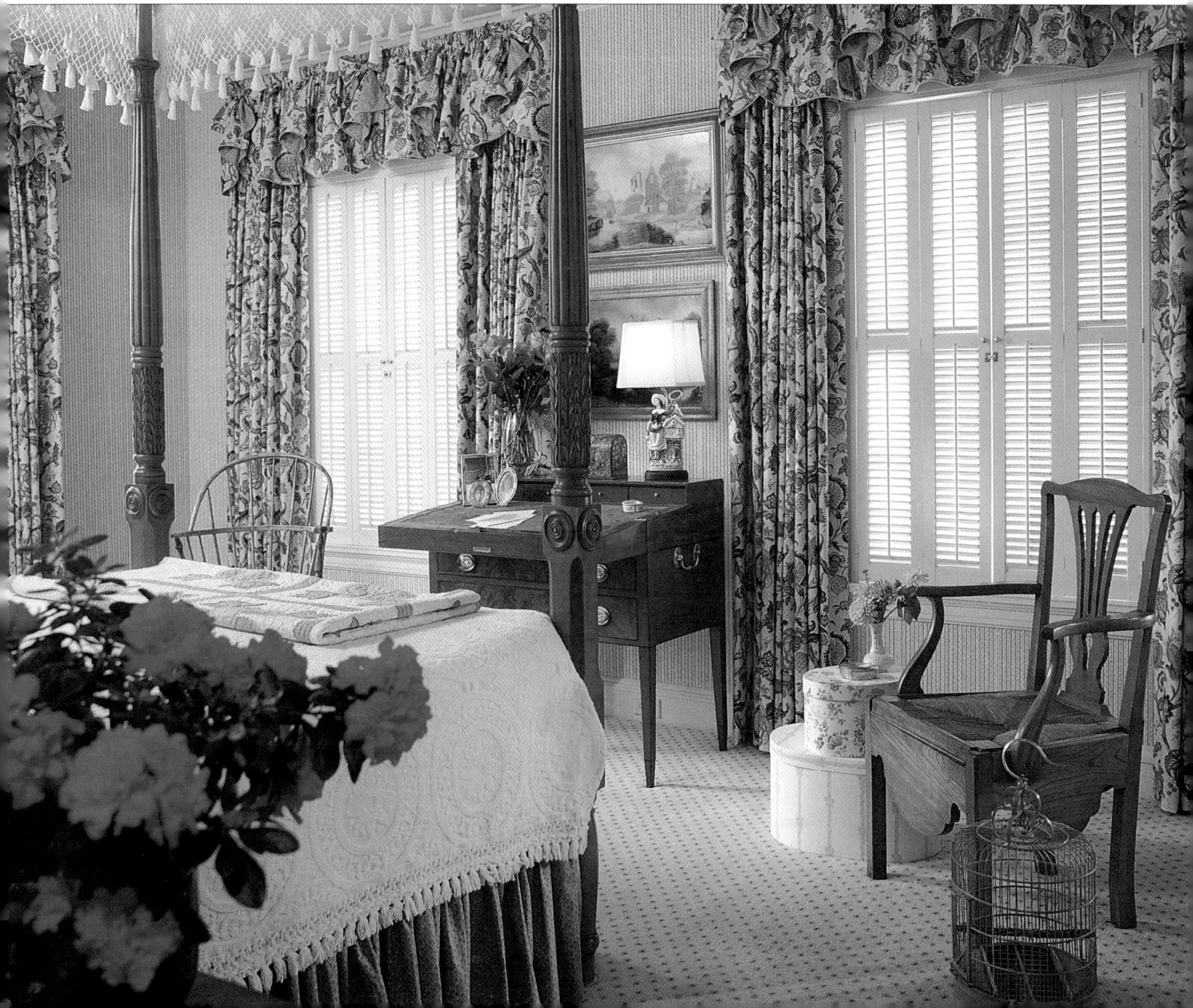

Wool/synthetic mix carpet was produced originally to reduce the cost of wool carpet and to add durability to it. The mixed carpet is not as soft as pure-wool carpet and is only slightly cheaper than wool.

Polypropylene is comparatively inexpensive and has good durability, although not as good as nylon, but is harsh to the touch. It also has a good resistance to soiling.

Grading

The life span of any carpet will vary according to fibre, quality and wear and tear. Areas that will wear most quickly include the stairs and turning points in any room or hall. As a result, it's important to assess the traffic areas in your house and use the correct grade of carpet.

Wool and synthetic carpets both come in grades that are based on the amount of fibre in the carpet. There are four grades—light, medium, heavy duty and extra heavy duty use. You should buy the highest grade you can afford for best durability.

Medium and light carpets are fine for bedrooms, although you may like heavy duty if you have children. Heavy duty or extra heavy duty are suitable for halls, entrances and stairs. Living areas should have heavy duty at least.

Underlay

Good underlay will absorb pressures, reduce wear on your carpet, prevent dirt from the floor getting up into your carpet, cushion carpet from uneven floors and insulate from heat and cold.

Felt underlay is good for sound deadening on wooden floors, but it's not used as much as rubber and foam. Rubber underlay is a waffle-like construction, and both it and foam are very good for use on concrete floors because they act as a barrier against moisture. Remember to choose an underlay that is firm rather than soft or the carpet will stretch.

Maintenance

Carpet will look better longer if it's properly maintained. At the very least, you should vacuum it once a week, moving the vacuum cleaner slowly over the pile to loosen the dirt. This will prevent the dirt from collecting in the base of the carpet pile where it can rub and cut fibre loose.

Don't forget to replace your vacuum cleaner bags when they are half full—if the bag is completely full the suction will not be as effective. It's also vital to treat stains and spills immediately after they occur. Apply stain removal techniques which are appropriate for your carpet.

With proper care your carpet won't need major cleaning for many years, but when you do want to clean it completely or revive the fibres, steam cleaning is the best option — however, make sure it's done by a professional. Once every two years should be sufficient, or even less frequently if your carpet isn't too badly treated.

Texture options

The main methods of making carpets are Tufted, Axminster and Wilton. Tufted is the most common and comes in three main textures — loop pile, cut pile or a combination of both.

Loop pile is made of loops of yarn of uniform or different length. It wears well and tends to hide footprints. Cut pile is achieved by cutting the tops off the loops so that they will stand upright and form an even surface. The most common cut-pile carpets are plushes and hard-twist piles. Plush carpet has been twisted slightly and heat set, while hard-twist cut pile uses yarn that is highly twisted and set. This type of carpet minimises footmarks, shading and shedding. Cut and-loop pile is a combination of loop and cut yarn with a sculptured appearance.

The Axminster and Wilton carpet-making processes produce the intricately patterned and multi-coloured carpets traditionally seen in heritage homes.

LEFT: Carpet is practical and warm in a sunroom.

RIGHT: A decorative rug under the dining table reduces noise and defines the area.

Dos and don'ts of cleaning rugs

- Rugs will last a lot longer if they are cleaned and moved regularly.
- Vacuum your rug regularly or use a flat-faced carpet beater to clean it.
- Deal with spills and stains as quickly as possible. Use warm water and a light detergent. Most importantly, do not use harsh chemicals.
- Use a proprietary rug-cleaning product to clean your rugs regularly — do not let dirt build up.
- Do not immerse your rug in water or hang it up to dry.
- Valuable rugs will need periodic cleaning by a professional cleaner.

Rugs

How to install a rug underlay

Underlay prevents your rug from slipping underfoot and will keep it perfectly even on the floor. There are several varieties to choose from (for a timber floor, polyester underlay is the most effective).

Most rug suppliers will supply underlay when you buy your rug for a minimal extra charge. Here's how to install it:

1. Roll out your rug into the exact position you want it.
2. Carefully roll it up again, ensuring it does not move out of line.
3. Apply underlay to the floor surface and ensure it is held firmly.
4. Align the rolled edge of the rug to the edge of the underlay, unroll the rug and use pressure to ensure the rug adheres to the underlay.
5. Use scissors to trim off excess underlay.

Laying new floor materials

Choosing and buying wood flooring

Wood flooring comes in strips and blocks. Strip flooring, which is by far the most common, typically measures from 50 to 150 mm wide with a smaller cover size due to the tongues and grooves. Most block (or parquet) flooring consists of strips that have been glued together into squares or rectangles.

You can purchase all these types of flooring finished or unfinished. Pre-finished flooring costs more

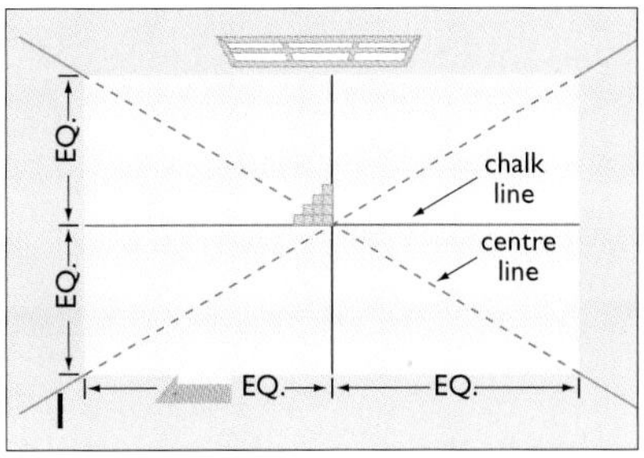

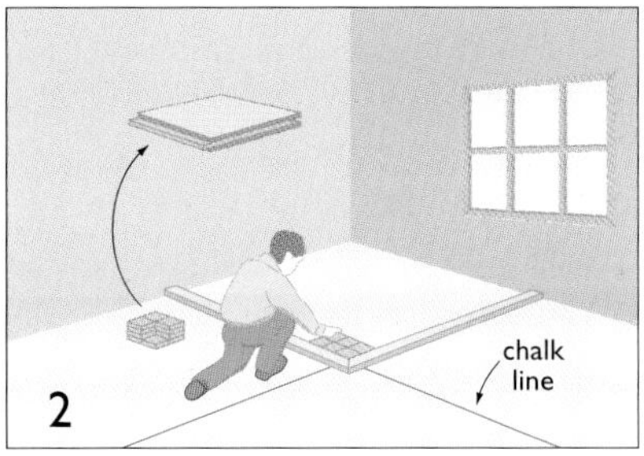

LEFT: Laying a parquetry floor.

1 Plan the installation by squaring off the room with chalk lines.

2 Lay a pair of 50 x 25 mm battens along the chalk lines and you'll get off to a square start. Tongue-and-groove edges keep later courses true.

and you must install it with extreme care so you don't mar the surface; unfinished flooring, on the other hand, must be sanded to smooth minor surface irregularities.

Flooring grades vary somewhat, depending on the kind of wood. Before you lay flooring, let the wood acclimatise to the conditions at your house. Have it delivered at least 72 hours in advance and spread it out in the room where it's to be laid.

Laying a parquetry floor

One reason for the popularity of parquetry flooring is that it's fairly easy to install, but it is not easy to do well. You don't need to use nails; adhesive will work just as well. On concrete it's best to put down a layer of polyethylene film, sleepers positioned 450 mm on centre and a subfloor material before laying the flooring.

Using a power nailer

Almost all wood flooring interlocks in tongue-and-groove fashion. To fasten it to your old floor or subfloor, blind nail at a 45–50° angle through the tongue along the length of each board, then set the nail so that the groove of the next board will fit over the tongue of the one you've just nailed.

A power nailer, available from flooring and tool rental dealers, speeds the job and saves your back. Clips of special nails load much like staples into a stapler. Using a heavy flooring hammer, simply strike the machine's piston drive mechanism to set each nail. With one of these tools, you can lay several hundred square metres of flooring a day.

Laying wood flooring over concrete

Strip-and-plank flooring can be cemented directly to concrete, but it is a job for a specialist. If you don't want to build a subfloor, lay a polyethylene vapour barrier, fasten down 100 x 50 mm 'joists', then nail flooring to the joists. First, be sure the concrete is

BELOW LEFT: Laying wood flooring over concrete.

1 Attach joists to the floor every 450 mm. Secure them with adhesive or masonry nails.

2 Lay the flooring, cutting the strips or planks so joints are centred over joists—a must for sound floor construction.

BELOW: A power nailer.

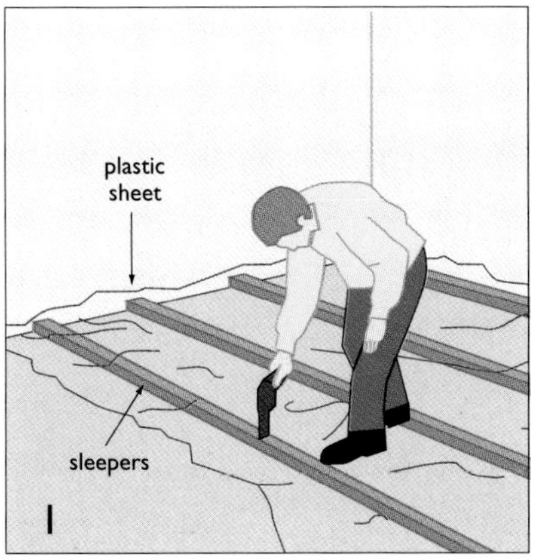

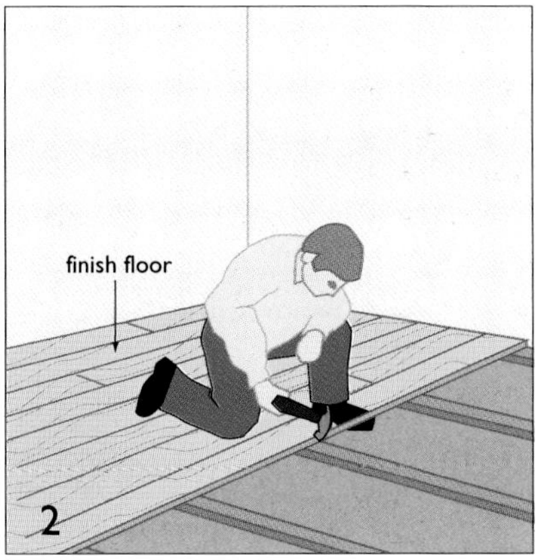

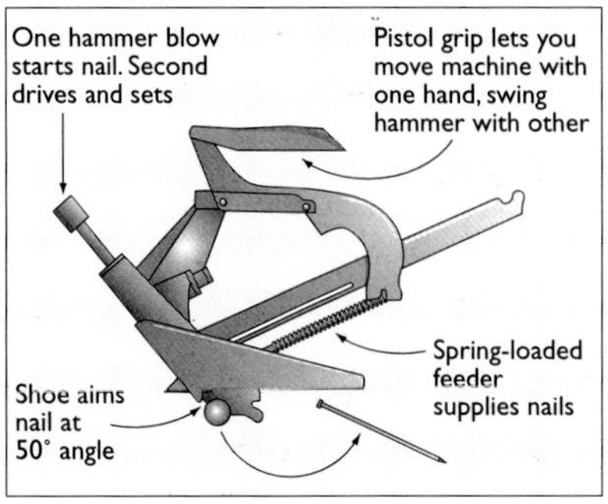

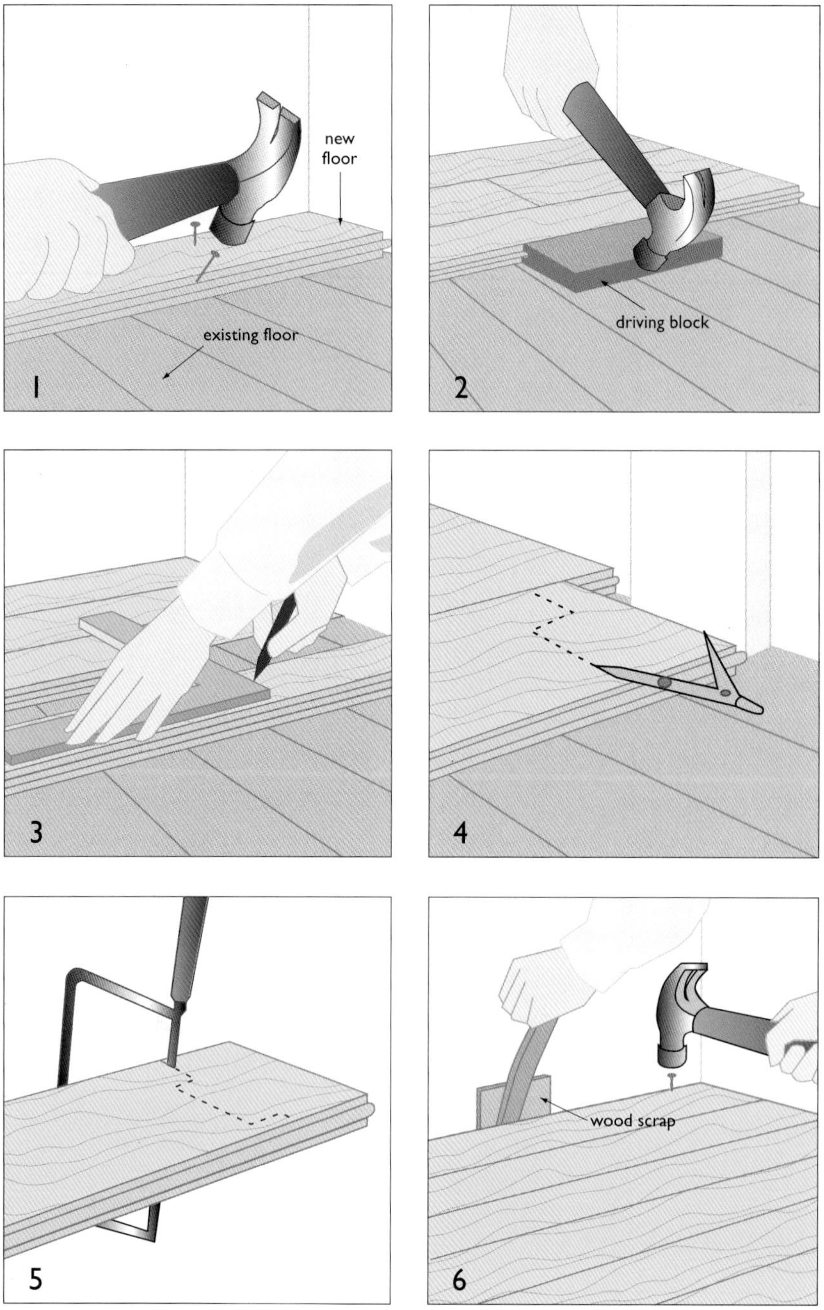

LEFT: Laying strip-and-plank flooring.

1 Place the groove of the first board 10 mm away from the walls. Blind nail through the tongue at 300–400 mm intervals.

2 To keep the courses parallel, tap boards together before nailing. Protect the tongues from damage by using a wood scrap.

3 Measure carefully before cutting the last piece in each course, and don't cut off the tongue or groove you'll need at one end.

4 To fit around irregularities, scribe a piece that's longer than you need with a compass, or use a contour gauge.

5 For scribed cuts use a coping or saber saw. If the board is the last one in the course make the cut-out first, then cut to length.

6 Pull the last few courses tight with a crow bar, protecting the wall with a wood scrap. You'll need to face nail the last course.

properly sealed against moisture. And if the floor is cold, you should lay rigid foam insulation between the joists.

Laying strip-and-plank flooring

Always lay strip-and-plank flooring across the grain of existing floorboards. But if you're nailing directly to sheets of plywood, the direction of the finished floor should be perpendicular to joists.

Start by sweeping the old floor well, setting protruding nails and removing skirting boards. Level bad dips by pulling up the old flooring, nailing shims to the joists and re-nailing the old boards. You can smooth minor irregularities by laying heavy building paper before you begin. Since wood expands and shrinks with humidity changes, leave a 10 mm gap between the floor and wall around the room's perimeter.

ABOVE: Top off the sanded floor with a decorative rug.

Do-it-yourself floor sanding

Whether your floor is made from brush box, blackbutt, blue gum, baltic pine or cypress pine, with a few days to spare, the right equipment and these tips you can have a beautiful polished floor. Although sanding floors yourself is not as easy as you might think, if you are careful and work methodically, you can end up with a very professional finish.

Once your floors are sanded and polished they're easy to maintain — all you need to do is mop them over with warm water mixed with a little methylated spirits to bring up the shine.

1

2

3a

3b

3c

1 Remove carpet. Pull up the old carpet and make sure you remove all the underfelt, battens and staples.

   If you are painting at the same time, it's a good idea to do the painting first as it's much easier to touch up the skirting board with paint than it is to fix up a paint-splattered floor.

2 Punch nails. Remove any nails that protrude above the level of the boards and punch down the rest. Be systematic when punching down the nails, and follow the rows. This way you are less likely to miss some of the nails along the way.

3 Fix problems.

3a
This floor had a strip of painted plywood filling a space where a wall had been knocked out.

3b
The plywood was removed and small struts were wedged across the space, held in place with screws drilled into the brick foundations.

3c
New planks were measured, cut to fit exactly across the space and nailed to the timber struts.

When patching floorboards, search your timber yard for the same type of timber as the old planks. Although the colour will probably differ because of age, at least the grain will be the same.

4

5

6

7

8

9

4 First sanding. The first sanding is done with a large-barrel sanding machine, using a coarse grade of sandpaper. It will remove most of the top layers of dirt, paint and even shellac. Do not be too fussy about this first stage, as it is mainly done to level the floor.

Working diagonally from one corner of the room to the opposite corner, start each run by holding the sanding drum off the floor until the sander is at full speed. Then repeat, working to and from the remaining corners to form a criss-cross grid and overlapping each run by 50 per cent. Never leave the sander stationary with the drum running as it will damage the floor.

5 Fill nail holes. Using a good-quality wood filler to match the timber of the floor, move along the rows of nails, leaving the filler a little proud as you go.

Make sure you choose a filler that is of the right consistency; not too dry and not too oily, as excessive oil will bleed into the wood and leave a stain. This will make any nail holes more obvious.

6 Edging. Using the small sander, go carefully around the edges of your room. You can do this twice — once with a coarse sandpaper and then with a fine one.

It is important that you don't press down too hard on the sander — guide it instead, using a circular motion. As there are several types of edging machine, make enquiries when you hire your machine to make sure you end up with the sander which best suits you.

7 Corners. Using a hand scraper remove the final layers that the sanding machine is unable to reach. Make sure you take particular care to get right into the corners of your room.

Check that your scraper is very sharp to ensure that you get a smooth finish. And try to go with the grain of the wood, rather than against it.

8 Second sanding. Change to a finer grade of sandpaper and go over the entire floor once more. Always work along the grain of the timber with this second sanding and never across it.

10a

10b

Safety tips

- Make sure the room is well ventilated; wear a dust mask.
- Empty rooms of all furniture, pictures and curtains.
- Don't smoke while operating the sander or applying any floor finishes.
- Make sure the machine is turned off at the switch before changing the sandpaper.
- Don't start or stop the machine while the drum is in contact with the floor.

This sanding is very important, as it will give you a good idea of how your finished floor will look. It is important to carefully go over sections that are marked, and if all else fails, you can gently use the scraper on areas where the boards have worn below the level of the surrounding floor.

9 Fine sanding. It is worthwhile employing a professional for this final stage.

After the fine sanding is finished, use a heavy-duty vacuum cleaner to make sure the floor is clear of all dust debris. Don't forget to clean the skirting boards as you go. Any dust left behind will spoil the finished job.

Rather than change to a finer sandpaper for this final sand, simply re-use any sheets that are left over from the last sand. As the tooth of the paper will have worn down, the effect will be more of a buff than a sand.

10 First coat.

10a

First go carefully around the hard-to-get edges and corners with a paintbrush to ensure an even coat.

Line a rectangular mop bucket with a heavy-duty plastic bag and then pour in your sealer. To pour any excess back into the can, simply lift the bag from the bucket and snip the corner off the bag to form a spout.

10b

Using a lambswool applicator and working quickly, spread on the sealer evenly along the grain of the timber.

11 Final coat. Repeat as for the first coat and then leave it to cure for at least 48 hours before moving the furniture back into place.

11

ABOVE: This striking floorcloth design is easily created with painted geometric patterns and simple flowers.

Other wood floor repairs

Here's how to restore wood floors' natural good looks — from smoothing away annoying scratches to replacing whole sections of damaged boards.

In both cases your success depends on how well you match your repair to the surrounding floor. So be sure to exercise all due care when removing the damaged flooring and when selecting stains and replacement boards. When purchasing new wood flooring, take a sample of what you have now so you can match it exactly.

Hiding scratches

1 To hide minor imperfections on waxed or varnished floors, first try rubbing the scratched areas with a rag that is moistened with stain that approximates the stain on your floor.

For surface cuts that don't 'disappear' when you treat the surface with stains, use steel wool and a solvent such as cleaning fluid. You must realise, however, that if you apply solvent, you'll need to rinse, then refinish, the treated area.

2 You can lift off most food stains and heel and caster marks by buffing the surface with the grain, using fine steel wool that has been moistened with mineral turps. This technique works especially well for oil-finished wood floors. With acrylic finishes, you'll also need to refinish the area you've abraded.

Replacing damaged wood flooring

1 To remove one damaged floorboard, make several cuts down the centre of the board with a circular saw. Adjust the cutting depth to the thickness of the flooring (usually 18–22 mm) so you won't damage the floor frame. Work from the centre towards the ends to avoid over-cutting.

Tips

- If your floors are slippery, there are several products available that will anchor rugs to the floor. Most carpet retailers will be able to advise you as to which will best suit your needs.
- The best way to look after your floor is with warm water and methylated spirits. For extra protection, glue small pieces of felt to the bottoms of furniture, especially chairs which are moved often, and ask your friends to leave their stilettos by the front door.

Restoring wood floors

Warped floors may require work to the joists beneath or a simple application of weight (bricks on a sheet of scrap plywood works well) followed by careful nailing with finishing nails to hold the boards in tightly against the joists.

Many old wood floors require finishing — something that can pose a major restoration challenge. The obvious, but expensive and disruptive, solution is to have them professionally sanded and refinished. A quicker and less costly option is to remove darkened, built-up wax and varnish with steel wool pads dipped in denatured alcohol.

If the varnish is spattered with latex wall or trim paint, first slather some lanolin-based hand cleaner on the spots and let them sit for 10 minutes. Then scrape off all the paint with a putty knife. Pigmented wood putty should be matched to the floor and applied to nail holes and small cracks. This won't work for large cracks or gouges; you'll have to replace, sand and refinish those.

That done, make sure the work area is well ventilated and that any nearby flames, sparks or heat sources are extinguished or removed. Then pour alcohol onto a 1 sq m area of the floor. Let it work for 3–5 minutes. Scour it with steel wool and wipe with a clean rag. The wood grain will shine through beautifully.

Comparing resilient floorings	
Material	**Properties**
Sheet vinyl	Solid vinyl. Several grades are available. Must be laid by a professional. Vulnerable to burns, but quite durable otherwise.
Cushioned sheet vinyl	Several grades of this material available, from moderately durable to very durable. Resistant to abrasion and discolouration. Durability ranges from that of commercial vinyl tile to cheaper imports which are approximately half as durable. Vulnerable to burns. This product usually contains a vinyl foam layer.
Roto sheet vinyl	Design is printed on a cellulose-felt or mineral-fibre backing, then coated with a thin film of vinyl. Easy to lay loose or with tape. Mineral-backed grade can be used from basement to bedroom. Cellulose-backed can be used only above grade. Less durable than other types listed. Vulnerable to burns and tears. This product usually contains a vinyl foam layer.
Solid vinyl tile	Basically the same composition and characteristics as sheet vinyl. Vulnerable to cigarette burns.
Commercial vinyl tile	The most popular of today's tiles. It ranks just a notch below solid vinyl tile in durability. Good resistance to burns, impact, scuffing, dents, oil and grease. Easy to install, especially if you choose adhesive-backed versions.
Asphalt tile	A pioneer among resilient floor coverings. Durable but difficult to maintain, grease will soften it; poor recovery from indentation. Brittle composition makes it difficult to cut.

Now chisel out the board, starting with the kerfed midsection and finishing with the sides. Be careful not to damage the groove of the adjacent board.

2 When you're dealing with more than one damaged board, you should begin by outlining the perimeter of the area to be replaced using a framing square. Go only as far as the edges of the nearest sound boards.

Now, with your circular saw adjusted to the proper cutting depth, cut along the ends of your outline (across the boards, not along their length). Again, cut from the centre to the edges. Then make a series of cuts only the length of the damaged area, as was done for the single-board replacement described previously.

3 To remove the boards, wedge or drive a crow bar between a couple of the lengthwise cuts, then work it back and forth until you're able to lift one of the boards. Continue prying boards loose one by one.

If you're working with parquet flooring, dispense with sawing and simply nibble away at individual tiles, relying on a hammer and wood chisel to do the job.

4 Secure replacement boards with finish nails blind nailed through their tongues at about a 50° angle. To fit the last board you'll have to chisel off the bottom of its groove. Now apply floor adhesive to the subfloor, tongue and half-groove of the board, then tap it into place.

Glue replacement parquet tiles with wood-tile floor adhesive.

Choosing and buying resilient flooring

Resilient flooring, so-called because it's softer underfoot than anything but carpeting, includes tiles and sheet goods. Tiles have been a popular do-it-yourself item since World War II, though they've changed considerably since that time in size (from 225 to 300 mm), appearance (from dull, streaked greens and beiges to vivid colours and patterns) and composition (from asphalt to varying blends of vinyl).

Sheet goods have been around a while, too, but because they come in bulky rolls up to 3.6 m wide, installation is best left to a flooring contractor. An exception to this is cushioned vinyl. Whether you choose to install tiles or sheet vinyl depends to some extent upon the use your new floor will get.

Cushioned vinyl is soft underfoot, has a minimum of dirt-catching seams and does a decent soundproofing job. Tiles, on the other hand, are less expensive, easier to install and more resistant to dents from items such as chair legs and pointed heels. For more comparisons, see the chart above.

Consider also whether you want a smooth or textured surface on your resilient floor. Smooth tiles and sheet goods mop up easily, show dirt more readily and inevitably collect a few scuffs and dents that won't come out.

Before you buy the goods, be sure you're clear about the manufacturer's installation recommendations. Most of today's resilient floorings can be installed on any grade. A few, though, shouldn't be laid on concrete in contact with soil. Most shouldn't be applied over an existing resilient floor, either.

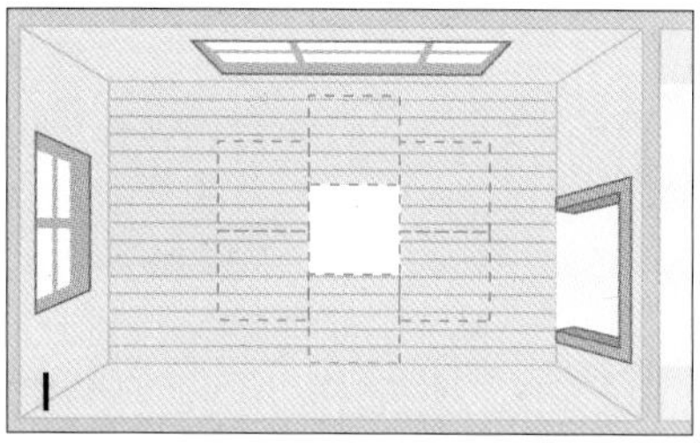

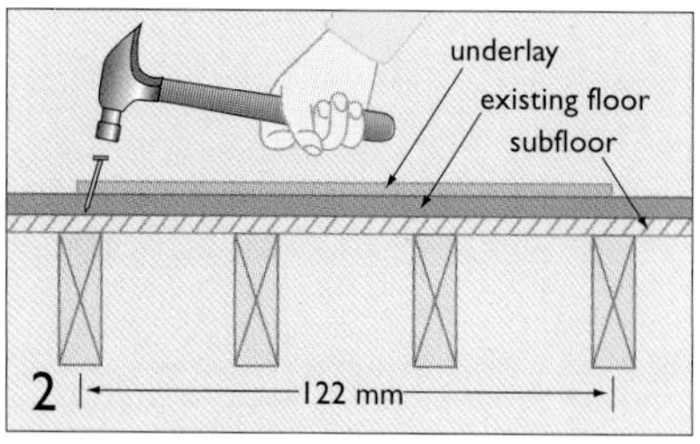

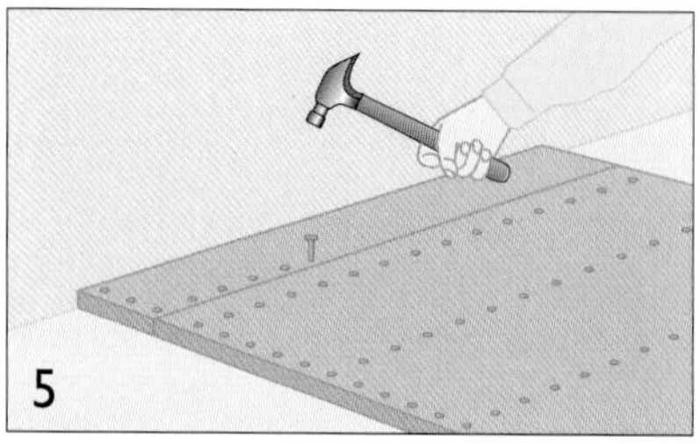

If an old wood floor is in good condition and has a subfloor underneath, you can successfully lay resilient materials directly over it. Otherwise, you'll have to put down an underlay first.

Since all but a few of today's tiles are 300 x 300 mm sq, determining how many you'll need requires only simple computations. Estimating the amount of sheet flooring needed is trickier, especially if there's a pattern involved and you have to seam somewhere. It's best to make an accurate plan of the room on graph paper and take it to the flooring dealer.

Preparing old floors for resilient flooring

Installing underlay

You must smooth badly worn wood floors with underlay before you install resilient tiles or sheet goods. But make sure that the material you choose is suitable for use as underlay (6 mm or thicker hardboard or plywood will work well). Hardboard underlay is available in standard 1200 x 2400 mm panels, but the 900 x 1200 mm sheets are easier to work with. It is a good idea to acclimatise the sheets to the room in which you plan to lay them. Do this by standing them on edge in the room for a couple of days.

To secure the underlay you'll need lots of ring-shank flooring or underlay nails. Drive one in every 150 mm across the face of each panel and every 75 mm at the edges. Stagger the panels and space them about 1 mm apart.

Laying building paper

A blanket of building paper quiets wood floors and smooths out minor irregularities in both wood and resilient floors. Cut the paper in strips that will stretch from wall to wall. Lay it at right angles across old floorboards, or in any direction across underlay.

Choosing and buying hard-surface flooring

Hard-surface floor materials—ceramic, mosaic, slate and quarry tiles—come in myriad sizes, shapes and colours. They're easy to maintain but some are difficult to install.

ABOVE: Installing underlay.

1 Begin at the approximate centre of the room and arrange the panels so you'll never have four corners converging at one point.
2 Tap with a hammer to locate a floor joist, then centre one edge of the first panel over it and nail through the subfloor.
3 At edges, slide a full sheet against the wall, overlapping it with previously nailed panels and squaring it up with them.
4 Next, using a scrap piece of underlay as a guide, draw a line along the entire length of the border piece. Cut along the line.
5 Lay the piece into place. Don't worry if it doesn't fit exactly— the skirting will cover irregularities. Nail the border in place.

BELOW: Laying building paper.

1 Apply adhesive with a serrated trowel and unroll the paper. Butt edges of adjacent strips; don't overlap.
2 Smooth out bubbles with a flooring roller, which you can rent from a tile dealer, or use an ordinary rolling pin.

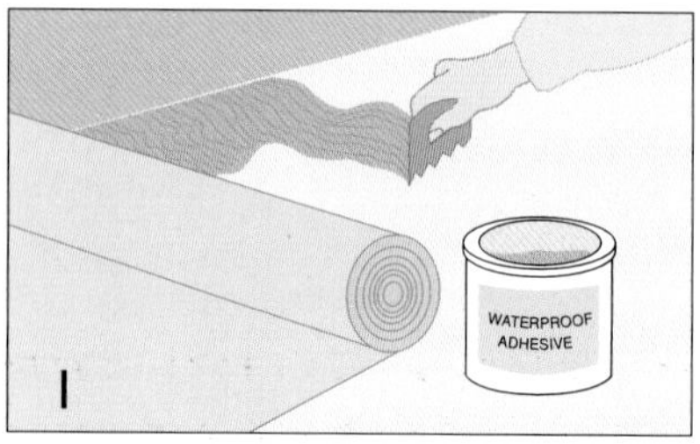

Comparing hard-surface tiles

Material	Description	Installation
Glazed ceramic tile	Sizes range from 19 x 19 mm to over 300 x 300 mm sq and thickness varies from 7 to 13 mm. The 300 x 300 mm is a popular size. Wide selection of colours, glazes, patterns and shapes.	Moderately easy
Ceramic mosaic tile	Available in 19, 25, 30 and 50 mm squares and various-sized rectangles, these are mounted to sheets of paper or mesh. Very popular with do-it-yourselfers.	Easy
Quarry and paver tile	Made from natural clays in large sizes, 150–200 mm squares and 100 x 200 mm rectangles and are normally 13 mm thick. They are also available as hexagonals. Earthen colours in reds, browns and buffs; also available in a variety of irregular shapes suitable for both indoor and outdoor use.	Fairly difficult
Special-purpose tile	Usually larger than 125 mm, with sizes up to 450 mm sq, 10 mm thick. Widest selection of colours, glazes, patterns, designs and shapes.	Difficult

Bear in mind that floor tiles are heavier than wall tiles, and those with mirror-like glazes will be slippery when wet.

Preparing your floor for hard-surface flooring

Because hard-surface materials are brittle and inflexible they can only be laid over a surface that's absolutely smooth and rigid.

Over wood floors you must lay down a 8–10 mm fibre cement underlay to prevent movement that could crack the grout. Install as explained on page 80.

Concrete also makes an excellent tile base. But check the floor carefully with a straightedge to locate any low spots, fill them with latex or vinyl cement, then sand smooth. Also, be sure to clean the floor thoroughly to ensure a good bond between flooring and base. A special dry-set mortar does a good job of bonding tiles to concrete, but don't use it over underlay.

Lay out the job so you'll have full tiles at the doorway by working away from the doorway to the opposite end of the room.

Snap a chalk line from the doorway to the opposite wall. Note that this line must be perpendicular to the door.

Now dry lay a row of tiles along the line, beginning at the doorway. If the tiles aren't self-spacing, allow room for grout.

Nail a guide board perpendicular to the chalk line at the point where the last full tile will be. Dry-lay along the board.

Adjust this row for even boarders. Snap a second line from the point where the border begins. Start laying here.

ABOVE: Natural coir used as a rug tones in with the polished timber and furniture in this elegant living room.

1

5

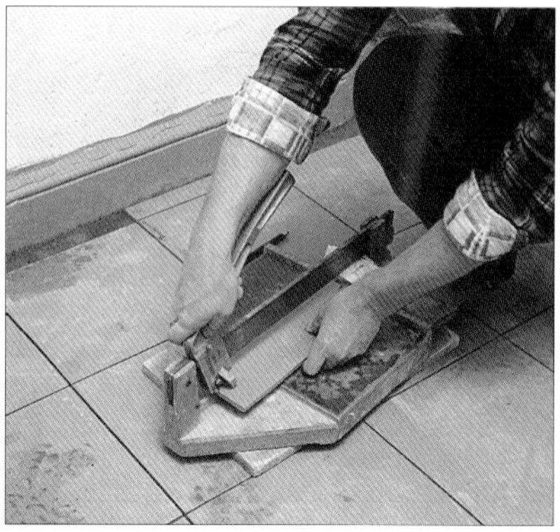

9

Tiling you can do

Here are step-by-step instructions to tiling your floors — a big job to take slowly and surely to its successful completion.

ABOVE: The finished tiling with its elegant grey squares makes a wonderful background for the old furniture. Maintenance is easy too — a simple mop-over is all that's needed to restore the tiles to perfection.

1 Cut and lay chicken mesh over the floor surface and fix mesh down with clout-head nails. The mesh provides a reinforcement bed for the cement.

2 Mix cement thoroughly in the proportion 3 parts sand to 1 part cement. Mix to a moist, spreadable consistency (not runny) and spread over a workable section of floor.

3 Where tiles end at doorways, fix aluminium angle edging to contain them and take cement mixture over them.

4 Spread cement mixture with a levelling stick or straightedge, making sure mesh is well covered.

5 Use a trowel to smooth the surface of the cement and check that it is even using a spirit level.

6 Sprinkle the immediate area to be tiled with a little dry cement to provide a 'key' for the tiles.

7 At this stage, stand on a board to distribute your weight evenly. Start laying tiles from the doorway.

2

3

4

6

7

8

10

11

12

8 Tiles should have approximately 5 mm of space left between them. You can use a slim batten as a spacer between the tile being laid and the previous one. Remove the batten as you go. Tamp down gently on the tile with a wooden block or hammer end to bed the tile firmly.

9 If you need to trim tiles to fit you can hire tools to help score and cut them.

10 Fit 'fill-in' tiles and tamp down as before.

11 When the tiles are laid, mix the grouting in proportion 1 part sand to 1 part cement, adding enough water to make it of a fairly loose consistency. Work the grouting over the tiles until all the spaces are filled, finishing the process with a rubber squeegee to remove any excess grouting.

12 Wipe off residue with an often-rinsed, wrung-out sponge or rag.

Step-by-step slate floors

Slate is available in a wide range of colours and textures to suit almost any area of the house.

1 Cover the floor to be tiled with hessian. Spread with slate membrane which will penetrate it. Leave overnight.
2 Sprinkle the floor with dry slate adhesive powder (you can stand on this), then mix adhesive as directed on the packet.
3 Spread the mixture with a notched trowel (10 mm) to key the surface of a manageable area.
4 Butter the back of a tile with an even layer of slate adhesive.
5 Position the tile accurately into the keyed surface.
6 Tap down to expel air and bed the tile firmly. Leave for one day.
7 Spread grouting, mixed as directed, over the floor in sections. Work in with a squeegee. Scrape off excess.
8 Sponge off the surface before surplus grouting sets on tiles, changing water frequently.
9 Give the floor surface a final clean with steel wool if necessary.
10 Coat with slate sealer, resealing traffic areas yearly if required.

Laying mosaic tiles

Mounted on 300 x 300 mm sheets (and faced with paper or backed by non-removable mesh), mosaics go down much faster than individual tiles. And you don't have to worry about equalising borders. Square up the room with guide boards and begin laying from a corner. Use spacers so that the gaps will be the same.

Align edges of the sheets carefully against the guide boards, lay sheets in place and twist slightly. Peel back paper to check that tiles line up.

After you've laid several sheets tamp them into the adhesive by pounding a piece of plywood on top of the sheet of tiles. Wipe off any excess mastic.

Mark for border cuts on the underside. Cut sheets between tiles by snipping the paper with a sharp knife or scissors.

Cut tiles themselves by nibbling at them with tile nippers. To make a hole, cut a tile in half and nibble notches in either side.

After the adhesive sets up, soak the paper thoroughly with warm water and, starting in a corner, peel it off.

A squeegee simplifies grouting floor tiles. Pack grout into each joint, then scrape off excess.

Cutting a ceramic tile

Whether you are tiling floors, walls or bench tops you will find the correct way to cut a tile is a good thing to have mastered. Tiles are very brittle and, if scored, will crack along that line of weakness. There are many specialist tools for the job but here we show you a simple method.

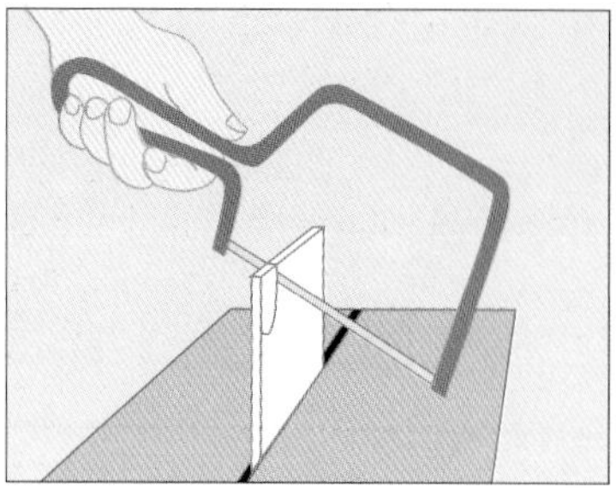

Tip

- When you are cutting a curve on a tile, make a template of the shape you want then mark the tile with a felt pen. Hold the tile vertically in a vice while cutting with a rod saw.

BELOW: Cutting a ceramic tile.

1 To make a straight cut on a tile, use a try square and the scribing edge of a tile cutter to score the face of the tile.

2 On a flat, smooth surface, position the scored line on the tile over a thin piece of dowel and apply gentle pressure with your hands.

3 If the cut is close to the edge of the tile, 'nibble' the waste away with a pair of pincers after scoring.

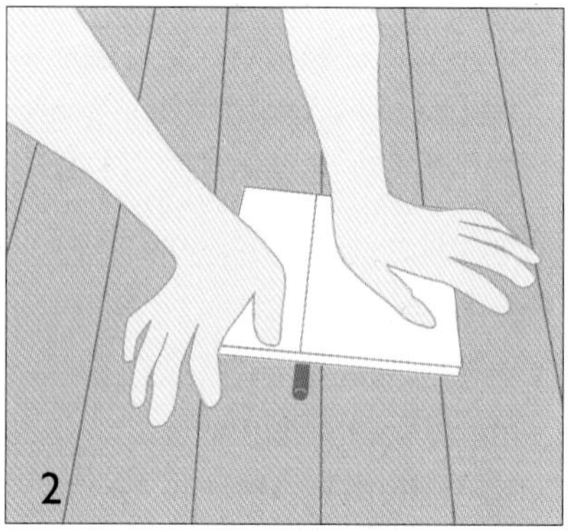

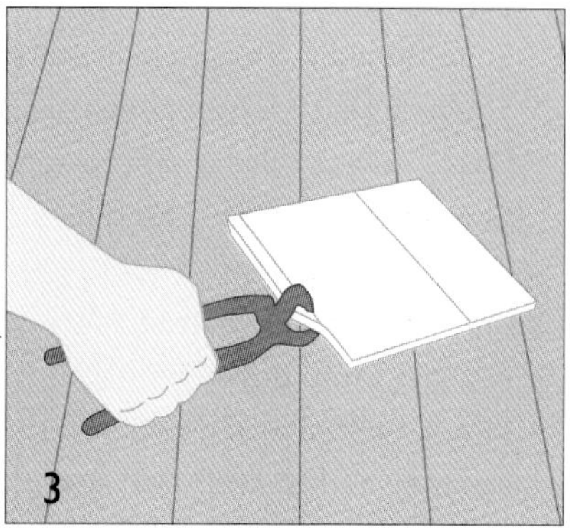

Hard-surface and resilient flooring repairs

Hard-surface floors require little maintenance. But occasionally you'll need to remove stains and patch or replace a damaged tile. Repairing resilient floors is not difficult, provided you can obtain matching tiles or sheet goods although the older and more worn the goods, the harder it will be to make the repair unobtrusive.

Removing common stains

Regardless of the type of stain you need to remove from your hard-surface floor, the sooner you do it the better. Always wear rubber gloves when working with harsh chemicals, and never use flammable solvents around an open flame.

The chart below lists cures for common stains on ceramic and quarry tiles, slate and brick, as well as on grout and concrete. For stains of an unknown nature, consult a flooring dealer for advice.

Filling cracks and voids in concrete

Prepare the damaged area by chipping away and brushing out all loose concrete. Then use a hammer and cold chisel to undercut its edges to 'lock in' the patch.

Now fill the void with latex or epoxy patching material, packing it in with a taping knife or a rectangular trowel. Check the manufacturer's instructions on whether to dampen or otherwise treat the area before filling.

Replacing resilient tiles

Begin by covering over the damaged tile with a dampened cloth. Now run a warm iron back and forth across the damaged tile to soften both the tile and the underlying adhesive. (Also use this technique when you simply need to dab more adhesive under a good tile whose corner has curled.)

If you don't have an iron handy, a propane torch works just as well. With this, however, take care that you do not scorch any of the surrounding tiles.

Score the perimeter of the tile with a utility knife and straightedge. Then, using a stiff-bladed putty knife, pry up the softened tile. If this doesn't do the job, use a hammer and chisel, working out from the tile's centre.

Scrape away the old tile adhesive and apply new adhesive with a notched trowel.

Before laying the replacement tile, warm it slightly under a damp cloth and then iron to make it more flexible. Then align one edge with an adjoining tile and press (don't slide) it in place.

Immediately clean up any excess adhesive and weigh down the new tile with a heavy object.

Patching sheet goods

Repairing a damaged area in sheet flooring is essentially like replacing a damaged floor tile: you lay in a 'tile patch' that you've cut from a piece of matching sheet goods. But

Treating common hard-surface flooring stains

Material	Stain	Treatment
Ceramic tile	Soap film	Scrub with vinegar; rinse.
	Grease	Keep wet 1 hour with a 1:4 lye-water solution, then rinse and dry.
	Gum, tar, wax	Scrape off solids; treat remainder with a rag soaked in kerosene; dry.
	Inks, dyes	Keep stain wet with household bleach. Warm-water rinse and dry.
	Food stains	Scrub with trisodium-phosphate solution (or bleach); rinse and dry.
	Paint	Soften and remove with acetone.
Brick pavers, concrete, grout	Efflorescence	Scrub with a 1:15 (for light bricks) or 1:10 (for dark bricks) solution of muriatic acid and water. Let stand, then rinse. (Don't apply acids to coloured concrete or grout.)
	Grease	Absorb what you can with sawdust or powdered cement, dissolve remaining with a de-greaser. Lighten with bleach.
	Paint	For wet paint, use the appropriate solvent. For dried paint, use a remover.
	Rust	Scrub in bleach, let stand, then rinse.
	Soot	Scrub in scouring powder, then rinse.
Slate or quarry tile	Blot all spills at once and scrub with detergent. Spills that penetrate these porous materials become permanent stains. To prevent stains, apply a sealer.	

unlike working with tiles, patching sheet goods demands a bit more attention to correctly sizing the patch and carefully matching its pattern to that of the existing floor.

Start by positioning the patch material over the damaged area, taking care to align it so the pattern matches the flooring exactly. Secure the patch to the floor with masking tape.

Cut through the overlay and the damaged flooring, using a utility knife guided by a straightedge. Make sure your cuts remain outside the damaged area. Cutting along pattern lines will help to conceal the patch.

Remove the old flooring just as if it were a tile.

Before you apply new adhesive for your patch, trial fit the patch into the cleaned out opening. You may need to lightly sand the patch's edges for a perfect fit. Finish by placing a weight on the patch and leaving it to 'set' for twenty-four hours.

LEFT: What was once a grim, grey inner-city courtyard has taken on a new lease of life with a simple painted geometric pattern in earthy terracotta tones which contrast sharply with the design highlight of blues and golds.

Stairs

The addition of an extra storey means the inclusion of a staircase. It also means additional storage underneath, although in a limited space you may opt for a spiral staircase.

Anatomy of a staircase

A staircase has many parts, all of them interlocked with sophisticated joinery that usually is concealed from view.

The basics are simple enough: a pair of stringers slopes from one level to the next. The composite illustration here shows both 'open' and 'closed-stringer' staircases.

The stringers support a series of steps called treads. A very simple staircase, such as you might have to the basement or a deck, consists of little more than stringers and treads. Complications begin when risers are added to fill the gaps between treads.

Finally, there's the balustrade consisting of the handrail, balusters and a newel post, which provides the safety of the staircase.

Stair edging can help to protect carpeted and hardwood tread fronts from excessive wear.

You can treat most of the ills that afflict staircases with patience and a few hand tools, as shown on the following pages.

Solving stair problems

Silencing stair squeaks

Every house has at least one: a floorboard or stair tread that groans and creaks every time it's stepped

ABOVE: Narrow vertical windows afford natural light onto the small staircase.

BELOW: The drop down ladder is the ideal form of access to the attic.

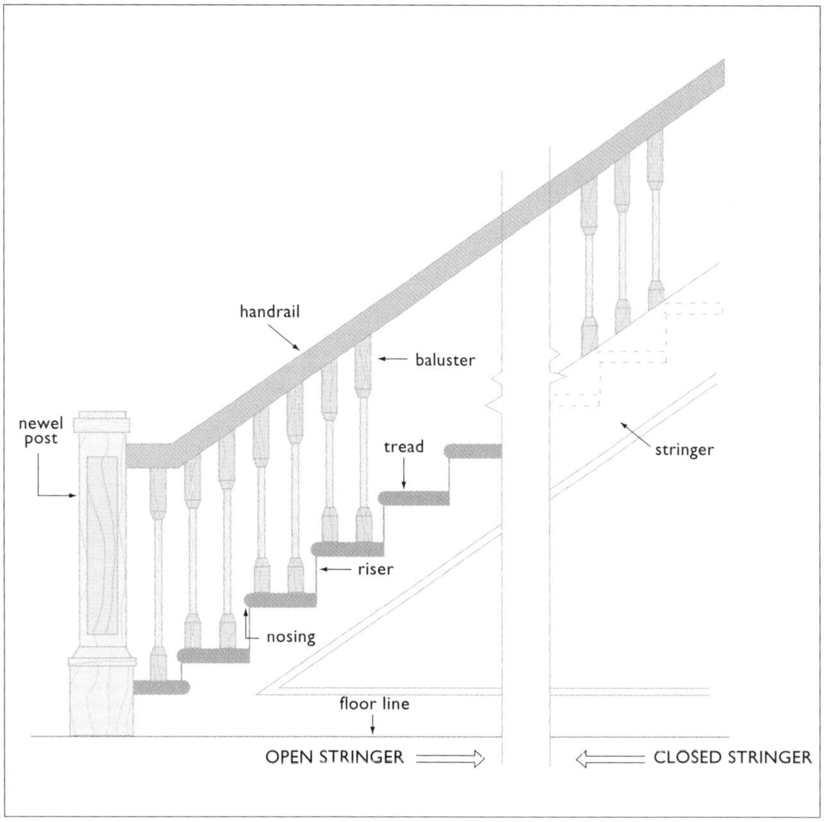

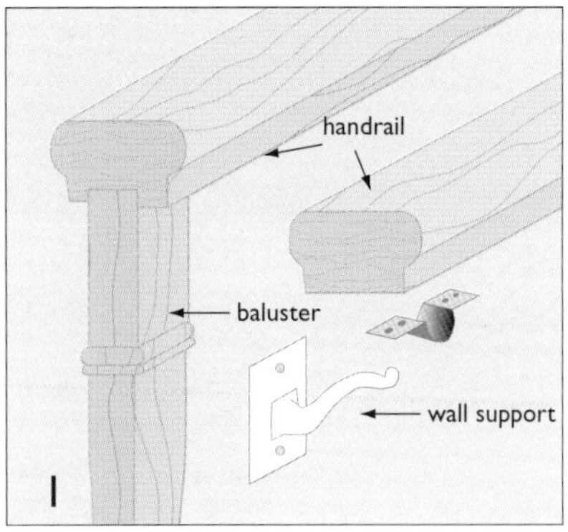

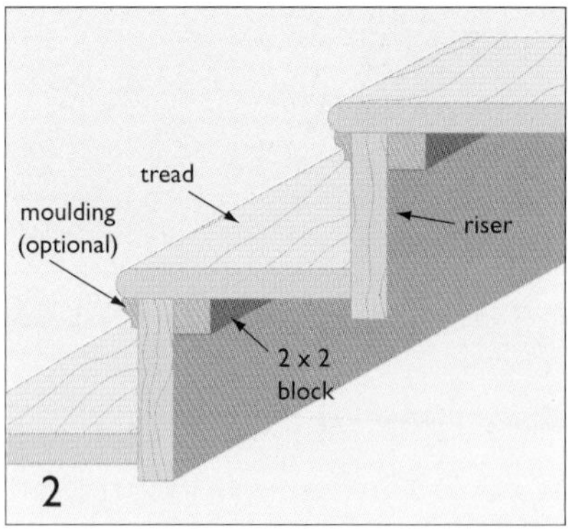

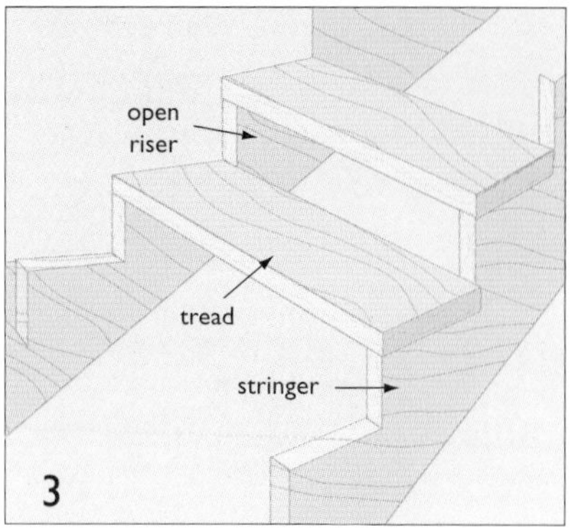

on. When you consider the weight and traffic borne by floors and stairs, it's not surprising that they may occasionally develop problems needing attention. Most staircase squeaks are caused by a tread rubbing against the top or bottom of a riser or a stringer.

Whether the wood stress causing the problem is in the flooring or the stairs, quieting these annoying squeaks is mainly a matter of locating them, then securing boards or stair components that have come loose and are rubbing against each other. If you're lucky you'll have access to these trouble spots from below. If not, there are ways to handle them from above.

Silencing stairs from above

To fasten down the front edges of a tread, drive spiral-shanked flooring nails at an angle into pre-drilled holes. (It's useful to have a helper stand on the tread as you nail.)

ABOVE: Anatomy of a staircase.

1 Some balusters fit into holes in the handrail and treads. Others are skew nailed and glued. Brackets support wall-mounted rails.

2 Treads and risers usually fit together with dado joints. Wood blocks underneath, which are optional, provide additional reinforcement.

3 Treads on open-riser staircases usually are nailed to the stringers. Note that this staircase also has open stringers.

LEFT: A good design for your builder to tackle is this simple and stylish staircase, made from natural wood, with a painted white finish. The uncomplicated lines give it both a sophisticated and country feel, making it suitable for either style.

RIGHT: What a breakthrough this is, in more ways than one. A short-cut stairway to an upper floor is achieved with maximum effect and minimum use of space with a spiral staircase; in this case a curve is the shortest distance between two points.

BELOW: Never overlook the excellent storage space which can be created under the stairs. Choose the storage system you need, then finish with doors and trims to match the staircase.

Next, set the nails and conceal the holes with wood putty.

To eliminate squeaks at the back edge of a tread, drive one or more wedges of scrap wood (coated with glue) into the gap between the tread and the risers. Later, trim away the protruding wood.

Silencing stairs from below

Squeaky stair treads that have parted company with their risers will respond well to treatments from below.

Drill pilot holes through small blocks of 50 x 50 mm of timber for the wood screws that will attach to both the tread and the riser. Then coat the contacting surfaces of the blocks with wood and glue and drive the screws in both directions.

Tightening rails and balusters

Wobbly handrails call for some detective work. Are the rails working loose from the balusters or are the balusters parting company with the treads? You can cure either problem as soon as you determine which one you are dealing with. If the rail is pulling away from a newel post, adapt these techniques. Loose newel posts require an expert's help.

Drill at an angle through the baluster and into the rail or tread, then drive a long wood screw to tighten up the joint.

Or work glue into the loose joint and drive nails through the railing's side. First drill pilot holes for the nails.

If the entire railing is loose, add blocking to its underside. Carefully cut angles for a snug fit, and then glue and nail.

Some good cases for stairs

A staircase should add a very special touch to your living area, as well as taking you from one level of the house to another.

Whether you're creating a room in your attic or adding another floor, you'll need a staircase. Building a staircase requires special knowledge—you'll need a specialist contractor or a staircase company.

Alternatively, you can consider using prefabricated stairs which are now available. And don't forget the space under the stairs—it can make great storage.

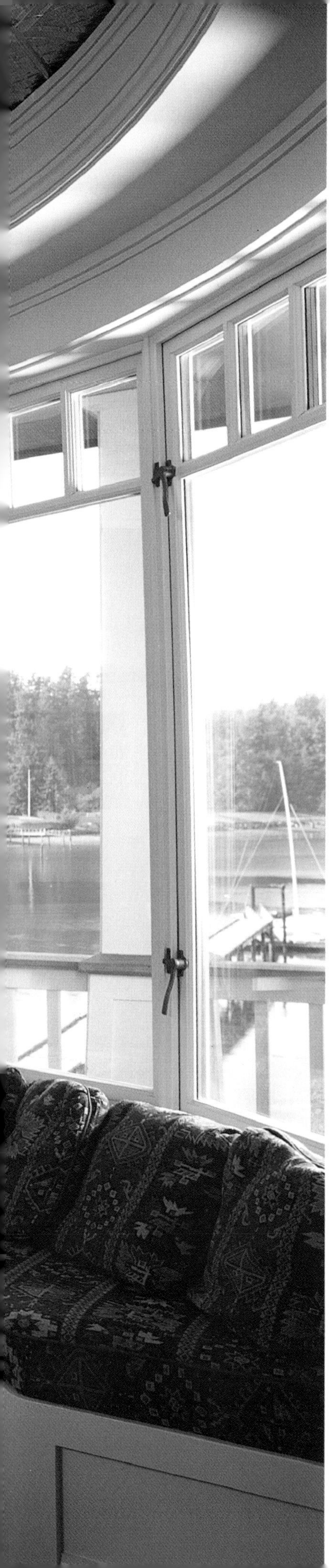

Doors and Windows

Doors and windows are such an essential and functional part of the house, providing entry, light and a view to the outdoors, that we seldom notice them or think about their style. Choosing the right type is not always easy. Interior doors are available in a bewildering variety of stock items from a number of sources, but most home renovators generally find something that suits their needs and their budget in the manufacturer's or retailer's showroom. There are also many outlets specialising in recycled doors and windows, which are especially useful to those wanting to match a period style. If budget is not a major consideration, a good joiner can custom make doors to suit the house.

Windows, both wooden and aluminium framed, are available glazed and ready to fit, although these too can be custom made.

The style of doors and windows should match the house. Good maintenance is most important for efficient opening and closing, as well as for security. This chapter shows you some of the variety of doors and windows available and how to build, maintain and repair them.

Casement windows are great for catching breezes because they act in the same way as sails, directing moving air inside. Notice that half the windows open from the left and half from the right. These windows, with their small panes at the top, create a Federation touch.

Doors

Whether they are heavy-duty exterior doors or decorative interior doors, they can be both stylish and functional. This is best achieved if they are in harmony with the style of the house.

Doors galore

The range is quite bewildering. Doors now have all sorts of different functions. There are front and back doors, French and sliding doors, internal and external doors, with or without any number of glazing and panelling designs. And then there are solid and hollow, timber or otherwise, security or not. Here are some ideas to help make you door wise.

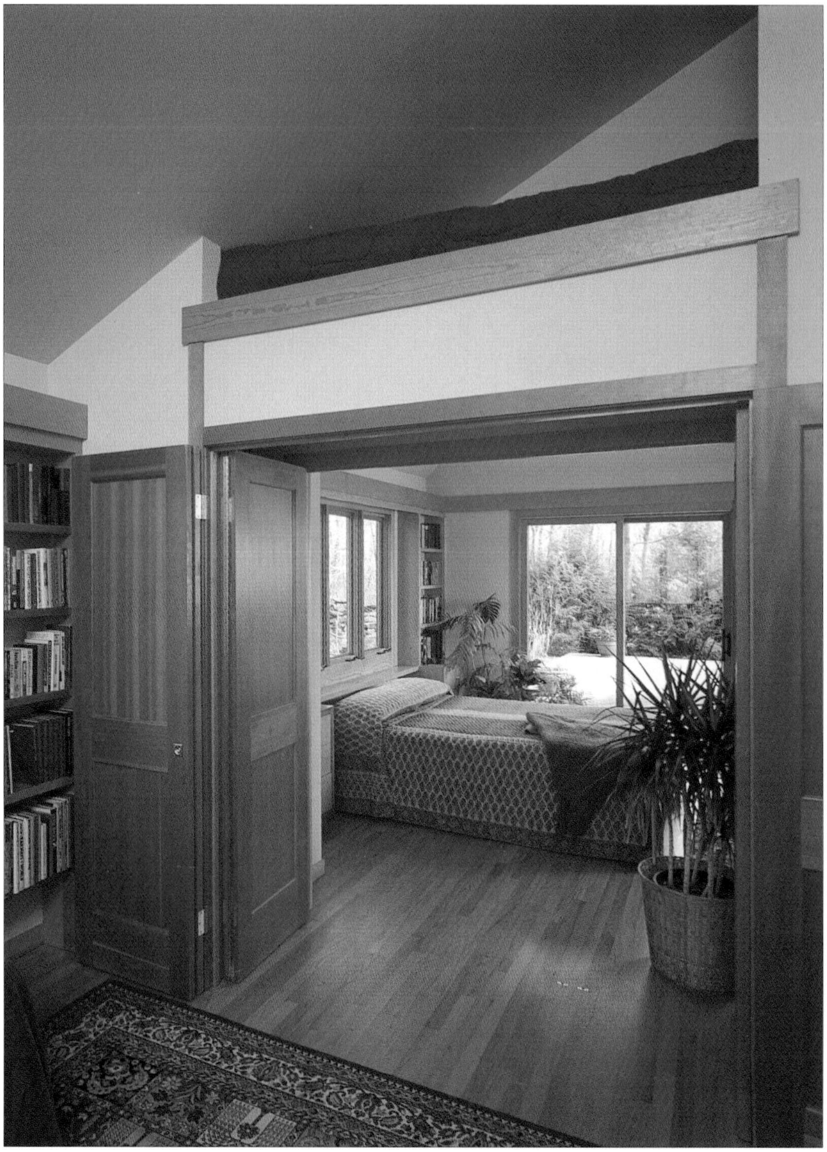

TOP: Glazed doors fill the entire end wall.

ABOVE: Overhead internal fanlights permit filtered light into the adjoining room.

RIGHT: Panelled and bi-folding doors provide interior efficiency with large-scale openings and small swing.

Door talk

- Most standard doors are 2040 mm high and 810 or 820 mm wide.
- Solid timber doors can easily be cut down but hollow internal doors can be cut down only a little.
- Plain, hollow internal doors are made with a light timber frame covered with a fine sheeting and filled with cardboard or chipboard. These are unlikely to hold coat-hook screws.
- Your front door should be in the style of your house. Beware of a hollow door using timber moulding to masquerade as a solid one.
- Aluminium doors, sliding or swinging, are always an option, but only if they match the period of your house.

Double doors

Interior double doors are not a new idea, but they have particular relevance these days. We live in houses with open-plan living and interior spaciousness, but we also need to be able to close off rooms from the rest of the house to be efficient with heating. Double doors give a wider-than-standard passage from one room to another, but keep the two rooms completely separate when necessary.

ABOVE: These glazed doors allow a visual link between the entry hall and the main drawing room.

LEFT: Throwing the doors open achieves an entrance on the grand scale, making the sitting area a natural extension of the hallway.

Folding doors

The idea of being able to throw the house open to the outdoors is very appealing. Traditionally, this is achieved with one or more pairs of French doors, but sometimes they just do not create a wide enough opening. By using folding doors, a whole wall can literally be folded away to merge the interior and exterior.

With this system of rollers and tracks at the top of the doors and guiding channels and pivots at the bottom, you can hinge as many doors together as you like. Each door should be no wider than 900 mm and weigh no more than 60 kg. Depending where you position the hardware, the doors can swing inwards into the room or outwards onto your deck or verandah.

Installing doors such as these is a job for the experts and, until recently, they have been used only for commercial application. For quotes, contact companies listed under 'shop fitting' in your Yellow Pages telephone directory. Alternatively, you could try your local window and door joinery. It may not have tackled a job of this nature before but, as long as it knows where to obtain the hardware with the correct specifications, there should be no problem.

TOP: This opening only measures 2300 mm but it is more than enough to make the terrace seem like a generous extension of the kitchen and breakfast room.

FAR LEFT: When opened wide, the doors protrude outwards onto the terrace. You can choose to have them opening into the room or even half each way.

ABOVE LEFT AND LEFT: The hardware is the key — rollers and tracks at the top and pivots and channels at the bottom. The right hinges are also important.

French doors

Taking an existing window from a timber-framed house and replacing it with a set of French doors is well within the reach of the experienced handyperson. Check with your local council to see if you need a permit. Conditions will vary, depending on the structure of the house and proximity to neighbours. Most window openings are not structural, but ask the advice of a qualified person.

French doors are usually purchased complete with frames and come in a range of standard sizes: those we used are 1685 mm wide x 2100 mm high, measured at the wall opening (including door frame). If you want the doors and frame custom made, expect to pay extra. The standard door size was used here and the opening adapted to fit the doors.

1 Check for any power points or switches close to the proposed opening. This may indicate there is wiring running through where you intend to cut the wall. If in doubt, don't take chances. Call an electrician to re-route the wiring.

2 Remove the architrave and any frame linings on the inside of the wall to expose studs to which the window frame is fixed. Mark the line of the inside edge of the studs on the wall surface (plaster or plasterboard) and cut out the opening as neatly as possible.

3 Drive a nail through the external wall cladding from the inside to mark stud location, then cut out the external cladding. If you have old fibro sheets or boards (asbestos) take special precautions with their removal and disposal. Your local council will

ABOVE: Before.

LEFT: After – additional space and light.

ABOVE: Glass doors in a wall of glass allow you to enjoy the aspect beyond.

RIGHT: French doors mean easy access from the outdoor living area.

refer you to the relevant authority. Don't dispose of pieces of external cladding until you've finished — they may be useful as in-fill pieces.

4 If your opening is narrower than the standard frame size you may have to add extra studs. Skew nail into existing top and bottom plates. Allow 5–10 mm around the frame for flashing and ease of fitting. The existing top plate in a non-structural opening does not need to be strengthened. If too high, add another top plate across the top of the opening.

5 Clout nail an Alcor flashing to the frame sides and top (sides first) and, with the aid of a couple of friends, put the frame, bottom first, into the opening. Use wedges and packers to square it up and secure by screwing through the frame into the studs. Use screws so they can be removed should more squaring up be required as you progress.

6 Unless your opening size is very different from a standard-sized frame, an extra-wide architrave will cover the gap between the surrounding wall surface and the frame. If the gap is too large for an architrave you are faced with replacing some external cladding and patching the internal plaster. If so, consider paying extra for a custom-made frame.

7 A variety of locks is available. All locks should come with fitting instructions and a cardboard template which shows where to cut and drill. Mortise locks (which fit inside the door timber rather than being mounted on it) are for the experienced only. To learn how to fit these, practise on an old door first.

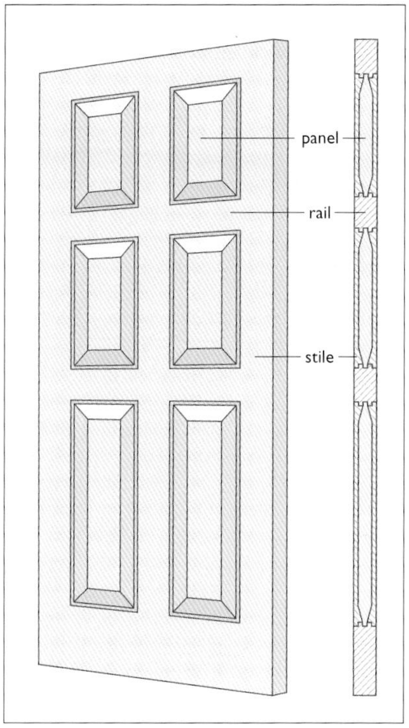

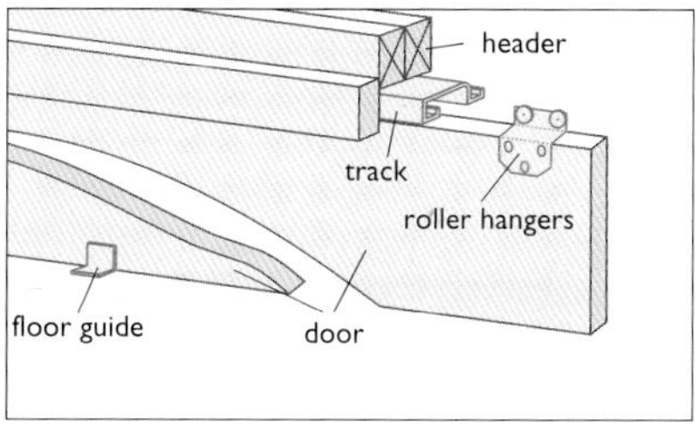

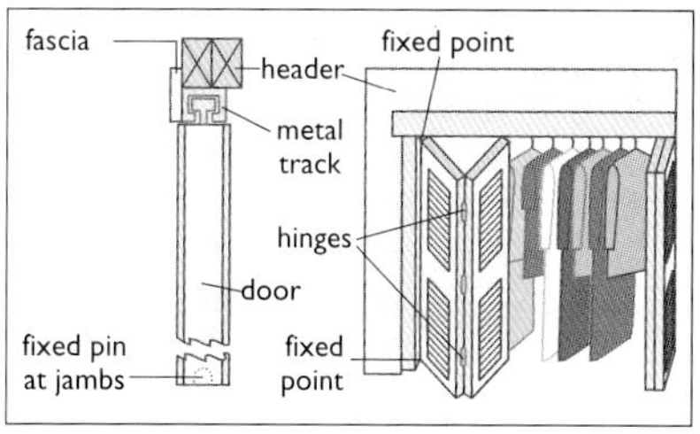

FAR LEFT: Anatomy of a panel door.

ABOVE LEFT: Anatomy of a sliding door.

ABOVE: Anatomy of a folding door.

Door construction

Anatomy of a panel door

Almost every modern door has a vertical stile and horizontal rail framework. This construction helps counteract wood's tendency to shrink, swell and warp with changes in humidity.

With a panel door you can see the framing. Spaces between frame members can be panelled with wood, louvred slats or glass.

Anatomy of a flush door

Flush doors hide their framing beneath two or three layers of veneer. Alternating the veneers' directions — called banding — minimises warping.

A solid-core flush door has a dense centre of hardwood blocks or particle board; a hollow-core door uses lighter material, such as corrugated cardboard.

Anatomy of a sliding door

Sliding doors come in pairs. Panel or flush, solid or hollow core, they roll along an overhead track and are guided by metal or nylon angles screwed to the floor.

Anatomy of a folding door

Folding doors — sometimes called bi-folding — are hinged together. One pivots on fixed pins; the other slides along a track.

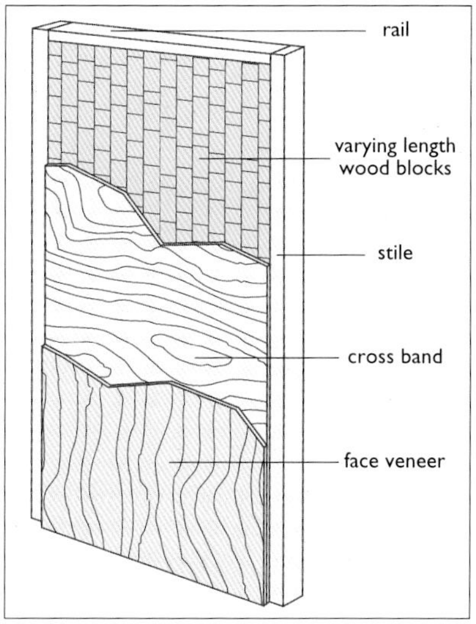

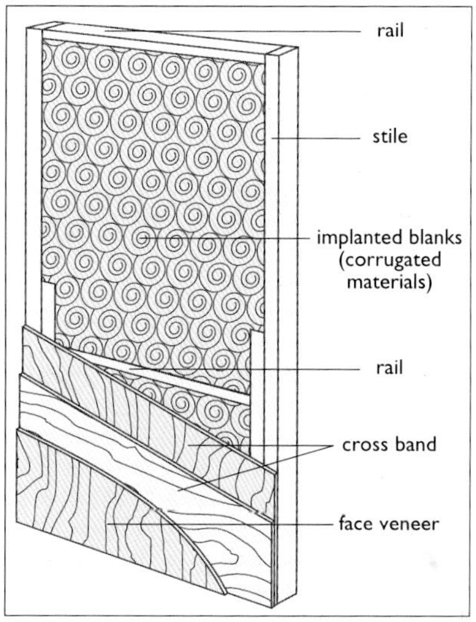

LEFT: Anatomy of a flush door.

ABOVE: Internal French doors leading to a glassed-in verandah maintain an atmosphere of light and warmth.

Solving door problems

A sticking door can be extremely irritating, but usually you need spend only a few minutes with a screwdriver, some sandpaper or a plane to get it swinging freely again. Finding the bind can be the trickiest part of the job.

At the time of construction care is taken to ensure that doors are plumb and square in their openings. Once the jambs are set and the door knob-and-latch set have been installed, a check is made to see that the door opens and closes as it should and that the latch engages the strike plate correctly. As time passes and the house settles, both the jamb and the door expand and contract at different rates. Also, the door is opened and closed countless times. These factors (and others) can eventually cause problems such as binding doors and loose hinges.

Repairing hinged doors

When a hinged door gives you trouble, don't be too quick to take it down and begin planing its edges. Many difficulties call more for analysis than for work — and they're better dealt with by making minor adjustments while the door is in place.

Almost all problems result from one or more of these causes: improperly aligned or loose hinges, an improperly aligned strike plate, warping of the door itself or a frame that's out of square.

If a door sticks or refuses to fit into its frame, close it as best you can and sight carefully around its perimeter. Look for an uneven gap along the hinge jamb; this means the hinges need attention. If the door seems too big for its frame — or out of square with it — mark the tight spots, then sand or plane them.

Freeing a binding door

If your door is binding near the top or bottom of the latch edge, first make sure that the hinge leaves on the door or jamb aren't loose. Then you may be able to solve your problem by shimming out one of the hinges. Shim the top hinge to cure a bind near the bottom and shim the bottom hinge for binds near the top.

To shim out a hinge, open the door and insert a wedge beneath the latch edge for support. Then remove the screws that hold the hinge to the door jamb. Trim a piece of thin cardboard to fit the rectangular mortise on the door jamb, and insert the shim between the jamb and the hinge leaf.

If shimming takes care of the bind on the latch but causes the door to bind at the top or bottom, or if your only problem is binding at the top or bottom, pinpoint the location of the trouble spot while opening and closing the door. Scribe a line along the door's face to denote where you want to remove wood. If the bind is along the top edge, partially open the door, drive a wedge under its latch edge and use a block plane to remove the high spot. Work from the end towards the centre to avoid splintering the end grain.

If the high spot is on the door's bottom edge or along the hinge edge, take the door off its hinges for planing. With a hammer and a crow bar, tap up on the head of the hinge pins.

Anchor the door in a floor-standing work vice. Hold it firm by wedging one end in a corner or by straddling it, and plane high spots. Then, for side planing, work a jack plane in the direction of the grain, holding it at a slight angle to the door. If you're planing end grain at the door's bottom edge, use a block plane and shave from the door's ends towards the centre.

Curing strike problems

When a door won't latch, or rattles when it's latched, examine the strike plate attached to the jamb. A minor adjustment here will probably solve the problem for you.

First, take a close look at what happens when the door closes. Is the latch engaging the strike? If it isn't, determine if the latch is too far from the strike or if it's hitting the strike but missing the hole. Often, scratches on the plate will give you a good idea of exactly how far it's out of alignment.

A door that doesn't fit snugly against stop moulding will almost certainly rattle. To silence it, you must either move the strike plate or reposition the stop.

If the strike plate is off only a few millimetres or so, enlarge the opening with a file. You may need to chisel away some wood, too.

Accommodate a bigger disparity by relocating the strike. You'll need to extend the mortise.

Use thick cardboard or thin wood to shim out a strike that's too far away to engage the latch. Resetting hinges can cause this.

What to do about warping

For latch-side door warpage, pry off the stop, close the door and draw a line along its inside edge. Re-nail the stop on this line.

For a hinge-edge warp, add another hinge to the centre of the door. Force the door into line before screwing down.

You may be able to straighten a warped door by weighting it. To prevent new doors from warping, seal all edges and surfaces.

BELOW: These floor-to-ceiling windows in a dining alcove have the effect of French doors. The top of the window follows the line of the ceiling, and the warm, natural timber is continued around the room by the picture rail.

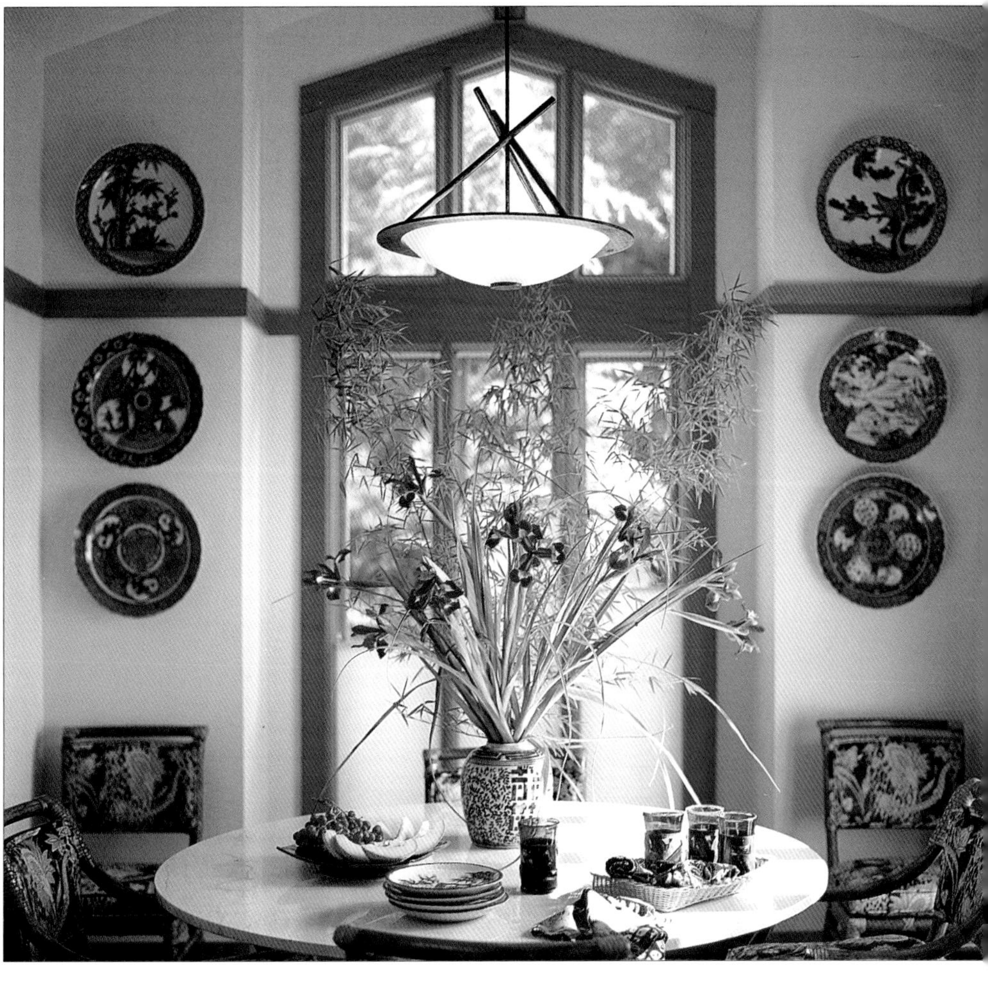

RIGHT: Glass above with timber panel below is a perfect combination for a back door. With the top open and the bottom closed, air and light are admitted while children and pets can be confined easily.

Lubricating balky latches

Turn the handle to retract the latch, then puff powdered graphite into the works. Lubricate collars of knob shafts on each side, too.

Lubricate a thumb-operated latch level by puffing graphite into the lock body. Never use oil — it will clog the mechanism.

Latch assemblies aren't terribly expensive, so if you find that lubricating won't free one, replace it.

Repairing sliding doors

Compared with swinging doors, sliding units rarely malfunction, and when they do, a few turns of a screwdriver will usually put them right again. Maintenance of sliding doors is practically nil, too, since almost all of them roll on self-lubricating nylon wheels.

If a sliding door sticks or jumps its track, it probably has alignment problems. Check first to see that the door hasn't warped. You may be able to compensate for minor warping by shifting the guides slightly; otherwise, you might as well replace the door.

A few sliding doors — most notably the glass versions — roll on wheels along a bottom track. You should adjust and maintain these as you would a sliding window (see p. 127).

To remove a sliding door, lift it and tilt slightly. With some designs, wheels will lift off at any point along the top track. With others, you can only free the door when its wheels are adjacent to a 'key' opening. This arrangement prevents track jumping. The plates holding sliding doors in position can work loose and slip out of alignment. If this happens, re-align them and tighten screws.

Fix or replace floor guides that are broken, bent or out of line. The doors should clear the floor by at least 1 cm.

Repairing folding doors

Use a wrench to raise or lower folding doors. A screw and slot on the lower pivot bracket helps you get them plumb, too. Don't lubricate the top assembly glides, as most of them are self-lubricating.

Installing new doors

Hanging a door

Replacing a door or hanging a new one in an existing opening makes a satisfying carpentry project, provided you keep everything square, measure and cut carefully, and visually check your work at every step.

Most doors measure 2040 mm high. If you have to alter the size of one, allow 3 mm for clearance at the top and sides, and 10 mm at least at the bottom — more if it must clear carpeting. Never cut more than 20 mm from either end.

Once you've hung a door, install stop mouldings on the jamb so the door can't swing against its hinges. To mark for stops, just close the door and draw a line on the jambs along the door's inside edge.

Check to see whether the frame is square, measure its height on both sides, then trim the door to fit. See above for clearances.

Now measure the frame's width, checking it at several points. If you have to plane, work towards the centre of the door's edge.

Unless the frame already has stops, you'll need help to prop the door in its opening. Square it up with shims at all edges.

Measure for hinge locations and mark with a pencil on the door and jamb. Solid-core doors should have three hinges. Position top hinges no less than 15 cm from the top and bottom hinges at least 23 cm from the floor.

Begin a mortise cut by scoring around marked edges. Take care you don't cut deeper than the thickness of the hinge leaf.

Next, make a series of parallel cuts across the grain. Work from the side to knock out chips, then lay in the hinge leaf. You may need to shave away more wood to ensure that it lies flush.

Finally, screw the leaves to the mortises, set the door in place and insert the pins.

Cutting in a doorway

If you've done little or no basic framing work, opening up an interior wall for a new doorway provides a great introduction. Just be sure to measure carefully and keep everything plumb and square.

Plot a location that won't involve having to move any plumbing lines. You may encounter wiring, in which case you must call for an electrician to relocate it.

Size the opening to fit accurately your new door and frame. Most will require about 6 mm clearance all around.

Use a hammer and chisel to break open a plaster wall. Cut wood lath with a saw; use snips on metal lath. A jigsaw or keyhole saw makes short work of cutting plasterboard.

BELOW: Solid doors are not always suitable in the interior of a house. In this hallway, a doorway was cut in and glass doors were installed so that light and warmth would still be retained in the sunroom.

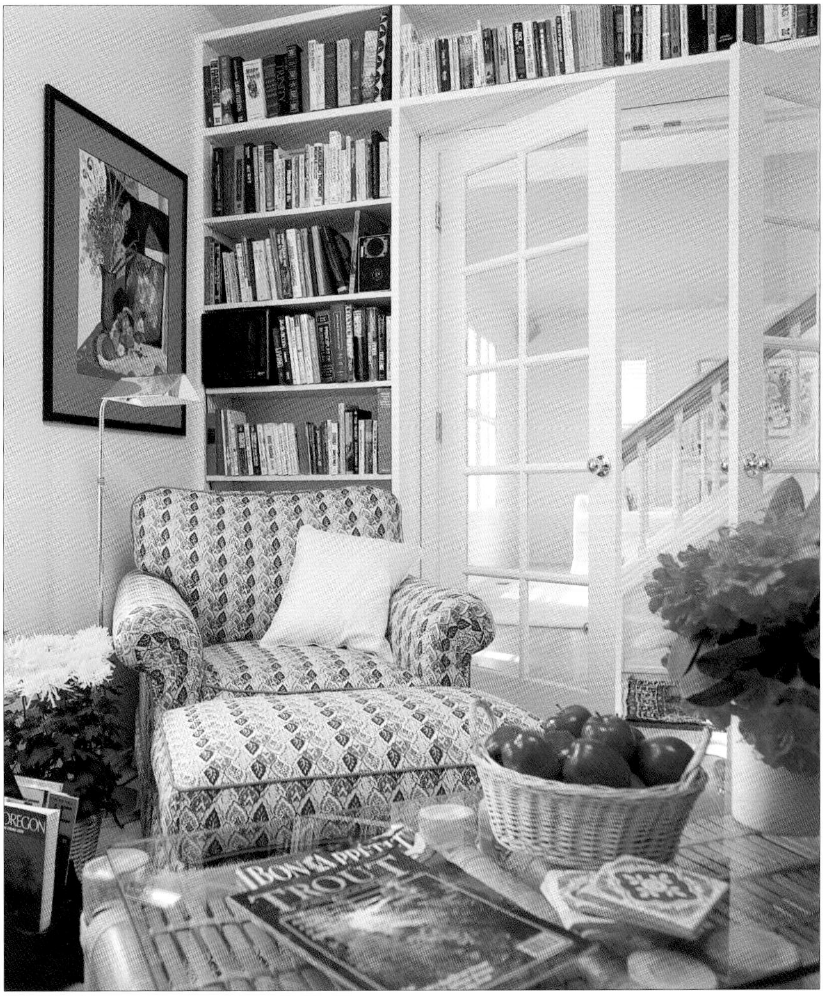

BELOW: A whole wall of French doors in this extension means there is plenty of natural light and the owner has the ability to adjust the temperature inside by opening one or several of them at a time.

Note that these instructions apply only to interior walls that are not load bearing.

Begin by marking stud locations. Open up the wall to the ceiling and nearest stud on either side of the new opening.

Before removing studs from the opening, measure down the appropriate distance from the ceiling. Make cuts along this line.

Build a header by nailing a 100 x 50 mm header between the studs on either side. Skew nail it in place.

To save timber, locate one side of the opening against an existing stud. Leave an additional 100 mm for jack studs.

Now cut jack studs for either side of the opening. These add support for the header and make the doorway much more rigid.

Cut the bottom plate last. You may need a chisel and hammer to pry it out. Patch the floor or install a saddle.

Closing up a doorway

Pry off skirtings on either side of the door, then slip a hacksaw blade between the frame and studs to cut the nails.

Once the nails are cut, you can remove the frame in one piece and re-use it. If the assembly sticks, tap lightly to free it.

Nail 100 x 50 mm timbers to the top, sides and bottom of the opening, then skew nail a stud in the centre. Apply plaster.

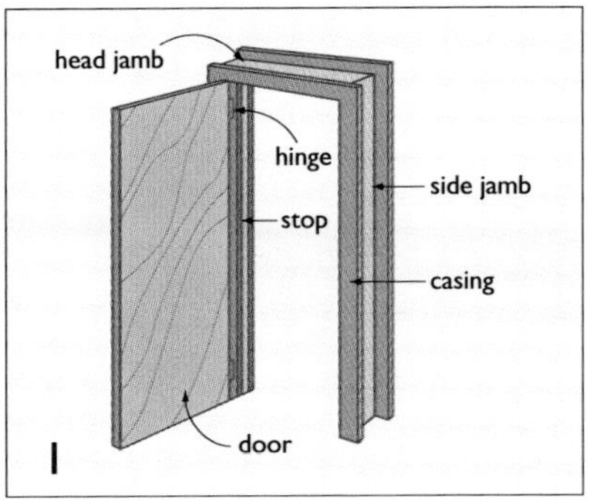

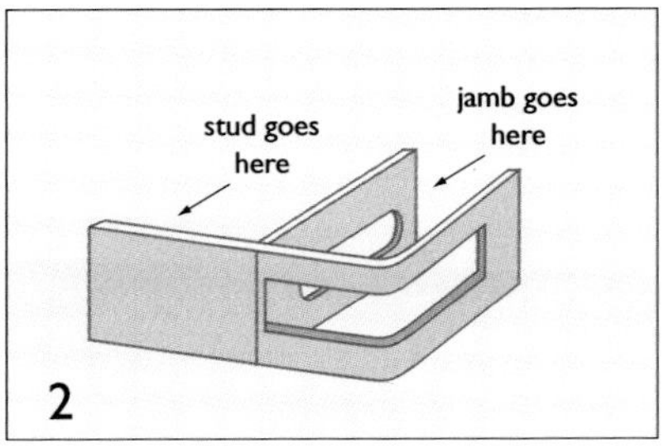

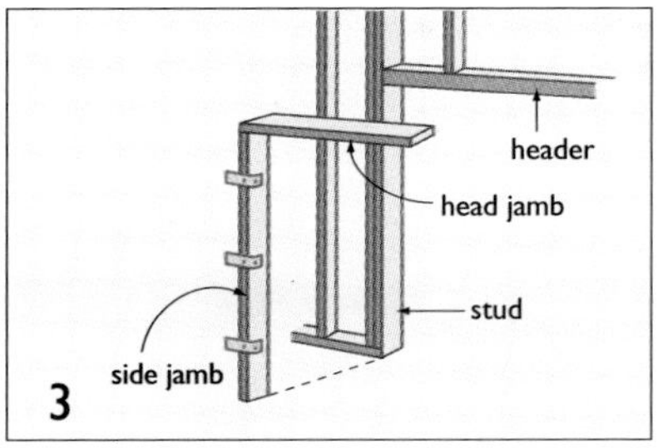

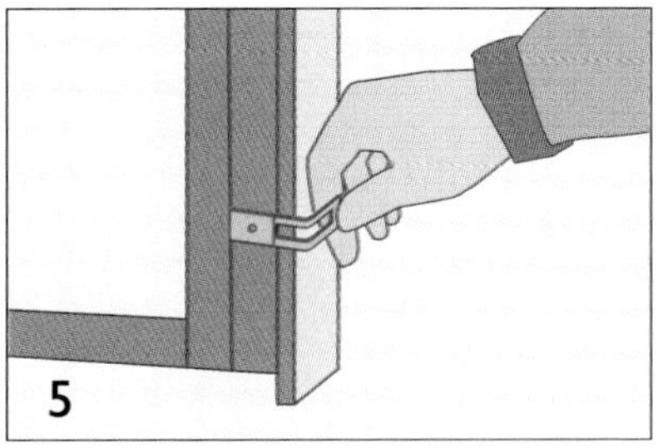

ABOVE: Installing a pre-hung door.

1 Pre-hung doors arrive like this, though they also include several braces you remove after shimming and nailing the unit in place.

2 Align a unit in its opening with wood shims, or use these metal versions. Some manufacturers include them with the door kit.

3 Clip metal shims onto the jambs after the door, jamb and one casing are in place. Then use a level to plumb side jambs.

4 Check to be sure that the head jamb is square. In the likely event that it isn't, shim wherever necessary before nailing.

5 Now drive nails through the jamb into the studs, then break off the shims' tabs. Finally, install casing moulding.

Installing a pre-hung door

Once you've made an opening for a new door you have two options: cut, fit and assemble a 12-piece frame, then hang the door; or slip in a pre-hung door-frame assembly, shim and nail it into place.

Custom building saves money but takes time — and you risk botching the job. A pre-hung unit costs more but you get everything you need — door, hinges, jamb, stop and casing mouldings, even a latch if you want it — all in one accurately made component.

Pre-hung units come in standard sizes, with a limited choice of casing mouldings. Some timber yards will order other sizes and styles.

Before you buy a pre-hung door, be sure to measure the thickness of the wall in which you'll be installing it; fibrous plaster and plasterboard surfaces call for different jamb widths.

The procedure shown here applies to door assemblies with a removable casing on one side. With another type, both casings are permanently attached, but side and head jambs are split down the middle. You plug half the unit into one side of the wall, then install the other half from the opposite side.

Choosing and buying hinges

Most full-sized doors hang on butt hinges. Besides the standard butts there are special-purpose butts that close themselves, carry heavy loads on ball bearings, even lift a door in mid-swing to clear carpeting.

If you're replacing a butt hinge, replace its mate, too. Before buying the new hinges, measure the old hinges, noting first their height, then their width when open. With some types you'll also need to know whether yours is a right- or left-hand door. A hinge's 'hand' refers to the side of the door it is installed on. To check this, stand opposite the door's swing.

Generally, it's best to get loose-pin hinges, as they permit you to remove the door more easily than the fixed-pin type.

Full-mortise hinges — the most common type — require 'gains' in both jamb and door edge. They make a neat installation.

For a half-mortise hinge, you cut a gain only in the jamb. You can fasten the hinge to the door with bolts for extra strength.

Surface-mounted hinges require no gains at all. This arrangement works only on doors that are flush with their casings.

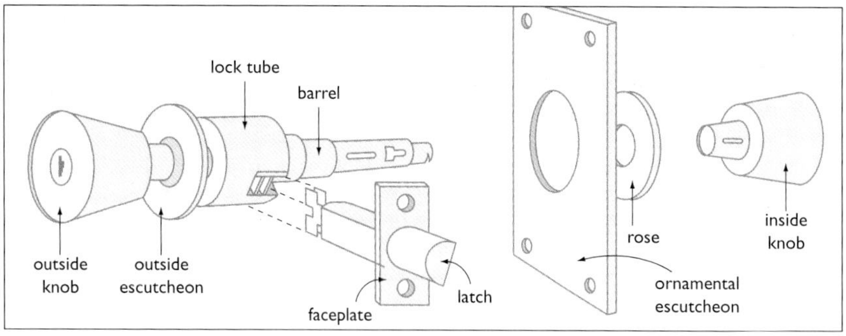

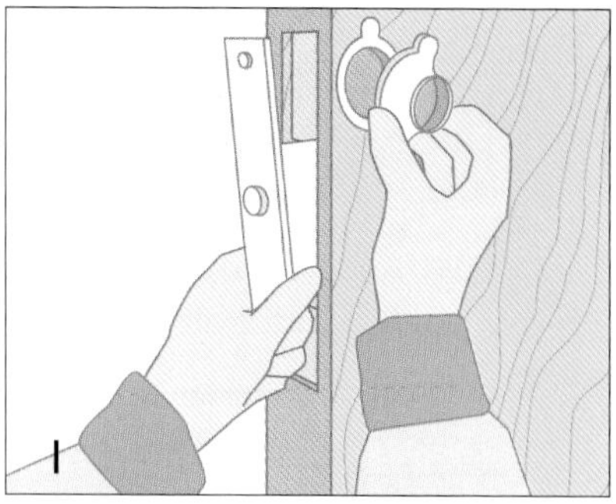

Installing a knob set

Interior knob-and-latch sets differ surprisingly little in overall design, though you can choose from different styles and quality levels. Most modern doors have the cylinder-type knob-and-latch set or a slight variation called the tubular lock.

Older mortise knob sets aren't used on interior doors any more, but you can easily replace one with a cylinder or tubular unit. Large-sized escutcheons will hide holes left by the old style knob-and-keyhole arrangement.

Measure the door's thickness before buying a knob set. Some units fit both 35 and 45 mm doors; others, only one.

If you're installing a knob set in a new door, you'll need a hole saw or an expansive bit and a spade bit in a size specified by the manufacturer. Most companies also provide fairly complete instructions, plus a template for locating the holes you must bore.

Be warned, too, that a cylinder set provides little protection for exterior doors or other points of entry to your home.

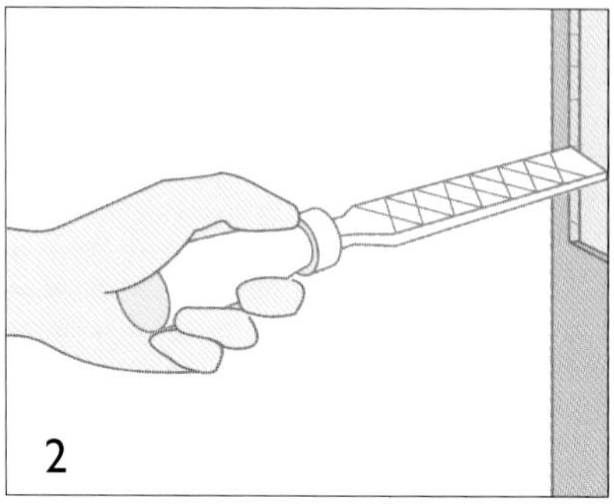

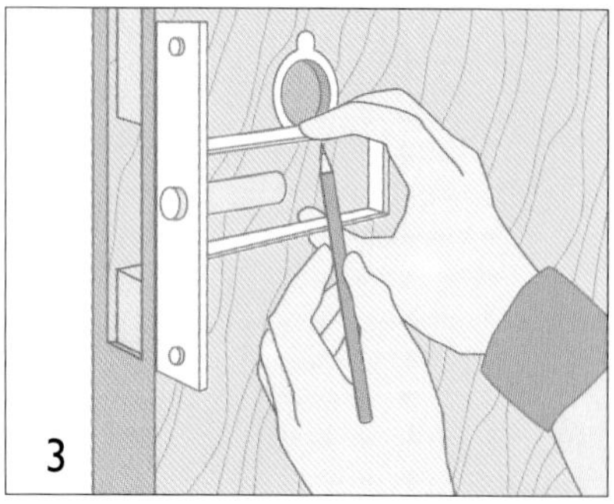

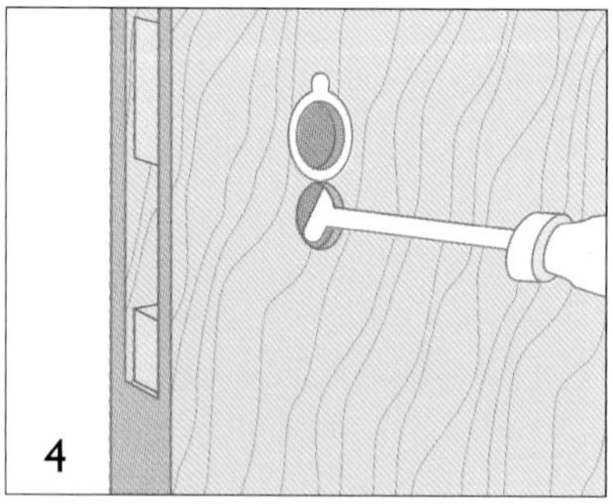

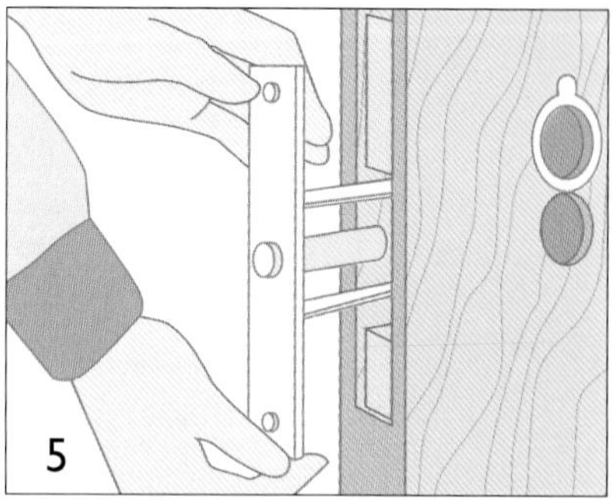

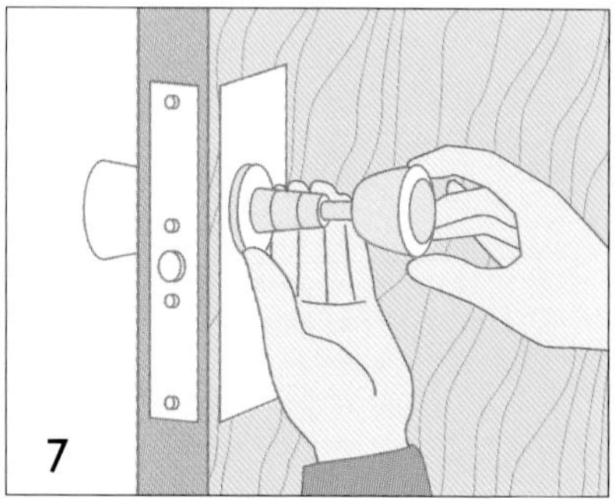

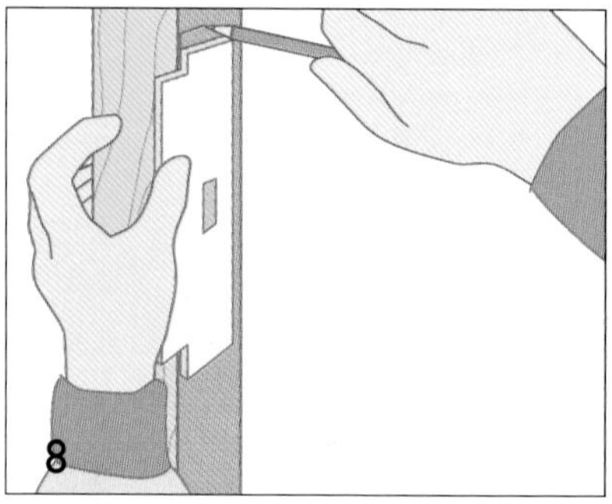

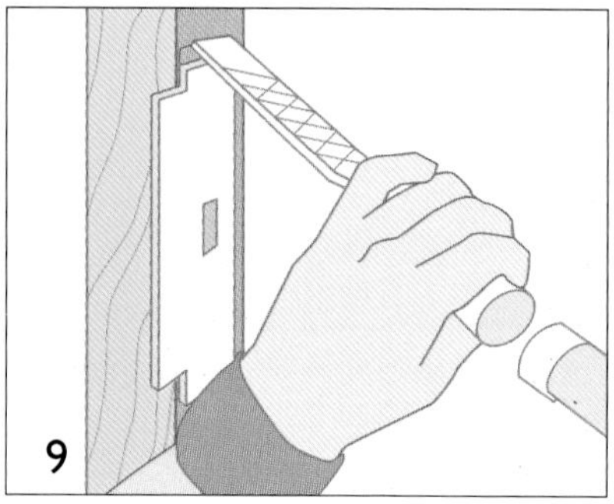

1 To remove an old mortise latch, take off the knobs, unscrew and pull out the latch assembly, and dismantle any trim pieces.

2 You'll probably need to rework the mortise to accommodate the new unit. Make adjustments with a file or chisel.

3 Now carefully position the new latch assembly as shown and mark where you must bore a hole through the door.

4 To avoid splintering, bore halfway through from one side, half from the other. Keep bit perpendicular to the door's surface.

5 Slip in the latch assembly and fasten it with screws top and bottom. On new doors, locate knob sets 90 cm from the floor.

6 Install the escutcheons, then slip on the outside knob assembly. Most catches can be set for left- or right-hand operation.

7 Complete the door work by securing the rose, then the inside knob. Before tightening, make sure the latch works freely.

8 Now close the door, carefully locate the strike plate, then open and mark its position on the jamb with a sharp pencil.

9 You'll probably need to enlarge the original mortise both top and bottom.

Improving existing doors

Weather-stripping doors

A poorly weather-stripped exterior door can leak up to twice as much air as a window in the same condition. Couple this with the fact that most doors also are used far more often than windows, and you can see why their seals merit a careful looking-at every so often. First, check for crimped, flattened or missing weather stripping at the top and sides. You might be able to adjust spring metal — the most commonly used door material — by prying lightly. Other types probably will have to be replaced.

Next, feel along the threshold. Air infiltration here means you need a bottom-of-the-door device to stop the air flow. And how's the door itself? Warping, an out-of-square frame or deteriorated caulk around the edges give air a chance to get through even the tightest weather stripping. Be sure to examine storm doors, too. Some metal versions have a bulbous gasket along their lower edges; others employ a sweep. Both should be replaced periodically.

Finally, check out any interior doors that open to an attic, garage, basement or other unheated space. Builders often don't bother to seal these big heat losers at all. Worse yet, some cut costs by installing hollow-core doors here. If that's the case at your house, you might save on heating bills by investing in the far greater thermal efficiency of a solid- or foam-core door.

There are many types of seals you can use:

- Foam tape installs easily. Just cut strips to length, peel off the backing and press in place on the inside of the stops.
- Tack rolled vinyl stripping to the stops' faces. Align so that the bulbous edge projects a bit.
- Nail spring-metal strips to the jamb inside the stop. With this type, be sure to fit carefully around the latch and any locks.
- Interlocking metal channels form a good seal, but are tricky to align. You must nail to both the door and the stop.
- Metal 'J-strips' look and seal best, but they're the most difficult to install because you must rout a channel in the door.
- Use special insulated moulding to seal the gap between double doors. Nail it to the face of the door that's usually closed.

RIGHT: Louvre doors filter the light and allow the air to flow through — ideal in a tropical climate. In this bedroom they provide direct access to the garden and a brick ledge at the foot of the solid window makes an ideal position for indoor plants.

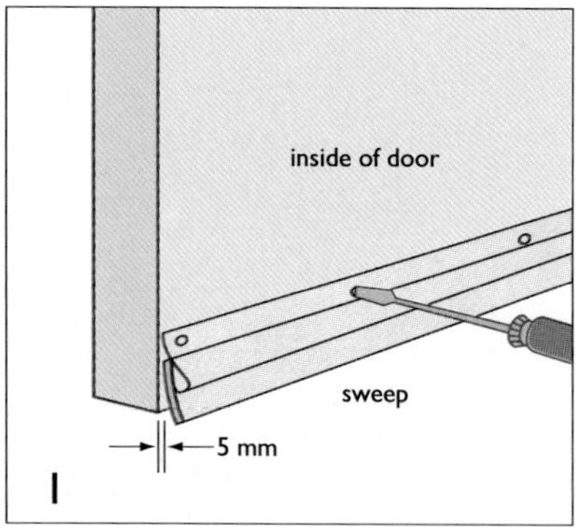

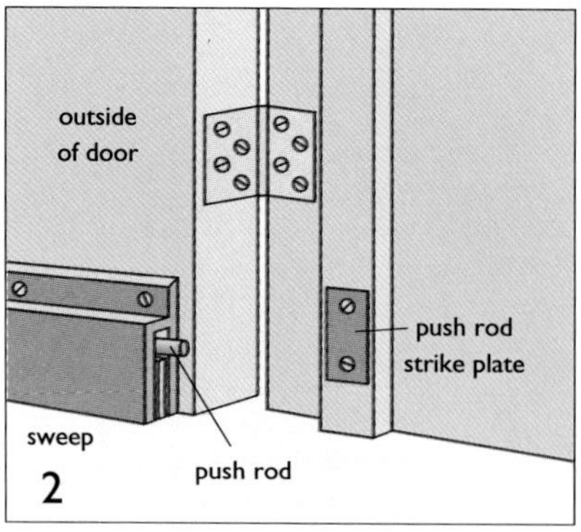

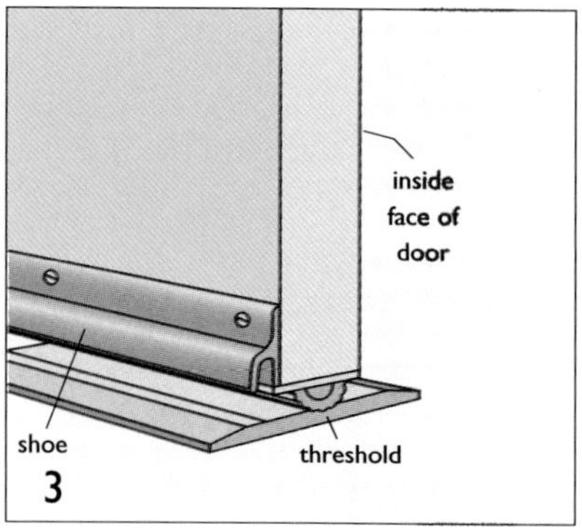

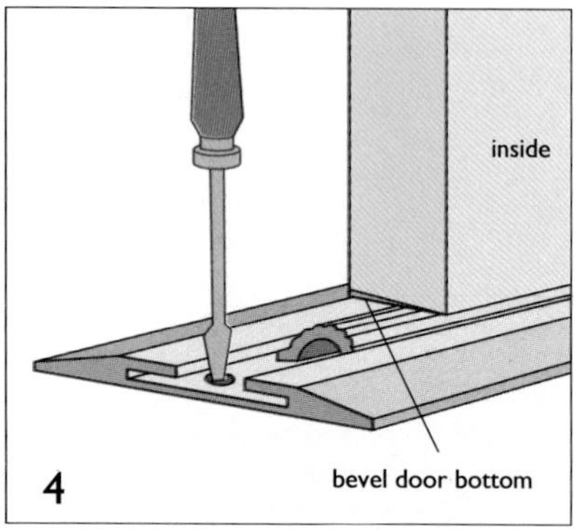

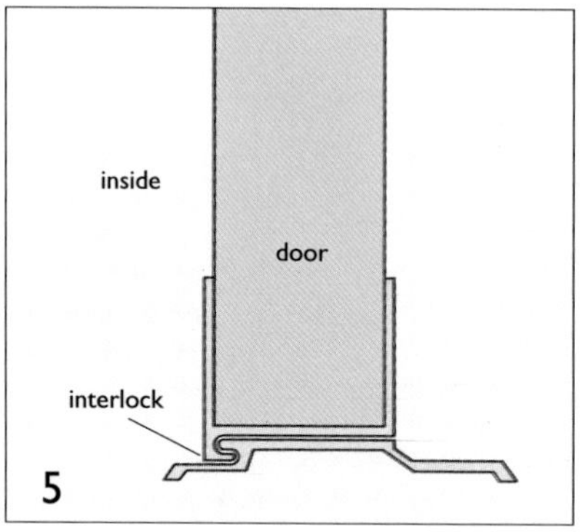

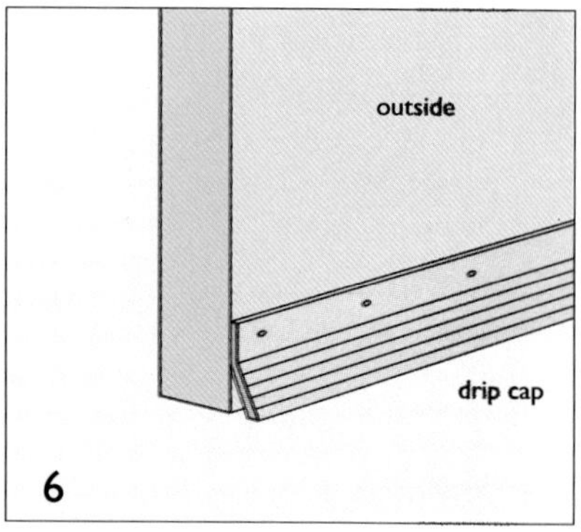

Sealing underneath doors

A door's bottom edge poses two special weather-stripping problems. First, its threshold — sometimes called a saddle — has to withstand lots of traffic. Second, any seal you attach to the door itself must be able to clear any carpeting or unevenness on the floor within the arc the door traverses.

The devices shown here solve these difficulties with varying degrees of effectiveness. If your door has a badly worn saddle, consider replacing it with one of these or with a wood version.

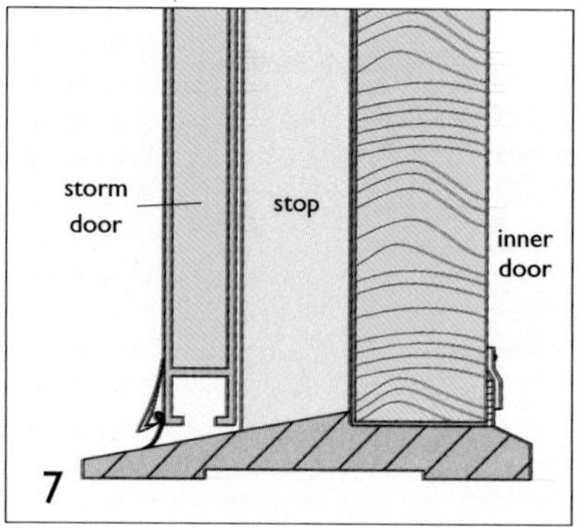

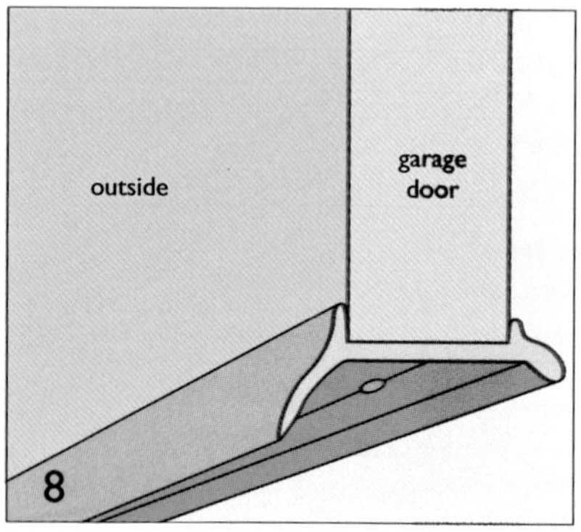

1 A sweep works fairly well if the floor is relatively even. You simply attach it so the sweep seals against the threshold.

2 An automatic sweep uses a spring action to hoist itself up as you open the door, then drops down again when you close it.

3 A shoe on the door's lower edge makes a durable seal. To install one, you'll have to remove the door and possibly plane it, too.

4 A bulb threshold works like a non-moving shoe. Bevel the door bottom. You'll need to replace the bulb periodically.

5 Interlocking thresholds make the tightest seal. Installing one calls for some tricky carpentry work and fitting, though.

6 If your door lets water into the house, nail a metal drip cap to its outside face. Stop air with a bulb threshold.

7 Don't forget to check weather stripping under storm doors, too. You can buy replacement rubber or plastic sweeps for these types of doors.

8 To weather-strip the bottom edge of a roll-up or swing-up garage door, you can purchase a special gasket.

Restoring a door

Many a dim room will live to sparkle another day with the additional light that shines through bright new glass panels. They're great for ill-lit hallways, but are also an excellent little lighting trick to play anywhere in the house. If privacy is a problem, use frosted opaque glass instead of transparent panes, or choose glass with an attractive Victorian pattern.

LEFT: Solid timber doors with glass panels inset look equally attractive as front entrance doors or as internal doors. Doors such as the one shown here can often be bought for a reasonable price at demolition yards. They can then be stripped and stained or repainted to bring about a complete transformation.

BELOW: Restoring a door.

1 Carefully lever beading off so the timber is not damaged.

2 Pull out nails with pincers.

3 Drill a hole at each inner corner of the beading line. Use a jigsaw to remove the rectangle formed by the holes. (The beading on the other side of the door remains.)

4 Clean the rebate.

5 Apply putty to the rebate.

1

2

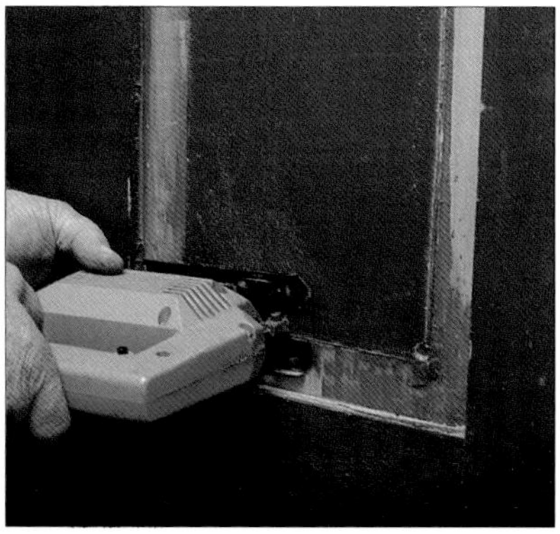

3

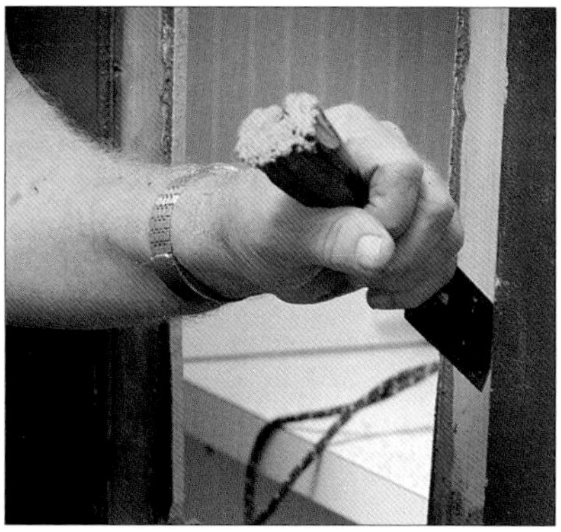

4

5

6

7

8

9

6 Press in the pre-cut glass panel, with the smooth side facing you if the glass is rippled or etched.

7 Secure the glass with pins.

8 Apply a little putty to the beading you have removed.

9 Secure with skew nails, punch in, fill and sand. Finish the door as desired.

BELOW LEFT: The timber on this door has been stripped and sanded. Coloured glass was used as a border with a transparent panel in the centre to provide a clear view to the next room.

Tips

Painting doors and windows

- When painting windows, work from the inside out, starting with muntins and progressing to sashes, casing, lintel and sill. Use a high-quality sash brush to paint narrow window elements. If your hand is unsteady use a paint shield or apply masking tape on the edges of the windowpanes.
- As with windows, paint doors from the inside out, starting with the door's recessed panels, if any. Mini-rollers and foam pads speed painting of narrow door elements. For tight spots around doors, use an angular sash paintbrush.

Do-it-yourself flyscreen door

No matter where you live, you share your abode with a range of little creatures that either want to bite you or annoy you. Here's how you can build a traditional flyscreen to keep them out.

The frame for this screen is made from clear dressed oregon. It is easy to work with and won't break your budget.

The sizes given on the drawing are indicative only, as they will vary to suit your individual door opening. The main perimeter frame is made from 75 x 25 mm timber (all sizes are nominal) with two 50 x 25 mm cross pieces. The dowels are 15 mm in diameter.

1 Cut the pieces to length, being very careful to make all cuts square (use a mitre box if you have one). Lay them out on a flat surface as they appear on the diagram. Check for square by measuring the diagonals and then glue the four corner joints and clamp them. (Be sure to pad the jaws of the clamps to protect the timber frame.)
2 All joints are glued and then screwed and plugged. (Use a spade bit with a diameter a little larger than the screw head and drill a hole about 20 mm into the frame edge. Using a drill the same size as the screw, drill the rest of the way through the first timber.) After you have screwed the joints together, take a square dowel—after shaping the end with a Stanley knife—and glue and plug it into the screw hole. Trim any excess with a chisel. You will see that the screw hole has almost disappeared.
3 Before fixing the two centre cross pieces, fit the dowels. Using a spade bit again, drill the holes about 25 mm deep and glue in the dowels.
4 The decorative corner pieces are cut from 75 x 25 mm timber using a jigsaw. Clamp the timber to a bench to cut it. (You can vary the pattern to your taste but once you choose one, make a template and use it to mark out all four corners.) Glue and screw them in place much the same as the frame pieces.
5 Lay out your screen mesh (available at most hardware stores) on the back of the frame and fix it in place with staples. Overlap the inside of the frame by about 15 mm. The edge of the mesh is then hidden by fixing a 25 x 10 mm beading over it, flush to the edge of the frame, with panel pins. (Mitre the corners of the beading and arris the edges.)
6 We suggest you hang the flyscreen with a spring-loaded screen-door hinge at the bottom and one regular easy-fit butt hinge (75–90 mm) at the top. This way, the door won't slam too hard. If you intend to paint your project, it is probably a good idea to paint the main frame before you fit the mesh.

ABOVE: With new balustrades on the steps and a decorative timber flyscreen door, the entrance to this house is neat and welcoming.

BELOW: Flyscreen door.

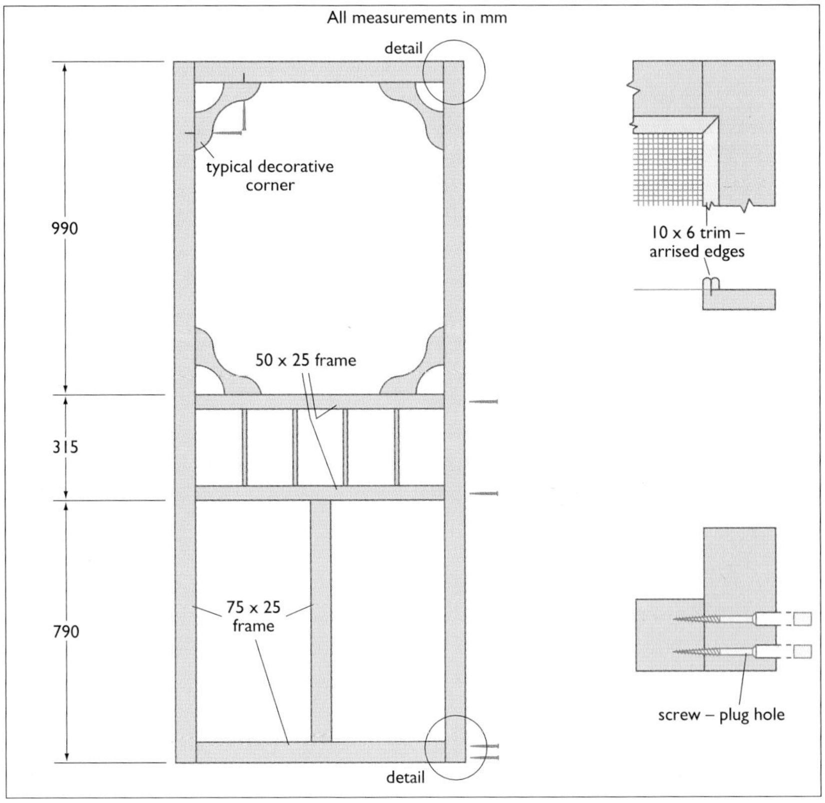

How to keep your home secure

Nearly four out of five household burglaries occur in broad daylight. It would seem most robbers like to work the same hours you do.

Insurance companies warn that only about a quarter of the houses broken into have adequate security at the point of entry. You can make your home safer by upgrading the security on your doors. There is a wide range of security devices to suit all types of doors.

Patio doors

A broom handle or dowel laid in the bottom track is an effective security device if the door cannot be lifted out of the frame.

A patio door pin is simply a chrome pin that keeps two doors together when placed in a hole drilled through the frames.

Anti-lift plates can be fitted in the head track of the frame to prevent lifting. They also can be used on sliding windows.

Patio door bolts are 10-mm-thick bolts that lock the stile to the frame at the head and/or floor.

The sliding door handle fitted to your door should have anti-lift pins to prevent the door being lifted from its track. It should also be capable of being deadlocked from inside and out for double security. If it doesn't have these features, consider replacing it with one that does.

Timber doors

The door chain, the old favourite, is now available in a keyed version. Also available is a door guard, a bit like a hasp and staple.

Interlocking deadlocks feature a clutching action which interlocks with the striker. They are available with single or double cylinders.

Deadbolts are very secure bolts that can't be opened without a key

ABOVE: A selection of locks and sensor lights for doors and windows.

FAR LEFT: For complete security this keypad provides access by PIN number only.

LEFT: Brass deadlock suitable for domestic doors.

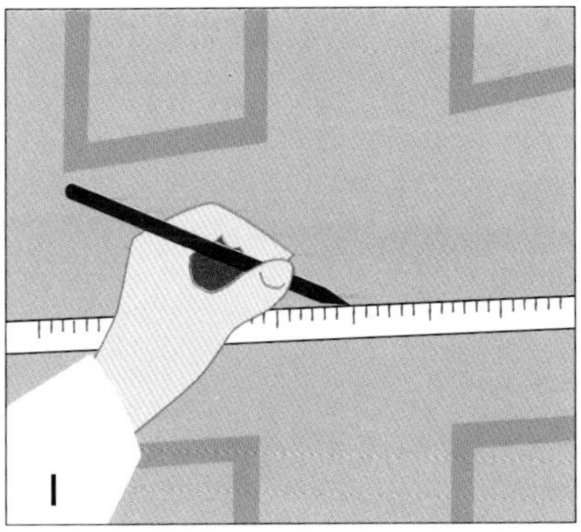

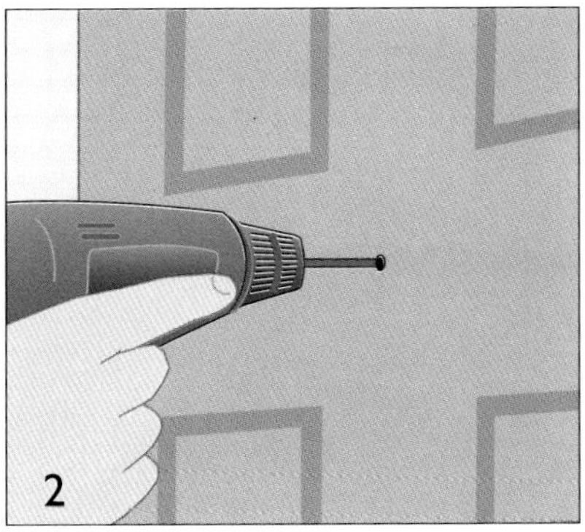

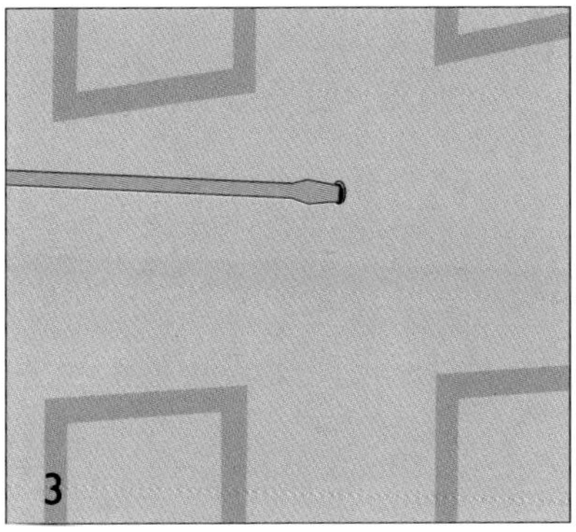

and are difficult to wrench off or cut. They have the advantage that the bolt itself goes into the meat of the frame. They can be placed a third of the way up the door to provide extra strength against it being kicked.

The double cylinder deadlock locks inside and out and easily covers marks left by previous night latches. Combined with a door frame strengthener, it gives greater protection against intruders kicking in the door.

The digital lock, a variation of the deadlock, is opened by punching in your own entry code, which is easy to remember if you use your bank PIN.

There are locks available for internal doors, but the consensus is that once intruders have gained access, they won't be inhibited about making noise and will simply smash doors down.

Fitting a security door viewer

The lens in a door viewer allows you to see what is happening outside the door over quite a wide angle. It is easy enough to fit to any door, whether solid or hollow, from 32 to 51 mm thick.

Fitting a safety chain

A safety chain on a timber front or back door allows you to open the door marginally to see who's calling, but won't afford an opening sufficient for anyone to enter. It also doubles the security of a lock and makes you feel a great deal more comfortable about being home alone.

Use a hefty safety chain, preferably one made from stainless steel. The screws supplied with it must be stout and at least 38 mm long (50 mm is better).

Position the safety chain close to the lock on a hollow-core door (so that you'll have something solid to screw to) and mark screw holes. With solid timber doors, the height is up to you. The fitting with the chain goes on the jamb side (the frame the door hangs on).

Pre-drill one screw hole to suit the shank size and one to suit the average diameter of the core around which the thread turns. Drill no deeper than shank length. Now use a twist drill to drill the rest of the hole slightly longer than the length of the screw.

Select a screwdriver that fits the head of the screw. It should be slightly narrower than the head diameter and fit tightly across the width. Excess movement could cause the screwdriver to turn out of the screw head and damage the slot.

Sink in all the screws until they are tight. Slip on the chain. The chain should be long enough to reach between the two fittings, allowing the door to open a few centimetres so that you can see who is there without allowing the person to enter.

ABOVE: Fitting a security door viewer.

1 With a tape measure and pencil, mark the centre of the door at a comfortable eye level.

2 Drill a 3 mm hole and then, using it as a guide, drill from both sides of the door with a 13 mm drill bit.

3 Screw the two halves of the viewer in from both sides of the door. When choosing the viewer, make sure you select one with as wide an angle of vision as possible.

Tip

- French doors look attractive but securing them satisfactorily can be a problem. Installing heavily made barrel bolts top and bottom plus a quality rebate lock will help give you good protection.

Windows

Because we use windows to allow natural light inside the house and provide a view of the outdoors, we seldom notice them. But occasionally, when an errant ball finds its way through a glass pane, when a sash absolutely refuses to budge or when a screen needs repairing or replacing, windows make their presence known. This chapter was written for those occasions.

ABOVE: If you are having a pitched ceiling in your renovation, this window treatment may give you some ideas. Colonial windows, capped by a fixed arch, French doors and vertical panelled dado create a very attractive room.

You should realise, however, that with proper maintenance you can do a great deal to prevent some window problems. To keep windowsills from rotting, for example, make sure they always have a protective coat of paint.

Check windows regularly. To keep movable sashes working, occasionally clean the channels they ride in. You will be amazed at how smoothly you can make crank-operated windows perform with a periodic squeeze of powdered graphite or drop of penetrating oil in and around the crank mechanism.

On the following pages you'll find the solutions to a host of window problems, including balky sashes, broken panes, damaged screening and many others. No longer will you have to go to the expense of hiring a repairer, or worse, ignore the repair completely.

The link between house and garden

Windows give the house personality. But as well as endowing interiors and exteriors with memorable impact, windows themselves can possess personality. When small, they can imply secrecy, intimacy and protection. Conversely, they are extroverted, welcoming and all-embracing when large. Medium-sized, they are just right. If a window is less than perfectly proportioned, its decorative (and frequently functional) treatment can create an illusion which will solve the proportion problem and promote the window from being a mere donor of light and fresh air to a focus for beauty. Additions and alterations to windows can make an incredible difference to a room and to the whole house.

Windows can also grow out into the garden if they are given sides, a base and a raked top and pushed beyond the boundaries of the wall to create miniature conservatories or glasshouses. These expanded windows are known as 'bump-outs' and they are a wonderful way of adding extra light and an unprecedented feeling of space to a dark and under-sized room.

Window types

Anatomy of a double-hung window

Often, there's more to a window than meets the eye. That's especially the case with the double-hung type shown on the next page. Its secrets include heavy sash weights concealed behind the frame's side jambs. Connected via a rope-and-pulley system, the weights provide a counterbalance that not only makes the sashes easier to open, but also holds them in any vertical position you choose.

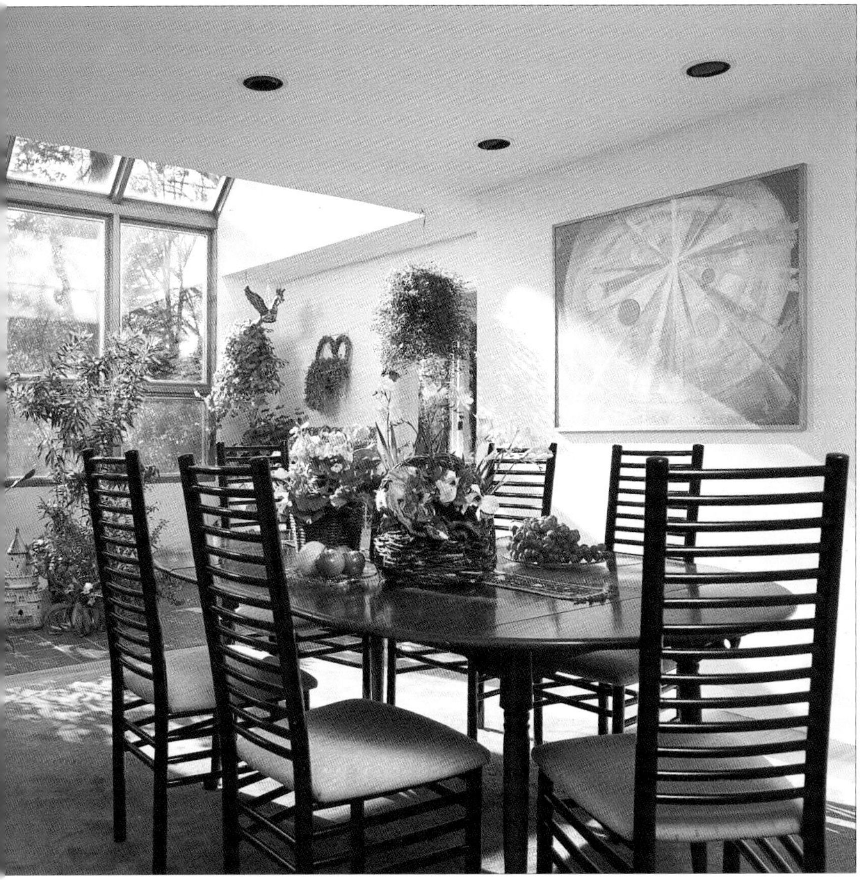

ABOVE: This charming little bathroom window, set into the outside of a double-brick wall, allows an extra-wide tiled sill. Western red cedar stands up to moisture and is very suitable for bathrooms.

LEFT: Conservatory-style windows can transform as well as extend your living area. If the addition is to house plants, use a floor surface which is appropriate to the use.

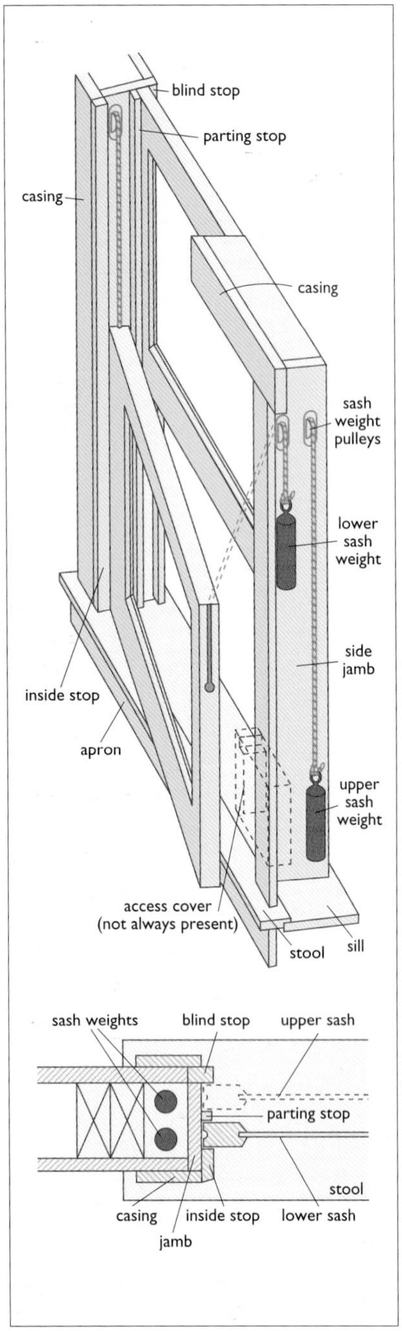

A series of stops fitted to the jambs provides channels in which the sashes slide. Check the top view and note that although the outside blind stop is more or less permanently affixed, the parting stop and inside stop can be pried loose if you want to remove the sashes.

Newer double-hung windows replace the weight-and-pulley mechanisms with a pair of spring lift devices.

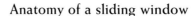

With both double-hung types the lower sash comes to rest behind a flat stool; its outside counterpart, the sill, slopes so water can run off. Trim — called casing at the sides and top, and an apron below — covers any gaps between the jambs and the wall material.

Anatomy of a casement window

Casement windows open and close inwards and outwards, usually with the help of a crank-type operator. In the version that is illustrated here muntins separate the panes. With some double-glazed casements the muntins snap to the inside of the window to facilitate cleaning, or are absent altogether.

Anatomy of a sliding window

As with double-hung windows, sliding sashes open up only 50 per cent of the total window area for ventilation. Some sliding windows have one fixed and one sliding sash, as shown here; with others, both sashes slide along continuous tracks. Sliding windows may have wood or metal construction.

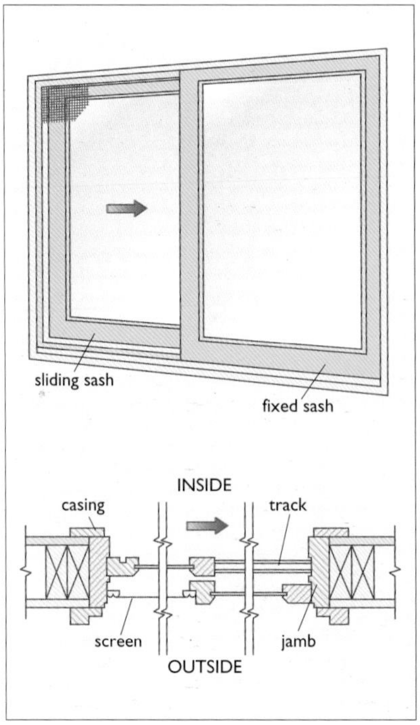

ABOVE: Consider two tall vertical windows instead of one large horizontal one to add a classic elegance to your rooms. These are double-hung, powder-coated aluminium with fixed colonial bars.

FAR LEFT: Anatomy of a double-hung window.

LEFT: Anatomy of a sliding window.

BELOW: Anatomy of a casement window.

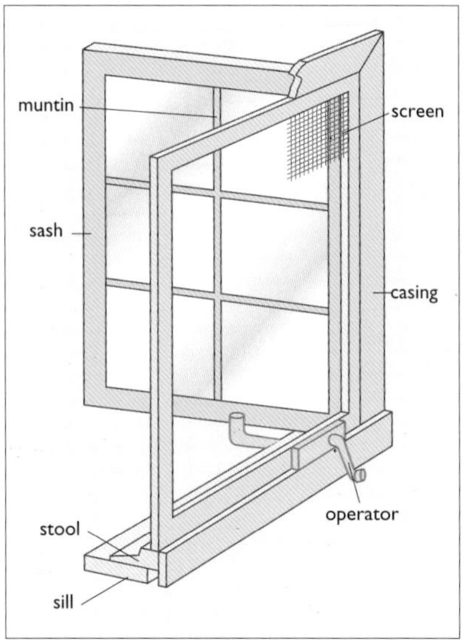

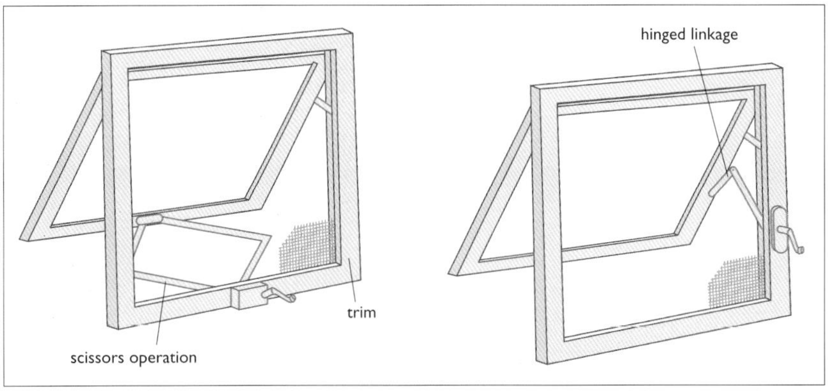

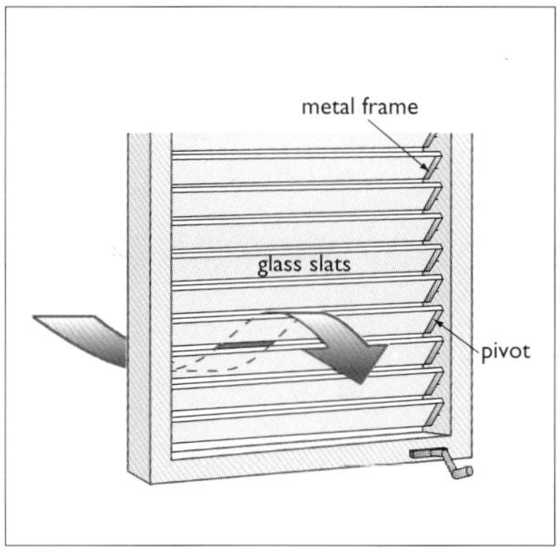

ABOVE: Anatomy of an awning window.

ABOVE RIGHT: Anatomy of a louvre window.

BELOW: Use windows as a decorative and practical room divider.

BELOW RIGHT: Custom-built windows can be any shape or size. This renovation made the most of the pitched roof with a sturdy sculptural window system.

Anatomy of an awning window

Awning sashes tilt outwards, under the direction of a scissors- or hinge-type cranking system. Some awnings slide downwards as they tilt, so you can open them to an almost horizontal position for maximum airflow. Sometimes awning units serve as the only operable elements in a big bank of windows.

Anatomy of a louvre window

Louvre windows let in lots of air and each turn of the crank pivots a series of glass slats for maximum flow control. The frames here consist of short metal channels at either end of the slats. Those glass-to-glass joints tend to leak air, so you usually find louvres only in areas that normally are not heated.

Improving natural light

There are both major and minor ways to improve the flow of natural light into your house. If you need to make major changes, chances are your house is an old one. Old houses are definitely the worst offenders when it comes to inherent darkness.

It's not that people once disliked light and built houses in such a way as to block it out — although you could be excused for thinking so. It's just that leadlights and the like have been replaced as a result of a revolution in the making of glass, frames and other window-related technology.

Major renovations

A common, major renovation is to move the bathroom from the back of the ground floor to an upstairs site. This allows the ground-floor room to be extended across the width of the house. Floor-to-ceiling glass doors or sliding glass doors can then be installed, allowing in masses of light, and bringing the garden or courtyard 'inside' as well.

A more radical major renovation might be to replace the entire wall or part of one with glass bricks, either clear or frosted, depending on privacy needs.

Removing unnecessary dividing walls also qualifies as a major

Tips

- Before you begin renovating or extending, collect lots of pictures and ideas for windows from magazines and brochures. Eventually the style that you really like will become apparent.
- If the existing windows in your home are vertical, your new windows should be also.

BELOW: A new bay window in traditional style.

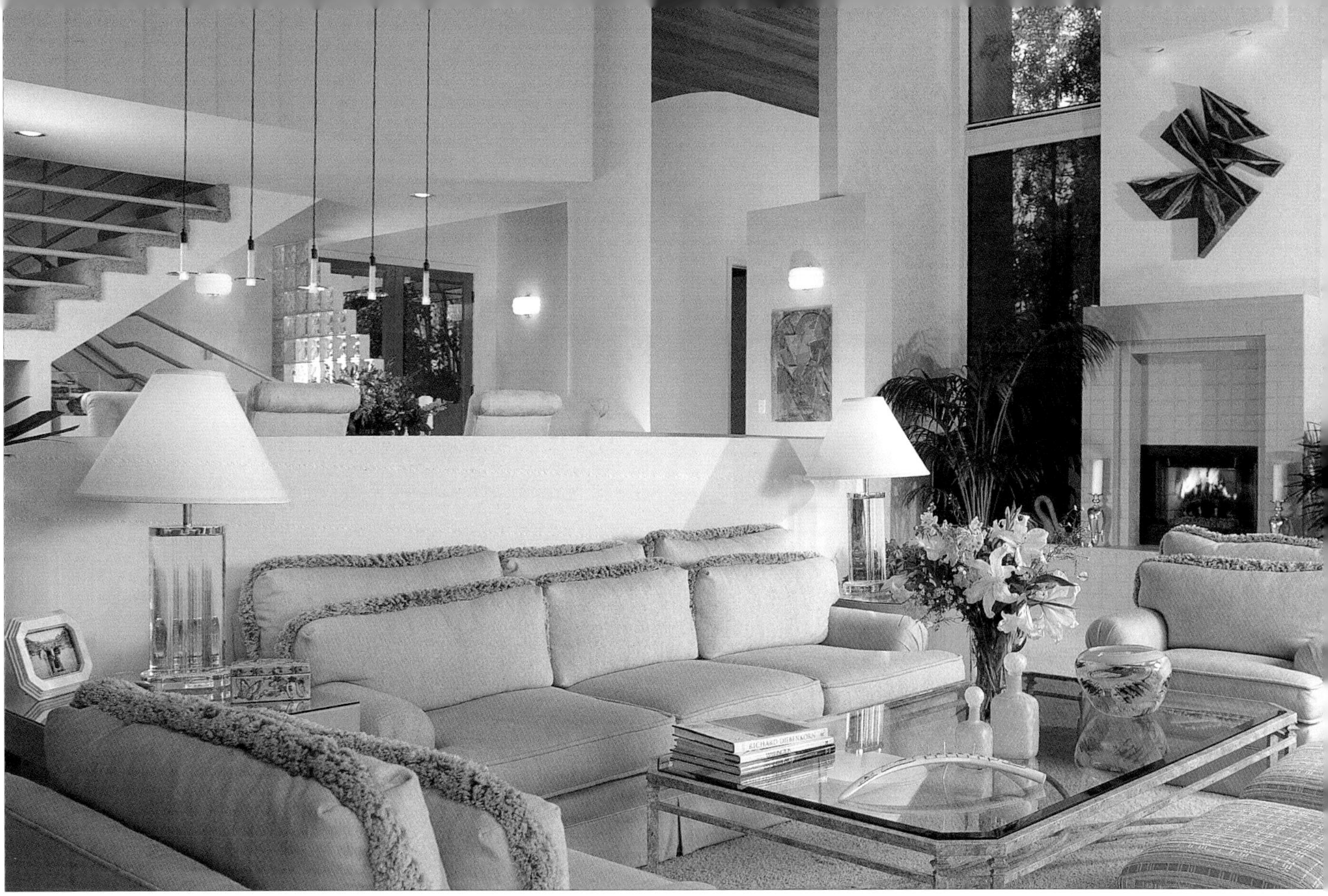

change. The fewer the walls and doors, the more light can flow through the whole house.

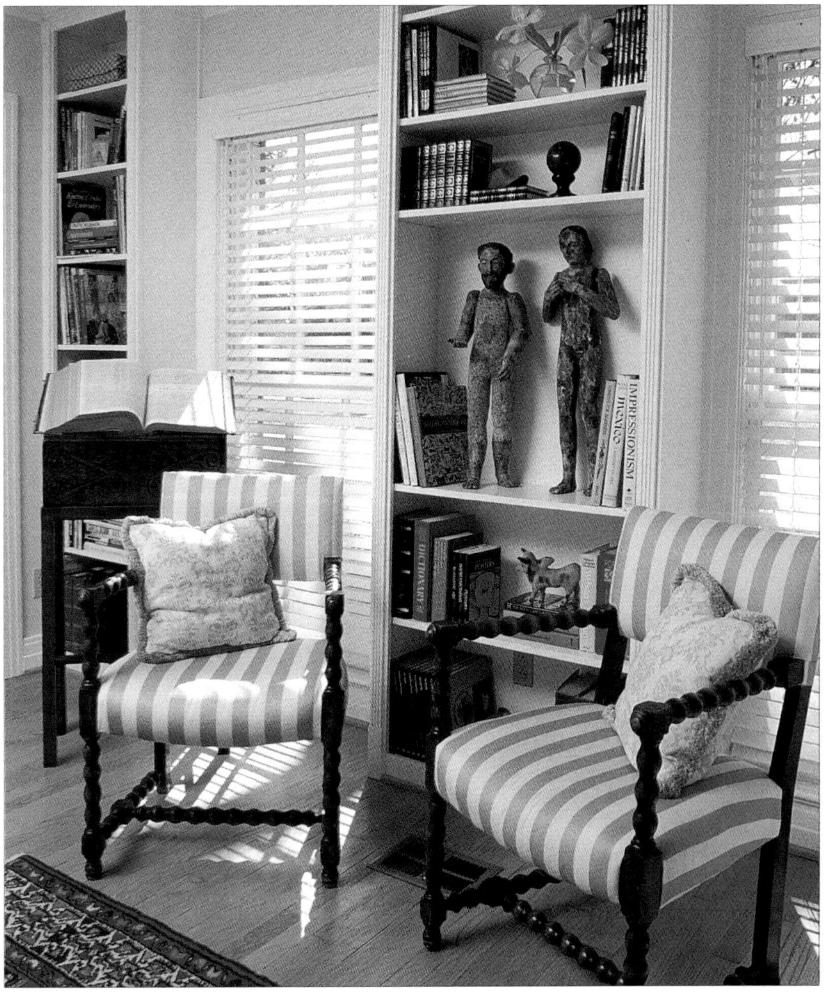

Inspirational windows

Window design can set the style of your home. Colonial, Federation, Mediterranean or modern, there's a shape for you. If you're planning a renovation, the ideas pictured here may inspire you to create interesting architectural designs to suit your natural lighting needs. There are lots of stock windows available, but you may like to have something a little different.

ABOVE: Floor to ceiling glass provides a dramatic glimpse of the outside.

RIGHT: Painted timber venetian blinds filter the light.

ABOVE: The mirror's position gives the illusion of space and reflected light plays on these classic windows.

LEFT: A fixed pane in a cosy corner beside a door.

ABOVE RIGHT: Wraparound windows can easily stop at normal windowsill height.

BELOW RIGHT: The absence of a corner window mullion and floor-to-ceiling glass give the wraparound window an unobstructed outlook.

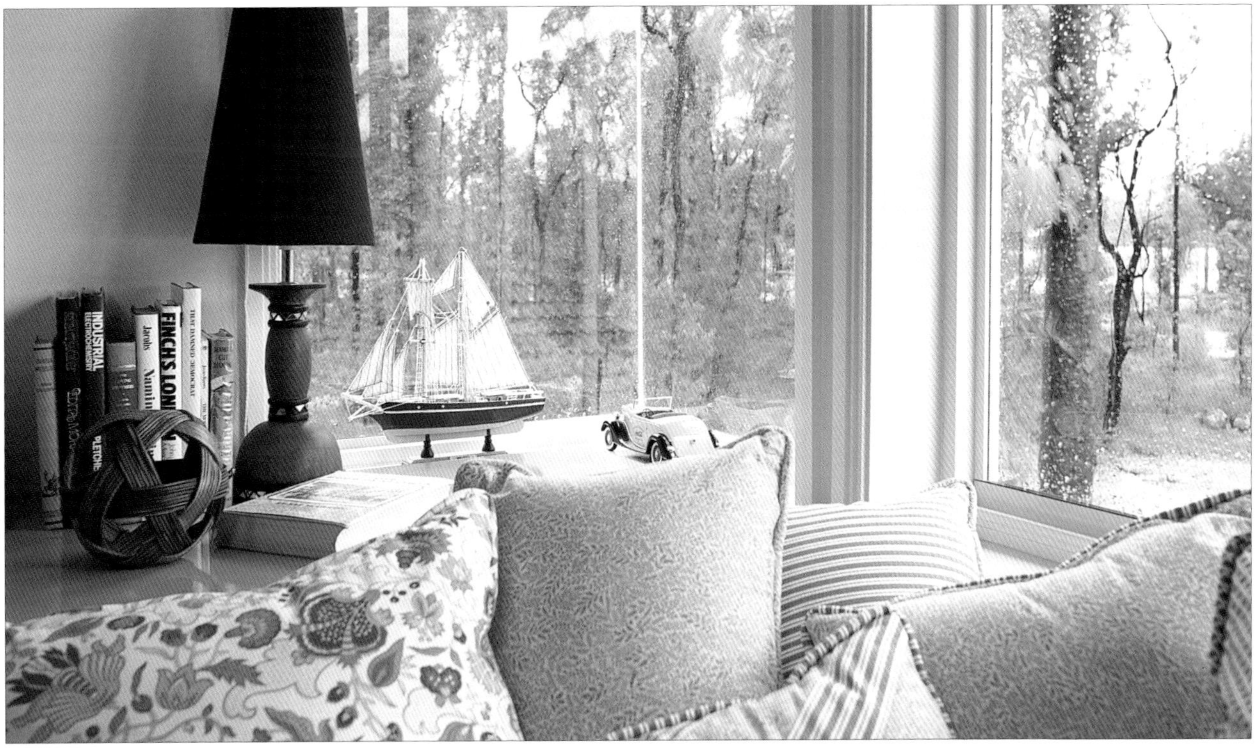

Corner windows

Windows that wrap around corners are a design feature which regularly comes back into fashion. Now, however, they've returned with a stylish refinement.

By placing verticals or posts approximately 300 mm either side of the corner, overhead beams can cantilever without being supported where they meet at that corner. This means that the two panes of glass can also meet with only a silicon seam to waterproof the join.

Because we are used to seeing the corners of our houses boxed in, the effect of them seeming to be supported by glass alone is both very stylish and eye catching.

This type of design detail was originally included in commercial architecture only. Now the larger window companies are offering silicon-joined corner windows in aluminium and timber for domestic application. The thickness of the glass varies from 5 mm to thicker laminated glass, depending on the size and application.

ABOVE: In the form of a large glass gable, this 'dormer' is lined beneath the roof's collar ties. Vertical blinds are one of the few ways of furnishing triangular window shapes.

ABOVE RIGHT: The space under this dormer was designed to take a double bed. The sill height coincides with the low, unusable section of the roof cavity and lines up with the low vertical walls.

BELOW RIGHT: The traditional proportions of the single dormer in this attic bedroom project outwards from the main roof, starting close to the ridge. The alcove provides a head-clearance area on the low sloping side of the room.

Tip

- Plan a gabled dormer to be the same pitch as the roof of the house; this ensures that it doesn't look like an afterthought.

Dormer windows

The word 'dormer' traditionally refers to a small roof shape, with a vertical window, which projects out from the main roof pitch to allow light into an attic room.

Dormers until recently have been the sole property of period building styles, but they are now appearing in contemporary architectural designs. The dormer is seen as an attractive device which is also practical as it turns roof cavities into useable spaces.

The modern-day popularity of the dormer has led to variations on its original format. Today's dormers can sit back from the facade of your house or be a continuation of it; they can spread across an entire roof or be scaled down to become an incidental roofing shape. You can use them to channel light into ground-floor rooms.

The photographs here will give you some idea of construction technique, but note that many builders claim that building a dormer is one of the most difficult building tasks. So you should seek expert help before you attempt to turn your dormer dreams into reality.

Shutters

Shutters come in all sizes and most finishes. They're a highly decorative means to an end; they help with problems with insulating from the sun, controlling light and privacy, while still allowing you to open doors and windows to fresh air. Lastly, they provide security.

You'll have no difficulty in fitting shutters to standard doors and windows, and special sizes and slat widths can be made to order.

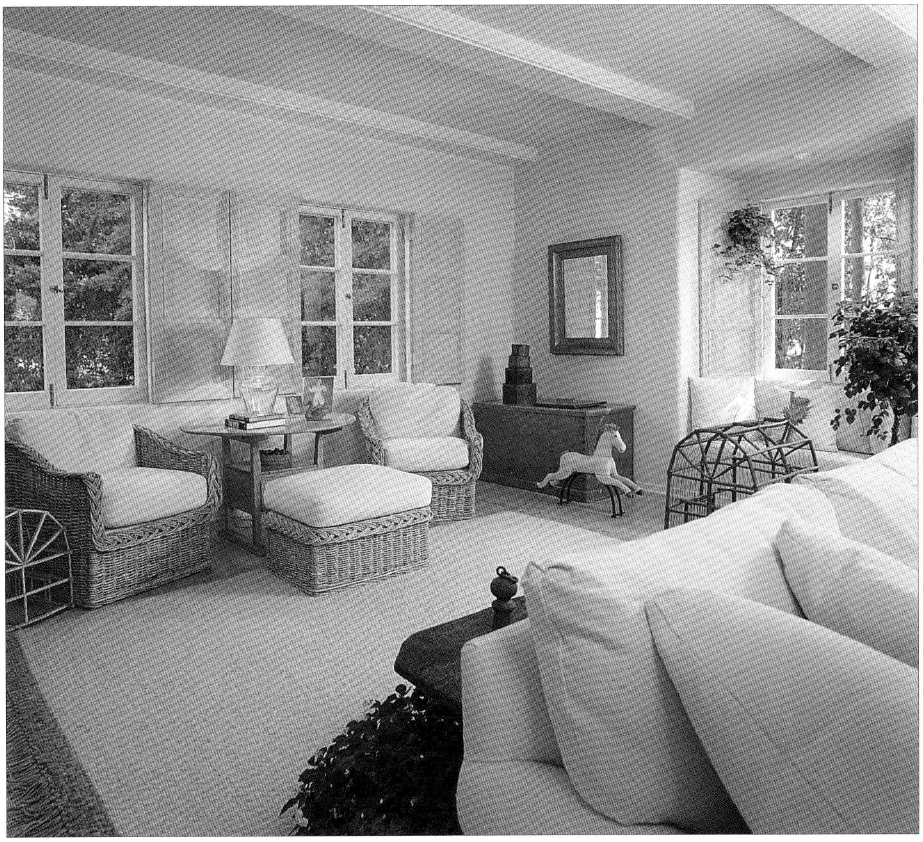

ABOVE RIGHT: Custom-made solid shutters.

FAR RIGHT: Shutters become an integral part of the wall.

RIGHT: Two part bi-fold shutters give plenty of options.

BELOW: Floor-to-ceiling shutters allow both light and privacy.

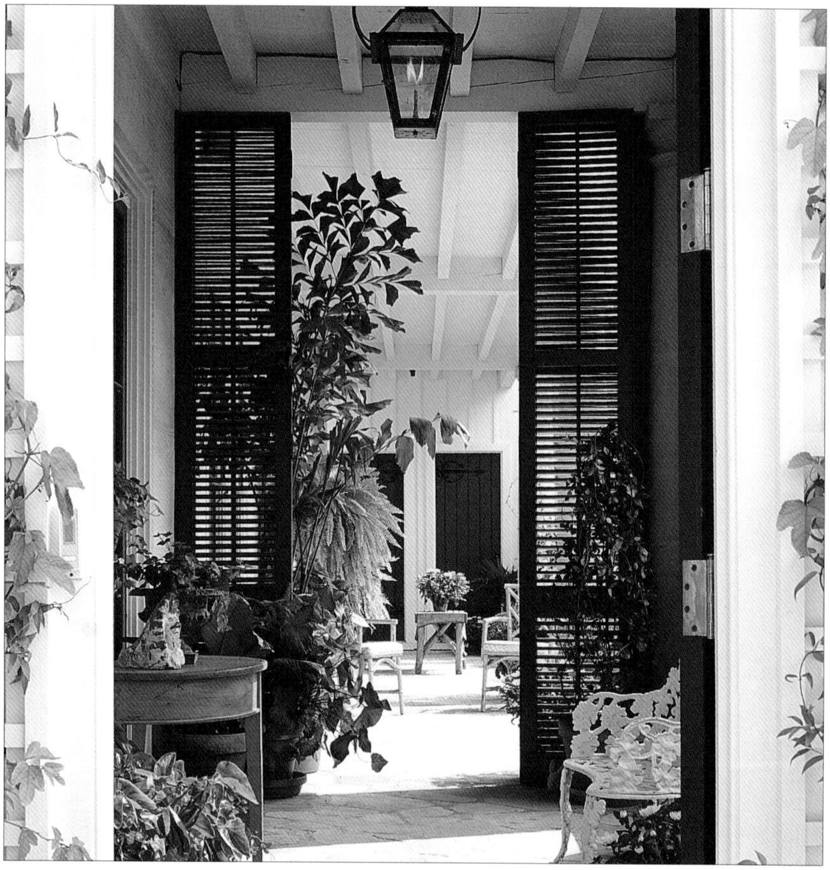

ABOVE: Window locks provide essential security on windows not covered by external bars. A keyed security lock for a window can be combined with the closing mechanism to make it unobtrusive.

RIGHT: For an easy way to partition off a section of verandah to make a more intimate space, consider an elegant folding screen of ground-to-roof shutters like these. They'll separate the area while leaving it visible through fine horizontal slats.

Tips

- Save window cleaning for a dull day. Bright sunlight will dry the windows too quickly, leaving smears on the glass.
- Polish with a pad of newspaper; the printers' ink will buff and avoid a smeary surface.

Fitting an architrave to a window

Varying the profile of an architrave and adding detail at each top corner will enable you to dictate a room's mood and period.

Architraves are simply timber mouldings. Try to find a moulding that matches your original at your local timber yard.

1 Measure the height and width of the window to determine the inside measurement of the pieces of architrave and where to cut them.
2 Cut the mitre joints on the architrave, cutting on the waste side of the pencilled lines.
3 Nail the architrave to the window frame at the top, bottom and centre, but don't drive the nails home until all pieces are in position and their alignment has been checked.
4 Drive the nails home and add extra nails at 300 mm spacings. Punch the nail heads below the surface of the timber, fill, sand and finish.

Window locks

The extensive use of glass in our homes makes it relatively easy for burglars to smash or cut their way in. However, you can make it difficult for them to remove your belongings if you install deadlocks on external doors and keyed locks on all the windows. Unless the burglars can locate the keys, they can't open anything and are forced to clamber out through a window edged with broken glass.

Putting locks on timber windows is relatively easy; it may even reduce your insurance premiums and, better still, may considerably reduce the likelihood of burglary.

Purchase a system with a single master key. Keep the key in a secure, secret spot. Locks featuring one-way screws are the easiest to install; a one-way screw can be screwed in but can't be screwed out.

Installing a window lock

Make sure the type and number of locks you select will suit your windows. If you're unsure, ask at your hardware store.

Window locks

More than 50 per cent of break-ins are through windows, so that makes them your number one weak point, unless you live in a fortress-like block of units. Listed below are window types and the locks that will suit them.

Double-hung windows

- keyed sash lock
- keyed security bolt, with various-sized bolts to suit either timber or aluminium windows

Both locks can be easily installed and have optional one-way screws to prevent removal.

Casement windows

- keyed security bolt
- window bolt. Again, one-way screws are recommended.

Sliding windows

- keyed security bolt
- sliding-window push lock

The sliding-window push lock is slimmer as it is intended for aluminium windows. It also prevents the window being lifted out of its tracks and can be locked in a partly open position to allow ventilation.

Awning windows

- keyed security bolt
- window bolt
- window lock that locks windows that have chainwinder operators
- key-operated lockable chainwinders are available. They give you the flexibility of locking your windows in an open position and can be wound shut from this locked position.

There are more sophisticated options to these standards, such as through-screen locks and a simple push-button lock which requires a key to unlock it. There is also the option of having four locks keyed alike, which saves space on your key ring.

BELOW: Installing a window lock.

1 Carefully read the instructions supplied with your chosen lock. Place the fitting in its recommended position and accurately mark around the screw holes with a sharp pencil or, alternatively, use a punch.

2 Using the correct-sized drills, pre-drill the holes, first for the screws and then for the locking bar. Drive the nail 3–4 mm into the centre of each screw position before drilling; this will help keep drill holes in the correct place. Drill the hole for the locking bar with a drill of a largish diameter which will be easier to turn with an electric drill.

3 Screw the fittings on with the 'one-way' screws and test. Continue until all the windows are lockable.

1

2

3

Solving window problems

When a window binds or refuses to budge, don't try to force it — you risk damaging the sash, the frame or both. Instead, take a look around the sash's perimeter, both inside and out. Chances are, you'll find that paint has sealed the window shut or that a stop moulding has warped. Both difficulties usually respond to the gentle prying techniques described below.

BELOW: Freeing a balky sash.

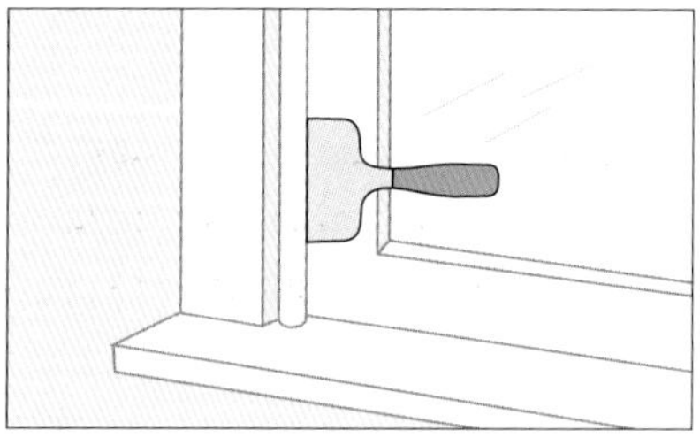

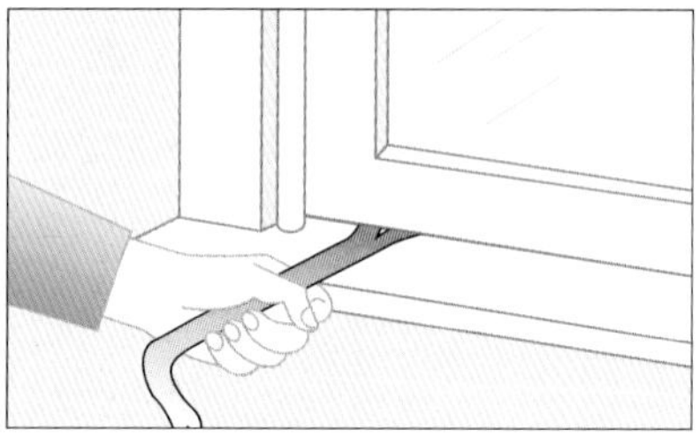

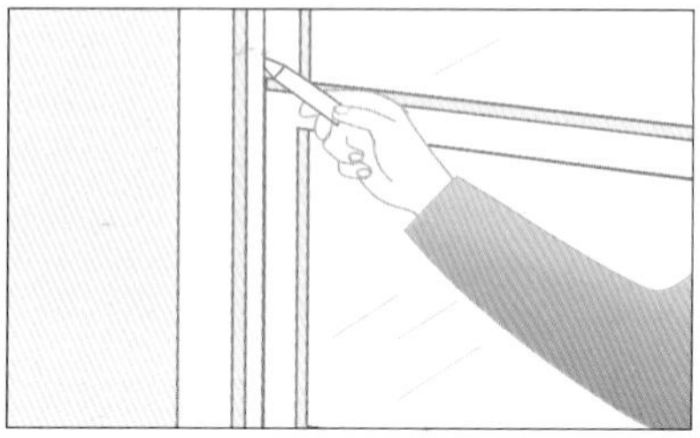

With double-hung windows, the culprit also could be a faulty spring lift or a broken sash cord. Having to replace these involves dismantling the window, which is a not-too-tricky job.

Repairing double-hung windows

Freeing a balky sash

To break a paint seal, tap a broadside putty knife between the sash and stop, then work it back and forth, or try prying from outside with a wide-bladed tool such as a crow bar. Work around the window's perimeter until the sash pops free.

If a sash is binding between its stops, you can often separate them slightly by tapping along their length with a wooden block.

Once you get the window moving again, lightly sand its jambs, then lubricate with paste wax, paraffin or a bar of soap.

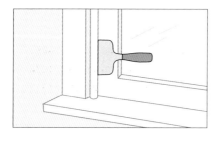

Tips

- Don't paint sash cords. It makes them brittle and prone to jam and snap. Parting and stop beads are quite common mouldings and should be readily available from good timber suppliers and some hardware stores.
- Check the conditions of the pulleys. They can rust and damage the cords. They are easy to replace.
- Be careful not to mix up the weights. They are fitted to suit specific sashes.

Replacing sash cords

Working from inside the window, first remove the stop (or staff) bead which holds the inside sash in place. Use a craft knife to break the paint seal with the frame, then use a chisel to prise it loose. It should bow enough to pop the ends out of the mitre joints. If not, push it back in place and pull the nails out (bowing the bead will have made them show through the paint). It should now come out quite easily. It is often possible to remove the inside sash only after removing the stop bead on one side. If this is not the case, take out the other, then carefully lift out the sash.

If one sash cord is broken, it's wise to assume they're all worn and replace them all at the same time. If only the knot at the counterweight has come undone and there are no obvious signs of wear, it is probably safe to deal just with the problem at hand. After removing the inner sash, disconnect the sash cord (mark where the cord reaches to on the sash and pull out the nails). If any counterweights are still attached, tack the end of the cord to the main window frame so they don't drop down inside the frame.

At the bottom of the frame is the weight pocket cover. Remove enough of the parting bead (often this is not nailed) to expose the cover and open it up (diagram 1). It will be screwed or nailed in place. The weights and any broken cords

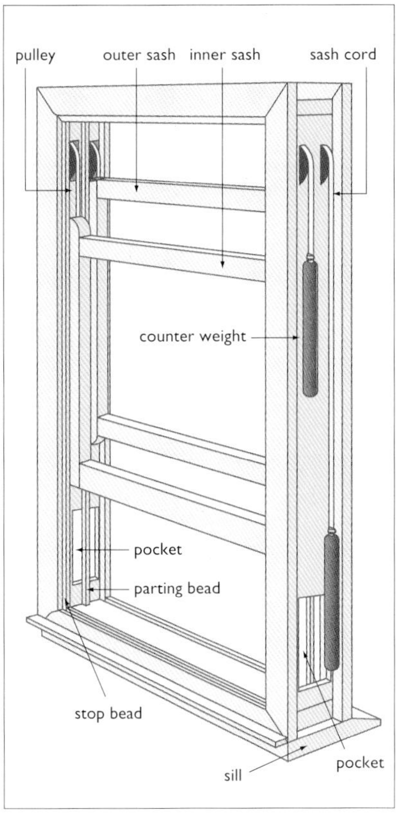

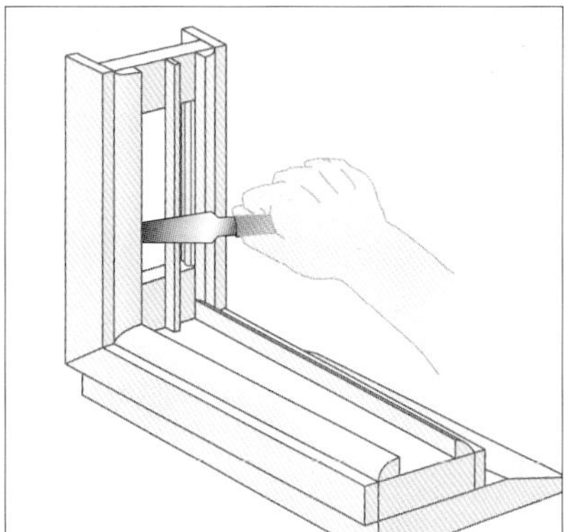
DIAGRAM 1

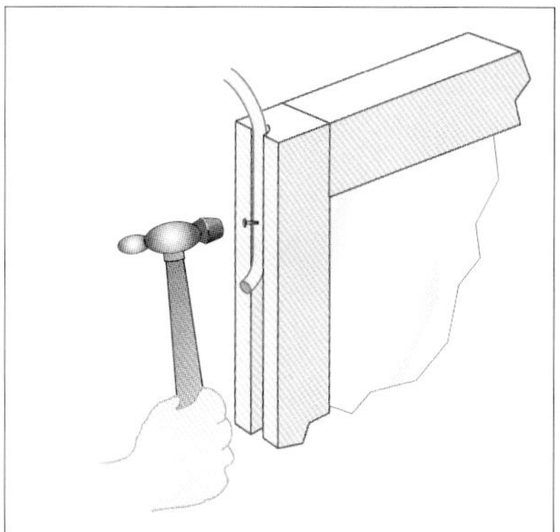
DIAGRAM 2

ABOVE: Replacing sash cords.

can now be accessed and cords retied or replaced. Measure the old cords (if they're broken, join the bits together) and make the new cords the same length (add a little extra for possible adjustment later). Use a piece of string with a small weight attached (a mouse), such as a bent nail, to feed the new cord over the pulley and down the weight passage. Thread the cord through the top of the counter-weight and then secure it by tying a double knot.

Attach the other end of the cord to the sash, lining it up with the mark, and fix it with a single clout nail (diagram 2). Make sure the nail is further down from the top of the sash than the distance from the top of the frame to the centre of the pulley. Nail gently so as not to risk breaking the glass. Try the sash in the frame when both cords are attached. If the weight hits the bottom when the sash is at the top, the fixing nail is too high up the sash. If the sash doesn't reach the bottom, the cord is too short. Make any necessary adjustments, then tap in a couple of more clouts.

Replace the pocket cover, the outside sash if it was removed, the parting beads and the inside sash. When replacing the stop bead, you should try to use the same nails and holes to ensure a neat fit. Add a couple of extra nails to keep them tight. The repaired sash should go up and down easily.

BELOW: This sash window-cum-door glides up to allow access to the enclosed verandah beyond.

Adjusting spring lifts

Tube-type lifting devices include a spring-driven twist rod or spring that helps lift the sash and hold it in place. Before tampering with one of these, first check to ensure the window hasn't been painted shut. If that's the case, follow the procedures explained previously. But if the device doesn't seem to be working at all, it's probably broken and needs to be replaced.

Get a good grip on the tube before you remove the screw holding it to the jamb. Otherwise, the spring will unwind in a hurry.

If the window sails up and down too easily, hang on to the screw and then let the spring turn for a couple of revolutions.

If the window is hard to move, tighten the spring by turning it clockwise. It may be necessary to adjust both lifts.

Replacing spring lifts

Begin by removing the inside stop from one side of the window. This should make room enough to remove the sash.

Next, remove the screw that secures the tube, let the spring unwind, then pull out the sash. You may need to pry a little.

Remove the twist rod/tube unit and replace it with a new one. Then re-install the sash and adjust as shown for adjusting spring lifts.

Repairing casement windows

Casement windows may stick because the frame has become loose or because the timber has swollen from the damp or from a build-up of paint. Take out the casement — it's only a matter of removing a few screws. Lay the window on a flat surface. Fit two sash clamps, being careful not to overtighten them and crack the glass, and square the frame. Screw through the side of the frame to tighten up the joints, countersinking the screws and plugging the holes with dowels. If the wood is at all suspect, it may be necessary to fit metal angle plates at the corners instead.

Before refitting, sand the window back to the bare timber and repaint. Be cautious of old lead paint. Wear a dust mask and carefully vacuum any dust for disposal in sealed bags.

When putty is not protected by paint it tends to crack and fall out. Carefully hack out any suspect putty and replace it, using a putty knife. Ask the hardware store for the putty to suit your frame type.

To replace glass, measure the opening, allowing 3 mm for clearance, and lay your new glass in a 3-mm-deep bed of putty. Secure

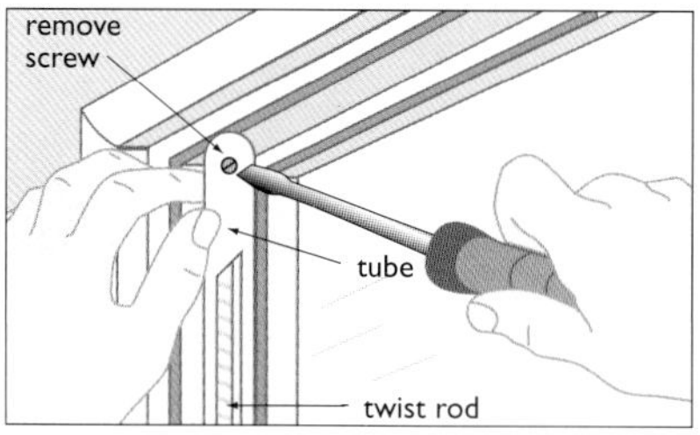

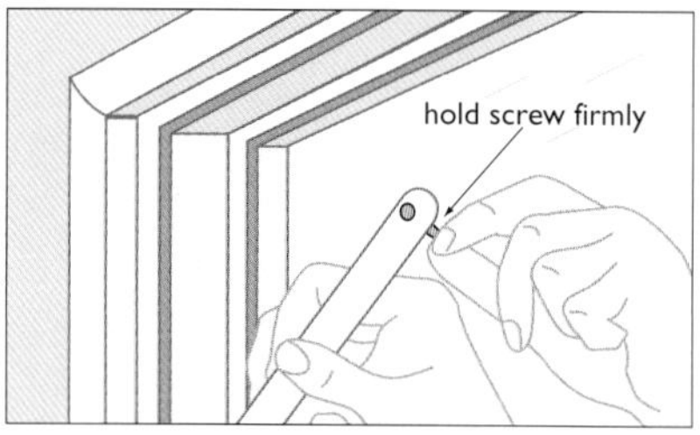

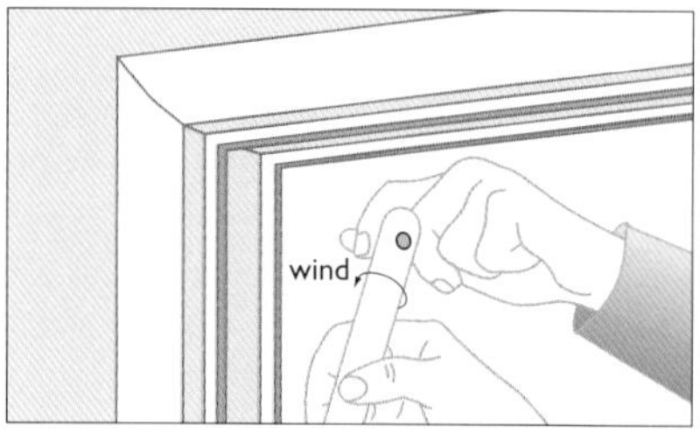

ABOVE: Adjusting spring lifts.

BELOW: Replacing spring lifts.

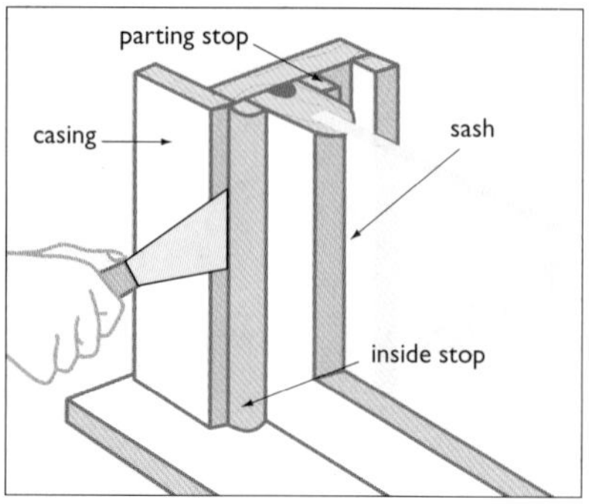

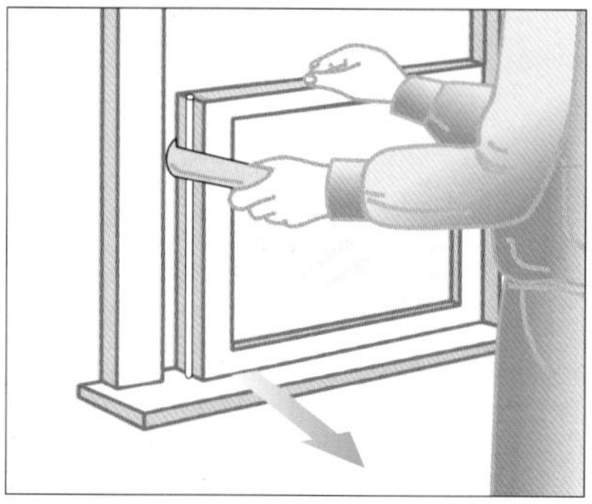

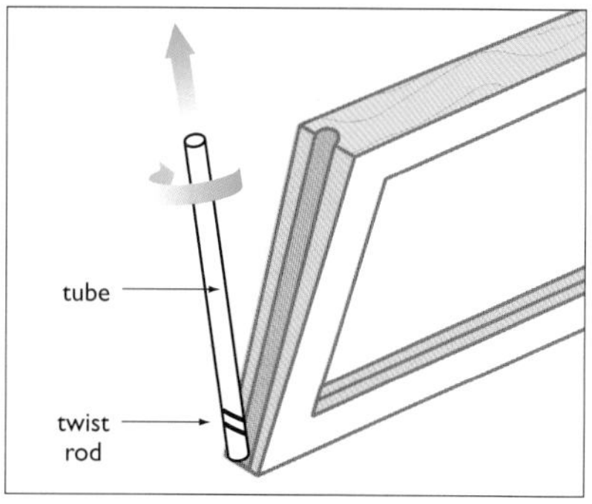

the pane with small nails (sprigs) at 200 mm centres, then apply more putty to the depth of the rebate. Smooth off the surface, dipping the putty knife in water to stop it sticking to the putty. Clean surplus putty off the glass with white spirit.

Finally, check that the external head and side flashings are in place.

Heavy accumulations of paint, grease or dirt cause most casement window difficulties. If you have one that's malfunctioning, open it wide and check all sash and frame edges. Usually, a few minutes with a wire brush, scraper or some sandpaper will remove the rub. If not, partially close the sash and check its fit. Wood casements sometimes suffer the same warping, swelling and out-of-square problems that can bedevil doors.

Finally, examine the unit's mechanical components. You will probably need only a screwdriver and the right lubricant to set things right again.

Bent, sagging or loose hinges throw a sash out of kilter. Replace, shim or tighten them up. Tighten loose latch screws. If a handle won't pull its sash snug, shim under it or — with lipped windows — add weather-stripping.

If a wood sash has warped, try counter-warping it with wood strips. Leave them in place for a couple of weeks.

Servicing operators

Operator mechanisms differ, but most of them consist of a sliding- or scissor-arm arrangement that may or may not be driven by a geared cranking device.

If a sash isn't opening and closing smoothly, check its arm first. You should look for loose screws, bent metal, rust and caked grease or paint that might be interfering with the action.

Next, turn your attention to the cranking system. You may have to remove it for servicing.

A sill-mounted sliding shoe device traps dirt. Unscrew the channel, clean it and the sill, then lube both with paste wax.

To keep crank assemblies turning freely, apply a few drops of light oil. With some, you may need to take off the handle first.

To dismantle an operator, first disconnect its arm from the sash, then remove the screws that hold it to the frame.

If the gears are encrusted with old grease, soak the unit in a solvent, then repack it with a multipurpose lubricant.

Sometimes you can free jammed gears with a coat-hanger. If they're stripped or badly worn, replace the entire assembly.

Repairing sliding windows

To keep sliding sashes moving smoothly, clear any paint or debris from their tracks and lubricate with paste wax, paraffin or silicone lube. When a slider jams, binds or jumps loose, you'll usually find that something's lodged in the lower track or that the track itself is bent.

If everything seems clear and straight, lift out the sash and check its grooved edges. Clean and wax these, too, if necessary.

Bigger windows and sliding glass doors roll on sets of nylon wheels called sheaves, which are self-lubricating and rarely need attention. If a sheave has been mangled, remove the assembly and replace it.

To remove a sliding sash for repair, unlock and partially open the window, then lift it and flip its lower edge towards you.

To straighten a bent track, cut a wooden block that just fits in the channel, then carefully tap the soft metal against it.

'Catch-and-dog' window latches sometimes get bent out of shape. Adjust them so that the dog's 'hind leg' hits against the catch.

Repairing awning windows

Awning windows, and their inverted cousins called hoppers, operate

ABOVE: Ensure window frames are well-maintained with regular painting.

BELOW: Repairing sliding windows.

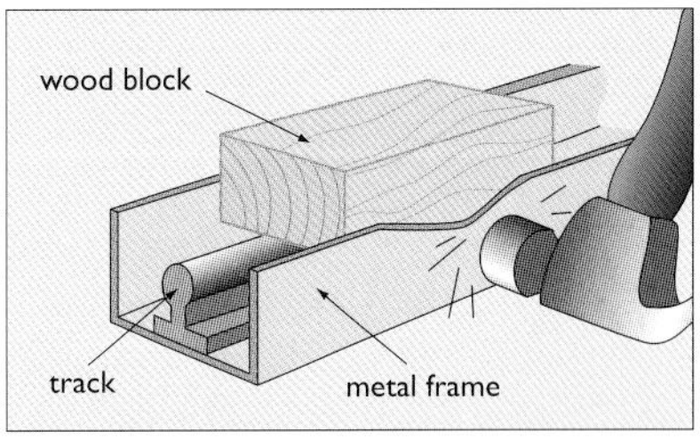

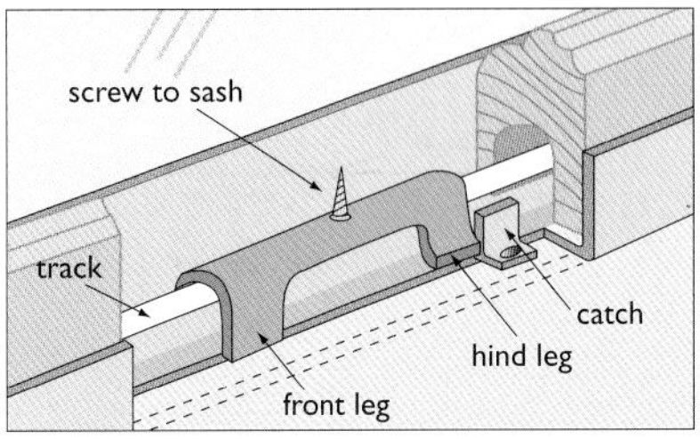

much like casements, and require the same repair procedures.

Keep latches, hinges and operators moving freely. If you neglect an arm assembly that's too stiff, it could pull screws loose, or even force sash points apart. Clean off any rust with steel wool, and lubricate with paraffin or graphite; never use oil — it attracts dust.

To remove an awning sash, first open it up as far as you can, then disconnect the operator's side or scissors arm.

Now tilt the sash to a horizontal position, disengage its sliding hinges, and pull the window free from its frame.

Repairing louvre windows

Louvre windows resemble venetian blinds, except that instead of cords and tapes, their mechanisms depend on a series of gears and levers that may be partly or entirely concealed in the jambs. This makes louvres relatively difficult to repair; often you have to dismantle the entire window to get at its vertical arms. If your unit jams, try freeing it with graphite or another non-oil lubricant.

Simple tab-like clips hold the louvre slats in place. To remove one, just bend open the tab and slide out the pane.

Don't force a balky mechanism. Instead, lubricate the crank shaft and all pivot points, then work the handle back and forth.

Getting balky operator mechanisms operating again

Start by opening the window far enough to disengage the arm from the track in which the arm slides. Clean both the track and the portion of the arm that connects to the track with a rag or a cotton swab soaked in alcohol or in some cleaning liquid. Lubricate with a light grease or petroleum jelly.

Next, squeeze a penetrating oil into all pivot points and work the parts back and forth until things loosen up. Wipe up any excess oil. The final step is to remove the operator itself, if possible, and coat the gears with a liberal amount of light grease. Replace the operator mechanism and see whether your effort has paid off.

Replacing an operator

If no amount of cleaning or lubrication can make the window work smoothly, you may elect to replace the entire mechanism. To do this, open the window to the point where you can disengage the linkage arm from its track. Remove the screws holding the crank mechanism to the window frame, then slide out the entire assembly. Buy a replacement operator and install it, reversing the procedures described here.

Snugging up a sash

After lots of use, many crank-operated windows lose their ability to close tightly. You can remedy this problem by installing weatherstripping or shimming.

Replacing broken windows

Expect to pay dearly if a repairer comes to your house to replace a broken window. Most won't even take on small jobs such as this, and the few who do are forced to charge what may appear to be an exorbitant amount. All the more reason to do the job yourself. The techniques for repairing wood- and metal-framed sashes differ considerably, but neither is difficult. Just be sure to wear heavy gloves whenever you work with glass panes.

Reglazing wood-framed windows

1 Start by removing any loose shards of broken glass, then use an old wood chisel to pry up the glazing compound that holds the pane in place. (Soften the compound with a propane torch if necessary.) Remove the old glazier's points which hold the pane in place.
2 Determine the size of the replacement pane needed by

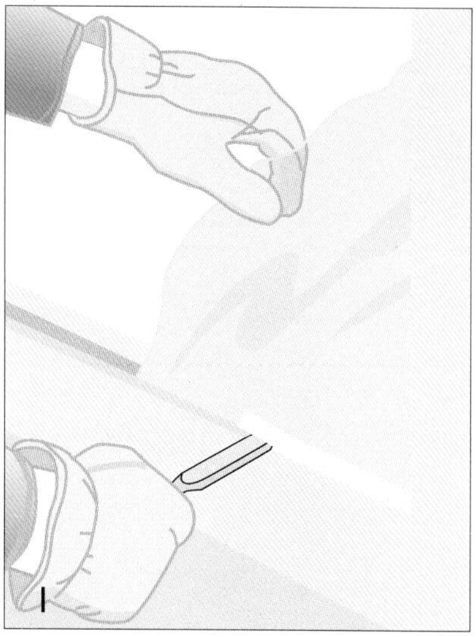

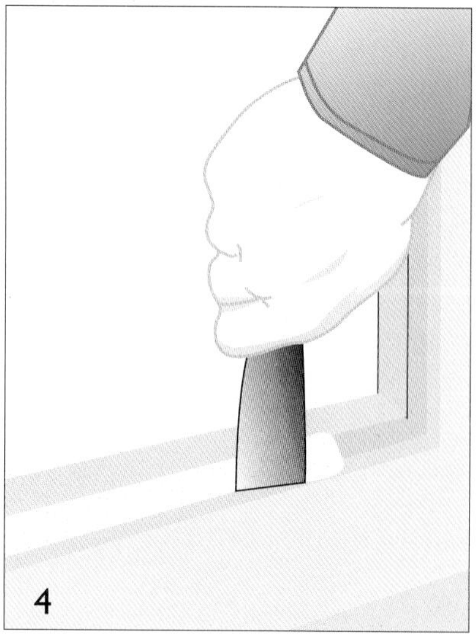

ABOVE: Reglazing wood-framed windows.

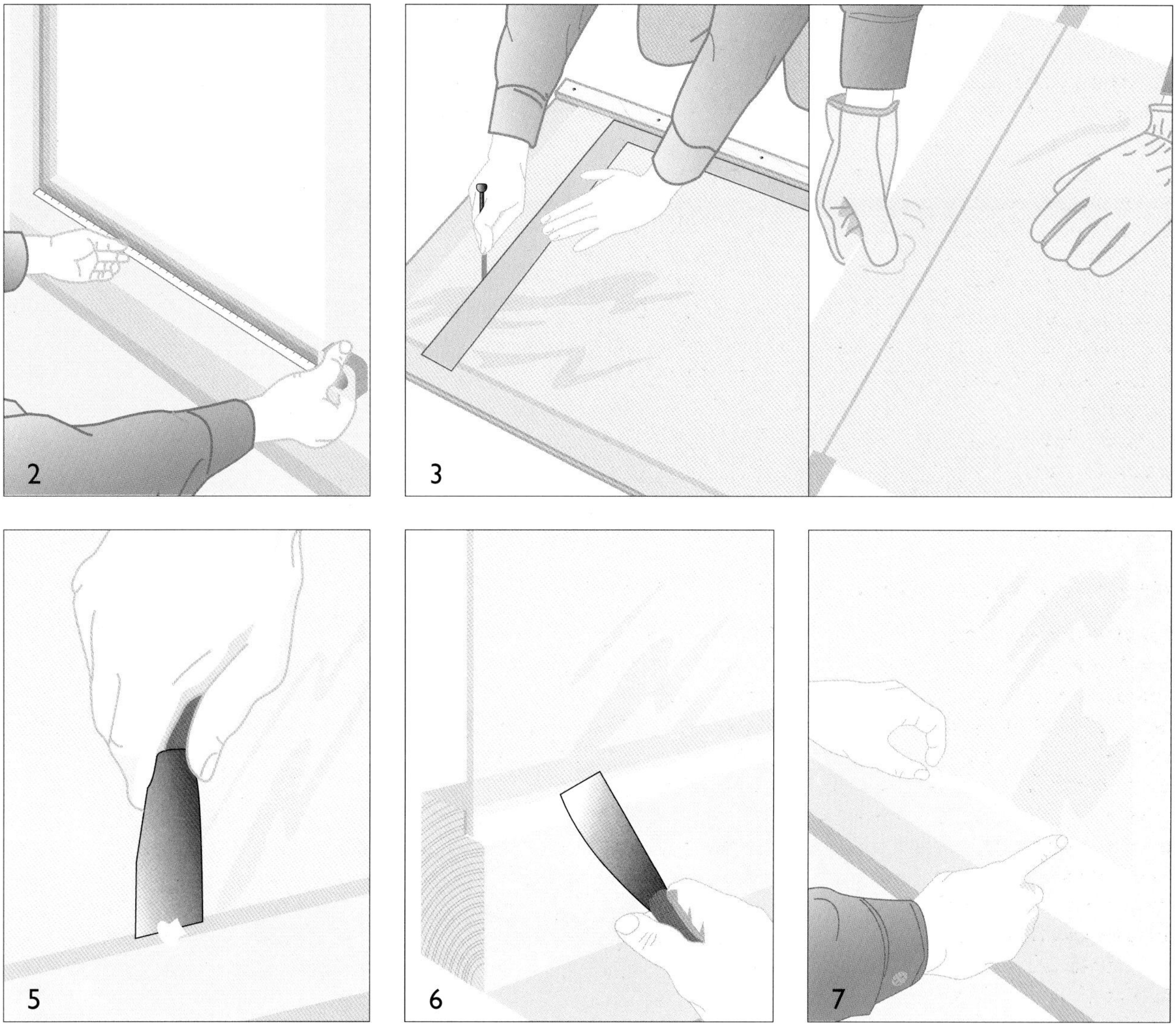

measuring the cleaned-out opening. Subtract 3 mm from each dimension.

3 Have a glass supplier cut your replacement pane to size, or cut your own. To cut your own, make a single score along each cut-off line with a glass cutter guided by a framing square. Then place the score over dowel or the edge of a table and snap off the scrap piece. Trim any rough edges with pliers.

4 Prime the rabbeted area of the frame in which the pane will rest with linseed oil, wait 20 minutes, then lay on a 2 mm bed coat of glazing compound.

5 Position the glass pane, insert matchsticks around the perimeter to centre the glass in the opening, and press into the glazing compound. Install two metal glazier's points per side.

6 To complete the installation, roll some glazing compound into a 6 mm 'rope' and press it around the sash edges.

7 Bevel the compound with a putty knife held at a 30–40° angle. Allow a week for the compound to dry, then paint around the installation, overlapping the glass about 2 mm for a tight weather seal. Don't clean the window until the paint has dried.

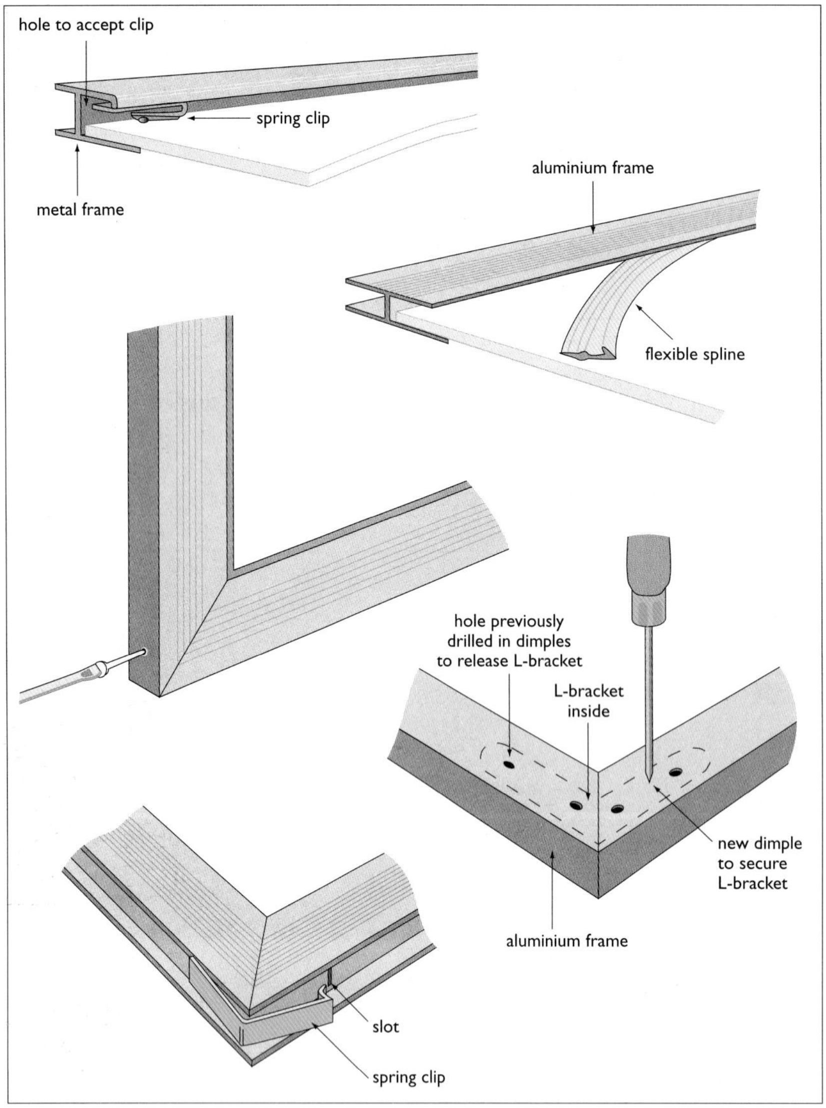

ABOVE: Reglazing metal-framed windows.

BELOW: Repairing screening, mending small holes.

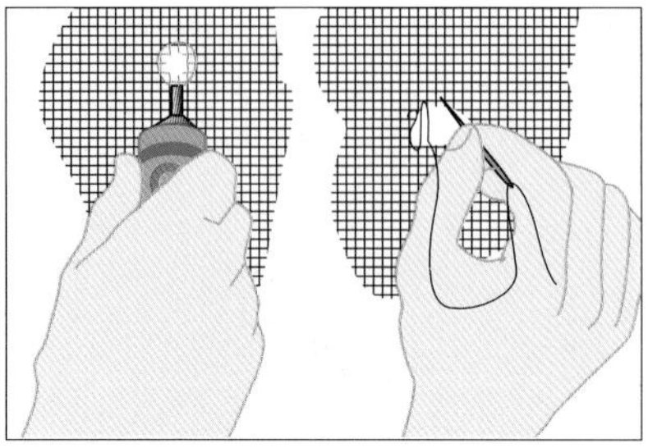

Reglazing metal-framed windows

Metal sashes come in a variety of configurations. Some are of one-piece construction in which glass is held in place by removable metal clips (augmented by glazing compound) or a flexible spline. Other sashes, the kind glaziers refer to as 'knock aparts', have frames that disassemble for reglazing. With the exception of some of the one-piece spring-clip types, you should remove all metal sashes from their frames when working on them.

Like wood sashes, the one-piece steel sashes (the kind often found in basement windows) hold glass in place with glazing compound. But underneath it, metal spring clips take the place of glazier's points. One-piece aluminium frames use a vinyl or rubber spline, which you can pry out with a screwdriver and re-install with a putty knife.

In the 'knock apart' category, many sliding sashes are held together with edge-driven screws at their corners. Once removed, you simply pull the frame members away from the glass. Some pin-type aluminium frames have internal L-brackets 'dimpled' in place at their corners. To release them, drill out the dimples. To reassemble, make new dimples with an awl to hold the L-bracket in place.

Repairing screening

Holes and tears in screens are among the most put-off repairs in many homes. That's probably because they're not as urgent as a leaking tap or a sticking door or some of the other must-do repair jobs. But you can only procrastinate so long because eventually you won't be able to get fresh air in the house without allowing a horde of flies or mosquitoes in with it.

If you have one or more screens in need of attention, there's no better time than now to take corrective action. You'll learn here how to repair both small tears and gaping holes in screening, as well as how to replace screening in both wood and metal frames.

The tools and materials for screen work are, with a few exceptions, as common home workshop tools as you can find. For mending, you'll need silicone glue or tin snips and a small amount of aluminium or fibreglass. To replace a wood-framed screen, you'll need a putty knife, a screwdriver, a staple gun, some scrap wood strips for stretching the replacement screening, a hammer and brads, and a utility knife. For work on metal sashes, you also may need a length of replacement plastic spline. To make screening replacement work easier still, consider investing in a special screening tool.

Mending small holes

Small tears in metal or fibreglass screens respond well to mending with clear silicone glue. If necessary, dab it on in successive layers until the tear is completely filled.

You also can 'darn' small holes in metal screens. Unravel a strand or two from a piece of scrap screening and sew the hole shut, weaving the strands into the sound fabric with a needle.

Patching large holes

To repair large holes in metal screens, start by neatly trimming the damage to a ravel-free square or rectangle using tin snips. Now cut a piece of patch screening that is about 50 mm larger (overall) than the damaged area.

Unravel a couple of the patch's strands on each side and bend them over at a 90° angle. Position the patch over the opening and thread the bent wires through the sound fabric. Then bend the wires over to hold the patch in place.

The technique is even simpler for fibreglass screens. Cut a patch of similar material with scissors and affix it to the screen with transparent silicone glue.

Replacing wood-framed screening

1 To remove the damaged screening from the frame, pry up the wood moulding strips with a putty knife. Start with the frame's centre rail, if it has one, and work from the centres of the strips to their edges. Now remove all the staples you have exposed and lift out the screening.

To cut your replacement screening to the correct size, unroll a length of it and cut a piece that is several centimetres wider and at least 300 mm longer than the frame. Fold over the top edge of the screening about 12 mm and staple this hemmed double layer as shown here, working from the centre to the edges.

2 Before stapling the remaining edges of the screening in place, you'll need to make an improvised 'stretcher' from a pair of 50 x 25 mm pieces of timber. Nail the bottom 50 x 25 mm to the floor or a bench, then position the bottom of the frame a few centimetres away from the 50 x 25 mm, with the excess screen lying over it. Now nail the second 50 x 25 mm atop the first so the screening is sandwiched between them.

3 Insert two wedges (made by cutting a 100 x 25 mm diagonally) between the 50 x 25 mm cleats and the bottom of the frame. Now tap the wedges with a hammer until the screening becomes taut. (Tap the wedges gently, alternating sides and being careful to avoid overstretching the screening.)

4 Now staple the bottom edge in place, followed by the sides (pull on the fabric to tighten it before stapling), and finally the centre rail, if there is one. Again, begin stapling at the centres, and as you work smooth the mesh out towards the edges.

Finish the installation by trimming away the excess from the frame side and bottom with a utility knife. Refit the screen moulding with countersunk brads. Fill the recesses with wood filler.

Replacing metal-framed screening

1 Unlike screens in wood frames, metal-framed screens are held in place by a spline that's friction-fit into a channel around the perimeter of the frame. Removing a damaged screen is simply a matter of prying loose this spline with the blade of a screwdriver.

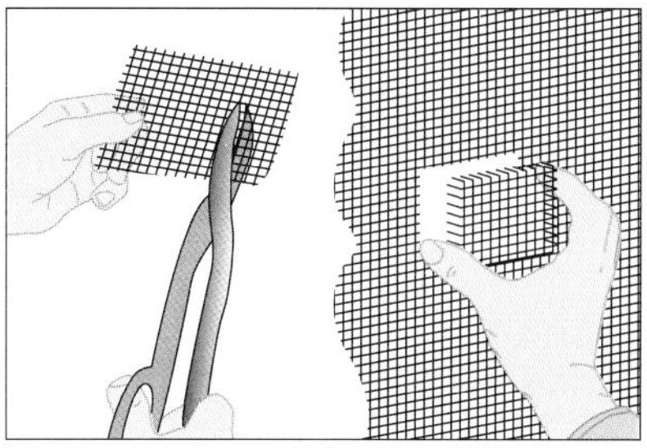

ABOVE: Repairing screening, patching large holes.

BELOW: Replacing wood-framed screening.

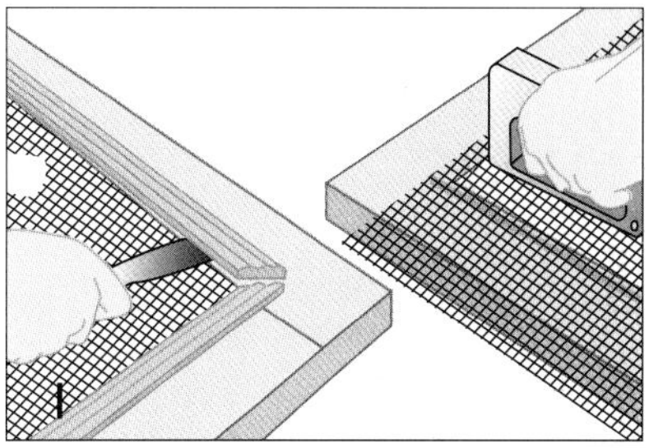

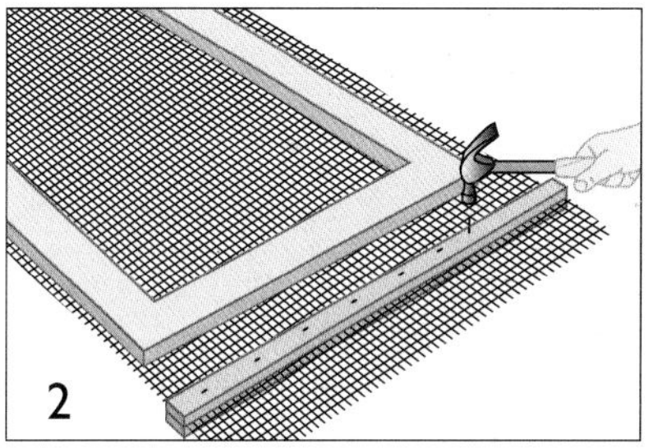

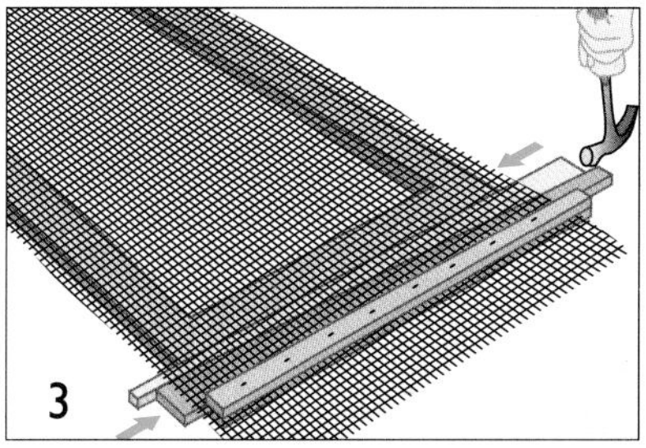

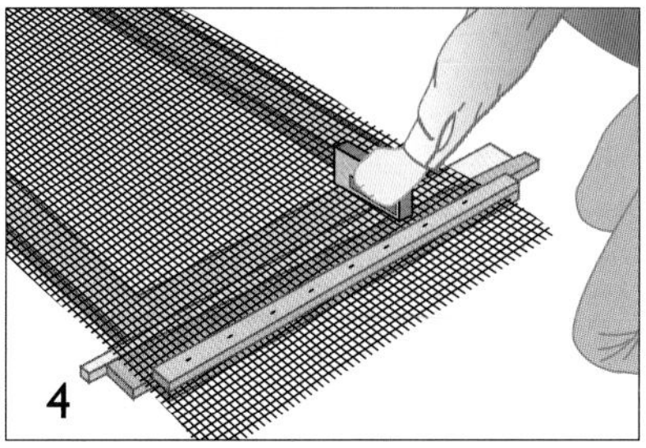

RIGHT: The bump-out window provides more space as well as light.

BELOW: Replacing metal-framed screening.

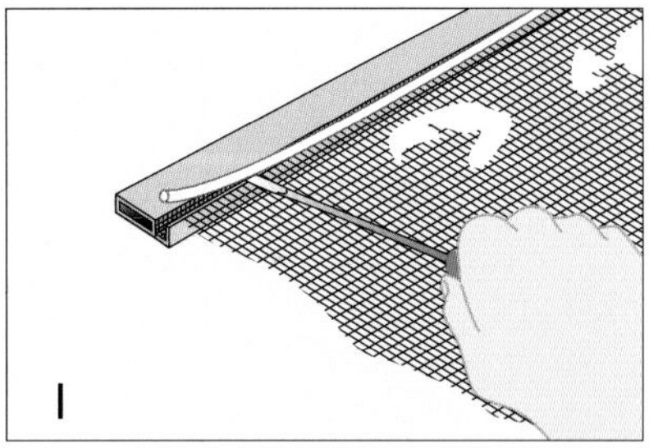

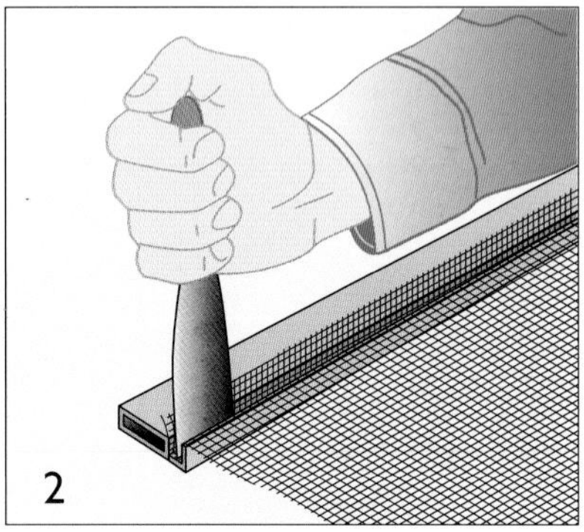

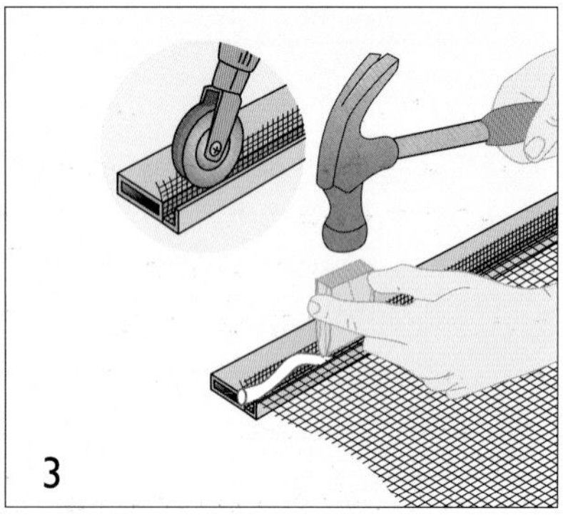

2 Cut your replacement screen to the same size as the frame's outer dimensions, trimming the corners at 45° angles (to make them easier to tuck in). Now use a putty knife to bend an edge of the screen into the channel along one side.

3 Secure this edge by driving a spline (the original or a replacement) into the channel with a hammer and wooden block. Have a helper pull the opposite edges taut, then pull the other two taut as you tap in the remaining splines. Trim away the excess screening with a utility knife. Note in the diagram the special screening tool that makes this task even easier.

Do-it-yourself bump-out window

Unless you're an experienced handyperson, this project may be rather ambitious. You can, however, use it to inspire your builder to be adventurous. A bump-out window will give any room an extra dimension, as well as being a cosy suntrap and a way of bringing the outside into your home.

Before you begin, decide whether you will fit your bump-out structure with custom-made windows or standard-sized aluminium-framed ones. Check the actual opening size required for each window sash and the standard heights available.

For the window pictured, the sliding side windows were custom made to a non-standard width of 350 mm and to a standard height of 1030 mm.

Building pointers

Use dressed oregon or cedar for the framework and follow the diagram as a basic construction guide.

Note that the inside end of the studs for the bump-out floor must be firmly anchored to the wall's timber frame. This will hold the cantilevered floor firm and counteract the weight of the entire structure, making the bricks become the fulcrum on which the floor studs rest.

The floor, or 12 mm plywood, should be no deeper than three times the width of the wall.

Note the three-way joint used where horizontals and vertical meet at the junction of the sloping roof.

Fit the window frames according to the manufacturer's specifications. The large front window is fixed glass. This could be an aluminium window sash or simply a sheet of glass sandwiched between strips of beading which is fixed to the bump-out frame.

Where the sloping sheet of glass that forms the roof of the bump-out meets the horizontal framing component, it should be allowed to overhang by about 50 mm.

Be sure to use a silicon-based sealer on all joints, especially those where the glass and timber meet. It is also vital to fix flashing at the junction of the house wall and the bump-out roof.

This kind of window alteration is marvellous when a room suffers from a deficiency of natural light. If a window opens into a light well where an extension would be out of the question, a bump-out can expand greatly the area of glass, and its deep shelf/sill is the perfect stage for a pretty array of plants. For the maximum light boost, paint the wood in white full gloss and house your pots in pale containers. Alternatively, you could also opt for clear-finished timber, as in our picture.

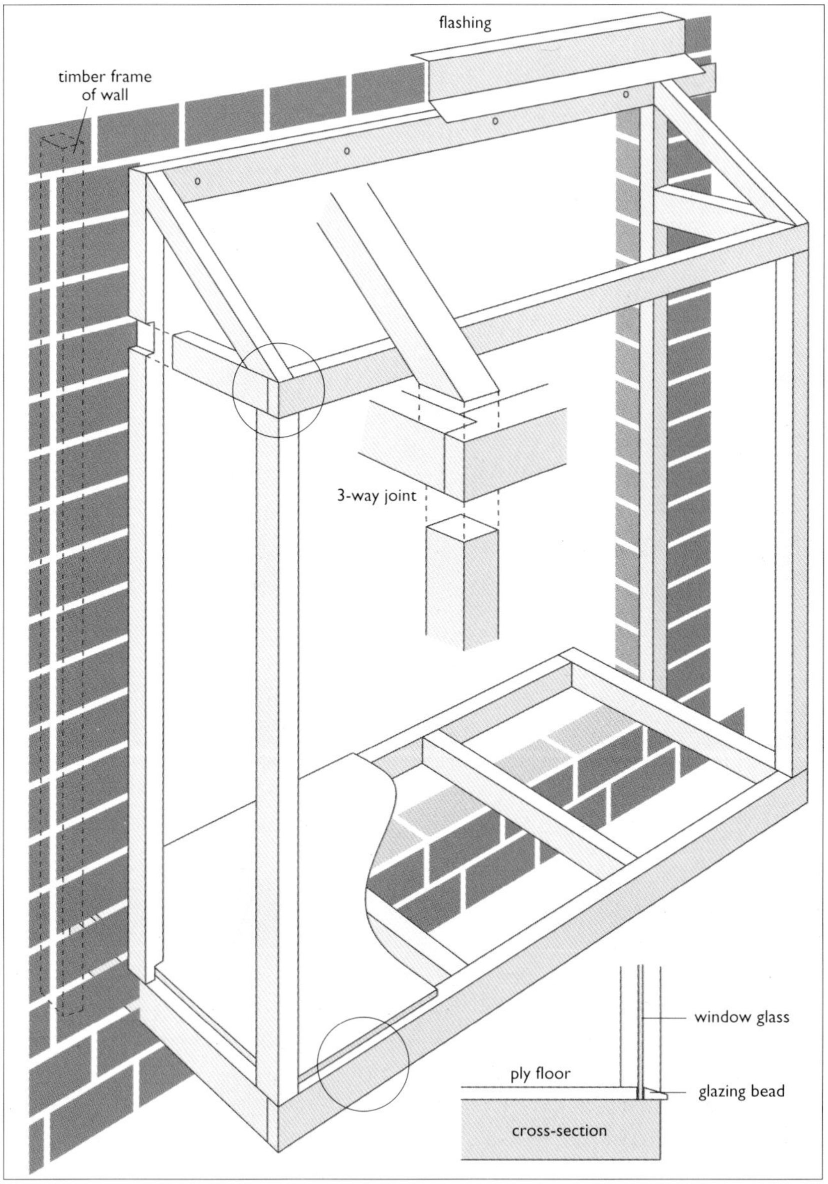

ABOVE: A bump-out window is ideal in a kitchen. Besides bringing in plenty of natural light and providing a view, it creates additional bench space that is an ideal position for herbs or delicate indoor plants.

LEFT: Installing a bump-out window.

FLOUR
PASTA CLASSICA

Wet Areas

Whatever your lifestyle, good design and planning of the kitchen, bathroom and laundry (the work areas) can make the tasks performed in these rooms easier and even pleasurable. The kitchen is often the most important room in the house and the bathroom's 'look' is now considered as important as that of the living areas.

Whether starting from scratch or improving an existing kitchen, bathroom or laundry, there is a variety of options available to the home renovator. Very often the kitchen is a gathering place as well as a work station. An open-plan kitchen close to dining and living areas ensures the cook does not have to work in isolation, away from social or family activity. Laundries with plenty of bench space for folding and ironing clothes may allow an additional work area for sewing. In smaller, older houses the laundry can effectively be combined with the bathroom, or even hidden in an alcove or cupboard in the kitchen.

If you are not limited by space, your first step is to decide what you want — a large eat-in kitchen, a bathroom with bath, twin hand basins and marble finishes, a laundry-cum-workroom — or something less grandiose.

If you intend to redesign your existing layout and move services such as plumbing, electricity or gas, the undertaking is considerable. As with any renovation, you need to be aware of the legal restrictions. The idea of moving a bathroom upstairs, for example, may sound great, but it could be a luxury you either cannot afford or will not be allowed. In all these rooms the cost of the fittings most often determines the final plan and, as with any renovation, it's all in the planning.

Today's kitchens are multi-functional and are usually the centre of household activity. A well-planned kitchen that allows room for children to do homework or visitors to sit without interrupting the cook makes a pleasant and efficient work space adjacent to the dining area.

Kitchens

The methods employed in planning a new kitchen are similar to those used in planning a good meal. Who will be using it? How many people are to be catered for? Do any of them have special requirements? What ingredients are required? Do they go together? Finally, and most importantly, how much will it cost?

Begin by making a wish list of the equipment you would like. If you cannot afford it all at once, be sure to allow some space in your design for future installation of these extras. Other important factors to take into account are the location and type of kitchen required. Is it to be open plan with a lot of passing traffic? Do you want to eat in it? If not, how accessible is it to the dining area? How much storage do you need?

If your cooking caters for a number of people, a walk-in pantry is a good idea; if you live alone and eat out often, a large pantry may be a waste of space. Remember, also, kitchens get a great deal of hard use, so choose work surfaces that are resilient and will mellow. The kitchen is a work area and should be practical and easy to use, so the positioning of cooktop, refrigerator and work surfaces should be in a logical order. Safety aspects are also a prime consideration, especially if there are young children in the house. Try to position gas burners or electric elements and equipment out of their reach. A dream kitchen may not be achievable but simply redesigning existing space, or even just a paint job, can work wonders.

ABOVE: When planning, consider the cook's view.

RIGHT: Appliances such as the dishwasher should be within easy reach of the sink.

Planning

It's not how a kitchen looks, it's how it cooks that matters; a million dollars worth of marble will do nothing to improve a bad design. After all, it's not only the quality of the ingredients that gives a good result, it's how you put them together. So before you start trying out taps and dithering over door handles, decide on the overall kitchen design by making a plan.

Templates are included here to simplify the process.

Work flow and the work triangle

The best way to conserve your energy in the kitchen is to create a more efficient work-flow plan. Look at the sequence in which regular tasks are done, as this will dictate the practical basic position of appliances and storage space. In its most simple form, this flow takes the shape of a 'work triangle' between the fridge (and pantry), the stove and the sink. In larger kitchens it's easier to look at these as part of the preparation centre, the cooking centre and the cleaning up centre.

These three kitchen elements form a triangle that plots the most frequent journeys the cook will make. As a general rule, a trip around the work triangle should be no more than 7 m.

Because the kitchen is a work area, it should be planned to make the tasks as easy to perform as possible. If the kitchen will allow it, the sink and stove should be positioned along the same wall with at least a 600-mm-long stretch of bench on either side of them. The refrigerator then needs to be located as close as possible to the sink and stove.

TOP: Easy to maintain surfaces are the most practical in a kitchen.

ABOVE: In a large kitchen an efficient work flow plan will conserve your energy.

LEFT: An island bench is ideal for extra storage.

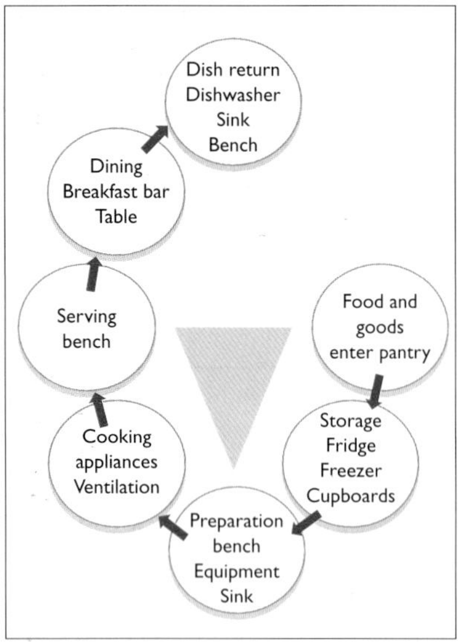

ABOVE: Work flow plan.

BELOW: Standard kitchen shapes.

BELOW RIGHT: Shallow U-shape.

Shown on these pages are some of the most common kitchen layouts to illustrate how the work triangle fits into each of them.

Kitchen shapes

The kitchen shape you use will depend on the space you have available. Consider the traffic flows, the minimum space you need between benches, and wall space for tall storage. The U-shape plan is usually the most efficient as it excludes traffic movement through the kitchen although, ultimately, it doesn't matter what shape the kitchen is as long as it follows the work flow shown here.

Shallow U-shape

Where one end of a much larger room is turned over to food preparation, the shallow U is the most likely configuration for a kitchen. The addition of an island bench will section the kitchen off from the rest of the room as well as compensate for the spread-out nature of this type of layout. In this instance, the work triangle takes in the extremities of the plan.

The cooktop and refrigerator are opposite one another with the sink placed centrally. The result is an expansive kitchen that is exposed to the rest of the room. This, plus the earthy finishes, creates a mood that is warm, generous and rustic.

Deep U-shape

This is perhaps the most popular kitchen layout. It automatically occurs where the kitchen is a smallish, self-contained room. The deep U combines the parallel bench advantage of the galley with the bonus of the third side to achieve maximum efficiency.

Especially where the space is very compact, this layout makes for multi-directional kitchen activity, allowing the cook to reach out equally in all directions from the centre space.

Similarly, the three sides of the work triangle are more likely to be equal. The refrigerator should be placed at the end of one of the arms of the U so it doesn't interfere with the continuous bench space.

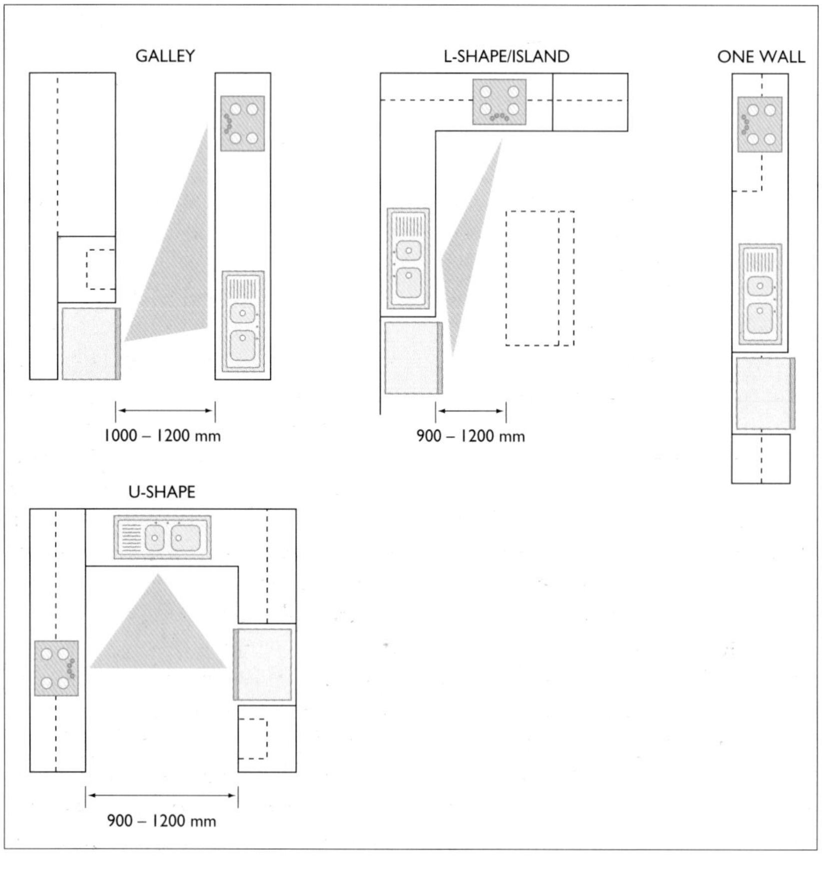

ABOVE: Before.

RIGHT: After — The deep U-shape is ideal in a small space.

BELOW: L-shape.

L-shape

Where obstacles such as doors, windows or even narrow room widths get in the way, your kitchen will not be able to wrap around two corners. Where one corner is the limit, the L-shape is the best option. Without the addition of an island or extra counter, your kitchen chaos will always be on show, and this is the major drawback with this type of plan. On the other hand, the open L creates a generous and accessible feeling.

There will never be human traffic problems because there is a total lack of floor space restriction. And because the layout is triangular in shape anyway, the work triangle is easily accommodated. The open space allows other rooms to spill into the kitchen area.

Galley

Where the plan is long and narrow with parallel benches, a galley is automatically created. It is important to remember that one metre is the absolute minimum workable space between the two benches. In this instance, the galley is prevented from becoming a U by the existence of a doorway at the end of the space. The sink and stove are situated adjacent to one another with as much bench space as possible between them.

Under-bench refrigerators have been placed opposite; using them has further maximised the amount of useable bench space.

In this case, much has been made of the small available space, which was made more problematic by circulation demands. What is

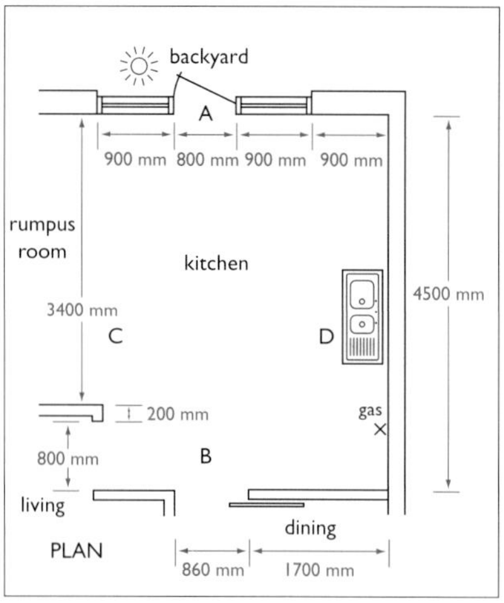

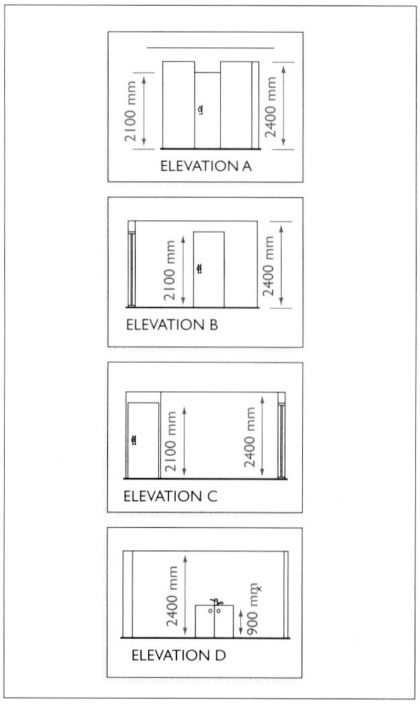

ABOVE LEFT: Galley shape.

TOP: A kitchen and living area plan.

ABOVE: Elevations for the plan.

essentially a thoroughfare has been carefully handled to become a thoroughly workable kitchen.

The fact that this is the smallest and most problematic of the four kitchen examples makes its success all the more triumphant.

Making a plan

To verify what you'll need, consider things such as: how much cooking you do (a large family will need plenty of storage and workspace); the type of cooking (TV-dinner chefs should make sure the freezer and the microwave are easy to get to, gourmets will be needing more specialised appliances and more storage); and whether you want to keep an eye on the kids while cooking. Collect brochures (with dimensions and installation specifications) of the appliances you plan to buy. Gather together the items you'll need and you are ready to draw up your plan.

Start by drawing up a rough sketch of the floor plan and each wall, then measure each dimension and mark it on the drawing. Show positions of fixed objects such as doors, windows, fireplaces, plumbing and gas connections, as well as the less tangible things, such as traffic flows, sun direction and views. Measure the appliances and fittings that you already have and plan to re-use.

Using the measurements of your rough sketches, draw the plan properly to scale on graph paper. Use a scale of 1:20 (1 cm on the plan represents 20 cm in real life). Once you have done this, pencil in a line 600 mm or 700 mm around perimeter walls allowing for traffic paths and door swings. If you prefer wider benches you can adjust that later. Mark in plumbing as this will influence where you put the sink (it's cheaper to keep it close to the original position). Turn to the templates and choose the ones that match your appliances. If the sizes are different draw your own templates to the same scale. Do the same for

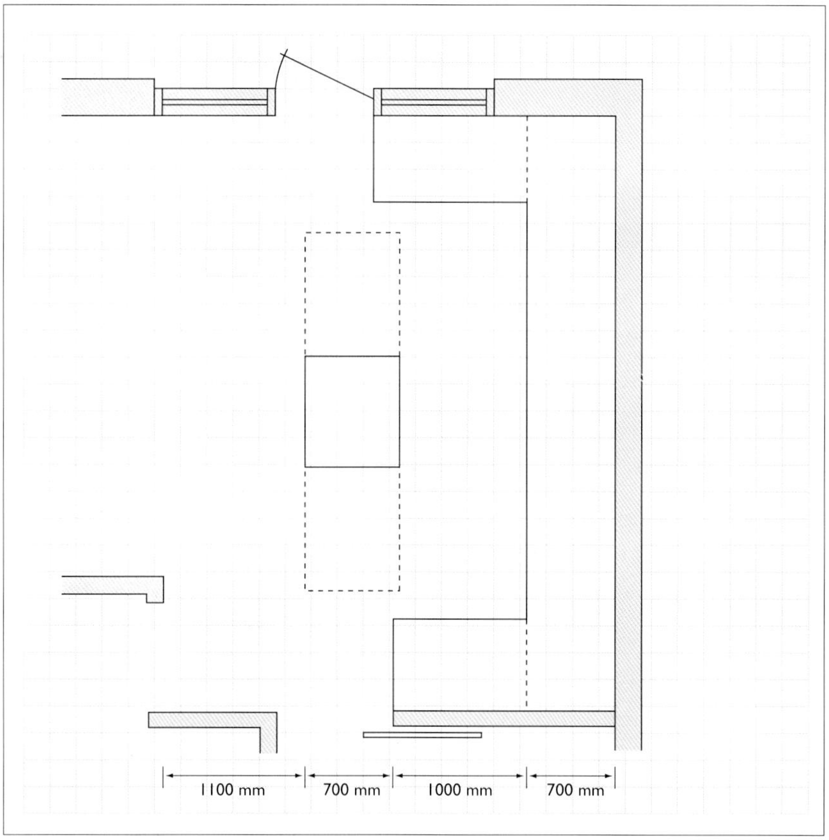

ABOVE: Photocopy and pencil in the best areas for benches.

RIGHT: Move the templates around and trace off some different options.

BELOW: Elevation B.

furniture modules if you are buying a kit kitchen.

Draw up the wall elevations as well (two are often enough) and pencil in the best areas for benches.

Move the shapes around the bench area until everything works well together and the work proceeds in one smooth flow. Position the main appliances (keeping in mind door swings) and the sink before you position cupboards and drawers. Trace different arrangements so that you have something to compare. Draw in the work triangle and arrow in the work flow: the most efficient design will stand out as being the simplest.

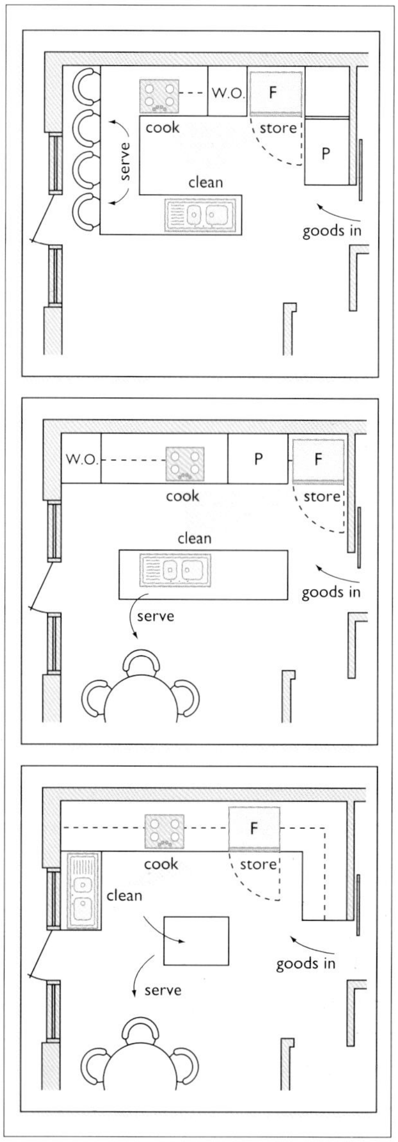

Move the templates around and trace off some different options.

Draw up an overall plan before you start dithering over details.

Choose the plan that works the best and glue the templates into position. Pencil in drawers and doors. Use a dotted line to show

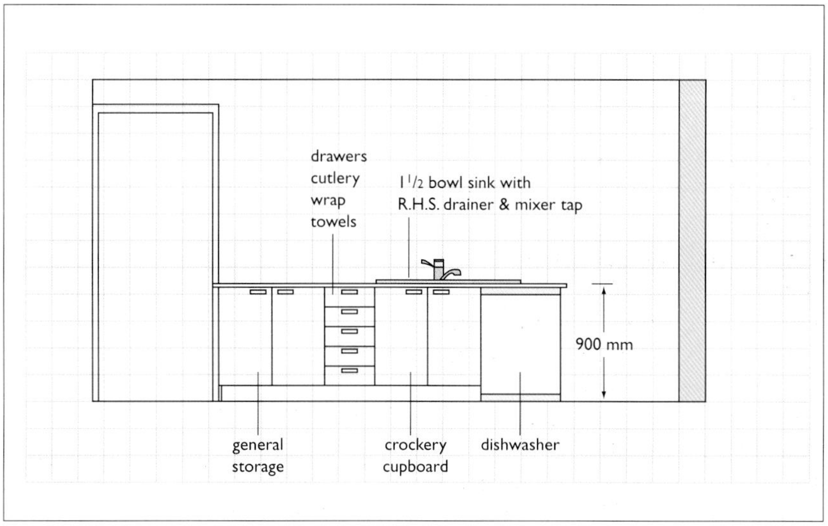

Kitchen design tips

Minimum bench lengths:

- for safety — 300 mm on both sides of hot plates;
- for preparation — at least 1200 –1800 mm;
- for unloading — 450 mm for fridges, wall ovens and pantries;
- for serving — 300 mm for two plates, 600 mm for four plates.

Storage

Working out where to put storage is easy; fitting it in is usually the hard part. The main thing to remember is that all food, utensils and appliances should be stored where they will be used. Consider accessibility (visual and physical), location (near use) and flexibility (allow for future change).

Ventilation

The best option is a powerful rangehood with easily accessed filters for cleaning. It should exhaust into the open air, not into the ceiling space, where it will create a vermin and fire hazard.

Lighting

Adequate natural, general and task lighting over the main work areas will help prevent eye strain and save you from slicing your fingers when chopping onions.

Safety

- Do provide bench space on both sides of the oven/cooktop and separate work areas from storage and eating areas.
- Do install a smoke alarm; they are straightforward and cheap to put in. Also keep a small fire extinguisher handy.
- Don't place an oven/cooktop near a doorway (allow at least 300 mm), in a corner or under a window.
- Don't store hazardous cleaning chemicals and sharp implements within reach of small children.

overhead cupboards and underbench shelves. Mark important dimensions and notes on the drawing. The finished drawing should show everything in place (you can mark all the power points, lighting and wall and floor finishes on the drawings) and, if you like, you can trace or photocopy the result to try

BELOW: Elevation D.

BOTTOM: The finished plan for Elevation B.

RIGHT: A coat of paint may be all that's required to update your kitchen.

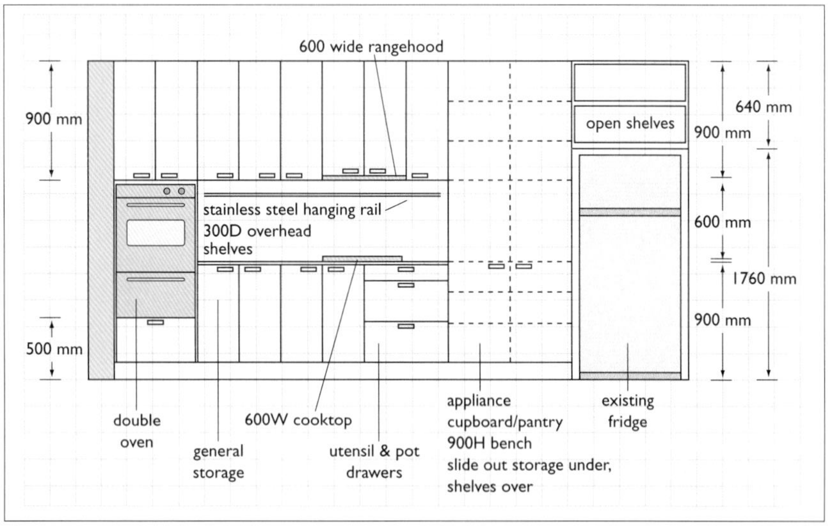

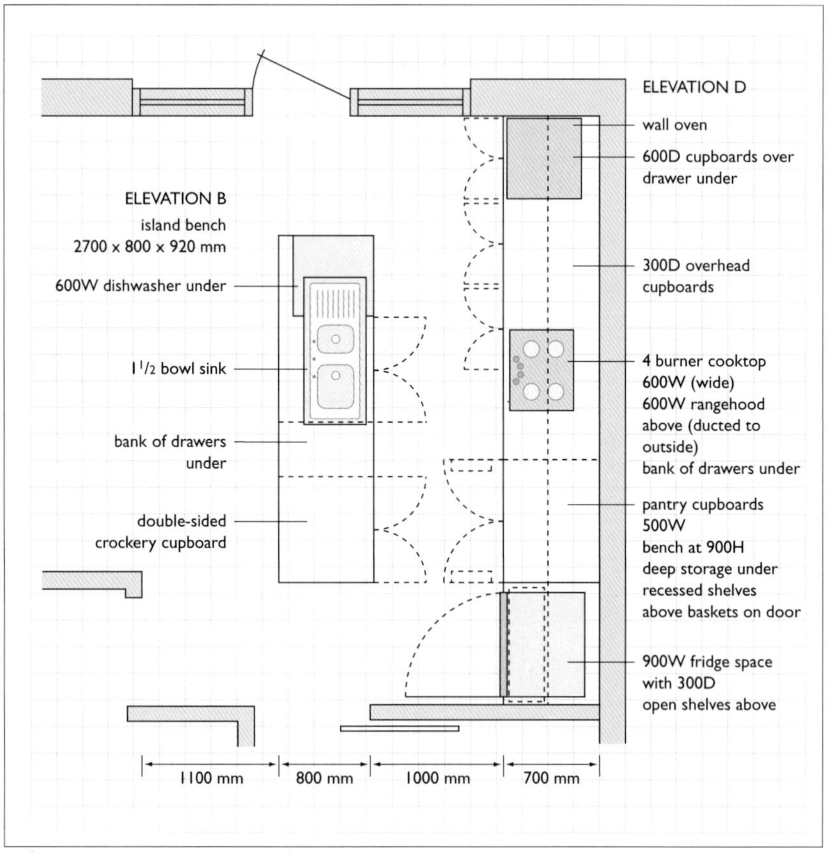

CENTRE LEFT: Fridge elevations and dimensions.

BELOW LEFT: Elevations for standard appliances.

BELOW: Sink elevations and dimensions.

BOTTOM: Oven elevations and dimensions.

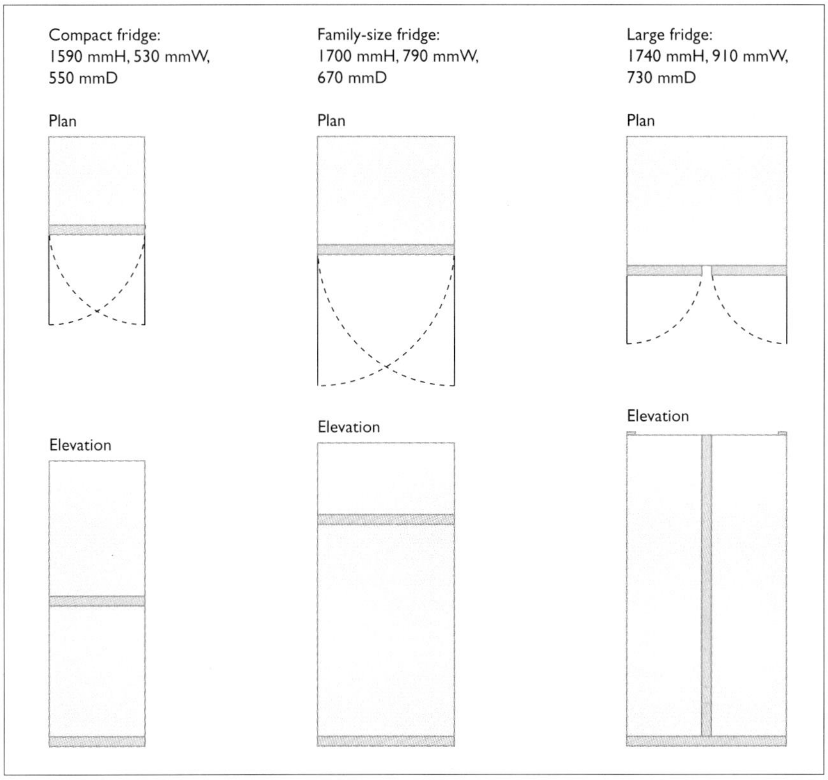

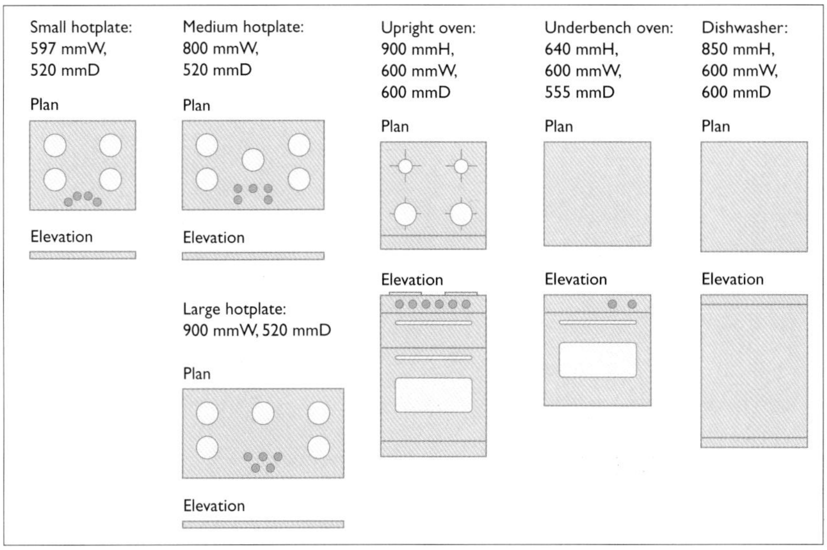

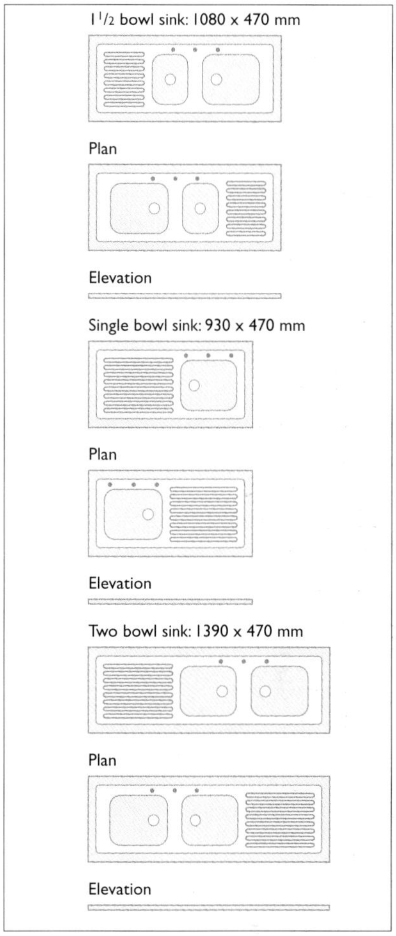

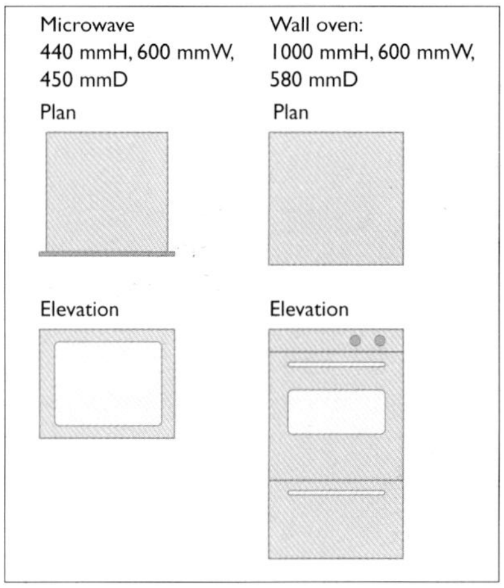

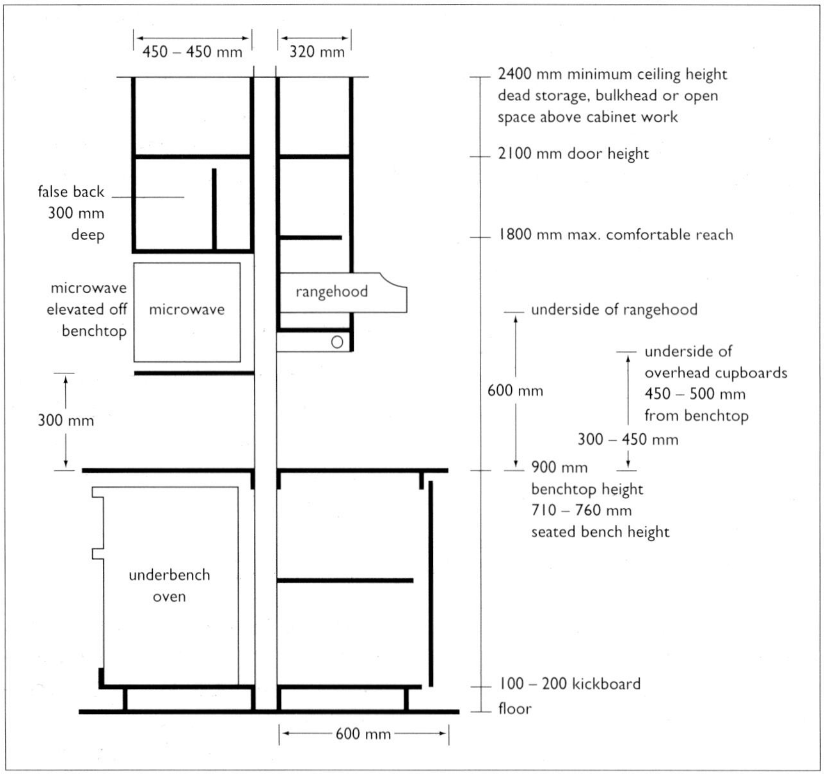

ABOVE: Average kitchen component dimensions.

FAR RIGHT: Floor plan for the customised kitchen.

out different colour combinations. If you are still a little unsure of your plan, you can check it with a kitchen designer. And don't forget to ring your local council to see if the plans are subject to approval before starting the job.

The right height

The recommended heights and depths shown above were arrived at through a study of what works best in the average domestic kitchen, for the average cook. If you are considerably taller or shorter or disabled in any way alter them to suit your needs, but remember that it may affect the resale value of your house.

Comparing cabinet materials	
Cabinet material	**Features**
Particle board	The better units have wood or plastic veneers, but some lacquered or photographed finishes work well, too.
Hardboard	Often used for doors, backs and sides on wooden frames.
Hardwood	Usually veneered plywood with hardwood frames. Sturdy construction, easy-care finishes.
Steel	Baked-enamel finishes. Some are noisy, prone to rusting. Not much demand for them.

Choosing and buying kitchen cabinets

Quality control and a broad range of styling options make today's mass-produced cabinets competitive with all but the most costly custom-made units. You can order stock cabinets, then assemble and finish them; purchase units which require only finishing; or select pre-finished versions ready for installation. You should also keep in mind that most manufacturers offer several lines, each constructed of slightly different materials and priced accordingly.

Judge construction by taking a close look at how joints are fitted and the way insides and backs have been finished. Check out the hardware, too. Quality cabinets have doors that swing freely and latch securely, and drawers that roll on metal tracks.

Measuring for new cabinets

Standardised dimensions and modular designs greatly simplify the job of tailoring cabinets to suit your kitchen. Just measure the space available, order a series of units that comes close to fitting it, then make up the difference with fillers between cabinets.

First, carefully plot your kitchen on graph paper, making both floor plan and elevation drawings. For base cabinets, measure at benchtop height as well as along skirting boards and note any variations. Make sure that you include door swings, power points, window casings, pipes, appliance sizes and any other features that could cause an unpleasant surprise.

Now fill in the layout you want, using the following information as a guide. Height measurements shown accommodate the reach of an average-height person and are accepted as standards throughout the kitchen and appliance industries.

Base cabinets typically measure 900 mm high by 600 or 450 mm deep. Wall cabinets are 300 – 450 mm high, 300 mm deep.

Manufacturers offer plenty of choices when it comes to cabinet widths. You can purchase them from 225 – 1200 mm wide.

Fillers fit between units, letting you adjust a bank of cabinets to the space available. Rip them to the width you need.

Installing kitchen cabinets

Achieving a built-in look with prefabricated cabinets might seem to call for some tricky carpentry. Not so! Examine a unit and you'll see that the manufacturer has done most of the work, providing you with perfectly square modules that you can interlock with screws or dowels.

Assembly consists of carefully levelling and plumbing each cabinet, then fastening it to the wall studs and to its neighbours.

Level the base cabinets. You'll probably need to use shims to accomplish this. Use the screw sizes specified by the manufacturer; drive the screws through the frame, not the thinner back and side panels. And never install cabinets with nails — they don't have the holding power of screws, and they might split the wood.

If a skirting board, door or window casing gets in the way, remove it and trim to fit after the cabinets are in place.

Cap off base cabinets with a bench top from a timber yard or a kitchen or building supplier. Most will cut one to size and even make a cut-out for the sink if you supply a pattern. (Measure carefully, though — mistakes are costly.) You can also make your own bench top by veneering exterior-grade plywood with plastic laminate.

Install the bench top by screwing angle brackets to the bench's underside and to the cabinet frame.

Finish off the job by installing moulding to cover any gaps that occur between the cabinets and the wall or floor.

To hang wall cabinets, first build a movable support you can put on the bench. Next, rest a unit on the support, shim behind to plumb the cabinet, then screw through the frame to the wall studs.

Begin the installation by marking the locations of the wall studs. Set a cabinet into place, then level it by tapping shims underneath. Level from front to back as well as from side to side.

Now drill pilot holes and drive screws into the studs. A screwdriver attachment on an electric drill speeds this job along.

Once you have levelled and secured the unit, chisel away any shims that protrude.

Sometimes a thin shim between cabinets will compensate for minor irregularities. The face edges must butt tightly, though.

Fasten units together by drilling holes and driving in screws. Countersink the screws' heads about 12 mm.

The customised kitchen

If you are disinclined or unable to build your own kitchen, consulting a kitchen professional is an excellent option to help you achieve your perfect kitchen.

A design plan

Illustrated below is the type of plan you will be given by a kitchen manufacturer. It includes the sizes of the standard kitchen components as well as the position of all the appliances and special fittings.

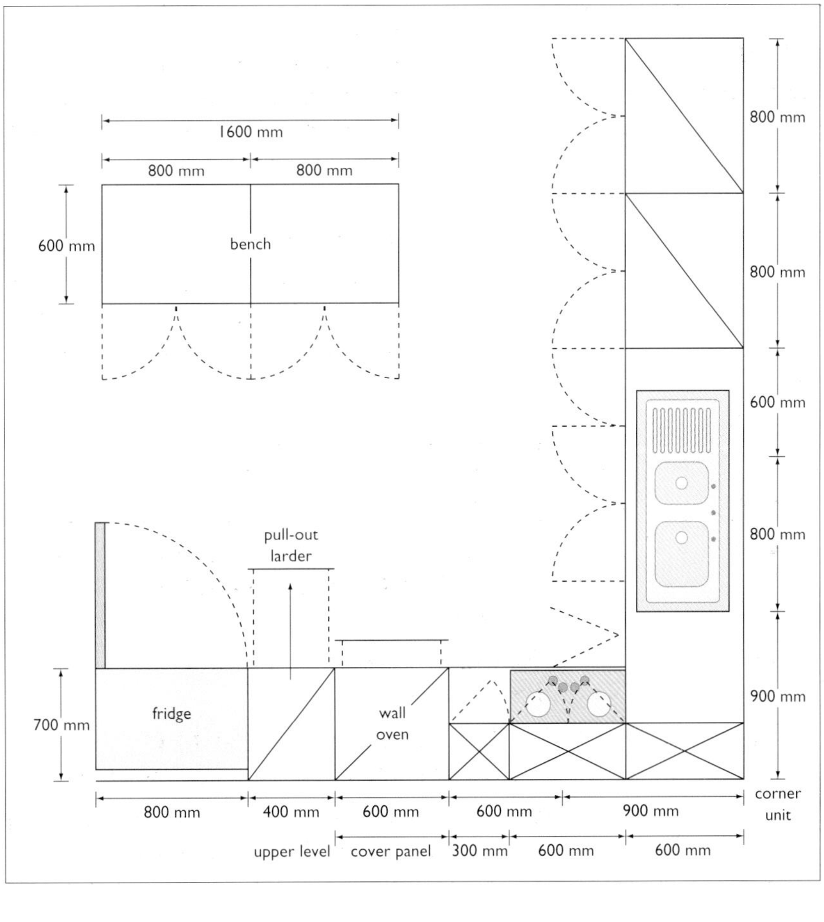

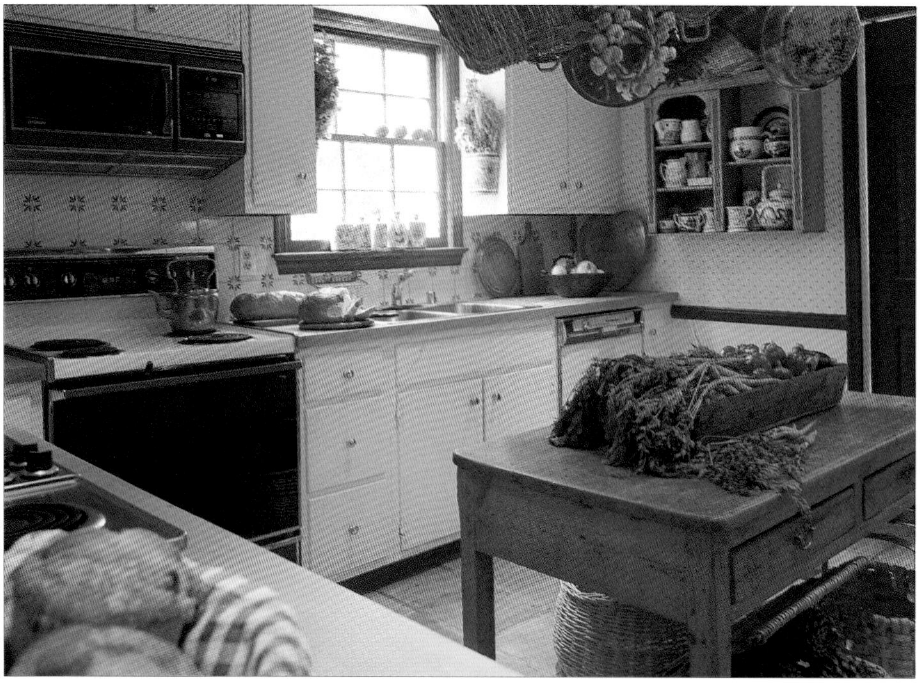

LEFT: The old island bench gives the kitchen individuality.

Know what you want

Study as many kitchen magazines and design catalogues as you can and keep a folder of pictures, products and ideas that appeal to you.

Look at how you use your kitchen at the moment. What are the things you like most about it and what annoys you? For example, you might have one of those corner cupboards which are difficult to reach right up the back.

Take along a measured plan of your kitchen space, noting where electrical, gas and water services, as well as windows, are located.

You should draw a rough plan of how you would like your kitchen to be. Show it to your kitchen manufacturer. It will be a good starting point.

Work out a plan with your manufacturer/designer

Be sure to discuss the range of kitchen options offered by your manufacturer/designer. You should be able to study a whole list, or catalogue, of standard fittings—everything from cutlery trays and sliding towel rails to pull-out, compartmentalised rubbish bins and vacuum-hose holders.

Work out how standard-sized cupboards or units will best fit into your kitchen space. Base cupboards will come in their own range of standard sizes as will wall and high (above-refrigerator) units.

Your kitchen design must, therefore, be the most space- and cost-efficient combination of all these component parts.

Investigate finishing options

Even if you have set your heart on plain white doors, there can be several different grades, from the cheapest of laminates to vinyls to super gloss, oven-baked enamel.

When it comes to bench tops, you can be as extravagant or thrifty as you like. If you choose a plastic-laminate top, run through the edging options your manufacturer has to offer.

Think about the type of door and drawer handles you want. For such small items, they have a great impact on the style and degree of quality of your kitchen project.

Although the standard bench height is 900 mm, you can always raise it by building your cupboards onto higher kick plates. Naturally, in the case of prefabricated kitchen components this will be more difficult and, therefore, more expensive. Some prefabricated types, however, have adjustable legs onto which the kick plates clip.

Unless you are happy with plain white splashbacks, you should go to a tile shop that has a large range and choose just the ones you want. Some kitchen companies will have tilers on hand, but with others you will have to organise that part of the operation yourself.

Similarly, kitchen companies are likely to offer a limited range of tap fittings as well as sinks. You will almost certainly be able to find something from this range that you are happy with. Otherwise, you will have to show them a brochure of what you want and ask them to organise it.

Arrive at an overall price and start the manufacturing process

With prefabricated kitchen component companies, the price of what you are buying is immediately calculable. If you are having a kitchen built, however, you will establish a quote and a time framework. Most custom-built kitchen manufacturers take about five weeks to deliver the goods. This will be laid out in a contract. (Take your time in signing any kitchen agreement contract.) You will pay a deposit, which is likely to be 25 per cent of the full amount. Materials should have a guarantee, as should the labour.

You can elect to have your old kitchen cupboards taken away or you can do the job yourself. You will have to establish this at the time of the contract signing. Remember, the more you do yourself, the less money you will have to pay out.

Having your kitchen installed

If you have already taken the old cupboards away, you will have the opportunity to repair the walls and paint them so your new cupboards will be able to slot into a perfectly clean environment.

Installing your kitchen cupboards will only take a day, but the trimming up and finishing will happen in short bursts over the ensuing week. You should make sure you are around during this time because minor adjustments can easily be made. For example, bench tops are usually cut on site to allow for irregularities in room shape. If you are available, you might even be able to change your mind regarding the actual sequence of component parts.

Both the electrician and plumber will have to finish their work after your cupboards are in place.

Don't remove any protective plastic coatings from appliances or fittings until all the work has been done. In particular, protect your kitchen from trades such as tiling, flooring and painting.

Make sure you fill any gaps where your cupboards and fittings abut the walls, floor and ceiling. Where the problem is very obvious, you will have to use timber beading; otherwise filler will do the job.

You're not obliged to pay the balance of the bill until everything is finished satisfactorily.

Installing a kitchen yourself

When the time comes to put in a new kitchen, there are several options you can choose. You can get a builder to do the lot, get a

Tip

- Most kitchen companies will do the design free of charge, as well as co-ordinate the work for you. The down side is that there's usually a limited choice of fittings and finishes, and you will generally pay more than you would when dealing directly with a cabinet-maker.

BELOW: Beautiful jarrah benches top tongue-and-groove timber cupboards which have been lime-washed in purple.

ABOVE: Pre-fabricated cabinets can easily be given a distinctive look with a painted finish.

BELOW: Pull out bins are tidy and save floor space.

kitchen supplier to make the fixtures and do the installation yourself or do the whole job yourself. A good option, if you are handy, is to combine a little of each.

Kitchen designers can advise you on layouts that ensure your kitchen is efficient. You won't be able to do the services yourself unless you are a licensed plumber or electrician. You can and should, however, pick out the locations, quantities and types of service fittings you require. Choose a sink and taps that suit you and have them located where you want them. Decide how many electrical outlets are required for your appliances and have them installed where they suit you. You will be using them, and the likelihood is that you will know best what you want.

When it comes to kitchen cabinets, there are also different ways you can go. Again, there are companies who will do it all: carcasses, bench tops, doors and drawers. You could buy prefabricated units to a basic design that you assemble yourself. The latter is probably the cheapest option if you have time. As doors, drawer fronts and bench tops generally dictate the overall appearance of the kitchen, you can truly customise it by building these yourself to your own design.

Take the time to look at the different types of hardware and fittings that are available for kitchens. They can make the difference between a kitchen that is easy to work in or a nightmare. Self-closing, adjustable hinges, slide-away work tops and slide-out storage racks are just a few innovations to consider. Be prepared to spend a bit more to get the best — it will be worth it in the long run.

Demolition

Before pulling the old kitchen to pieces, get the appropriate tradespeople to disconnect the services. Try not to disturb too much of the surround finishes, such as plaster, so there's less to fix up later.

Splashbacks

Tiles look great and are easy to keep clean. Fix them with tile adhesive to a cement sheet. The sheet should be glued and nailed or screwed to the wall behind. Remember, if the sheet comes loose, so do the tiles. Where your tiles sit on the bench top, make the grouted joint a silicone joint so that it doesn't crack.

Carcasses

Ensure that the carcasses are constructed from HMR (high moisture resistance) board and that all raw edges are sealed with either ironed-on or glued-on laminate. Make sure they are seated on a good base, which is level and securely fixed to the floor. Screw through the sides of the walls of the carcasses to join the individual units together, but don't fix them to the rear wall if they are already fixed to the floor.

Doors and drawers

A huge variety of off-the-shelf doors is available. Oregon and pine

Tips

- Rubbish storage and disposal has gone beyond the days of a garbage bin in the corner. Check out what is available from the specialists.
- Your new kitchen probably won't suit your existing lighting. Work this out early or you will be cutting holes in new finishes to take the altered wiring runs.
- Colours of fixtures, walls, doors, bench tops and so on all need to complement each other. Get out the colour cards and stain samples early. Don't be talked into a colour or stain that you haven't actually seen demonstrated and matched.

ABOVE: Timber for floors and bench top are a practical choice for a country cottage.

ABOVE RIGHT: An exterior door from the kitchen is useful in providing ready access to the garden or utilities.

CENTRE: This kitchen has well defined work areas even though the space is small.

CENTRE RIGHT: A bump-out addition incorporates a dining space into the kitchen area.

RIGHT: A wall was demolished between the kitchen and dining room making one usable and inviting space.

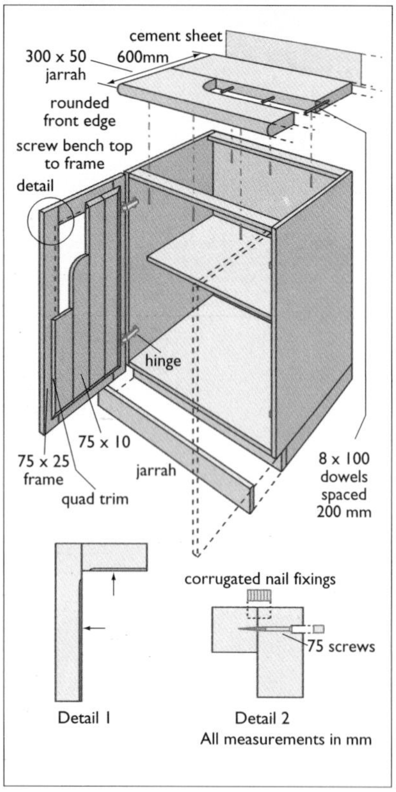

look good together. Simply construct a frame, then glue and nail pine lining boards to the back. Keep them far enough back from the edge of the frame to clear the hinges, and trim the edge with a quad bead. Round off the edges of the frame with a router or a sander. Alternative drawer fronts can be fixed directly to the drawer frames most cabinet companies supply. Use a piece of solid oregon or pine and stain it to your taste.

Bench tops

Beautiful 300 x 50 mm jarrah has been used here, joined with dowels (see diagram) to make it 600 mm wide. The front edge was then rounded and bottom-fixed through the top of the carcasses. Smaller jarrah pieces were fixed to the carcass fronts to make the matching kick boards.

Inspirational kitchens

Country

The country style suits those who enjoy home cooking, collecting and displaying pretty plates, and working in a clutter and bustle. The style is warm and welcoming with

ABOVE: Bench top and cabinet dimensions.

ABOVE RIGHT AND RIGHT: Modern appliances and the warmth of timber bench tops in a country kitchen promise generous hospitality and the freshest home-cooked food in convivial surroundings.

Tip

- An old garden ladder makes a great hanging rack for saucepans, baskets or strings of garlic. Suspend from chains and use butchers' hooks.

bunches of herbs drying and bottles of preserves displayed. For those who are less exuberant, the scrubbed and bleached timber, wooden bowls and blue-and-white simplicity of a farmhouse kitchen may be more suitable.

Modern/urban

One cook's attractive piles of pots, pans and collectable clutter may well be another's nightmare dust trap. Those who are highly organised and disciplined are driven to madness unless there's a place for everything and everything is in its place. A purpose-built kitchen is best, ensuring that all things have their allotted space, surfaces can be kept spotless and the cook will be in control at all times! Such kitchens are calm and spatially satisfying. There's room for art and even sculpture.

Mediterranean

This is for gregarious, active and hospitable people who like a touch of the exotic and luxuriate in tangible reminders of fabulous holidays and even more fabulous food. For them, entertaining is a relaxation, and is often spur of the moment. The colour in decoration and in food is often summed up by the Mediterranean look, whether authentic or not. At the other end of this same style is the whitewashed, rather spare decoration of the Middle East, with its brass lamps and coffee pots, sweetmeats and honey cakes. Or you can try coolly tiled, shady, vine-laden Tuscan simplicity.

ABOVE: Streamlined and sophisticated, this kitchen is a practical, well-planned combination of function and beauty. The decorative elements are pared down but the result is definitely not austere. Symmetry and order rule, but the hard gleam of stainless steel is softened by the gentler glow of honey-coloured parquetry. The surfaces are all easy to clean.

LEFT: This kitchen takes its cue from the Mediterranean. The focus is on earthy pottery, tiled surfaces, flowers, herbs and brilliant colours.

Tip

- If you don't have terracotta tiles on the floor, help the look with bright, striped, washable rugs. If there's room, a cafe chair and table will look right and be useful, too.

Kitchen storage ideas

You don't need to redesign a whole kitchen to make it work better for you. Examine your cooking habits and the way you use your kitchen to help come up with specific storage solutions. Cut down on clutter. Think corner cupboards, open shelves, drawer dividers and extra bench-top pull-outs, and utilise a nearby cupboard as a walk-in pantry if necessary.

With the clever storage ideas pictured here you can easily find a place for everything, streamline your time and make your kitchen work for you.

ABOVE: Utilise space between the tops of cupboards and the ceiling and even over doorways. Use high shelving to store things you rarely use.

LEFT: Note how simply this clever storage space for glasses can be made. Cut the shapes, then just glue and screw to the bottom of your cupboard. But first measure between the bowls of the glasses so they slide in and out with ease.

ABOVE: Store your platters side by side so you can get at the large ones, which are often hard to reach when stuck at the bottom of the stack.

RIGHT: Shallow, pull-out drawers are ideal for storing cookware and kitchen gadgets — much better than cavernous cupboards. Even those seldom-used things stowed at the back are easily accessible.

ABOVE: Storage need not be just for storing. Give cupboards glass backs and fronts and create an attractive room divider which can be easily accessed from both sides whilst still letting in light.

ABOVE RIGHT: Large hanging racks can house all your pots and pans. Make sure the rack is above a bench and not where you will bang your head on it.

Tip

- Pay a visit to your local storage shop. You'll find gadgets and fittings that will solve many of your clutter problems plus some that will open up a whole new way of looking at the places and spaces available to you. And don't forget, there's always a ceiling to hang a rack from!

ABOVE: It's surprising how much easier cupboards are to use if you remove their doors. Foodstuffs don't have to be hidden inside cupboards. They are decorative on open shelves and it's easier to see items that are running low and will need replacing soon.

ABOVE: A pantry with doors creates extra space when you attach shelves to the inside because you instantly double the storage area. Use heavy-duty hinges to carry the extra weight. If you install a power point, you can store and use appliances there as well.

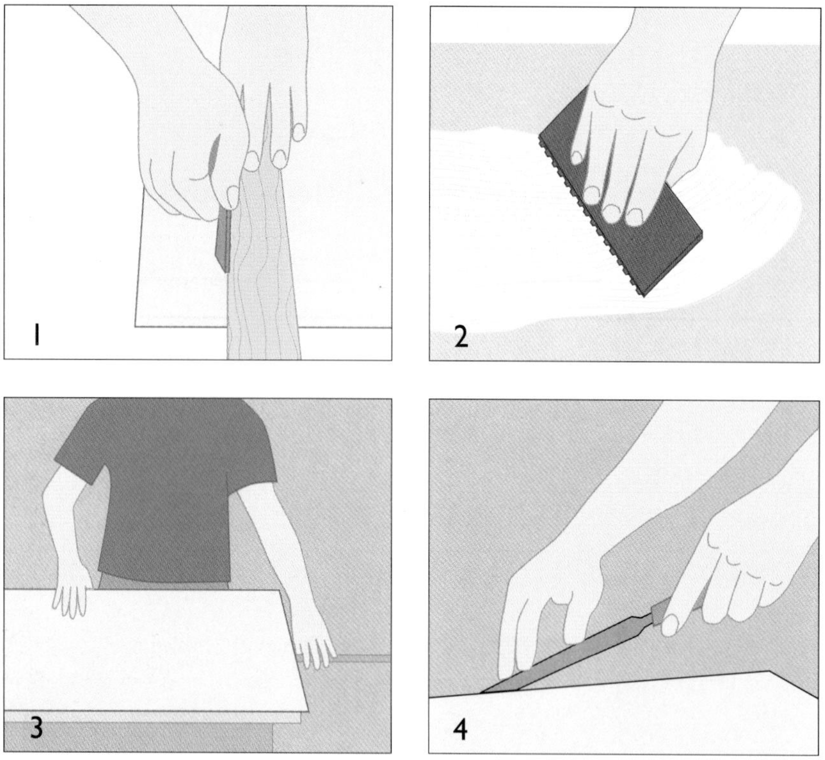

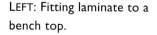

LEFT: Fitting laminate to a bench top.

1 Measure the size of the bench top. Mark the size of the new laminate panel with a felt pen, making it 5 mm larger in length and width than the bench top. Cut along the lines with a laminate cutter.

2 Using a notched spreader, apply the contact adhesive to the surface of the bench top and the underside of the laminate. Allow time for it to dry to the touch.

3 Place the long side of the laminate in position, using a dowel to separate the surfaces. Lower the laminate onto the bench top and slowly move the dowel back. Bump the surfaces together with your palm.

4 Trim the edges with a block plane, then file smooth with a warding file. For the final strokes, hold the file at a 45° angle to the cupboard.

Fitting laminate to a bench top

You can remove old laminate by working in from the edges with a wide-bladed chisel. Force the chisel between the laminate and the bench top. It doesn't matter if the laminate tears, but you should take care not to damage the particle board underneath.

Fixing drawers and doors

When a drawer with metal side glides sticks, remove the drawer and thoroughly clean both glides. Apply powdered graphite or silicone lubricant. Make sure the screws holding the glides are tight and secure.

Over the years, wooden centre glides can become rough and worn. First smooth the glide with sandpaper, then rub it with crayon or candle wax to help eliminate friction when the drawer slides.

Loose hinge screws cause cabinet doors to sag. If the screw holes have enlarged, tightening the screws won't help. To reduce the size of the hole, insert into it a toothpick coated with glue and then re-insert the screw.

To work properly, magnetic catches must be in near-perfect alignment. Screws let you adjust a catch back and forth. A sliver of wood, forced underneath as a shim, lets you adjust vertical alignment.

LEFT: Drawers either side of the cook top are ideal for pots and ovenware.

FAR RIGHT: The mobile butcher's block is an asset in any kitchen.

Building a butcher's block

A good chopping board is indispensable. It is even more useful with legs and wheels so it can be used as extra bench space as well. This mobile butcher's block is a great project for using up any old off-cuts, as it takes a lot of short pieces. Even if you have to buy all the materials, it will be considerably less expensive than purchasing a ready-made bench.

Source the hardwood from a demolition or recycling yard; 80 x 80 mm finished is a convenient size. Obviously the bigger the section you use, the bigger your block will be. Per metre, finished, straightened hardwood is inexpensive. If you are using recycled timber, it must be fully seasoned—this is essential.

You can mix and match different timbers in the block for visual appeal. Look for medium-density timbers (not too hard so they don't blunt your knives) and avoid those with dirt-gathering, gummy veins. A mix of blue gum, tallow wood, red stringy bark and iron bark was used here. (Other excellent woods for the purpose are New Zealand beech, Tasmanian myrtle, tulip oak and Tasmanian blackwood.)

Avoid oily timber, as this will inhibit the gluing process. For the same reason, do your gluing and assembly as soon as possible after the timber has been dressed to avoid any dust or grease build-up from the air.

The block is built in two halves and then bolted together. A bit of 'jigsaw puzzling' will be required between the individual pieces to get the best (squarest) fit.

1 Working on a flat bench, lay out one side with two legs and three blocks. When you have them square, drill two holes through their length so you can bolt them together. If you have a long enough drill (an expensive item), you can first glue the pieces together with PVA woodworking glue, clamp them with a sash clamp and then drill through the full length. Otherwise, drill each piece individually, making sure the holes all line up. Sand off any drill burrs, thread the rods through and, after applying glue to one face of each join, put on the washers and unions and tighten the rods, clamping the five pieces together. Don't worry if the top is out of level a little—you can sand it later. The holes in the legs should be drilled large enough to take the unions (see diagram) and the rods should be cut so that they don't protrude beyond the hole.

2 Repeat step 1 with five block pieces, squaring them up on top of the first section.

3 Glue the two sections together; clamp them securely.

4 After giving the glue 24 hours to set (you can assemble the other half of the block during this period by repeating steps 1 to 3), drill two 140-mm-deep holes through each block of the second section into the first section. Squeeze glue into each hole, then hammer in the dowels. Repeat this on the other half of the block after its glue has set.

5 Drill holes for the six threaded rods which will hold the two halves together in a similar manner to step 1.

6 Cut off and sand any pieces of protruding dowel. Position and glue a spacer to the leg of each completed block half, then glue and bolt the two halves together.

You will need:

Components	Material	Length or size in mm	No.
Legs	80 x 80 mm finished hardwood	830	4
Blocks	80 x 80 mm finished hardwood	250	16
Spacers	80 x 80 mm finished hardwood	200	4
Bands	150 x 25 mm finished hardwood	370	2
		450	2
Dowels	8 mm hardwood dowelling	150	20
Corner angles	30 x 30 x 3 mm mild steel angles	120	4

Other: handle; brass towel rail; 10 mm threaded rod (buy six 1 m lengths and cut to suit); 26 threaded rod joiners (in lieu of nuts); 26 washers; pair of castors (get a good solid pair with its own base plate); a thick-walled length of metal pipe (preferably copper or brass for appearance) 320 mm long.

7 Drill a hole through the centre of each pair of spacers, then bolt the metal pipe in place.
8 Shorten two of the legs by the overall height of the castors and fit them.
9 Sand the top of the block and any other out-of-line edges with a belt sander.
10 Mitre the corners on the timber for the bands and glue and tack them in place. Drill holes in the corner angles to take 60 mm round-headed, black no. 8 screws, then fit the angles, screwing into the mitred corners.
11 To finish, stain or seal the block, but use only an edible oil such as vegetable oil on the top working face. Finally, fit the brass rail.

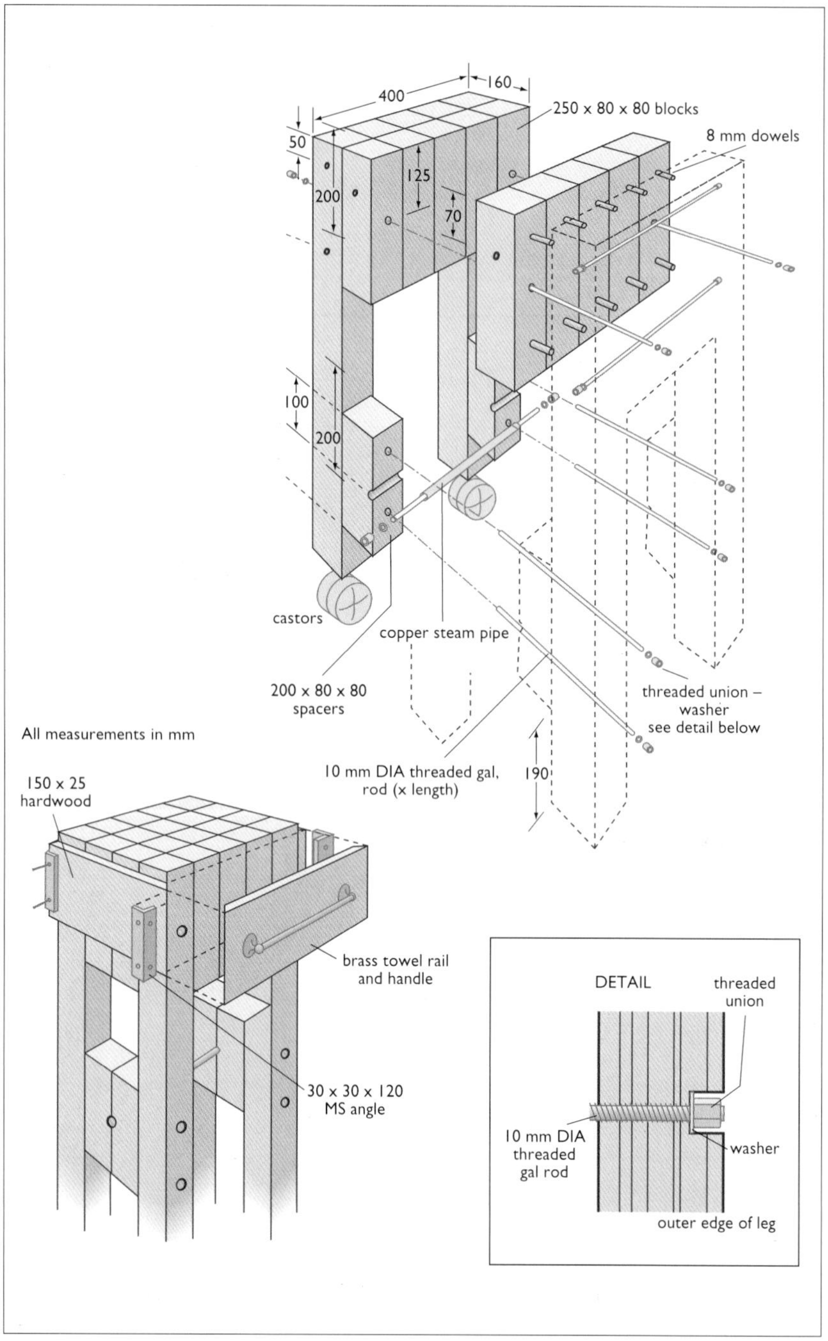

ABOVE: Butcher's block.

LEFT: The island bench can also double as a breakfast bar.

Tips

- You can vary the height of the block to match your bench simply by choosing longer legs than those we have nominated.
- The key to success with this project is to ensure that all joining faces are clean and square, so take a bit of time over the 'jigsaw puzzling' to get the very best fit.

Bathrooms

Before you begin remodelling your bathroom, determine your needs and educate yourself about your options. This may save you much time and effort in the long run.

A bathroom at its most basic consists of an enclosed space and some plumbing fixtures. Yet, bathrooms can be among the most complex and challenging parts of a house to design and remodel. Yesterday's gloomy closets have evolved into today's appealing cleansing and relaxation rooms. Recent trends in bathrooms include sunnier spaces, whirlpool baths, luxurious showers, twin basins' barrier-free design, improved lighting, more storage for bath accessories and supplies, and even twin bathrooms in master bedroom suites.

The best new and remodelled bathrooms reflect the way people live today. Life has speeded up considerably in recent decades, and family members are now under more pressure than ever to get up and out of the house quickly. Smart bathroom design can smooth the way by making efficient use of every available square metre while adding visual interest and beauty.

Renovating or adding a bathroom is one of the best home improvement investments you can make. The main benefit is the added enjoyment and pride of

ABOVE: A generously proportioned bathroom in an older house.

ABOVE: Early remodelling decisions can help get the look you want—such as choosing to keep the wainscoting and pine flooring, then using new wainscoting for the bath surround for a rustic setting.

TOP RIGHT: White with a touch of warmth added by terracotta tiling and the blue accessories gives a feeling of spaciousness in this small bathroom.

RIGHT: This light, luxurious bathroom has the bath positioned in the bump-out window so that the bather can take advantage of the garden view.

ownership you'll feel while you continue living in your house. You'll also realise benefits if you decide to sell. An adequate number of eye-catching, fully functioning bathrooms is one of the first things people look for when shopping for a house. The money you spend on a bathroom facelift, expansion or addition almost certainly will increase the value of your real-estate investment.

The key to a successful remodelling is planning. The following pages offer you a systematic approach to the phases of bathroom design, materials selection and construction.

Assess your wants and needs

Before rushing into drawing your floor plans and choosing the fixtures, step back and determine exactly what you want and need in a new bathroom. You probably have general ideas about this already, but the more thorough and specific you can be from the outset, the more satisfying the final results will be.

Start by taking detailed stock of your present bathroom situation. Consider everything from surface materials to more fundamental issues, such as layout and location. Perhaps new flooring, wall coverings, bench tops, cabinets or fixtures would do the trick. Or maybe you'll need to rearrange the layout of an existing bathroom, add onto it, or create an entirely new one.

ABOVE: Tiling to sill height is practical in a bathroom; the use of colour and pattern here create an Art Deco look.

BELOW: The use of frosted glass on exterior windows and on the screen between bath and toilet ensures privacy without sacrificing light.

Sometimes a bathroom doesn't work well because it has too much space. This happens most often in houses that were built before the advent of indoor plumbing. When the outdoor privy came indoors, it often was placed in a bedroom or some other space that lacked the right proportions or scale to function as an efficient bathroom. These old-fashioned bathrooms may contain all the essentials yet look and feel awkward in actual use, so they offer many opportunities for improvement.

Wants and needs must always be balanced against the budget. Remember not to let your planning decisions get out of touch with financial realities. If you're updating a bathroom in order to make the house more marketable, make sure you don't overdo it. You could lose money by spending more than you realistically can hope to recover on resale or by installing unconventional products or materials. If, on the other hand, you plan to live in your present house for the next 10 years, indulge yourself a little. Remember the trade-off strategy: by choosing, say, stock ceramic tile from a retail outlet as opposed to a specialty tile, you'll save money and retain a high resale value. Simple choices can save money you can put towards a feature you really want, such as a spa, marble vanity top or deluxe shower hardware.

The list of questions on the next page will help you analyse what you need in a new or renovated bathroom. These questions are only a beginning — a springboard to get you started in evaluating your particular situation.

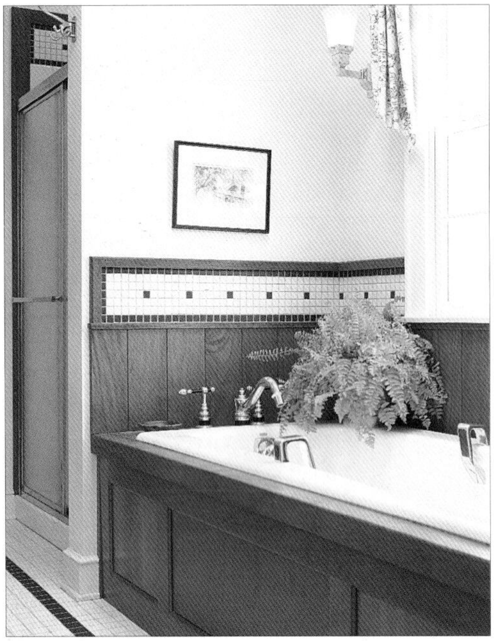

ABOVE: The facelift to this bathroom was achieved with a coat of paint and the installation of new tapware and a timber bath surround.

Take stock of your existing bathroom

- Can two people comfortably and conveniently use the bathroom at the same time?
- Is the basin of adequate size? Would two basins be better?
- Do you use the bath for relaxing soaks or do you prefer to shower? A built-in shower tray with extra-high sides will render a bath redundant.
- Is the bathroom just for kids? Do they like using it? Why or why not? Is it child-safe?
- If this is the main family bathroom or a children's bathroom, is it close to the bedrooms? Second bathrooms are sometimes essential, but you might consider one with a shower only, as this can often be squeezed into a very small space. It makes economic sense to place a bathroom next to or above a room which has existing plumbing.
- Does the bathroom relate to adjacent rooms the way you would like it to?
- Are there frequent traffic jams in or near the bathroom?
- Is there a door that swings into the traffic path? Doors can be re-hung on the other side of the door frame to make space more efficient.
- Is the room primarily a shower/bath/toilet area or is it also used as a place to shave or apply make-up?
- Are you forever bumping your elbow on a side wall when you brush your teeth?
- Are all the cupboard and entrance doors sliding ones? This will save a great deal of space, especially if you have a small bathroom.
- Is the toilet visible through an open door? Multi-use bathrooms will work much better if the toilet is separate from them. The addition of part-partitions can help with privacy problems. Also, wall-mounted toilets, bidets and basins enhance space and make floor cleaning easier.
- Are there enough power points near the basin and mirror?
- Are there places to put a towel close to the shower and/or bath?
- Are there allotted spaces for such items as a laundry basket, bathroom scales, towels and a toilet brush and plunger?
- Is there ample, convenient storage?
- Are the lighting and ventilation adequate?
- Is there a grab bar next to the shower or bath?
- Is there enough bench space?
- Is the bath or shower big enough?
- Are there signs of water damage anywhere?

Level of change

Once you've decided what kind of bathroom you want, it's time to plot your strategy for getting it. Can it be done with a simple facelift, will it require adding onto your house, or does it fall somewhere in between? The following five basic remodelling categories are arranged from the least costly to the most.

Facelift

If an existing bathroom works well but needs an infusion of style, it may need only a facelift. This involves re-covering, refinishing or replacing any or all of the existing wall, floor, ceiling and bench-top surfaces. It also can include replacing the plumbing fixtures and/or adding new lighting, a heater and an exhaust fan. With the right combination of well-chosen materials, you can make a dramatic change to your bathroom for relatively little money and labour.

Minimal remodelling

With a few changes to your existing bathroom layout, you can make a small bathroom function and feel like a larger one. A bathroom as small as 1.5 x 2.5 m, for example, can be divided into sections by adding a wall, and perhaps a pocket door, to separate the bath from the toilet. Create a sense of expanded space by adding a large mirror or two, installing recessed or strip lighting fixtures, or raising or vaulting the ceiling. When decorating, keep the colours light and the patterns simple.

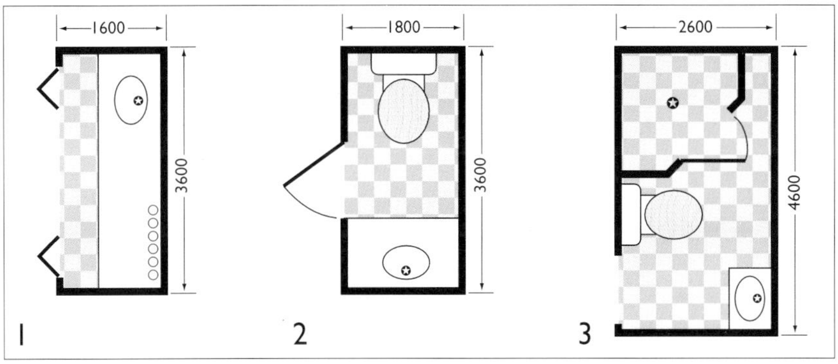

Expansion

If space is tight, consider expanding the bathroom into space borrowed from adjoining areas. You may be able to incorporate all or part of a cupboard, hallway or bedroom to gain the bathroom space you need. A few extra square metres can make a world of difference.

Finding space

This option involves carving out space from your home's existing floor plan for a new bathroom. To find the space, look first to rooms that already have plumbing — the kitchen or laundry, for example. In multi-storey homes, look to second floor areas above an existing bathroom, kitchen or laundry. Often, little nooks can be expanded or hidden spaces opened up as shown in the floor plans above. You can make use of space beneath a staircase, for example, or under the eaves in the attic.

Building an addition

If expanding your current bathroom or finding space for another one within your home just won't work, you may need to add onto your house. Often a simple extension under a roof overhang can yield enough space for a full bathroom. Alternatively, by adding a 90 cm bump-out window you might create all the space you need. If you're remodelling on a second or third storey, think about making attic space useable by building a dormer. Extra bathrooms and toilets can be fitted into surprisingly small spaces and can add considerable value to your house.

Designing or redesigning your bathroom might seem to be a fairly straightforward undertaking, but because bathrooms are compact, high-activity areas, every small decision is important, every centimetre crucial. Outlined on the following pages are some of the basic space requirements demanded by a range of bathroom products and aesthetic considerations you might like to take into account.

ABOVE: A half bathroom in an attic can be a convenient solution if you need to add a bathroom, because you often can locate it directly above existing plumbing, making tapping into the supply and drain lines an easy matter.

ABOVE LEFT: Building an addition.

1 A make-up centre can be installed in an existing cupboard.

2 This half bathroom fits under a staircase or in a coat cupboard.

3 This 1 x 2 m cupboard space has room for a shower.

LEFT: Black and white is dramatic in a small space.

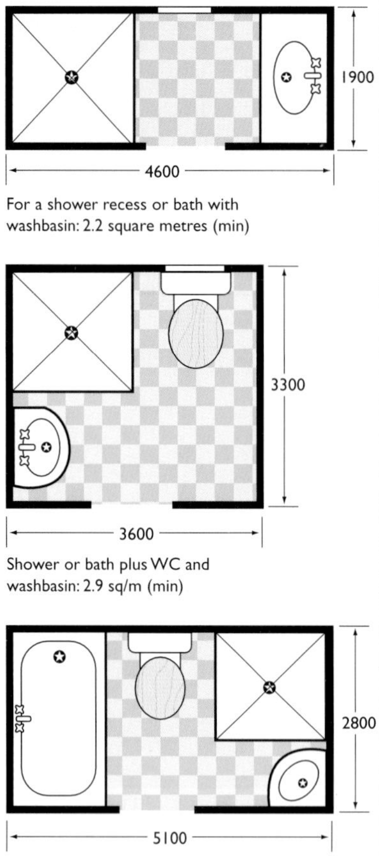

For a shower recess or bath with washbasin: 2.2 square metres (min)

Shower or bath plus WC and washbasin: 2.9 sq/m (min)

A bath as well as a shower, WC and washbasin: 3.5 sq/m (min)

Planning

You should plan carefully before you start spending.

Bathroom layouts

Theoretically, you can build a bathroom as small as you like. As an indication, however, of the types of bathrooms your local council is likely to allow, the following minimum sizes are given:

- for a shower recess or bath with basin — 2.2 sq m (min.);
- shower or bath plus toilet and basin — 2.9 sq m (min.);
- a bath as well as a shower, toilet and basin — 3.5 sq m (min.).

If you have no room for a separate laundry, you should allow an additional 0.7 sq m for a washing machine, 1.7 sq m for a washing machine and bath, and 0.5 sq m for a clothes dryer.

How to plan your bathroom

Most bathrooms are rectangular or square, so we've concentrated on these two shapes when suggesting possible layouts. The diagrams are designed to help you plan your available space and determine the size and shape of the fixtures you can accommodate.

Use the examples of floor plans on the following pages to decide on your own particular layout, remembering that preventing mistakes at this stage will save you much worry and money later. (Note that sizes given for fixtures are standard.)

Ventilation

Planning to install a ceiling exhaust fan? Then remember, heat and moisture sucked into roof cavities can cause mouldy ceilings, as well as other problems. That steam has

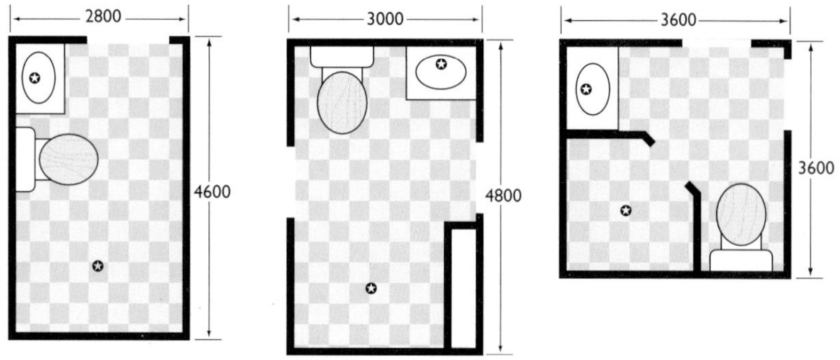

ABOVE: An all white colour scheme always gives a bathroom a clean, spacious atmosphere. The narrow shelf behind the cantilevered basin looks stylish and the marble and embossed tiles add texture.

ABOVE RIGHT: Bathroom layouts.

RIGHT: Toilet/powder room layouts.

Some important legal dos and don'ts

- Your local council needs to know what you propose to do, as requirements vary in different localities. You may have to submit an architect's plan for its approval.
- Your local council will tell you what its requirements are in specific circumstances. For example, if the bathroom opens into a kitchen, there must be proper ventilation and self-closing doors.
- Internal bathrooms must have adequate ventilation; you may need a skylight and/or mechanical ventilation.
- Always use licensed tradespeople; plumbers and electricians will automatically get in touch with the appropriate authorities on your behalf.

to go somewhere and the best place is outside. Roof ventilators can be installed by a home handyperson and many operate on wind power.

Bathroom sizes

Once you've decided what part of the house the bathroom will serve best and who will be using it, the next basic question is: 'What type of bathroom am I planning?'. To find your answer, make an inventory of the shortcomings of your current bathroom. Keep a list of your general wants and needs as you start to get more specific about your remodelling plan and what size bathroom you want to create.

Don't rush the process. According to many design experts, you should spend as much time planning and designing your new bathroom as it takes for the construction phase of your project. Take the time to visit real-estate open houses and design shows to gather design ideas,

ABOVE LEFT: Storage need not always be built in. Free-standing furniture can be suitable for storing rolled up towels or even books.

ABOVE RIGHT: The richness of dark-stained timber is complemented by white woodwork and hand-painted blue and white striped walls.

ABOVE: A pleasant and practical bathroom with innovative tiled storage.

Avoiding perils

Commonsense reduces risks in the bathroom. Here are some simple steps you can take to make your home safer for the whole family:

- Store chemicals, cleaners and medicines in upper cupboards where children can't see them.
- Make sure the cupboard can be locked.
- Install grab rails in the bath and shower.
- Purchase child-proof packaging for dangerous substances whenever possible.
- Make sure that the flooring is slip resistant.
- If you have a rug in the bathroom it should have non-slip backing.
- It's best if benches have rounded corners.
- Water-heater temperature should not be too hot.
- Never leave a small child unattended in the bathroom .
- Install locks that can be opened from inside and out.
- Provide a sturdy step-stool so children can reach taps and bench tops easily.
- Shower enclosures must always be of safety glass or acrylic material.
- Make safe provision for electrical outlets if you plan to use hairdryers, heaters and so on.
- All electrical installations must be fitted by a qualified electrician.
- Never touch live electrical appliances with wet hands.

and check out plumbing supply firms for product ideas.

Following are the three basic bathroom options, along with size requirements for each.

Half bathroom

A basin and toilet constitute a half bathroom. Typically, half bathrooms are located close to the main living areas. They're intended primarily for visitors' use and to provide backup for the main bathroom. Common dimensions for half bathrooms are 1.2 x 1.5 m or 1 x 2 m. At a pinch, they can be as small as 1 x 1.8 m or 1.4 x 1.4 m and still work effectively.

Half bathrooms are often the most overlooked part of the house. It's tempting to ignore a room that's not used often, but you should think of your guests and the impressions they'll take away from their visit. Because they are generally small, half bathrooms offer an opportunity to indulge in fun, offbeat or lavish decorating. They also can fit a lot of convenience into a small space.

Three-quarter bathroom

Equipped with a shower stall instead of a bath, a three-quarter bathroom can be squeezed into a space that measures 1.8 x 1.8 m.

If your family prefers showering to bathing, a three-quarter bathroom could solve your morning traffic jams. Other good uses for this kind of bathroom include as a guest bathroom, a bathroom for older children and a backup for the main family bathroom.

Full bathroom

Typically located close to bedrooms, a full bathroom consists of a basin, toilet and bath. It may contain a separate bath and shower or a combination of the two. The minimum room size needed to accommodate this full range of fixtures is 1.5 x 2 m. Many different floor plans are possible, though it all depends on your particular wants, needs and budget.

At least 20 cm should separate the top of the vanity backsplash from the bottom of the medicine cabinet or mirror.

RIGHT: A separate bath and shower are useful in a family bathroom.

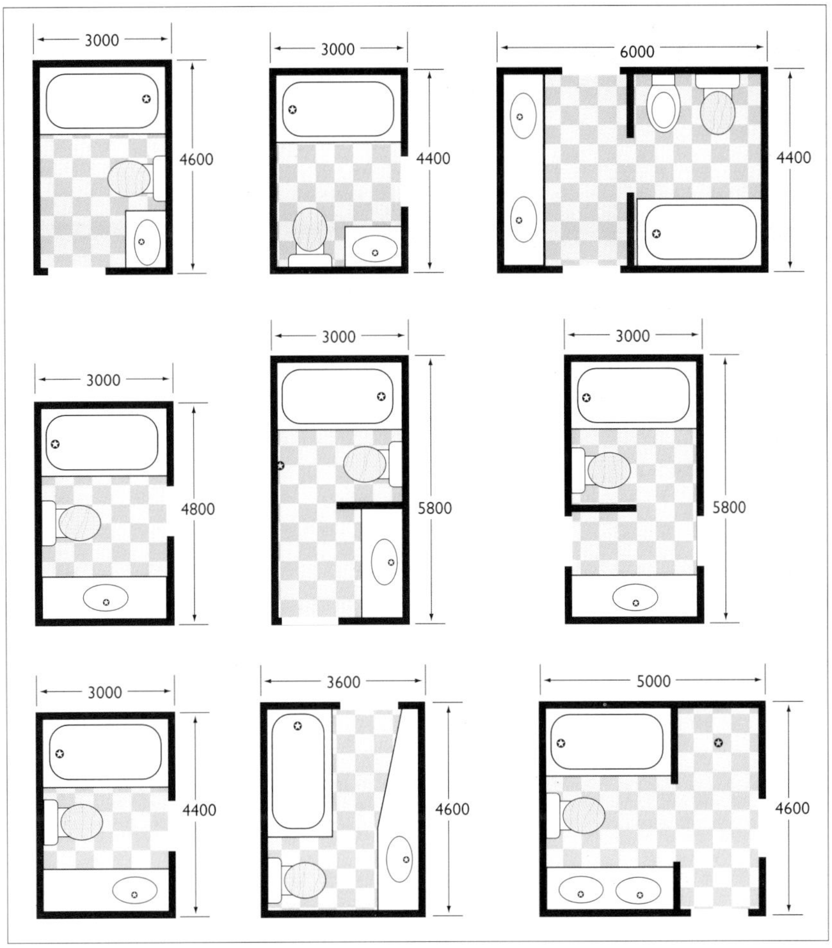

LEFT: Bathroom floor plans.

BELOW: A glass brick wall lets in the light but maintains privacy. The inexpensive vanity provides ample storage for everyday items, while a glass soap jar is practical as well as decorative. The carpet flooring matches the pastel theme.

Allow at least 40 cm from the centre of the toilet to any obstruction, fixture or equipment on either side. For clearance in front of the toilet, provide an open floor space of 1.2 x 1.2 m. A good 40 cm of that floor space should extend to each side of the toilet's centre line. You should allow at least 2.5 cm between the back of the water tank and the wall behind it.

The toilet-paper holder should be positioned 15 cm beyond the front of the seat with the roller 65 cm above the floor.

Minimum interior shower dimensions are 85 x 85 cm, but most people prefer more room. Swinging shower doors must open into the bathroom, away from the shower's interior.

The standard height for vanities is 75–80 cm. Adjust the height upwards for tall users. In bathrooms with two vanities, one can be 75–85 cm high and the other can be 85–105 cm high.

Toilets isolated in a separate compartment should occupy a space 90 cm wide by 165 cm deep, with a swing-out or pocket door. Dividing walls are normally about 15 cm thick (including trim at the bottom of both sides), so allow space for them.

Shapes and sizes

Do lots of homework! Shop around for basins, toilets, baths and bidets so that your choice of shape and material will suit both your taste and your pocket. You'll find they come in materials including enamelled iron, vitreous china, plastic and fibreglass, and bath shapes can be rectangular or square, circular or oval, even triangular. You can find

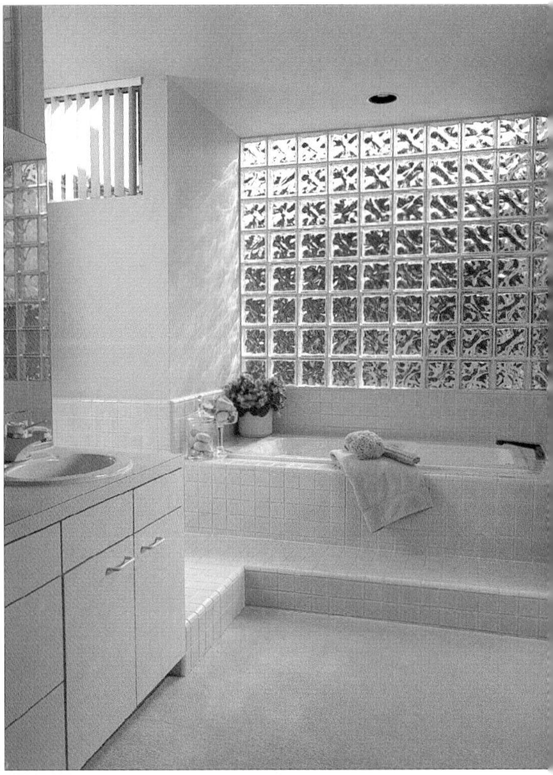

basins that cantilever, pedestal basins and ones that are built into a bench top.

Then there's the importance of storage. It's wise to work out what you need and choose to store in the bathroom. Certainly toiletries, towels, cleaning materials, soaps, toilet paper and toothbrushes come to mind, but you may want more areas for specialised storage—now's the time to plan them.

It's also the time to work out your lighting needs. All fittings and power points must be located safely, well away from wet areas.

Hand basins

Before you choose a bathroom basin consider how the basin material will influence the way the basin looks, how durable it will be and how much maintenance it will require. Each of the following materials has its own characteristics.

Porcelain-enamelled cast iron is extremely durable and is easy to care for, but it's heavy and needs a sturdy support system.

Stainless steel is durable and unaffected by household chemicals. The steel, however, tends to collect spots from hard water and soap.

Vitreous china has a lustrous surface, is easy to clean and is the most resistant to discolouration and corrosion. However, it can chip when struck by a heavy object.

Fibreglass-reinforced plastic can be moulded into novel shapes, but doesn't hold a shine as well as other surfaces and is not as durable as the other materials mentioned.

Simulated or cultured marble and other solid-surface materials are handsome, but they may chip when struck by a heavy object, and abrasive cleaners may spoil the finish. Shallow nicks and scratches can be removed by sanding gently with fine-grade sandpaper.

Styles of basins fall into three categories: those that stand on pedestals, those that hang on the wall and those that rest in vanities.

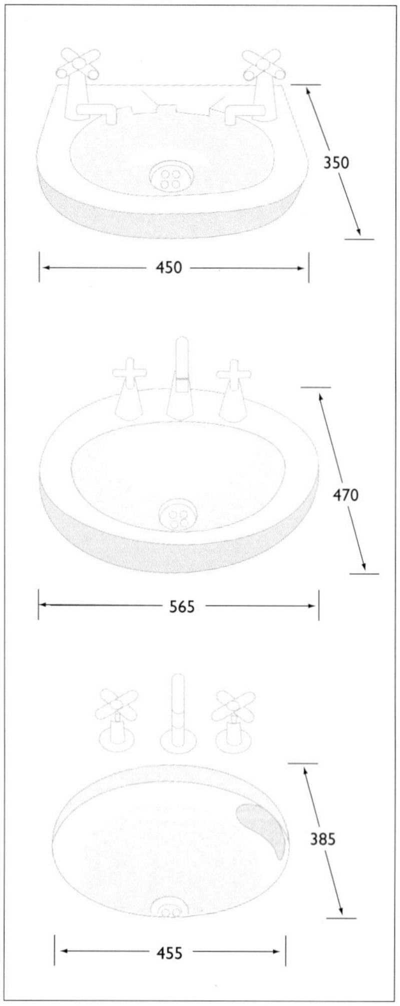

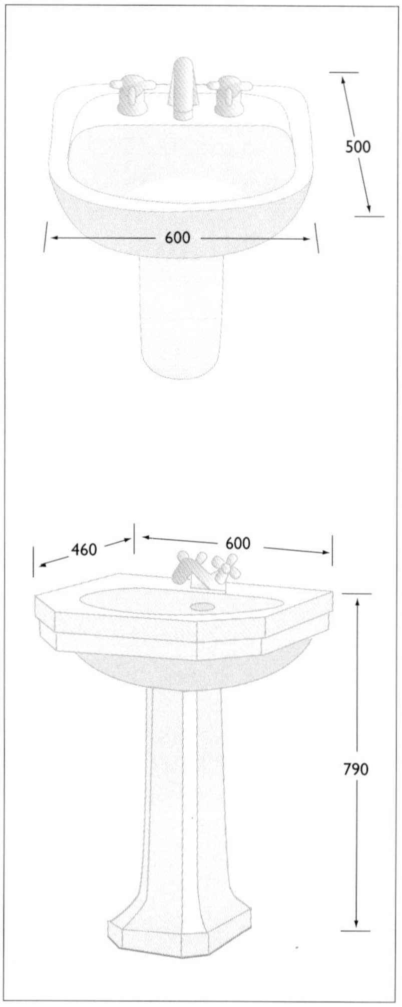

ABOVE LEFT AND ABOVE RIGHT: Hand basin styles.

For both pedestal and wall-mounted basins you should allow a minimum of 50 mm either side for elbow room. In front of the basin you will need a metre, but this can also be the all-important room circulation space.

Pedestal

A pedestal basin not only gives a bathroom distinctive charm, it also can make a small bathroom look larger because there isn't a wide bench top around the basin or storage below the basin itself. These advantages are also the main disadvantages with pedestal basins since they make for a lack of bench space and less storage.

One criticism of pedestal basins is that there is nowhere to put items down on them. However, this can be overcome with a larger pedestal basin.

Wall-mounted

Usually designed for compact spaces, wall-hung basins have the advantage of squeezing into small bathrooms. However, like pedestal basins, wall-hung basins have no storage below and don't conceal the plumbing below. Wall-hung basins often are used in bathrooms designed for people with disabilities because they can be installed at any height and have a clear space underneath that allows for easy wheelchair access.

Vanity

Vanity basins have lots of bench-top space around them and handy storage below. Their main drawback is they require the most floor space of any basin style.

Basins in vanities can be attached to the vanity units in a variety of ways:

- A self-rimming or surface-mounted basin sits on top of the counter after the basin has been dropped into a hole large enough to accommodate the basin bowl but smaller than the outside rim of the basin. The outside rim is a ridge that forms a tight seal with the bench top. These types of basins are perhaps the easiest to install because the hole in the bench top need not be perfect as it's hidden once the basin has been installed.
- Rimmed basins sit just slightly above the bench top with a tight-fitting metal rim joining the basin and the bench top. The rim is made with different finishes to match whatever tap you have. Disadvantages with rim basins are that the rim joint can be difficult to clean, and they are difficult to install.
- Undermounted basins are attached to the bottom of the bench top giving a clean, tailored look. Undermounted basins, like rimmed basins, are sometimes difficult to clean where they attach to the bench.
- Integral basins are part of the same piece of material as the vanity's bench top. Because there is no joint between the bowl and the bench top, they are easy to clean. The main disadvantage is that the entire unit must be replaced if any part of it is damaged.

Bench tops

When it comes to bench-tops, look for something that will stand up to water, soap, alcohol- and acetone-based liquids, toothpaste and cosmetics. Replacing a bench top or adding a new one is a feasible do-it-yourself project, and you don't have to replace the whole cabinet if you don't want to.

Most bathroom bench tops are surfaced with plastic laminate, tile, solid-surface material, wood or marble or granite.

Buyer's guide

- Basins can make a stylish statement with bowls that are round, oval, rectangular or asymmetrical, all available in a rainbow of colours. Some of the more expensive models are adorned with available hand-painted designs.
- Choose the largest basin you can fit into your bathroom. Larger basins are more comfortable to use and they reduce the amount of water that splashes out of the bowl.
- If you are purchasing all new fixtures for a bathroom, look for matching basin, toilet and bath combinations.

BELOW: Laminate is widely used on bathroom bench tops.

installed particle-board bench top, although a professional will do the job best.

Tile

As it does for floors and walls, ceramic tile makes an attractive, durable finish for bench tops. It's available in many colours, designs and textures. Grout lines that trap dirt and encourage mildew are a drawback, but new grouts and sealants help alleviate these problems.

Getting professional results with tile is a challenge for do-it-yourselfers. A slightly irregular look can be appropriate for rustic, unglazed quarry tile, but other tile varieties demand greater precision. Using pre-grouted tile sheets, or sheets of mosaic tile on a mesh backing, makes it easier to space tiles evenly.

ABOVE: Tiles are the most commonly used surface in bathrooms.

BELOW: Floor tiles can also be used on bench tops.

Plastic laminate

Plastic laminate offers good value and performance. As a result, it is the most widely used bench-top material in bathrooms, just as it is in kitchens. Various manufacturers market laminate under different brand names, but they're all basically the same material—a stack of thin plastic layers bonded together under heat and pressure. Laminate is easy to clean and resistant to water and stains. On the negative side, laminates can burn, wear thin and dull over time. Hard blows can chip or dent the plastic, and there's no remedy short of replacement.

Available in many colours and patterns, laminate finishes range in texture from high-gloss smoothness to a mottled, leather-like look. Dealers usually have a few standard patterns in stock; you can order others after looking at colour charts in the store.

Do-it-yourselfers can buy prefabricated laminate vanity tops or have them made to order with a hole cut for the basin. Installing the finished bench top is a fairly easy matter. It is possible to apply pieces of laminate material to an

Solid-surface material

Solid-surface bench tops offer many of the advantages of stone with few of the drawbacks. Cast from an acrylic resin, solid-surface material demands little maintenance and is extremely durable. Intense heat and heavy falling objects (which shouldn't pose much of a threat in bathrooms) can cause damage, but scratches, abrasions and even minor burns can be repaired with fine-grade sandpaper. The methods and tools needed for working with this material are similar to those required for woodworking. However, some manufacturers require that a trained professional install their material.

Solid-surface material is available in white, beige, pastels and imitation stone. It comes in flat sheets and in ready-formed bench tops with integrated basins.

Wood

As a bench-top surface, wood is attractive, versatile and easy to install. It is, however, especially vulnerable to water damage, and its porosity makes it hard to keep clean. All hardwood and softwood species must be well sealed with polyurethane or marine varnish. Special care should be taken to seal around the edges of plumbing fixtures so standing water can't seep in and cause wood rot.

Marble and granite

Though marble and granite are unrivalled for their beauty, these classic materials warrant careful thought before being used in a bathroom. Marble stains easily. Granite shrugs off most stains, except from grease (especially if the granite is unsealed). If a solid sheet of stone for your bench top is beyond your budget, marble or granite tiles may be substituted as a cheaper alternative.

Cultured marble is less expensive and is made from real chips of natural marble embedded in plastic. It's available in sheet form and in standard dimensions. Although it is easy to clean, cultured marble must be well cared for. Once scratched, it cannot be resurfaced. Follow the manufacturer's recommendations for what type of finish to apply to cultured marble to best protect it.

Taps

Most bathroom taps receive heavy daily use, so don't choose one that simply looks good; you must also consider ease of use, safety and durability. With taps, price is a fairly accurate measure of quality. A warranty is a good indication of a higher quality tap.

Tap finishes include chrome, polished brass, coloured epoxy coating, pewter, nickel and gold. Polished brass finishes usually are coated to keep them from tarnishing. Chrome is the standard finish for most taps because it is durable and cleans up easily.

The best sets are made of brass and come in various finishes and designs. Some brass taps can contain relatively high levels of lead. If lead in your water is a concern, look for lead-free brass taps and always allow the tap to run for a minute before drinking the water.

Before you buy make sure the tap set is the proper size and design to fit your plumbing fixture. Most basins have holes pre-drilled in their rims to accommodate standard taps and plumbing.

Taps come in three standard types: centre set, spread fit and single control. Centre-set and spread-fit taps are similar, since they both have two separate control handles (one for hot water, one for cold water) plus a spout. The difference between them is that centre-set taps are connected above the basin deck and appear to consist of a single unit, whereas spread-set taps have no visible connection between the controls and the tap because the valves and mixing chamber connect underneath the basin. Single-control taps also consist of a single unit but have one central control device (usually a prominent

ABOVE: Marble is classic and durable.

BELOW: Gooseneck taps on the basins match that on the bath.

lever or knob) instead of two separate control valves.

Although single-control taps can be elegant and convenient, they sometimes are trickier to operate with the desired results for basins, baths and showers. Choose them with caution for bathrooms intended for use by either the very old or the very young. To prevent the possibility of hot water burns, you might want to choose a tap with a built-in temperature-limiting valve.

Toilets and bidets

The amount of space required for a toilet varies greatly from model to model and style to style, so you will have to check your brochures. The average depth, however, from the back of the cistern to the front of the seat is 650 mm. Widths of cisterns range from 350 to 580 mm. For the overall space requirements, you should allow at least 450 mm from the centre of the seat to a large obstruction (to the side) such as a wall or bath. Allow 400 mm from the centre of the seat to the edge of a basin at the side.

Obviously bidets require less space because they don't have a cistern. They are generally about 570 mm front to back and require a 140 mm space behind them. In front of both the toilet and bidet seat, you should allow 650 mm (minimum) floor space.

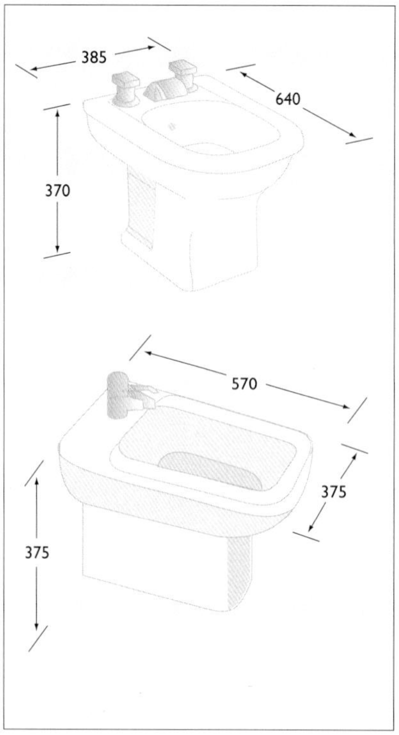

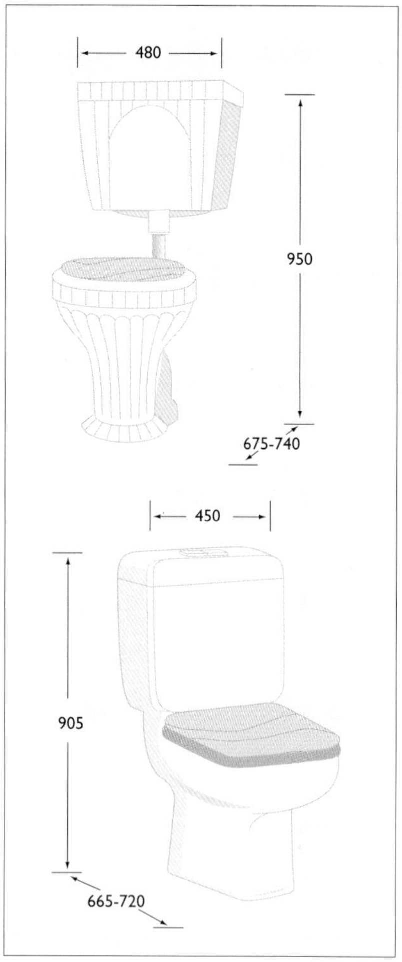

Accessories

These days you can choose any style from old world, fancy and colonial to ultra-modern, acrylic and plain. Some people prefer not to have these matching perfectly, though this is the most obvious way to go. Consider building in the odd shelf with tiles or adding a battered old recycled shelf rather than automatically resorting to immaculately matching 'suites' of bathroom accessories. Always remember, there's more than one way to accessorise a bathroom.

Showers

Square showers should be no smaller than 900 x 900 mm, but rectangular showers can be as narrow as 760 mm.

Some shower trays are about 300 mm deep and incorporate a

ABOVE LEFT: Bidets.

ABOVE RIGHT: Toilets.

LEFT: This luxurious bathroom has an outlook to the garden and is large enough to accommodate shower, bath and twin basins.

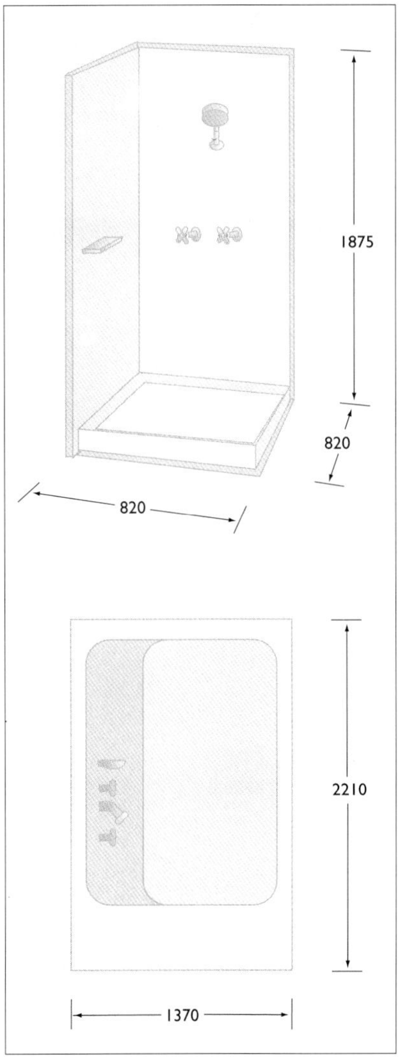

ABOVE: Shower styles.

BELOW: Two types of spa bath.

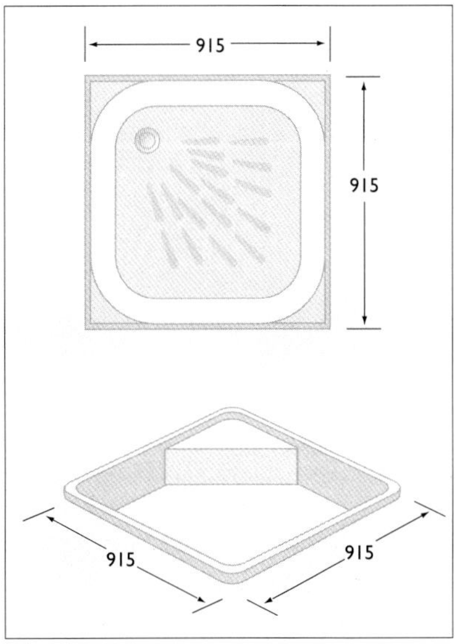

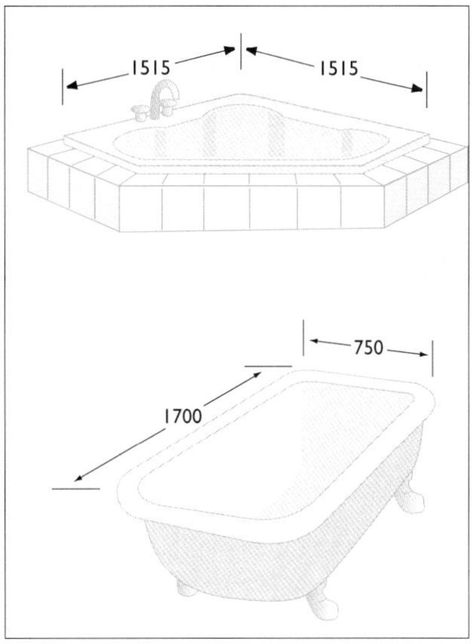

ABOVE: Old and new bath styles.

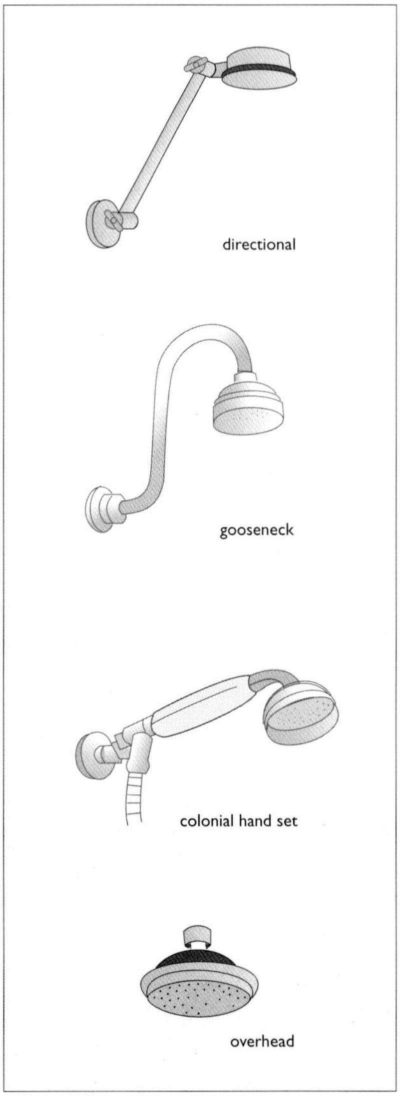

ABOVE: A tiled ledge alongside the bath can also be used as a storage bench.

LEFT: Four types of shower head.

seat. These are particularly suited to the elderly. Tiled shower recesses require copper, stainless steel or fibreglass shower trays. These are fixed in place and sealed in before being covered in mesh reinforced concrete and tiles.

Prefabricated shower compartments come with two or three fibreglass reinforced walls combined with the tray.

Baths

Today you can have the bath of your dreams—anything from the freestanding, old style on legs to a luxurious spa with as many as 16 jets. Similarly, you can have baths that take up as much or as little space as you have available. Corner-style bath/showers are the space-efficient solution when there is not room for a full bath and separate shower cubicle.

ABOVE: Shelving units that glide out work better than drawers, because storage items stay neat instead of getting in a jumble.

ABOVE RIGHT: This bathroom built for two is outfitted with compartments so there's no question where items go. The double vanity houses pull-out towel racks, tilt-out drawers and a rubbish bin.

Storage

In bathrooms, as in kitchens and houses as a whole, it's nearly impossible to include too much storage space. Having easy access to grooming supplies and toiletry items is most critical near the basin, bath, shower and toilet.

Basin area

The basin includes two primary storage facilities: the vanity and the medicine cabinet. When selecting a vanity, consider how you will use it. Will it store cleaning supplies? Towels? Underwear? Cosmetics? Hair dryers? All of the above? Your answers to these questions will determine the most efficient combination of cabinet space and drawers. Some stock vanities resemble chests of drawers; others are simple base cabinets; most combine drawer and cabinet space. By elevating the height of the bench top, you can gain additional storage space below.

If you are keeping an existing vanity, you probably can improve its storage capacity by making a few simple modifications. Mount wire racks inside cabinet doors to hold cleaning supplies, a hair dryer or a curling iron; add shelves or half shelves to create more space. Take a cue from kitchen cabinetry and include pull-out elements such as a rubbish bin, shelves and towel rods. If budget and space allow, create built-in nooks for stashing your toothbrush, razors and other grooming aids.

A mirrored medicine cabinet above the vanity provides ideal storage for cosmetics and toiletries. Choose between surface-mounted and recessed units in a variety of styles. Look for models with adjustable shelves to accommodate items of various sizes, and use cosmetic organisers to keep small items in order. Larger, three-door units provide even more space.

Bathing area

Look for bath and shower surrounds that have ample built-in

niches for storage for shampoos, conditioners, soaps and bath oils. For more space, buy a rust-proof plastic shower caddie. Some versions hang from the showerhead; others attach to shower walls with suction cups.

Use wall space at the ends of the bath to mount towel rails. To keep bath salts and lotions handy, you can place shallow display shelves above the towel rails or on the back wall above the bath. If you have a shower stall or a bath/shower combination, select doors with towel rails on the outside — an ideal spot for hanging wet towels to dry.

Toilet area

Wall space above a toilet is a fine place to put a wall-mounted cupboard or a freestanding shelf unit that straddles the toilet tank. A low-profile toilet, one with a cistern that rises only slightly above seat level, frees more wall area for storage. This may be an especially attractive option when the wall behind the toilet contains a window.

Other storage tips

Use wall space wisely. Hang towel bars above one another. Top a row of hooks or pegs with a shelf; hang towels on the hooks and stack washers on the shelf.

Add shelves wherever practical. This could be almost anywhere in the bathroom, since many shelving products come in a variety of widths and can be cut to any length. Corner shelves take advantage of frequently wasted space. Create an illusion of spaciousness (and more storage space) with glass or mirrored shelves.

Revamp an existing cupboard by converting the bottom half into a chest of drawers or a built-in laundry hamper. Install open shelves or cubicles for rolled bath towels in the upper portion.

Bring in items from other rooms. Chests of drawers, china cabinets and antique kitchen cupboards add character and storage space. Just remember to finish wood furniture with a moisture-resistant sealer to prevent warping.

Develop a colour scheme

Creating a good colour palette for your bathroom can be a challenge, but there's nothing forbidding or mysterious about it. The following general guidelines will help.

For the sake of continuity, carry your home's overall personality into the bathroom. Link the bathroom with adjoining rooms by matching colour values (that is, the colours' darkness or lightness) as well as actual hues. For example, if the trim in the hall outside the bathroom is painted a high-gloss creamy white, consider using that colour somewhere in the bathroom.

Most successful colour schemes use a minimum of three and a maximum of six colours. Three-colour schemes consist of a main colour (the prevalent colour used on most surfaces), a secondary colour (often used on cabinets, trim and/or some wall or ceiling surfaces) and an accent colour (the least-used colour to provide interest, variety and balance). The accent is often the brightest or darkest colour in a scheme; use it in at least three places (or on one major design element) to establish a definite presence.

Give thought to the colour of every component: walls, ceiling, window and door trim, wainscoting (if any), floor, furniture, benches, fixtures, curtains and accessories.

When determining your colour placement, decide what you want the main focus of the room to be. It is important to remember that the eye is attracted first to the lightest colour. If the walls aren't the main focus, they should not be painted the lightest colour.

White (including ivory and cream) fixtures are not only less expensive, but they also are easier to clean than dark fixtures.

White comes in many tones, and choosing from among them can be

ABOVE: Framed with mouldings that match the door, this built-in storage unit was carved from space often overlooked in bathrooms — the area between the end of the bath and the wall.

ABOVE: A large mirror framed by individual lights is the ideal cosmetic centre.

difficult. Decide if you want a cool white or a warm white, then choose one specific hue. Match all the white or off-white elements so various tones won't be competing with each other.

If you use the bathroom for applying make-up, choose lighter versions of the colours of the clothes that look good on you. The lighter colours reflect flattering light, allowing you to get your make-up colours correct.

Bench-top colours that keep their good looks are lighter mid-tones, greys and beiges. Dark colours have poor reflective qualities, solids tend to show marks and white shows stains.

White cabinets can make a small bathroom seem larger. Dark cabinets will have the opposite effect. Be sure to use dark cabinets only in a well-lit room.

Planning a cosmetic centre

Plan for enough power points. If you have two curling irons and a hair dryer, you'll need more than one outlet.

Keep everything in its place. Purchase drawer organisers for cosmetics and hooks for hanging your hair dryer and curling iron.

Light it right. If possible, light the cosmetic centre to duplicate the lighting in the place where you're

Make your bathroom children friendly

Protect your children against potential dangers in the bathroom by heeding these additional safety precautions:

- Keep washers and toys beside the bath so you won't be tempted to leave your child unattended in the bath.
- A cushion around the bath-tap spout, as well as edge and corner cushions on cabinets, can help prevent cuts and bruises.
- Install child-proof locks on all cabinets. Even the toilet lid should have a latch.
- Use only non-breakable drinking tumblers in a bathroom. Store them where children can reach them without having to climb precariously.
- Add slip-resistant strips in front of the basin and bath. Anchor rugs with non-slip pads or double-faced carpet tape.
- Block all electrical outlets with safety covers or plugs.
- Make sure grab bars inside the bath and shower stall are low enough for children to use.
- Choose taps and handles that are easy to use and have rounded edges.
- Locate towel bars or rings 15 cm or less from entrances to the bath or shower so children don't have to reach too far for them.

ABOVE RIGHT: A children's bathroom should allow space for toys.

RIGHT: A well lit bathroom with slat blinds to control the amount of natural light.

BELOW: The easiest way to give a room a facelift is with paint. In this case, white contrasts with coffee-toned wallpaper and bench tops in aubergine and chocolate to make an unusual but striking colour scheme. The main storage area, reflected in the mirror, is decorative as well as functional.

preparing to spend the most time. That is, if you work in a setting with fluorescent lighting, your make-up centre should have fluorescent lighting. The best make-up centres allow users to switch from one type of light to another, but these can be expensive.

Plan for the proper distance between yourself and the mirror. When applying eye make-up or lipstick, it's hard to get close enough to the vanity mirror, so supplement it with a hand mirror.

Place the centre out of high-traffic areas so you're not jostled as you apply your make-up.

Do a facelift

Small changes can add up to big results. A well-planned facelift will not only bring a fresh, updated look to an older bathroom, but it also can make a small bathroom look and feel more spacious.

Facelifts normally involve paint, wallpaper, bench-top surfacing materials, light fixtures and accessories. They also can help solve spatial problems. Using space better and making minor adjustments to doors, accessories and cabinets can improve the way the bathroom functions.

Take a moment to consider what kinds of problems you experience when using the bathroom in question. Just correcting what bothers you can make a big difference and doesn't always require major changes. For example, if the bathroom door bumps into fixtures or blocks cabinets, you might improve matters by changing the direction of the door swing. If you need to keep costs down, don't relocate fixtures, especially the toilet. Sometimes pointing the toilet in a different direction (which can be done without changing any plumbing) can give you more manoeuvring room. Also, you can angle the vanity into a corner. If there's a severe space shortage, install a smaller vanity—or a pedestal basin—and a lower-profile toilet.

When you do a bathroom facelift, re-evaluate the room's storage potential. If the room is more than 1.5 m wide, you may have room to add a cabinet or shelves at the foot of the bath. Shelves above the toilet or on the back of the entry door also add storage.

Make a small bathroom feel big

You don't have to add square meterage to an existing bathroom to make the space seem larger and work better for you. Just keep the following ideas and areas of improvement in mind. Some of them fall into the facelift category while others require more extensive remodelling strategies:

- Light. Install adequate lighting to eliminate shadowy corners. Create an illusion of height by focusing low-wattage, indirect lighting on the ceiling.
- Downsize. Swap large fixtures for smaller ones. Switch a bath

for a corner shower or a bulky vanity for a sleek pedestal basin.

- Design. Use no more than two dominant horizontal lines. The top of wainscoting, for instance, establishes one line. Aligning tops of doors, windows, mirrors and bath/shower enclosures establishes the second line.
- Minimise. Don't mix a lot of materials: stick with one, such as tile for floors, walls and bench tops. Get rid of any clutter. Keep wallpaper patterns light and small in scale. Stay away from frilly curtains and furry mats.
- Reflect. Use large mirrors to make walls look like windows.

Resurface the bath

Pedestrian as it may seem, resurfacing an old bath can go a long way towards brightening a tired bathroom. A new coat of epoxy paint can cover up an unsightly colour or chipped finish without the mess and expense of replacing the whole fixture. It's a job for professionals but can be done without moving the bath. The procedure takes four to six hours, then the new finish should cure for a few days before the bath is used.

Renovate

Renovation goes beyond cosmetic changes to encompass replacing fixtures, changing the layout, adding lighting, enlarging or replacing windows, and making any structural changes short of expansion. You'll save money if your plan calls for replacing, rather than moving, the bath, basin and shower. You'll have to balance your need to move any fixtures against your budget.

Space-stretching strategies

As the smallest rooms in most houses, bathrooms pose some of the biggest decorating and remodelling challenges. Almost every centimetre of space must count. Putting one or all of the following ideas into practice will help you end up with a stylish, affordable, hard-working bathroom.

Go for more bench space

Forget balancing grooming items on the edge of a small basin. Augment bench-top space by extending the vanity as far as possible on both sides. You'll get even more space if you extend a narrow piece of the bench top over the toilet (remember not to block access to the cistern).

Increase storage

Just as older homes never have enough cupboard space, older bathrooms invariably lack storage. In addition to the other storage ideas in this chapter, replacing a narrow medicine cabinet with a wider one and building cabinetry above the bath for seldom-used items are good storage solutions.

Add light

There's no better way to bring daylight into a bathroom than by adding a skylight, if the location allows it. Be careful—condensation

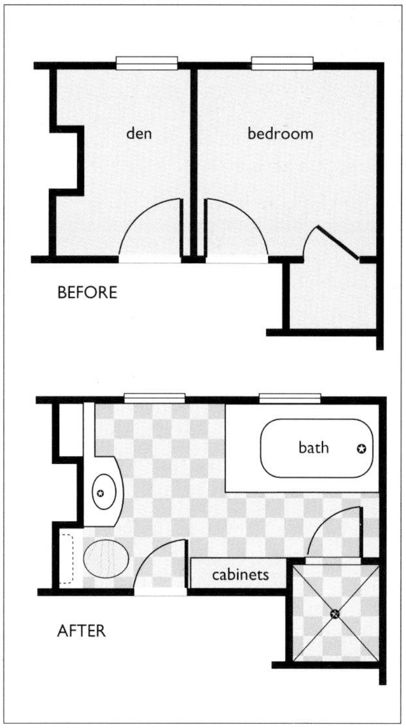

ABOVE: Here, space for a bathroom was gained by knocking out a wall.

BELOW: The installation of a bay window added light and an alcove for the bath in this renovation.

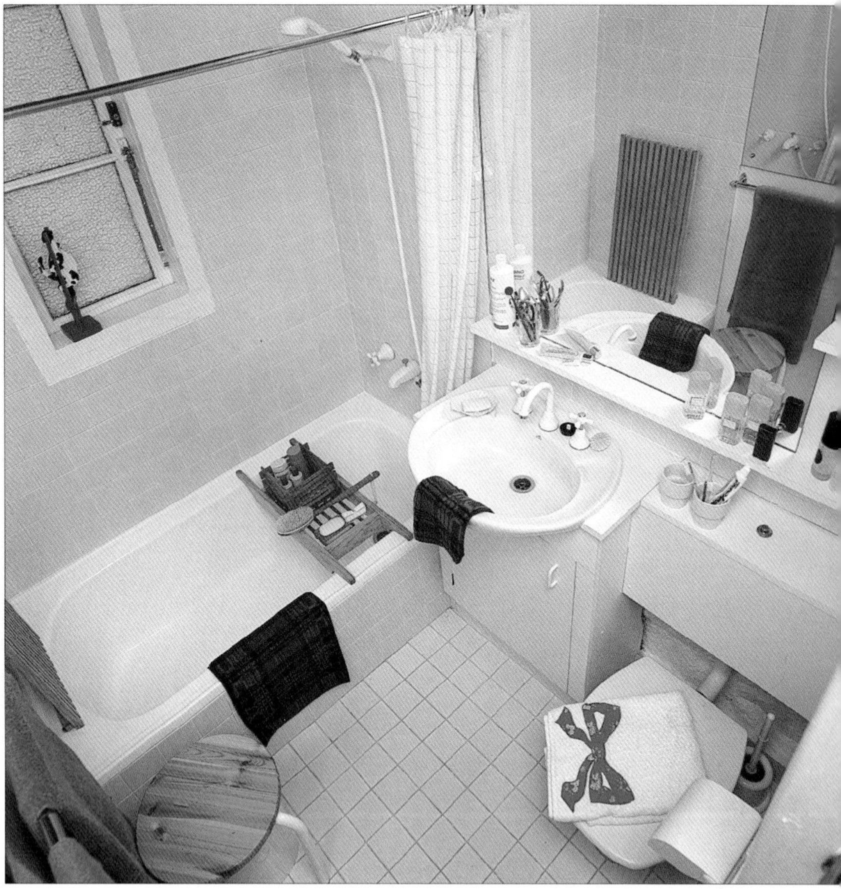

on skylights can cause moisture problems, especially during winter in colder areas. It is important to buy only a high-quality unit and be sure it's installed according to the manufacturer's specifications.

Putting in a skylight requires installing new framing between the bathroom ceiling and the roof to create a skylight shaft. Shafts that flare outwards towards the bottom admit more daylight. Paint the shaft white for maximum light transmission and the illusion of more space, or paint it a colour to give the bathroom a glow.

Divide and conquer

One popular approach to making the most of existing bathroom space is to divide it into compartments. Separating the bath, shower and toilet from the vanity area with a wall and pocket door creates a division of functions and enhances privacy. This can make it possible for the room to serve more than one user at a time.

Expand

If the amount of space in an existing bathroom simply won't do, borrow square meterage from adjoining areas. Look first to cupboards and other spaces that adjoin your current bathroom's 'wet wall'—the wall, that is, that already contains plumbing pipes. It's far less expensive to install fixtures when you can connect them to nearby plumbing lines. If you want to expand a main bathroom, for example, think about keeping the toilet and bath in their original locations and expanding adjacent space to accommodate the basin (or double basins) and dressing room. That way you save money and labour by not moving the plumbing fixtures that are the most difficult to move.

Carve out space for a new bathroom

Facelifting, overhauling and expanding can do only so much good if what you really need is another bathroom. Before concluding that you need to build an addition to your house, however, examine the existing floor plan. You may find some under-used space where a new bathroom would fit in well.

ABOVE LEFT: Before—This tiny bathroom, only the length of a bath wide and slightly more than that long, needed to be made both functional and visually much larger. It had only three small windows — two of them high up, and no storage at all.

ABOVE: After—The new grey and white colour scheme is streamlined and works perfectly in the small space. The high windows were replaced with a flat skylight. The use of small tiles on the bath and walls and two large mirrors facing one another help the space look larger. The new built-in vanity created much needed storage space.

But where should you look? Often, a half bathroom near the family room can take the burden off a one-bathroom house, as can a secondary bathroom with a shower in the basement. Basement laundry areas are good candidates for conversion because they're already equipped with plumbing. Look, too, at spaces close to the bedrooms. A vacant corner of the master bedroom is a likely spot for an additional bathroom, provided that the bedroom has one dimension that measures at least 5 m.

Another possibility is to divide a large existing bathroom into two smaller bathrooms, providing access to one of them from a hallway. Alternatively, you could transform a small bedroom into a full bathroom, then (if necessary) add another bedroom in another area of the house, such as the attic or basement.

Putting a bathroom in an existing space doesn't have to be a major project that puts you into debt for decades. If you're careful, practical and place new fixtures near existing plumbing vents the cost will be reasonable. The main question is where you'll locate the toilet. If the new fixture cannot easily be plumbed into the existing vent stack, the resulting complications can add thousands of dollars to your remodelling budget. In

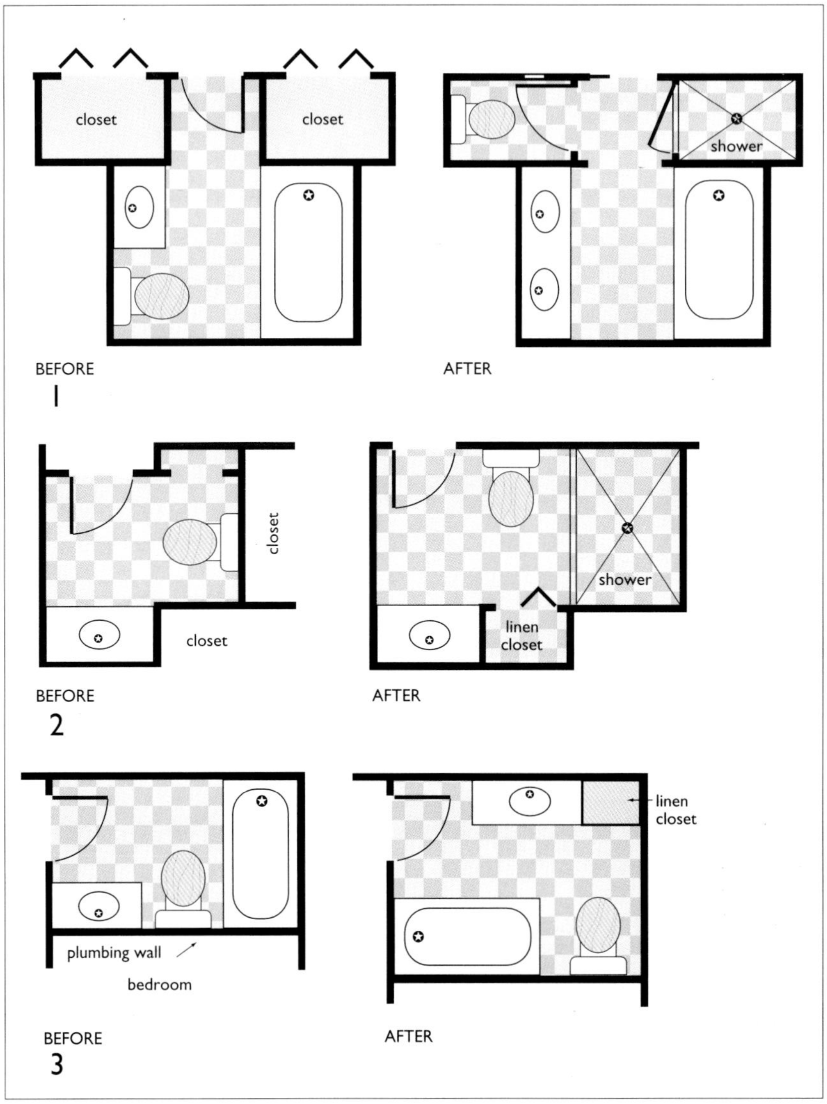

LEFT: Plans for expansion.

1 Cupboards located between bedrooms and bathrooms provide an opportunity for expansion. Simply annex one (or both) cupboards.

2 By expanding into cupboard space, this small half bathroom was transformed into a full bathroom with a large shower and linen cupboard.

3 The plumbing wall in this small bathroom was moved 450 mm into an adjacent bedroom, creating enough space for fixtures to be placed opposite each other. Moving and adding plumbing were less expensive than adding onto the house.

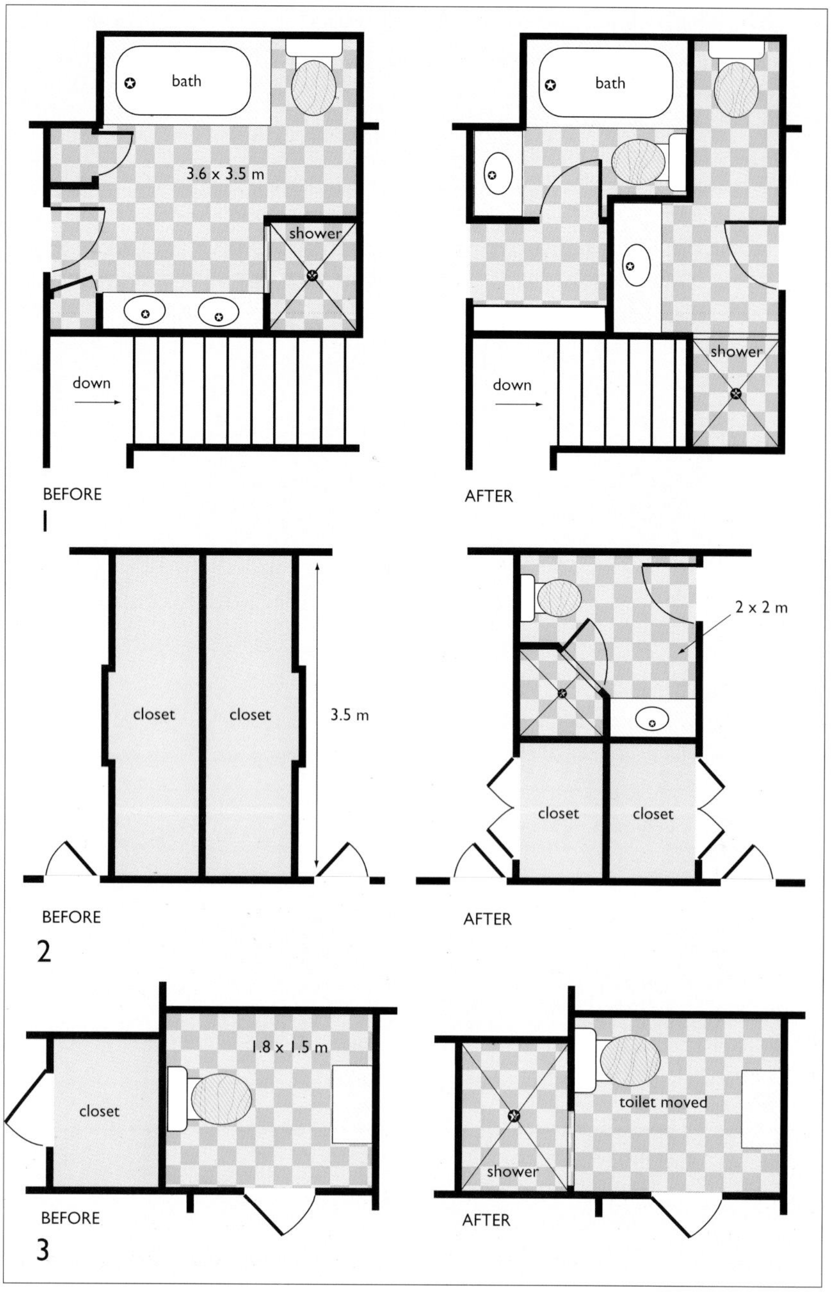

ABOVE: Plans for finding space for a full bathroom.

1 In this project, a large master bathroom was divided into two bathrooms. One opens onto the master bedroom, the other onto a second bedroom.

2 Two back-to-back cupboards yield enough space for a modest bathroom with shower and two reduced-sized cupboards.

3 This powder room was transformed into a full bathroom simply by relocating the toilet and adding a shower in what used to be cupboard space.

two-storey houses, it's most economical to stack the bathrooms directly on top of each other.

Put ease of access first when locating a new bathroom. Many homeowners fail to consider this and make the mistake of putting it in an out-of-the-way place. Size, too, is extremely important. Fitting all the necessities of a bathroom into too small a space is probably an unwise investment. If you don't have the necessary room, think about adding on.

Make it snappy

A remodelled bathroom is the perfect place for design flourishes. Because bathrooms are smaller than most other rooms, the quantities of finish materials required are relatively modest, so you may be able to splurge on extra architectural details and fancier materials without breaking your budget. Here are a few design tips to help make your new bathroom a comfortable, even inspiring, place to be:

- Gain drama and impact in a modest-sized bathroom with special tile designs.
- Make views within the room interesting. The least costly way is to use mirrors.
- Allow subdivided spaces to share light and air. Add an interior window or transparent glazing to walls of compartmentalised spaces.
- Don't skimp on windows. Light and ventilation are especially important in bathrooms.

Surface materials

A remodelled bathroom that looks good but doesn't work from a practical standpoint is bound to disappoint its owners. Assuming that you've designed the room's layout to meet your wishes and needs, the next most important factor is the finish materials — the surfaces, fixtures and flourishes that both set the style and determine how the room will hold up over time.

Your top priority should be choosing materials that will be appropriate to the way you and your family typically will use the bathroom. Beyond that, the best idea is to equip your bathroom with materials, fixtures and features that have become standard in new, comparably priced homes. If you're planning to live in the house for a while, however, make the materials as personal as you please, since resale will be less important than enjoyment value.

This section discusses bath/shower enclosures, floors and walls and materials that are available to cover these surfaces. Some materials have more than one application but may function better for one surface than for another.

Bath and shower surrounds

Any surface material for a bath or shower surround should be applied on top of water-resistant wall material. The most common type is wet area or water-resistant plasterboard. A more durable and popular product is fibre cement which is also water resistant. Fibre cement products may be more expensive than wet area plasterboard, but the added expense gives you a foundation you know can stand up to the moist environment of the bathroom. The surface material itself must be waterproof, not just water resistant.

Various manufacturers offer prefabricated surrounds made of fibreglass, acrylic, vinyl, plastic laminate or synthetic stone. Remodellers should avoid buying a one-piece surround (typically made of moulded fibreglass) unless they choose a unit that can be moved into the bathroom through available openings. Multi-piece surround kits which can be assembled inside the bathroom also are available.

If you decide you want to create your own bath or bath surround, you will have a choice of the following surface materials.

Solid-surface material

For durable, stylish, easy-to-care-for shower enclosures, solid-surface material is hard to beat. Though sometimes pricey, today's options

ABOVE: A basic white tiled bathroom with little ornamentation can be transformed into a warm room simply by adding colours. Here, bright-coloured wainscoting, striped wallpaper, and whimsical soap dishes and holders add sparkle without major changes to the bathroom's design.

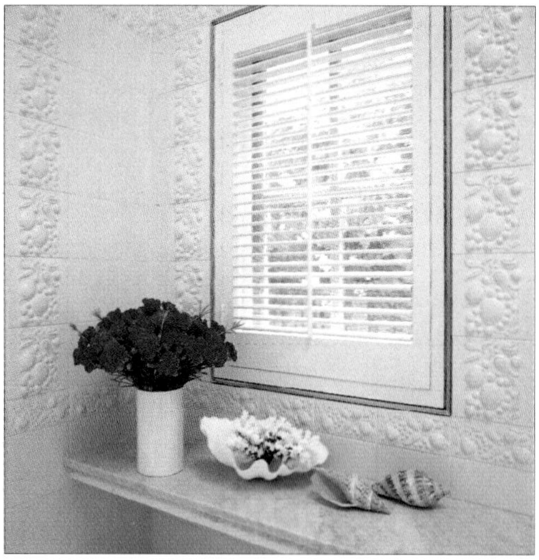

ABOVE: Ceramic tiles are a logical choice in bathrooms.

in this category have a lot to offer. Nothing beats this smooth acrylic surface for ease in cleaning, and the material lasts a lifetime.

For do-it-yourselfers, solid-surface bath and shower kits offer easy installation. These kits generally consist of pre-cut panels and curved corner mouldings. They are designed to go with standard fixtures; non-standard installations require professional help.

Ceramic tile

Waterproof, durable and easy to maintain, ceramic tile is a logical choice for bath and shower surrounds. There is one drawback: the grout can mildew, making it difficult to clean.

Small mosaic tiles come bonded to sheets of fibre mesh. These sheets go up faster than loose tiles, because you don't have to set each piece individually. Pre-grouted sheets of larger tiles have flexible synthetic grouting. You stick the sheets to the substrate surface first, then apply a thin bead of caulk around the edges. As with mosaic tile sheets, installing pre-grouted tile sheets is not as time consuming as laying loose tiles, nor does it require as much skill.

Fibreglass

Fibreglass is waterproof, durable and simple to clean. Many companies manufacture three- and five-piece shower/bath surround units in various sizes. Installing these units isn't difficult if your walls are straight and plumb and have been properly prepared. Most kits consist of two moulded end panels and one or more centre panels.

Floors

Before installing a new floor, check the condition of the subfloor (the material between the floor covering and the floor joists) and the supporting joists. Decayed subflooring, especially around the toilet and bath, is a common problem in older houses. Spot repairs may be adequate or you may need to replace the entire subfloor. This is an ambitious undertaking, so consult a professional if you're not sure how to proceed.

Unless you can inspect the underside of the subfloor from the basement, you'll have to pry up a bit of the existing floor covering. Prod around the base of fixtures and cabinets with an awl or a screwdriver in search of soft spots.

When choosing floor finishes, remember that your bathroom is the site of daily family traffic and the occasional bath overflow. Look for a durable material that is both beautiful and slip resistant.

Floor tile

Properly installed, tile is one of the most durable flooring materials. It's the number one choice for bathrooms because it's waterproof, easy to maintain and stain resistant. Ceramic tile is available in a wide range of sizes, shapes and colours and comes plain or decorated, glazed or matte. The grout that fills the cracks between tiles can be smooth or sandy, white or colour tinted. You can use the grout lines as a design element by choosing a coloured grout that contrasts with the tile. Once the grout has set, you must coat it with a latex sealer to repel moisture.

As a bathroom floor covering, however, tile has some drawbacks: it's hard and cool underfoot, and without a textured surface it can be slippery when wet.

Laying a tile floor can be a good do-it-yourself project, although it requires patience and care. All tile must be installed on a level, clean, unmarred subfloor. Most tile retailers carry the necessary installation supplies and offer instructions for do-it-yourselfers. Always use tiles specifically designed for a floor installation. Tiles manufactured for walls or bench tops are not designed to be used as floor tiles.

Warm floors

Ceramic tile, vinyl and hardwood floors are popular flooring choices for the bathroom, but they can be bone chilling in winter. That problem is easily solved with radiant heat panels installed in the floor joists. These operate only when you want them to and can be limited to defined areas, such as in front of the vanity or beside the bath. Look for radiant heat panels in retail building centres and through ceramic tile installers.

Resilient flooring

This category includes various vinyl and rubber flooring, in sheet and tile form. Resilient flooring is soft underfoot, yet stands up to heavy traffic and resists water penetration. It's available in an array of colours, patterns and textures. At the bottom end of the price range, vinyl is the least expensive flooring option. High-end vinyl products are comparable in cost to a good carpet or softwood floor.

Vinyl composition tile (combining vinyl resins with filler) costs the least. Rotovinyl (a printed pattern covered by a clear topcoat) costs a bit more. Top-of-the-line inlaid vinyl (vinyl granules fused together in a solid pattern that goes through to the backing) is the most durable.

Solid rubber tile is another option. Because rubber tile is used mainly in industrial and commercial settings, you may need to work through an interior designer or contractor to get it. Installation is tricky so hire professionals.

Resilient flooring can be installed over most other materials as long as the floor surface is smooth, clean and solid.

Marble

The costliest of surfacing materials, marble provides a smooth, classic covering for floors. It comes in colours ranging from neutral grey to pastel rose and can have either a polished or satin finish. Although marble is durable, it can be slippery when wet, so you should think twice before using it in or around showers and baths.

You can purchase marble in large, thick slabs or in smaller tiles. Slab marble is difficult to install, and its weight may require reinforcing the structure beneath. Check with a professional before choosing marble. Marble tiles are 10 or 12 mm thick, 300 mm sq, and less costly than the larger slabs. The price of marble varies greatly and, because marble is so heavy, is usually dependent on how far it must be shipped.

BELOW: Marble feels luxurious and is extremely durable, but it can be slippery when wet so you should ensure there are non-slip floor mats in place if you use it around the shower or bath.

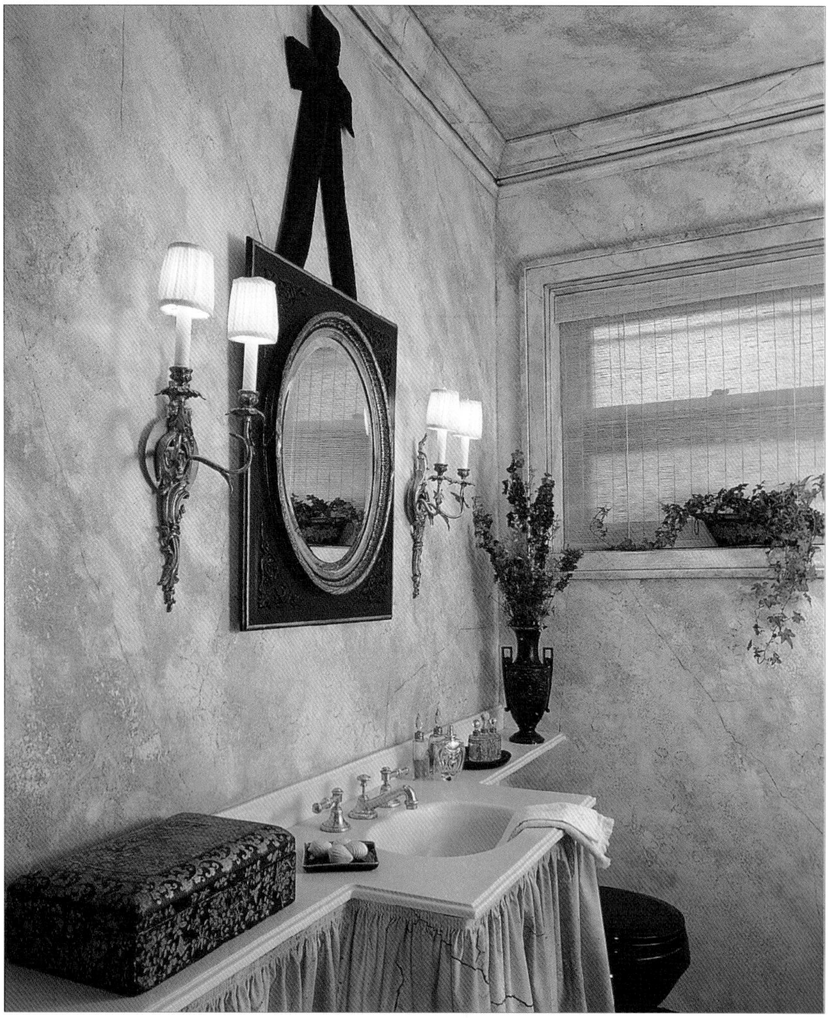

ABOVE: The faux marble finish in warm, earthy, ochre shades teams beautifully with the black and gold to achieve an elegance and style with a minimum of expense.

ABOVE LEFT: As long as you choose moisture-resistant paper, wallpaper can be used effectively in the bathroom as shown here, but on the panelling below dado height paint is a more practical choice.

Carpet

While it's comfortable underfoot, carpet has several drawbacks for use in the bathroom. Stains from cleaning products and make-up can be hard to remove, and poor ventilation in the room can cause moisture to collect and mildew to grow. As a rule, carpets are more practical in dressing and grooming areas of the bathroom than in wet areas.

If you do choose carpeting, look for types that resist mildew, don't retain odours and are less prone to water absorption and staining.

Wood

Wood floors are common in bathrooms, even though the potential for moisture damage is high. If your heart is set on a wood floor, be sure it's well coated with a urethane finish to protect against moisture penetration. You might consider using one of the newer wood look-alike products made of plastic laminate to have the look of wood but the water resistance of a laminate floor. Avoid wood planks that have bevelled edges as these form water-collecting grooves on the floor.

Walls

The quickest way to transform a bathroom is to change the look of its walls. Whether you choose paint, wallpaper, panelling or tiles, remember that a bathroom wall covering must stand up to heat, moisture and frequent cleaning. Mixing and matching materials for their strengths in different areas works well, especially if the bathroom is divided into compartments.

Paint

Paint is the least expensive covering for walls and ceilings, and it's the most easily changed for cosmetic make-overs. Besides choosing a colour, you'll also need to settle on a finish type, from flat to high gloss. Gloss and semi-gloss finishes work best in bathrooms because they repel water and clean easily. Glossier paints exaggerate all the lumps and bumps on a wall, however, so they must be applied to a flat, smooth surface.

Bathroom surface materials

Floor, wall and wet area coverings must be moisture tolerant or they won't stand up well in a bathroom. Look for durable materials that won't trap moisture or mildew and that can be cleaned easily. With flooring, avoid materials that become slippery when wet. Keep an eye on costs: finish materials demand a major portion of the budget of a bathroom remodelling project.

Type	Life	Maintenance	Comment
Flooring			
Hardwood	Indefinite	Moderate	Not highly recommended
Vinyl	20+ years	Easy	Yes, recommended
Laminate	10+ years	Easy to moderate	Yes, but avoid laminates with wood-based cores
Carpet	11 years	High	Not recommended
Marble/Granite	Indefinite	Easy	Yes
Tile (high-grade installation)	Indefinite	Easy	Highly recommended
Wall covering			
Paint	5–10 years	Low	Mould resistant additive
Wallpaper	7 years	Low	Moisture resistant
Ceramic tile	Indefinite	Relatively low	Highly recommended
Mirrors	Long life	High	Yes, highly recommended
Solid-surface material	Indefinite	Easy	Highly recommended
Wet areas			
Ceramic tile	10–15 years	Moderate	Yes
Plastic laminate wall panel	10–15 years	Easy	Yes
Marble, granite	20+ years	Easy to moderate	Yes
Solid surface material	Indefinite	Easy	Highly recommended
Glass	20+ years	Easy	Safety glass essential

Whichever paint you use, be sure to follow the manufacturer's instructions for preparation and application. Most surfaces must be primed first to ensure proper paint adhesion.

Wall coverings

All bathroom wall coverings should resist moisture and hold up to frequent scrubbing. Ordinary wallpaper is not the answer. Vinyl coverings (particularly vinyl that is laminated to fabric) weather bathroom conditions much better. Products labelled 'scrubbable' will tolerate more abrasion than 'washable' ones. Most wall coverings can be applied to a solid, clean surface.

Wood

Wood adds a natural warmth that complements many interior design schemes. As a wall-surfacing material it comes in the form of pre-milled, solid wood wainscoting, tongue-and-groove beadboard, veneered plywood or melamine-surfaced hardboard. Hardboard panels coated with melamine (a thin layer of white plastic) are well suited for bathrooms because melamine is water resistant and easy to clean.

> **Tip**
>
> • Never allow tile adhesive or grout to dry on the face of the tiles. Be sure to wipe it off as you go with a just-damp sponge — otherwise it will set permanently.

BELOW: Regluing loose tiles.

1 Remove taps and spout.

2 Take out loose tiles.

3 Sand off old adhesive.

4 Apply new adhesive.

5 Fix in place; grout.

6 Polish finished job.

Ceramic tile

Ceramic tile is attractive and durable. It won't fade or stain, it cleans easily and it is not merely water resistant but, when installed correctly, fully waterproof. It can be expensive, but its advantages make it well worth considering for at least some areas in a bathroom.

As with tiles intended for floor use, wall tiles come glazed and unglazed, plain and patterned, and in an unlimited palette of colours. Be sure that you use only wall tiles for walls and floor tiles for floors, since the two are made and finished differently.

Glass block

Glass block is popular in bathrooms because of its sleek modern look and its ability to transmit light while preserving privacy. It can be used to create both walls and windows. Glass block is very expensive when compared with other materials you might use. The cost can vary depending on the complexity of the job, labour costs and the block you select. It is a difficult job for do-it-yourselfers to do well, even with mortarless, 'do-it-yourself' systems. For professional results, it's best to call in a mason.

Making bathroom repairs and alterations

Regluing loose tiles

Regluing a few loose tiles in your bathroom (or kitchen) is not very difficult. The materials are readily available from the tile supplier or hardware store, and you can hire what tools you need.

First establish the reason for the looseness. One possible cause is that the previous subsurface

1

2

3

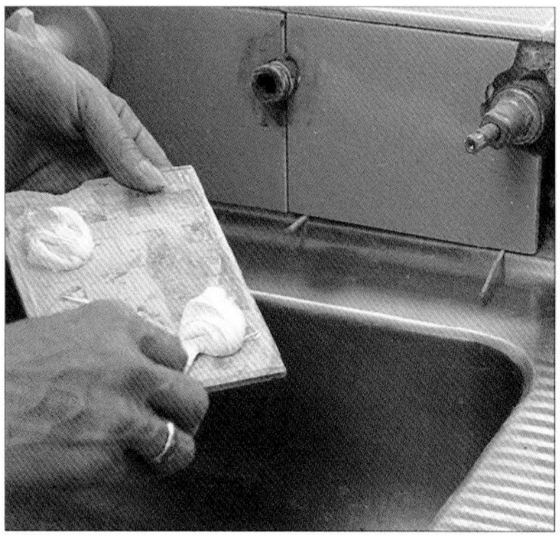

4

5

6

preparation was faulty. The subsurface must be DCFAF: dry, clean, flat and firm. In some cases it should also be sealed; for example, bare gypsum plaster must be thoroughly sealed with a multi-purpose primer or polyurethane paint to ensure good adhesion.

A leak in the plumbing can also cause loss of adhesion. Evidence of this will be a wet or damp subsurface. Unfortunately, only a plumber can rectify this problem.

Another explanation could be that the wrong adhesive was used or insufficiently applied. Regluing and regrouting should fix this.

A final possibility is that the grouting could be deteriorating and letting moisture in behind the tiles. If this is the situation, once you have reglued the offending tiles, rake out and regrout all the joints for complete peace of mind.

1 If you have to remove tap covers or spouts, you'll need a pair of multi-grips or a wrench. Wrap a tea-towel or cloth around the fittings to avoid damage.

2 Now remove the loose tiles, taking care that you don't drop them. An exact replacement could be difficult to find.

3 As always, preparation is all important. Carefully scrape or sand the old adhesive off the back of the tiles and the subsurface. Clean both surfaces with a strong detergent, which must be rinsed off.

If the subsurface is painted, scrape off any flaking paint. Avoid using a chemical stripper as this may leave a residue which could weaken the adhesion. If the surface is uneven, plaster it smooth, using a suitable filler. Roughen the surface with sandpaper for a better bond.

Once preparation is complete, allow patch to dry thoroughly.

4 Spread adhesive evenly over the area to be tiled. In hard-to-reach areas, as shown here, apply in thick dobs to corners of the tile. Press each tile into position, working from the bottom up. Push spacers (see our matchsticks in the picture) into place as you go to maintain an even joint. Make sure that the replaced tiles line up with the existing ones. Wipe off excess adhesive.

5 When the adhesive has dried, mix the flexible grout to a paste then press it firmly into the joints with a putty knife. Sponge off excess immediately.

6 When it is dry, polish the area with a dry cloth to achieve a truly professional finish.

Fixing a fitting to a tile wall

Fixing fittings to tiled walls is easy if you know how to do it properly. Remember, lasting bathroom fittings should always be screwed in place, not nailed.

Regrouting tiles

While your tiles may well last a lifetime, the grout between them will need to be replaced every

BELOW: Fixing a fitting to a tile wall.

1 Place the fitting in position and check for level. Stick some masking tape to the wall where the mounting screws will be located and mark the position of the holes with a felt pen on the masking tape.

2 Mark vertical and horizontal lines through the centre of the proposed holes. Use a 3 mm masonry drill bit to bore a pilot hole 25 mm deep and take care that the drill doesn't move off centre while you are doing this.

3 Enlarge the pilot hole using a drill bit that will fit the plastic plugs you are using. Tap the plugs in with a hammer and cut any waste off with a Stanley knife.

4 Position your fitting so the two sets of holes line up and screw the fitting firmly in place on the wall.

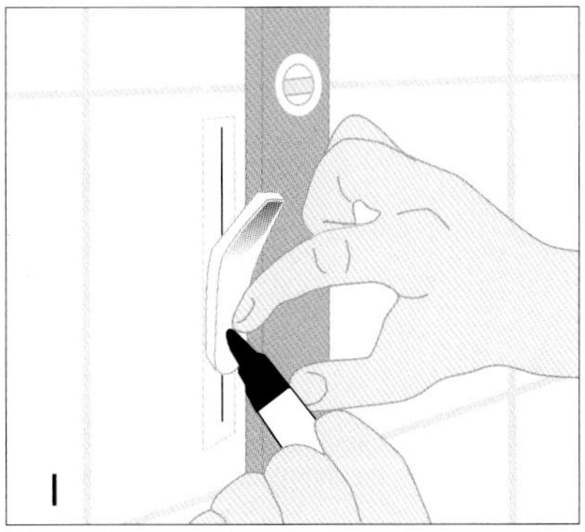
1

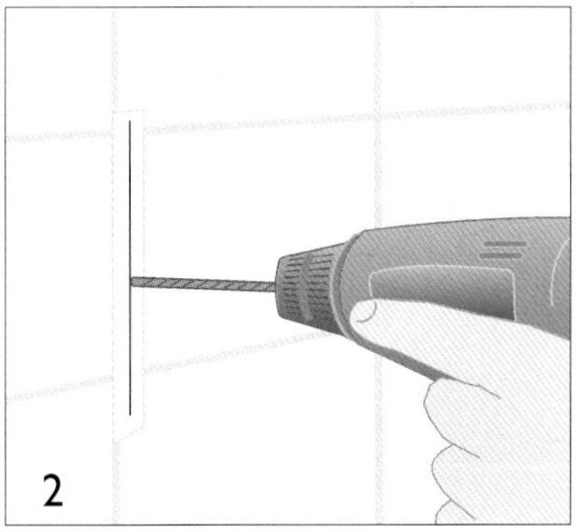
2

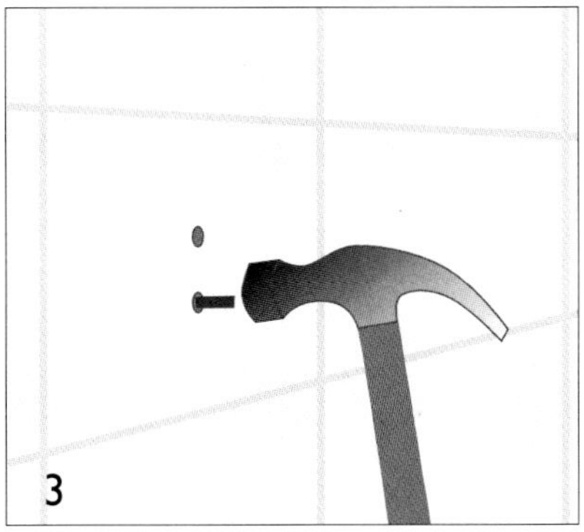
3

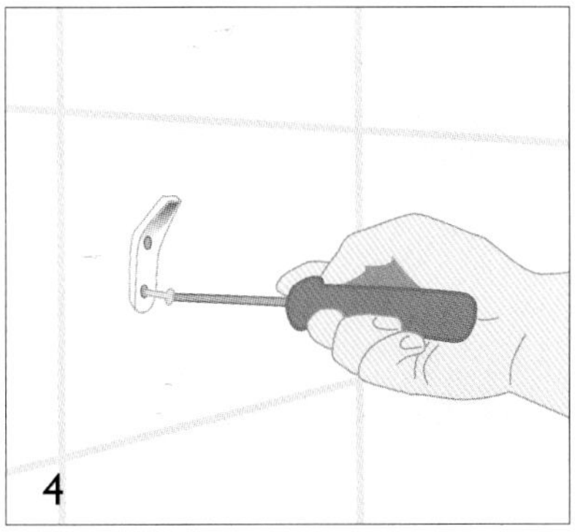
4

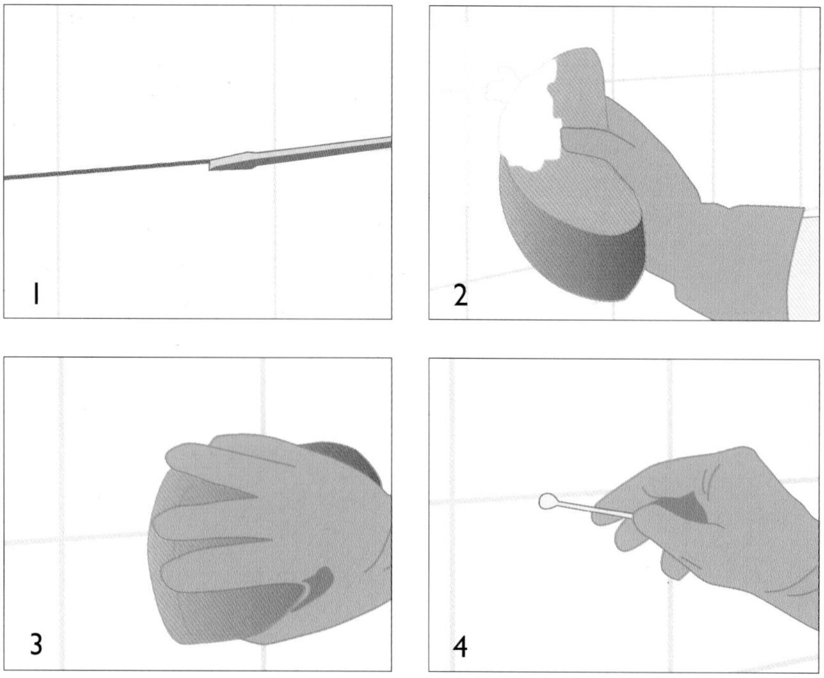

ABOVE: Regrouting tiles.

1 Scrape out the old grout using a large screwdriver or a grout rake. Be gentle, making sure not to damage the edge of the tile. Brush out loose bits of grout with an old toothbrush.

2 Mix the grout as recommended on the packet and apply it with a moist sponge. Work the grout firmly into the joins and wipe any excess from the face of the tiles.

3 Wash the sponge repeatedly with clean water and wipe the tiles clean while the grout is still wet. Do not have the sponge too wet or you will remove the grout from the joins.

4 While the grout is still wet, draw a small dowel, pencil or knitting needle over the join to give a smooth surface to the grout. This will give your grouting a professional finish.

few years because it can become discoloured with grease and dirt.

Sometimes gaps can occur because standard grout has been used instead of waterproof grout. Follow the steps pictured here for a professional result.

Replacing a showerhead

Changing a shower fitting is so easy you'll wonder why you never did it before. You need to be very careful when tackling anything to do with the water supply. It is illegal to interfere with existing plumbing by cutting into, replacing or extending pipes. This is not only because you might flood your home, or your neighbours' homes. You could also create a potential health hazard by unwittingly contaminating the water supply.

If alterations to pipework need to be done, you should call in a plumber. And if you are in doubt about local regulations, check with your water supply authority.

Shower arms and roses come in a variety of shapes and finishes; many have specific uses. For example, by varying the number and diameter of holes in the showerhead some actually save water. This is useful if water and heating bills are excessive or if water pressure is low.

Another innovation is the 'bubbling' showerhead. This mixes air with the water to provide the illusion of a fast-running shower. There are other showerheads that are pulsating. These mete out the water in spurts of varying intensity and volume and are claimed by the manufacturers to be therapeutic as well as stimulating.

If your existing showerhead is too low, it's easy to buy one with an adjustable arm.

To see the best range, go to a plumbing supply outlet or builders' hardware store. Take along a diameter measurement of your current shower fitting connection to make sure the one you choose will screw onto your wall outlet. Most do.

If you should have problems fixing onto your outlet (you might, for instance, find you don't have a proper male/female connection), you may need to buy a hexagonal nipple to make the join. There are all manner of adaptor fittings sold by your plumbing supply store.

1 To remove the existing shower fitting, place the adjustable spanner on the collar at the base of the fitting and unscrew (in an anti-clockwise direction).

2 Wrap a layer of thread tape around the thread on your new shower fitting or at the wall outlet. This helps ensure a watertight connection.

3 Screw the new shower fitting to the wall outlet, remembering to place the backplate in position as you do so. Be very careful not to cross thread the connection. This occurs when the fitting is put on crookedly and can damage the thread, which will then need replacing — a costly job if it's at the wall outlet!

4 Adjust the fitting for height if necessary, then turn on the tap to check performance.

1

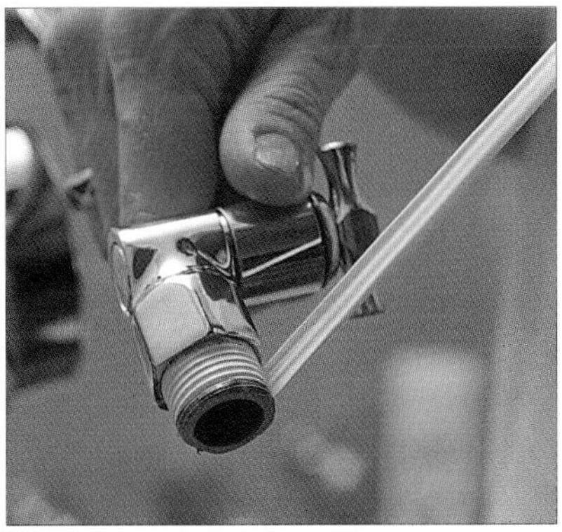

2

3

4

LEFT: Replacing a showerhead.

1 Unscrew old fitting.

2 Wrap thread with tape.

3 Screw on new fitting.

4 The finished job.

BELOW: It may seem obvious, but the use of mirrors will make a small space appear larger. This laundry leads off a small bathroom. The white tiles bordered with terracotta and the clever placement of the mirror give both rooms a light, spacious feel.

Opening clogged drains

Impossibly clogged drains call for a professional with the electrical equipment only experts can afford. Fortunately, most drain problems don't fall into this category, and often you can handle them yourself.

First you must realise that your home has three types of drains: fixture drains, such as those at basins and toilets; main drains, which lead from the fixture drains to the main pipe that carries waste from your home; and sewer drains, which run underground to the community sewer or septic tank.

Your problem can originate in any of the three, so your most immediate task is to locate the blockage. Almost always it will be in or next to a pipe connection that makes a turn, or in a trap.

To pinpoint the difficulty, open a tap at each basin, bath or other fixture, but don't flush a toilet—it could overflow. If only one fixture is clogged, the problem is right there or nearby. If two or more fixtures won't clear, something has lodged itself in a main drain. And if no drains work, the blockage is further down the line, either near the point where the main drain or drains connect to the sewer drain, or in the sewer drain itself.

If you bear in mind that waste water always flows downwards through pipes of increasingly larger diameter, you can find an obstruction you'll almost certainly never see.

Basins

Hair, bits of soap and other debris can gum up a stopper. To remove some types of stoppers you just turn and lift.

A plunger with a moulded suction cup is ideal for toilets or rounded lavatory bowls. Flat plungers work best on flat surfaces.

If a basin has an overflow outlet, plug it with a cloth and make sure the plunger seals tightly over the drain outlet.

If a plunger won't work, try an auger snake. Thread it down and through the trap, or open the cleanout and work from there.

If augering doesn't do the job, remove the trap and flush it. This also lets you get the snake into the main drain.

Baths

Remove and clean the stopper/strainer. Try the plunger treatment, blocking the overflow drain with a wet piece of cloth.

If the plunger doesn't work for you, remove the bath's pop-up or trip-lever assembly and run a snake through the overflow pipe.

Some baths have a drum-type trap — accessible by removing a plug in or under the floor.

Toilets

Use a plumber's friend over the hole in the bottom. Work the plunger hard and vigorously, and don't give up too soon.

If the toilet doesn't have water in the bowl, fill it to the rim. Spread petroleum jelly on the plunger's rim; this aids suction.

If a plunger doesn't work, use an auger. As you crank, it wends its way through passages.

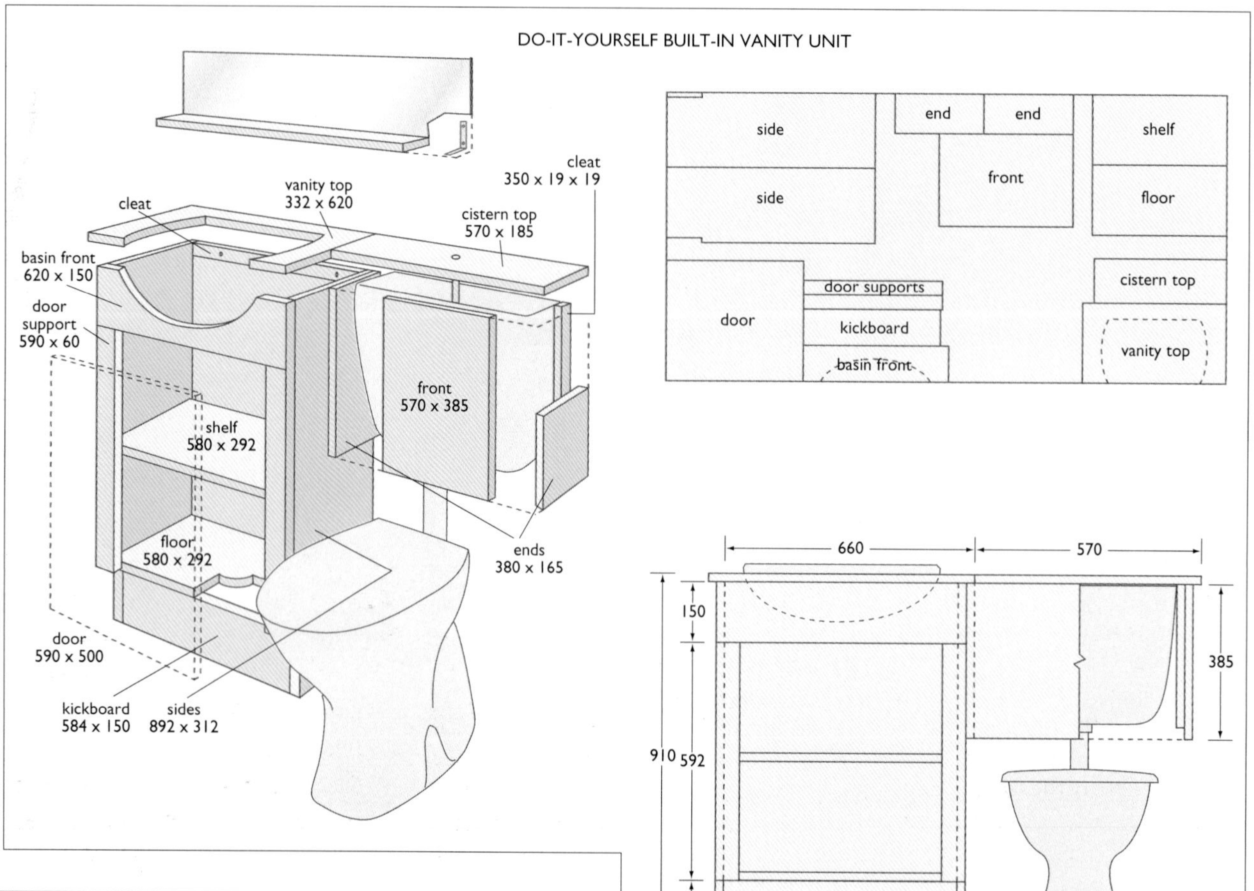

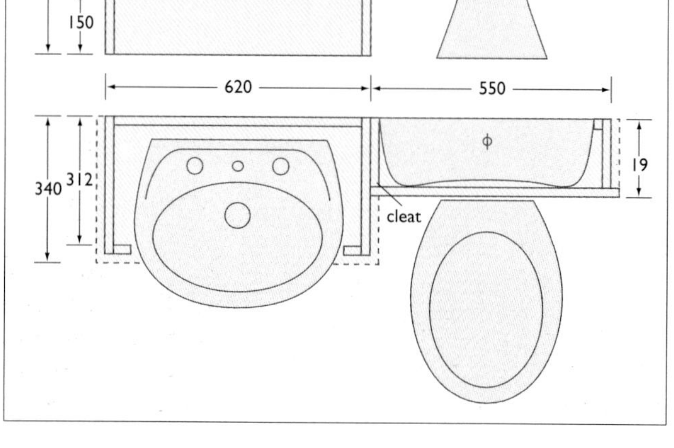

1

2

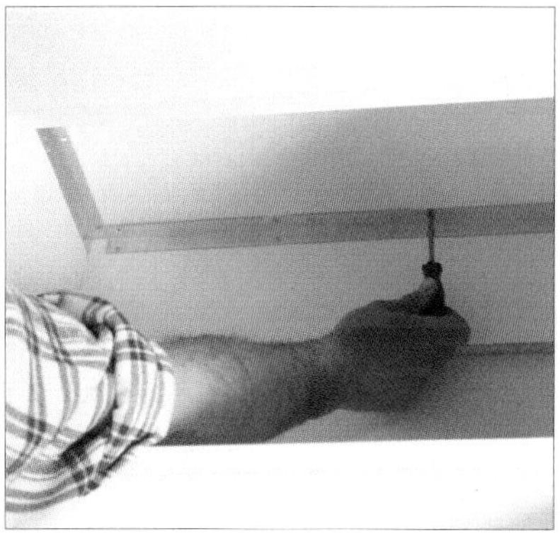

3

4

5

6

Do-it-yourself — Building a built-in

Building in vanity units and toilet cisterns creates a streamlined appearance as well as giving more space, especially in a small bathroom such as the one pictured here.

We boxed in the cistern which was adjacent to the vanity unit. By closing the gap between them we tied the two elements together to help cut down on visual confusion in the confined space.

You will be able to get all the components to make the built-in out of one 2400 x 1200 mm sheet of 19-mm-thick white board (see cutting diagram). Use any scrap material for shelves above the cistern. If you have a board supply factory nearby, you can get someone there to cut and edge all the components using our cutting diagrams as a guide. Include end components where the unit does not abut a wall and the sides will be on show.

LEFT: Building a built-in.
FAR LEFT: The built-in vanity unit and toilet cistern creates a streamlined appearance as well as providing a storage shelf.

Efficient medicine cabinet

Storing potions and prescriptions calls for a special type of shelving: it needs to be small in scale and shallow. By making this cabinet so that it opens halfway through its depth, its compartment-type shelves are not too deep and they

ABOVE: Building a built-in.

1 Line up the two basin cupboard sides and mark the position of the shelf, kick plate and cupboard floor, as well as that of the basin front.
2 Drill and screw through the sides into the edges of the horizontals.
3 Use aluminium corner strips to strengthen the internal corners, especially for the bench top itself.
4 Attach the facing components using 25-mm-long 9-mm-thick dowel pegs.
5 Hinge the door using 35 mm concealed hinges or similar.
6 Screw a 3 mm plywood back to all the rear edges of the unit. Conceal any screw heads with snap caps where necessary.

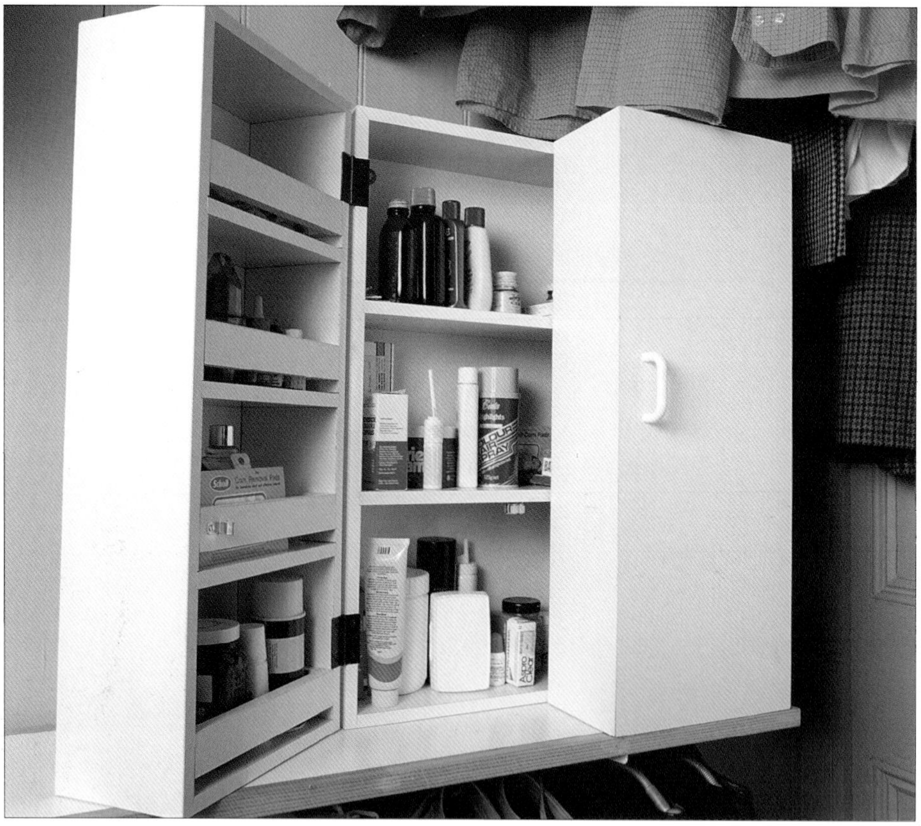

You will need these components, cut from 13 mm plastic-laminated particle board:		
Item	**Size (in mm)**	**No.**
Cabinet sides	625 x 135	2
Cabinet top/ bottom	474 x 135	1 each
Cabinet shelves	474 x 122	2
Cabinet back	599 x 474	1
Door sides	625 x 135	4
Door top/ bottom	222 x 135	2 each
Door fronts	599 x 222	2
Door shelves	222 x 122	6
Door shelf fronts	222 x 30	8
Other: iron-on plastic-laminate strip edging; 1 sheet or off-cuts plastic laminate; wood glue; 30 mm panel pins; four 50 mm butt hinges; two spring door catches; door handles.		

therefore allow a clear view and easy access to contents.

For easy cleaning, all components were made from 13 mm plastic-laminated particle board. Cut out all the components from the smallest pre-laminated shelves available as these already have laminated edges. Cut out all the components with the finished edges to the front of the shelves and the corresponding edges of the top, bottom and sides. Finish all other visible raw edges with iron-on laminate. To finish the outside surfaces of the doors and obscure the sawn edges of the sides, top and bottom, score and cut the entire surface from the sheet of plastic laminate and use contact adhesive to fix the sheets in place.

Cut out all the components listed at left and indicated in the diagram and assemble the three boxes with wood glue and 30 mm panel pins. Although the photograph shows mitre joints, it is easier to use butt joints — dimensions given are for butt joints. Carefully punch and fill the nail holes and retouch with enamel paint to match. Fit the 50 mm butt hinges and spring door catches, and drill through the doors to fit the door handles.

Leave the cabinet doors plain as pictured, use them as a source of decoration with an applied 'frame' of timber or plastic beading, or face them with a mirror.

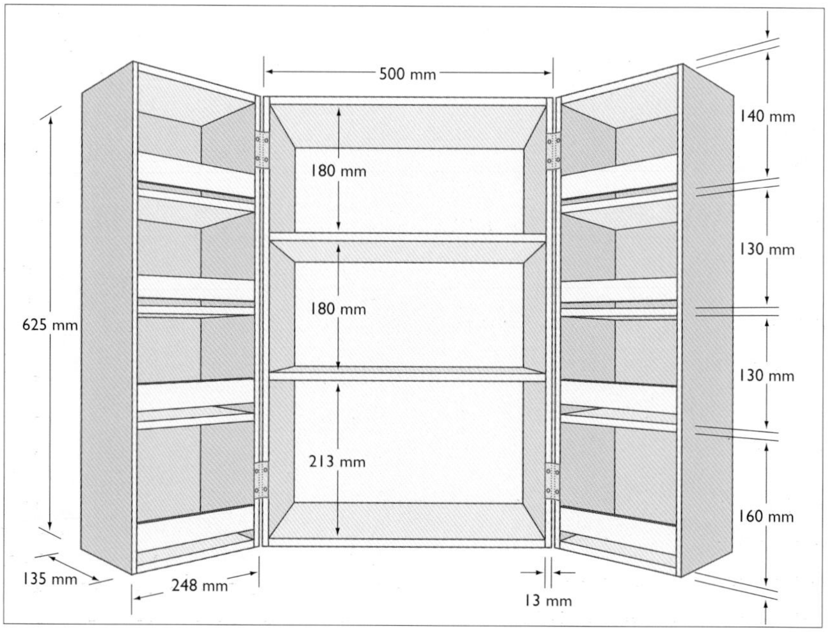

Build a bathroom

Make a set of timber accessories to create a bathroom with stylish appeal that complements a range of decors and reflects your individual sense of creative flair.

Vanity unit

Cut the components as you proceed, not beforehand.

Begin by gluing 150 x 19 mm planks together to make the side, door and top panels. Use sash cramps and epoxy resin glue for the job. Make the two side panels in one 1700 mm length, the two door panels in one 1300 mm length and the top 1100 mm long.

Cut them to the lengths listed at right. Glue and screw all battens in place as indicated on the diagram (side bottom batten 75 mm up). Draw the shape of the cut-out required for your basin on the underside of the top. Glue and screw the top battens (not shown on diagram) to the underside to correspond with its sides. These will reinforce the edges of the cut-out. Bevel the ends of the outward-facing door battens.

Cut 20 x 12 x 150 mm rebates down from the top of the inside rear corners of the back uprights to take the back rail. Glue and screw through the four uprights to the ends of the side panel battens.

Make the cupboard bottom, cutting out 50 x 20 mm notches to take the uprights. Turn the sides upside down and sit and screw the bottom in place underneath the lower side battens.

ABOVE LEFT: The finished medicine cabinet.

LEFT: Medicine cabinet components and dimensions.

ABOVE RIGHT: The timber vanity unit combines with the other components to offset this bathroom's painted surfaces.

You will need for the vanity unit:

Component	Material	Length in mm	No.
Side board	150 x 19 pine	825	6
Door board	150 x 19 pine	640	6
Top board	150 x 19 pine	1100	4
Side batten	50 x 19 pine	450	6
Door batten	50 x 19 pine	450	4
Top batten	50 x 19 pine	500	2
Corner upright	50 x 40 pine	825	4
Front upright	50 x 19 pine	745	1
Door stop	100 x 19 pine	650	1
Front rail	100 x 19 pine	950	1
Back rail	150 x 19 pine	950	1
Back rail	150 x 19 pine	570	2
Plinth side	150 x 19 pine	1070	1
Splashback	150 x 19 pine	1030	1
Splashside	75 x 19 pine	450	2
Bottom	12 mm plywood	990 x 550	1

Other: epoxy resin glue; wood glue; wood filler; clear satin polyurethane varnish; 30 and 50 mm countersunk screws; 30 mm jolt-head nails; two magnetic cabinet catches; two cabinet knobs; four 50 mm brass butt hinges; 4500 x 19 mm scotia moulding.

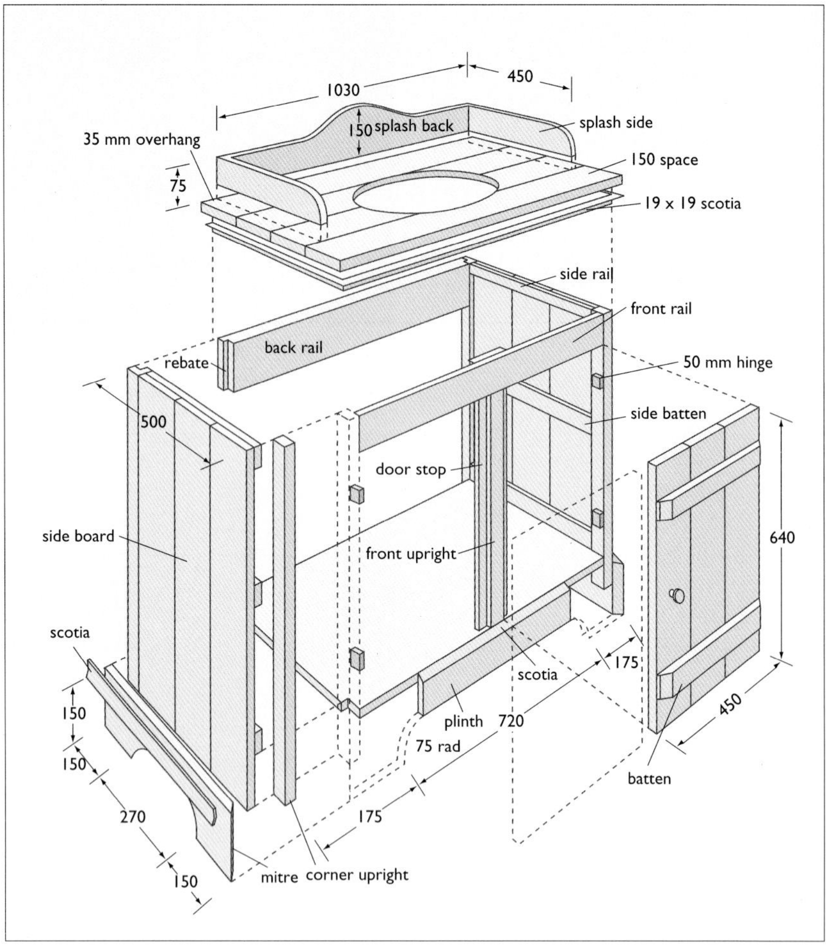

ABOVE: The right vanity unit can be one of the most elusive of household items, especially if you prefer the country look. One solution is to make it yourself. You can do this by following the step-by-step instructions here.

ABOVE RIGHT: The vanity unit components.

Cut 20 x 12 mm rebates into the ends of the back rail and then glue and skew nail the front and back rails in place.

Cut the curves to the plinth sides and front as indicated, using a jigsaw. Mitre the corners and glue and nail the plinth in place. Trim around the plinth's top with scotia moulding.

Glue and screw the doorstop and front upright together, flush at the bottom, and fit in place.

Similarly, cut the curves to the splashback and splashsides and mitre the corners before screwing in place from under the top.

Cut out the hole for the basin according to the dimensions and specifications given on your basin brochure.

Sand the bench-top edges to a rounded finish and fix the top in place by gluing and pinning the scotia to its undersurface and the top of the sides.

Hinge the doors in place and screw magnetic catches to the inside of the cupboard bottom. Drill and fix door knobs in place.

Punch, countersink, fill and sand before applying three coats of semi-gloss clean polyurethane.

Wall shelf

Cut out all the components as illustrated in the diagram. Use a jigsaw to cut the two shaped ends. Give the edges a rustic irregularity with a spoke shave or plane.

Drill and insert 30-mm-long countersunk screws in three places through the back into the rear edge of the shelf and twice through each of the sides into the shelf ends.

Drill four 16 mm peg holes 40 mm up from the bottom (see

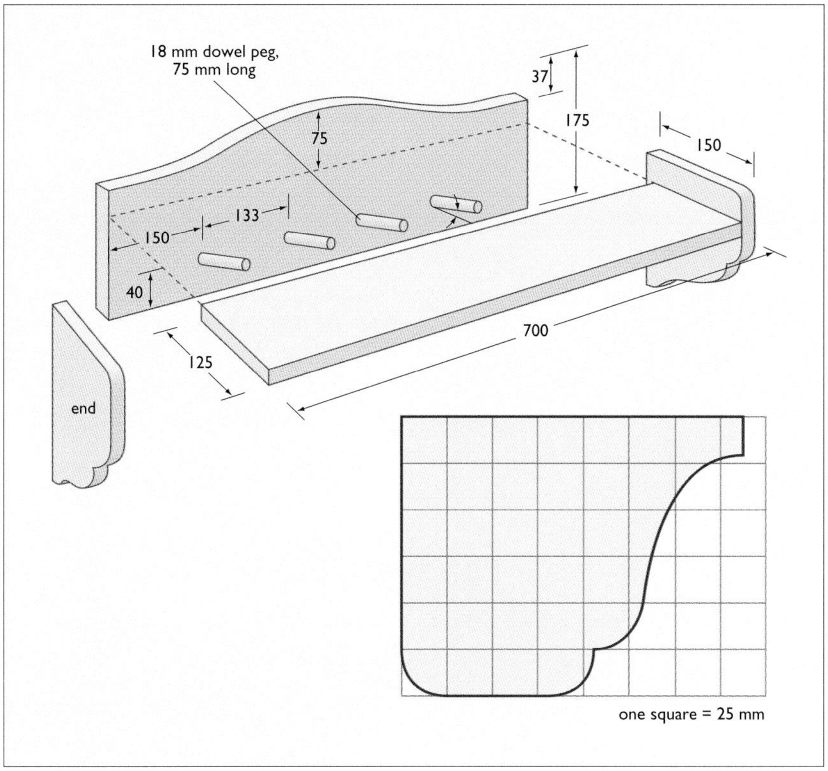

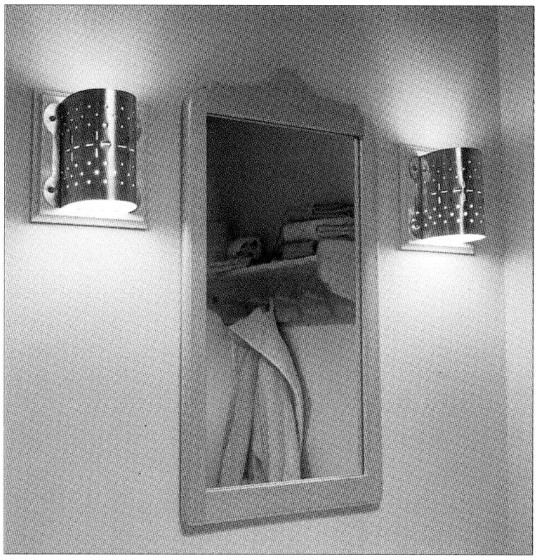

diagram for spacing). Allow the drill to rest against the bottom of the shelf as you proceed. This will give your pegs an even upwards tilt. Glue and insert pegs.

Sand and triple varnish before screwing to the wall through the upper back.

Light shades

Cut the 19-mm-thick block to the dimensions shown on our diagram and trim the edges either with a plane to make a simple chamfer or with a cove bit on your router to make a concave trim. If you prefer

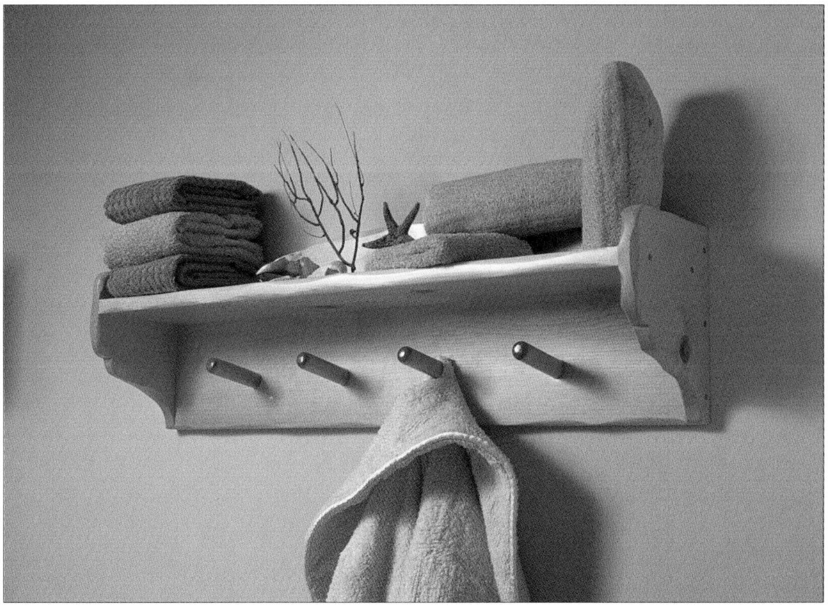

ABOVE LEFT: Details of the wall shelf.

ABOVE: A well-lit mirror is essential in the bathroom and a do-it-yourself one will save you money. With their perforated shades these wall brackets will give a perfectly diffused light to your vanity area. Make the fitting, screw it together and have it professionally wired in place.

LEFT: It's a handy occasional shelf anywhere in the house, but in the bathroom you'll find it ideal for hanging and folded towels. It's compact enough to position wherever you need it.

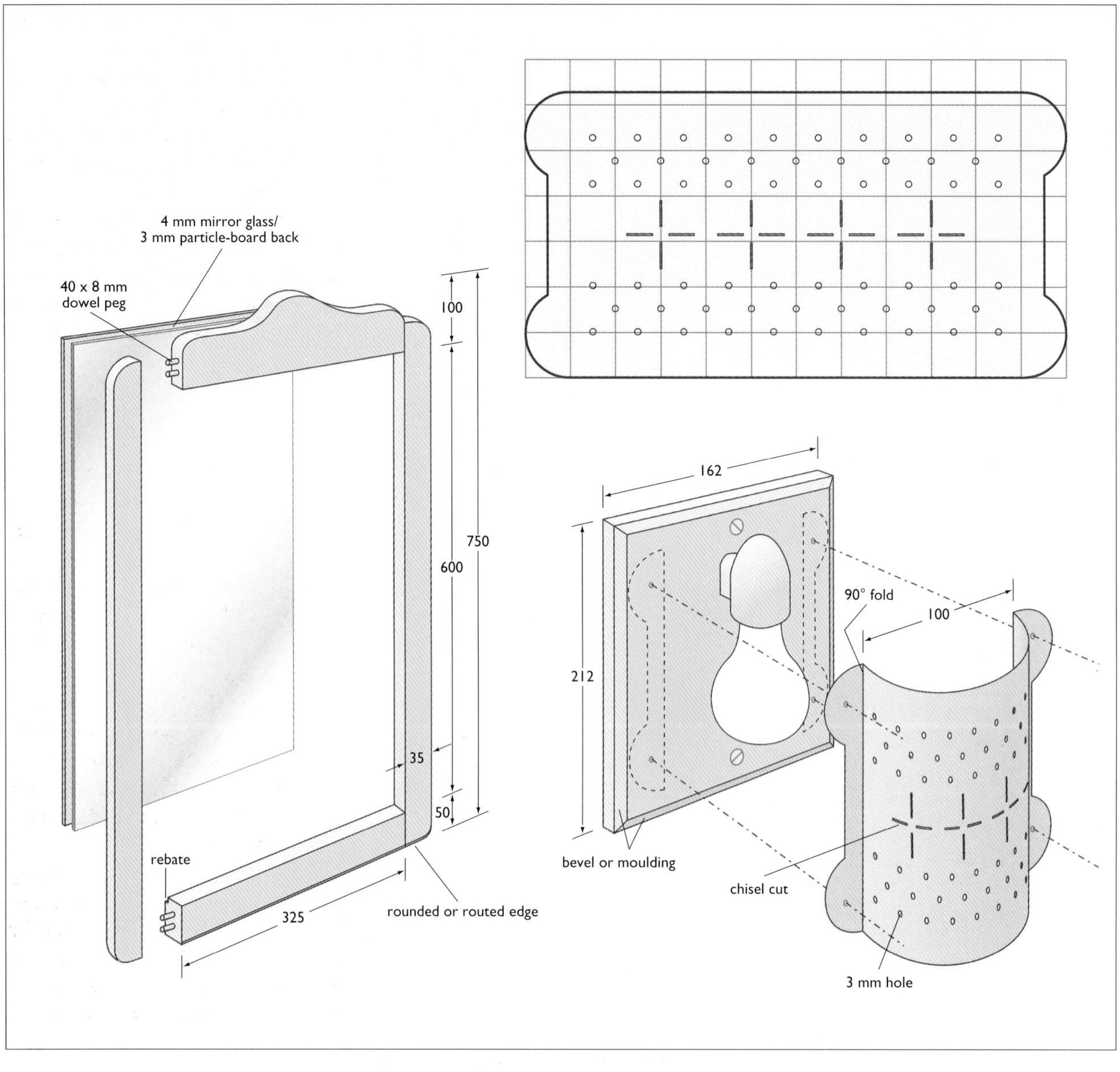

ABOVE: Mirror and light shades details.

you can trim the four edges with scotia moulding.

Make the shade using a 20 gauge aluminium sheet. Cut it according to our cutting diagram using tin snips and then file the edges. Use a nail punch to make the holes and a screwdriver for the slots. Use steel wool to give the shade a buffed patina and drill the four fixing holes. Bend the sheet over a round surface, such as a tin can, to make the 100 mm diameter and then fold the mounting flaps on the side of the shades over a hard edge to 90°.

Mirror

Begin by cutting two side 700 mm lengths of 35 x 19 mm pine or Tasmanian oak. For the top use 100 x 19 mm and for the bottom 50 x 19 mm. Cut these 325 mm long.

With a jigsaw, shape the top piece making it 50 mm high at the ends and the full 100 mm height at the centre. Similarly, round off all the corners.

Now cut a 10 mm square rebate into the rear inside edges of each of the four frame components to take the mirror glass and back. Make

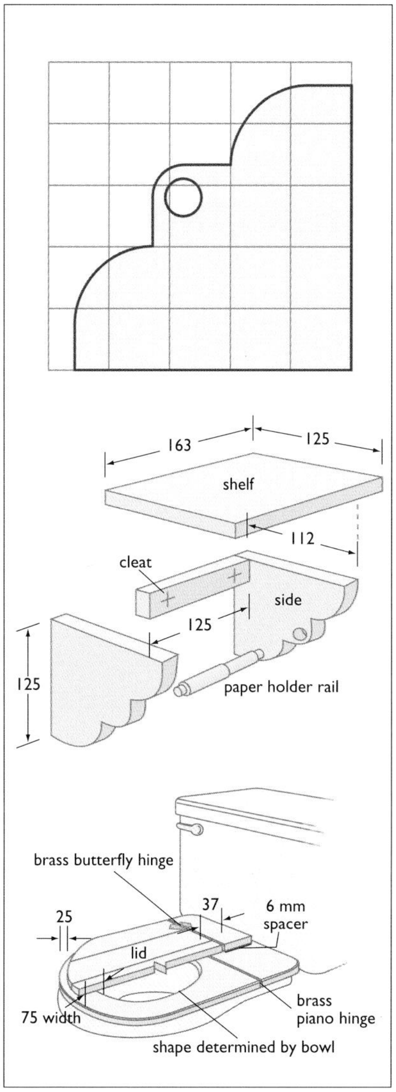

TOP: Give every bathroom accessory the country look. The shelf and sides of the paper holder have irregularly shaved edges to match the wall shelf.

ABOVE: A timber toilet seat completes the country look. It is not an easy thing to make. Details depend on the style of the toilet bowl.

ABOVE RIGHT: Paper holder and toilet seat details.

the corner joints by drilling two 40-mm-long 8 mm dowel pegs into each one. Now glue and assemble the frame.

You can simply round the front edges of the frame with an electric sander, but for a better trim, rout the edges with a 12 mm round-over bit.

Have mirror glass cut to size and fit 3-mm-thick plywood or particle board inside the back rebate. Use panel pins tapped into the inside edge of the frame to hold the back in place.

Paper holder

From a 450 mm piece of 150 x 19 mm timber, cut out the four components using our diagrams as a guide.

Drill 12-mm-deep holes (to take the paper-holder rail) in the position indicated in our side component cutting diagram. Assemble the holder by drilling and screwing through corners of the sides into the ends of the cleat.

Glue and nail the shelf to the top of the sides and cleat, checking the inside width against the length of the sprung rail (available from hardware stores). Fill, sand and varnish before positioning.

Toilet seat

To calculate the dimensions that are shown on our diagram, measure the bowl and add a 30 mm overhang to the front and sides. You will have to draw the seat and lid to the actual size on cardboard, observing the setbacks and suggested dimensions.

Glue and clamp four 100 x 19 mm planks together to achieve timber sheet sizes large enough for both the seat and lid. You can make the rear seat and lid components from a single length.

Mark out the components using your cardboard pattern and cut the curves with a jigsaw. Cut out the central void in the seat to suit the shape of your bowl. Reinforce the glued joints in the seat with a wriggle nail inserted into the end grain of the timber. Sand all edges to a rounded curve.

Both the seat and lid will need to rest on 20 mm diameter (approximately) rubber grommets screwed to their undersurface. To allow the rear sections to finish level with these, you will have to include timber spacers that are the same height as the grommets, glued and screwed to the undersurface of the rear sections.

Hinge the two pairs of components together (piano hinging for the seat). Glue and pin the packing to the underside of the rear components.

Drill and countersink coach bolts through the rear section of the seat to correspond with the fixing holes at the back of the bowl. Glue and nail the two sections together (the seat rear section will cover the coach bolt heads).

Sand, triple varnish and secure under the back of the bowl with wing nuts.

Pelmet

The timber pelmet adds the finishing touch to your new, country-style bathroom. All you will need to make this pelmet is a length of 200 x 19 mm timber which is the same width as your window; allow an additional 60 mm each side for overhang. Use your jigsaw to cut the curved shape, and then sand all the edges.

Drive a nail into the top of your window frame and insert a corresponding cup hook into the back of the pelmet as indicated in the diagram.

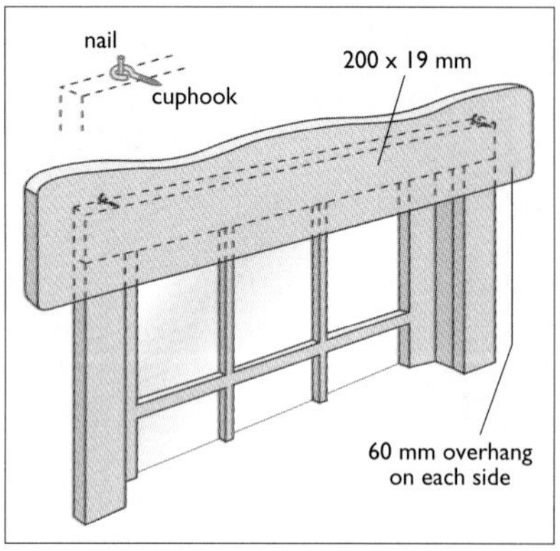

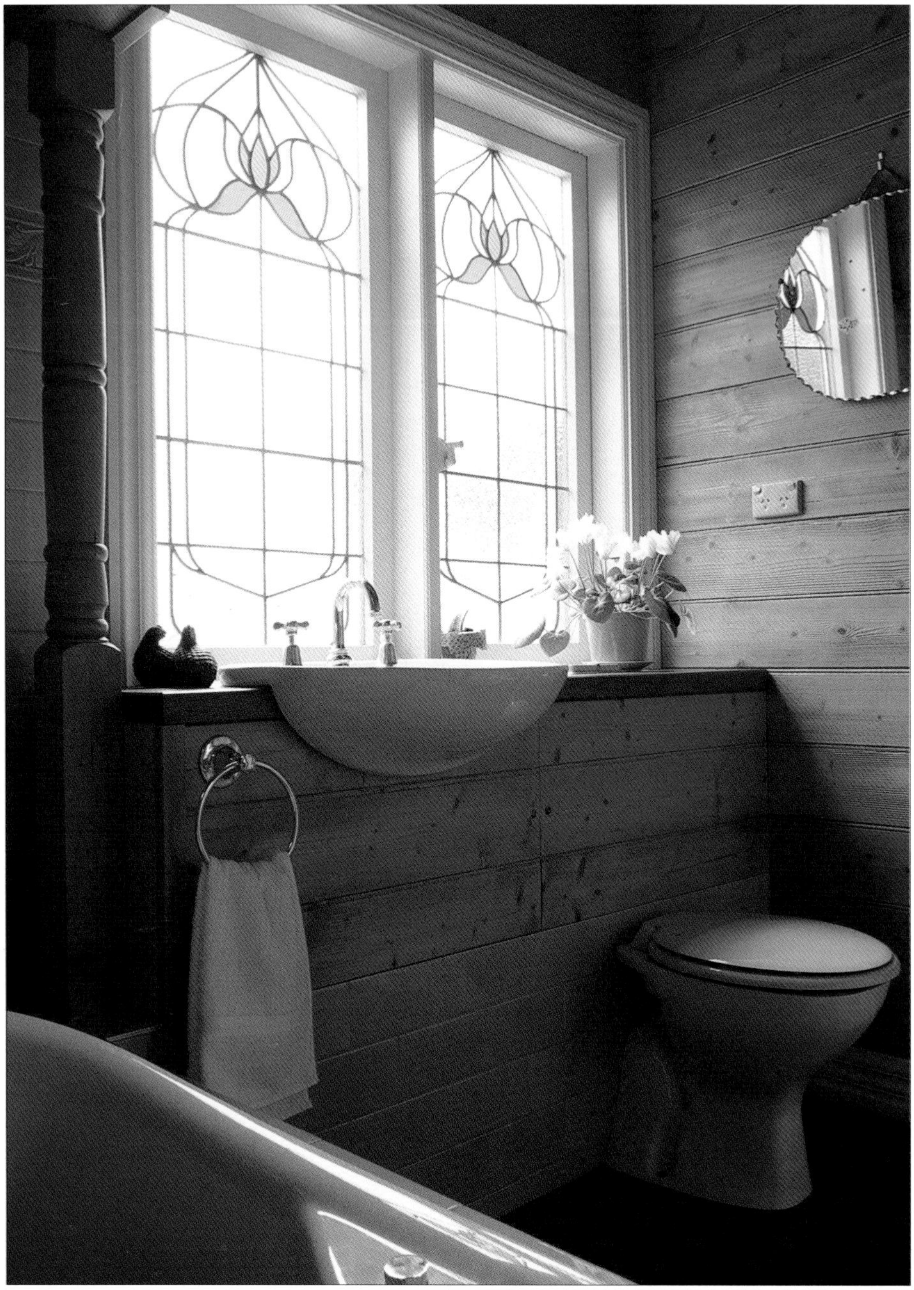

TOP: This pelmet will dress up any window.

ABOVE: Pelmet detail.

LEFT: The natural timber walls, old tiles and stained glass windows, although combined with modern fittings, give this bathroom a country look.

Laundries

More than any other room in the house, the laundry is a utilitarian space. Because it is purely functional, you have to take a practical approach with its design. Spatial efficiency, adequate storage and ease of maintenance are the main considerations. Regardless of the period or style of your house, the laundry aesthetic comes from slick, easily cleaned surfaces, tidiness and the comforting feeling that the home is being kept in order by this household nerve centre. It's pretty logical really. To do the work, it has to work.

Planning

Laundry essentials

Even if you can't afford the space for a big laundry, you should plan to include as many of the following items as you can (some of them you just can't do without):

- Washing machine. Compare the benefits of front loaders and top loaders in terms of price, space, energy usage, water efficiency and capacity, according to what you need.
- Tumble dryer and/or airing cabinet. Also, if you have a backyard, a clothes line outside.
- A tub for scrubbing stains and handwashing delicate items.
- Storage for detergent and bleaches, and anything else that is stored in the laundry.

ABOVE: When not in use the ironing board can be folded into the cupboard.

LEFT: Laundries are utilitarian, but they can be attractive as well.

RIGHT: With plenty of space you can have a large laundry with areas designated for specific tasks and storage.

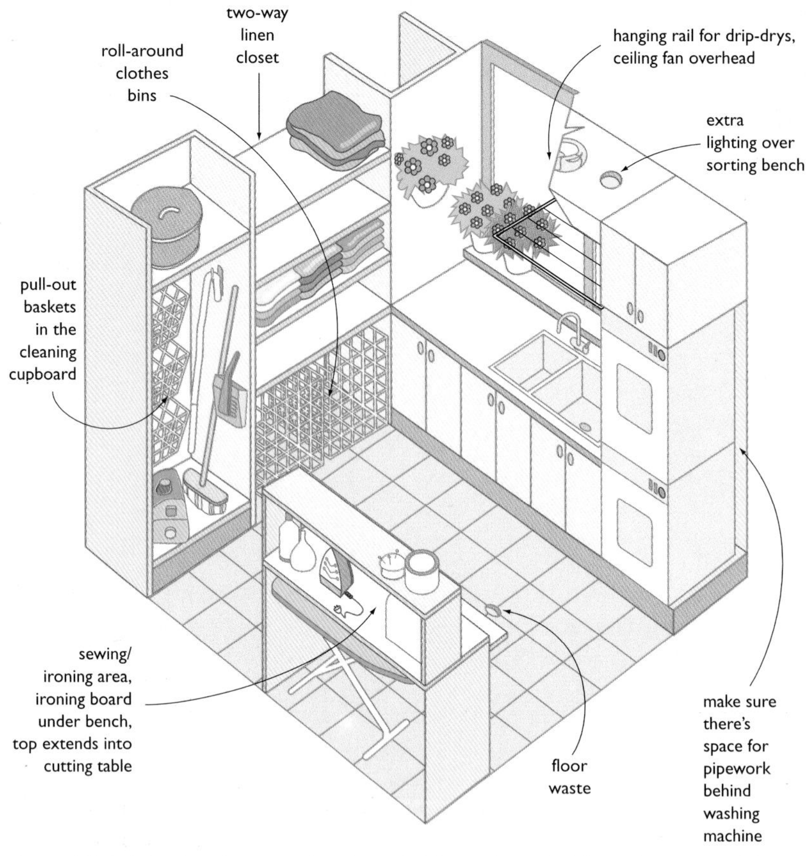

- Bench space for sorting. If you haven't got much space this sorting area could be a fold-down or pull-out table.
- A place for drip-drying. This will need drainage, so the easiest thing to do is put a hanging rail over the tub. This also gives you somewhere to hang freshly ironed clothes.
- Space for ironing. This includes the ironing board, iron, storage for sprays and somewhere to stack or hang the ironed clothes. The ironing board can fold out from the wall, or swing out from or sit under the bench.
- Linen storage. This should be close to the sorting bench and ideally should be two-way with direct access to the hallway or the bedroom.
- A laundry sorter. This is simply a divided bin or basket for organising clothes into different machine loads.
- If you have the space, the laundry is also a good place to put a mending centre and the cleaning cupboard.
- Remember that good ventilation and lighting are an absolute must in any laundry.

Space-saving ideas

The laundry centre on the right is tucked away in a well-located cupboard, so it's handy to get to and easy to hide away. Although it doesn't take up much space, it's packed full of good ideas to use in any laundry.

As well as a hanging rail above the tub, there's also provision for drip-drying dresses or gowns which are too long to fit above the bench top. The drips drain away in the drip tray.

When the hanging space is not required, the bench top drops down to become a sorting and folding

Tip

- Store the most-used boxes, bottles or sprays so that they're within easy reach — not tucked away under the tub.

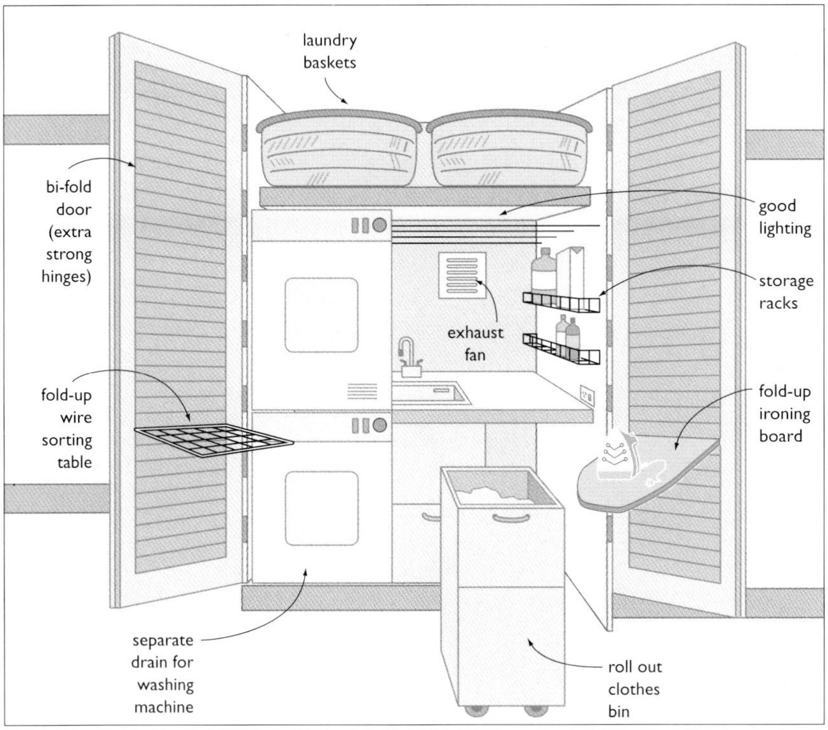

ABOVE LEFT: Careful planning is required for a small laundry to work efficiently.

ABOVE RIGHT: This galley layout combines the laundry with storage.

BELOW LEFT AND RIGHT: The table folds down into position when the hanging rail and tub are not in use.

table. Even the tub converts to valuable bench space.

High-necked taps (also called gooseneck taps) make it easier to get a bucket out from under the tap without drowning yourself!

Colour co-ordinated appliances look great, and you don't have to paint them yourself. If your washing machine and dryer exteriors are metal, you can have them electrostatically spray painted in any colour for a durable and professional-looking finish. To find a painter look in the Yellow Pages under Office furniture reconditioning.

ABOVE LEFT: A rail over the tub is handy for freshly ironed clothes or for allowing wet items to drip dry.

ABOVE RIGHT: Tall cabinets make long items such as mops and ironing boards easily accessible and see-through, pull-out baskets make smaller items easy to find.

BELOW: Work flow plan.

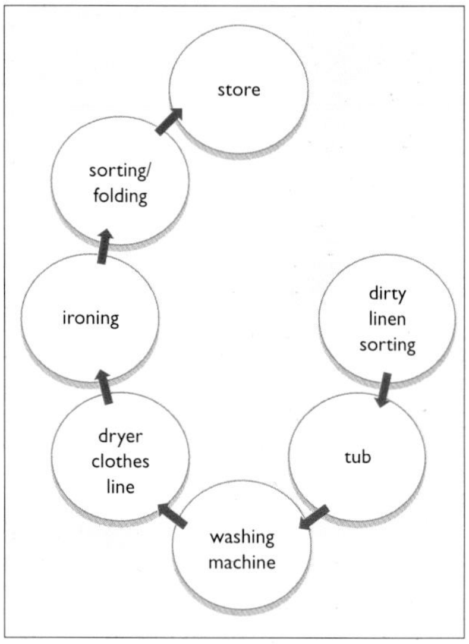

The labour-saving laundry

Laundries have come a long way from the copper and scrubbing board days. Apart from having an efficient design and layout, there are a few other labour-saving devices and tricks to help you get through the loads of washing and ironing faster. Although it's important to create a laundry that's pleasant to be in, it's even better to create one that you don't have to be in for too long.

Work flow

Work flow is simply arranging things so that the work follows a logical, smooth progression, rather than a to-and-fro trip across the floor. Laundries don't need to be big to work efficiently; in fact, the less distance you have to travel, the better.

Washing machines

Fully automatic washing machines are no longer a luxury, and there are many available at reasonable prices. There is also a machine on the market that is a combined washer and dryer — an extra space saver in a small laundry. Make sure the appliances are large enough for the household; doing a few large loads is easier than doing a lot of small ones.

Clothes dryers

Tumble dryers with stainless steel drums are easier to maintain, but make sure you vent them outside. Airing cupboards are great for drying damp clothes.

Laundry tubs

An overflow will save you from mopping-up operations after floods.

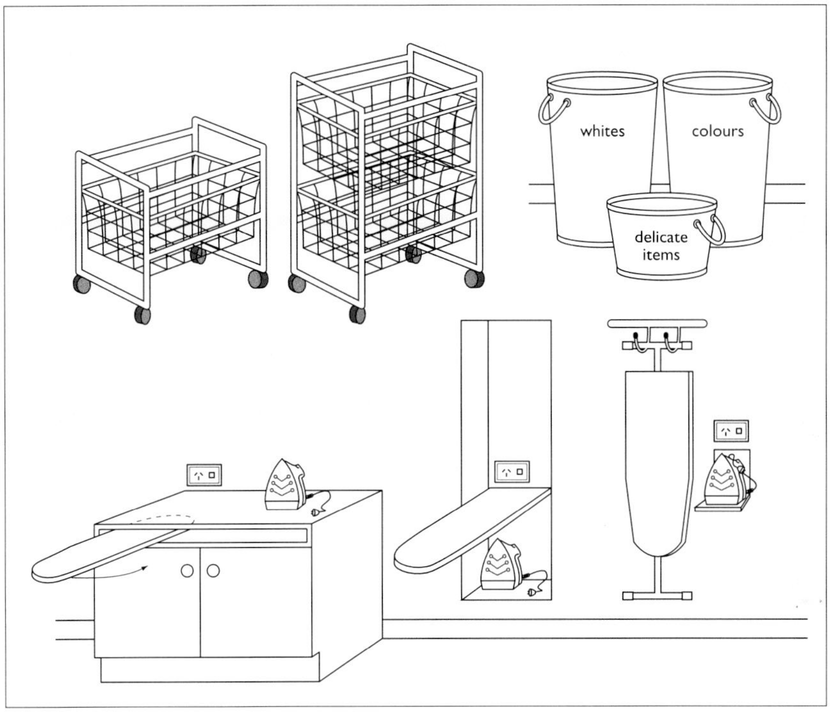

LEFT: Laundry storage ideas that save time.

Wire drawer frames/baskets on castors can be wheeled from room to room or dryer to ironing board. They are available from large hardware stores and storage shops.

A divided clothes basket, or two or three separate containers, will save you from having to sort the wash into loads later on.

Unless you can leave it up all the time, you'll need somewhere to put the ironing board so it's convenient to use.

Deep tubs are more versatile than shallow ones and twin tubs give you the option of soaking in one while handwashing in the other. There are different finishes available, but stainless steel is the easiest to clean if you plan to use the tub for dirty jobs such a cleaning the barbecue grill or washing out paintbrushes.

Taps

Lever-action handles are simpler to turn on and off; tall goosenecks make it easier to fill buckets without splashing water everywhere.

Surfaces and finishes

These should be waterproof and easy to clean, as well as bleach resistant. Non-gloss paints will help prevent condensation and wallpapers should be vinyl, scrubbable and suitable for the wet. Save finishes from flood damage by having a separate outlet for the washing machine and a floor drainage hole.

Lighting and ventilation

There's no reason to put up with a dark stuffy environment. Make sure all work surfaces have adequate lighting and you should install an exhaust fan to save you from sweltering in summer.

Deciding what you need

These questions and answers can help make the laundry less of a chore in your house.

Q Is everything positioned so that the work flows in a logical order?

A If not, consider rearranging things so they are; plumbing is usually located together, so this often only involves rearranging the storage or putting up some extra shelves.

Q Is the washing machine fully automatic or a hard-to-work manual? Is it large enough?

A Trade it in for a better model.

Q Are things stored right where you actually use them?

A Arrange things so they are.

Q Is the clothes basket divided to save you from sorting out the wash later on?

A Cut a piece of ply to fit the basket, or simply use two baskets instead of one.

Q Do you have a tub overflow?

Storage ideas

The easier everything is to get to the better. Make sure you have a place for things where you actually use them.

Items you'll need storage space for:

Washing powers, bleaches and so on, soiled clothes, and clean clothes.

Items it's useful to have storage for:

Iron and ironing board, linen, sewing and mending equipment, cleaning materials, mops and brooms, vacuum cleaner, raincoats, wet shoes, gumboots (use the laundry as the rainy day or workers' entrance), vases (and other flower-arranging bits and pieces), potting and gardening equipment, and luggage and/or sporting equipment.

ABOVE: The lattice inserts make the mellow look of these cupboards more interesting. Make sure the wood is well sealed from moisture.

TOP RIGHT: Laundry tubs do come in forms other than a metal cabinet. Insert models can be cut into almost any bench top surface to blend with surrounding finishes.

BOTTOM RIGHT: You can buy solid frame doors such as these or use plain ones and glue on timber mouldings to give the same effect. Paint them to protect against the wet and fit the room's colour scheme.

A Buy a plastic attachment that fits into the drain; it may save you from having some expensive flood damage.
Q Have you enough space for sorting clothes?
A Install a pull-down sorting table.
Q Could you install a two-way linen cupboard that opens from the laundry and the hallway, or even a two-way clothes basket that is between the bathroom and the laundry?
A Book a carpenter or DIY.
Q Is the ironing board easy to get access to?
A Look at the alternatives.
Q Is the lighting and ventilation good enough?
A Put in an exhaust fan and/or additional task lighting.

Laundry styles

Thoroughly modern, old-fashioned laundries

Just because you want your laundry to be an up-to-date, labour-saving, low-maintenance model doesn't mean you have to miss out on old-world charm — it's simply a matter of choosing the right finishes.

Small laundries

Laundries don't need large areas. When it comes to the crunch, you can fit them into the smallest room in the house, and find space somewhere else for the ironing board and broom cupboard.

The minimum requirements are around one square metre of floor space for the washing machine and dryer (if it's overhead), and a little less than that will take care of the tub. If you can manage it, it's a lot better to have some space for sorting dirty clothes into loads and

folding clean ones into various owners' piles.

Use light colours, which reflect more light, to make the room seem larger. It's also handy to have direct access to the clothes line.

Dual-purpose laundries

Inspired renovating can turn an old laundry into a multi-purpose utility room that will be a pleasure to use. If there's space in your laundry, here are some great ideas to adapt.

Imagine the luxury of having a complete sewing centre with a see-at-a-glance wire basket storage for fabrics and patterns beneath the workspace. The laundry is the ideal place to locate a sewing machine: it's close at hand for mending tasks and the ironing board is always at the ready.

By building a timber framework along one wall, you can instigate a 'take-away' system for clean clothes in one stack of wire baskets and allow for multiple storage in others. A fold-away ironing board frees floorspace when it's not in use, while fixed shelves beside and above it make an ideal linen press, conveniently placed so you don't have to trek through the house with piles of towels or sheets.

A high shelf takes care of off-season storage, and in the lower section you can add a bin for clothes and linen waiting to be washed. If you can, make it two-way to take dirty clothes from the bathroom on the other side of the wall. A drying rack with a collection of assorted coat hangers gives clothes a chance to dry wrinkle free and cuts down ironing time. Walls painted with a scrubbable paint and floors covered in hard-wearing rubber help to provide a good-looking, low-maintenance room.

ABOVE: The laundry is the most logical room in which to place an extra toilet.

RIGHT: If you have the space, the laundry can become a utility room which contains enough storage facilities to keep everything well organised and allows sewing and ironing to be done with ease.

Tip

- Hard water is hard on your wash because it doesn't always rinse well and leaves a detergent residue behind so clothes feel stiff. In hard-water areas, add a few tablespoons of baking soda to the load.

Liberate the laundry and double its duty

Happiness is a laundry and work centre with plenty of light and oodles of space. A tiny laundry has more good features than you'd imagine at a single glance. The three major units — washer, dryer and tub — can be stacked along one wall, to minimise the cost of plumbing. Open cupboards can be used to store frequently used linen. An ironing board will tuck into a cupboard and all the necessary ironing paraphernalia can be stored within it.

Building a laundry and sewing centre where every sliver of space is used to its best advantage isn't difficult. Standard unpainted cupboards can be fitted in where space permits and then laminated bench tops added.

Best dressed in the laundry

For the swishest of all laundries, a combination laundry/dressing

ABOVE: The galley style layout can work as well in a laundry as it does in a kitchen.

RIGHT: The wall opposite the laundry appliances provides plenty of storage for children's clothes and sports equipment.

room must surely be the ultimate in dignified living. The secret here is that every item has a given position, so the clutter is actually a picture of organisation.

Even in a small room, every bit of space can be called into service to achieve a look of busy order that will make you want to keep up the good work. The walls can do wardrobe duty, modified by the addition of hanging rods, with the area under the bench used for folded items and a custom-made shelf system on the opposite wall for shoe racks.

Hide-away laundries

Laundry location need not be confined to the conventional areas such as a strip off the kitchen or a corner of the bathroom. Any house with a staircase has a little goldmine of unused space just waiting for conversion into a compact family wash area. Just one weekend's work could create an efficient workplace from the wasted triangle beneath the stairs.

How you arrange the laundry depends on your individual priorities, but by using the sleight-of-hand approach you easily can incorporate the whole workings into the empty space conveniently and all but invisibly.

You can use louvred doors to conceal built-in shelves and allow access to the wedge-shaped space above from folding doors on one side. The under-stair area can house mending, ironing and cleaning gear as well as the laundry equipment.

A coat of paint will give a cheery welcome when the doors are open. If the doors themselves are finished in a clear polyurethane and are splash safe and easy to clean, they will complement the surrounding ceiling and floor.

By utilising the under-stair area, the house loses no effective floor space and the laundry is only visible when in use.

The open-and-shut case

With a little planning and perhaps some remodelling, a long, narrow cupboard can give almost as much useful space as a small room — if it's filled efficiently. Build in a smart slide-out bin for soiled linen between the washing machine and dryer. A laminate top, flush with the appliances, will provide a surface for sorting and folding. And with storage, it's a good idea to make your shelves adjustable. This way you can create special spaces for jars and packets of different sizes. Folding doors give the finishing touch, taking less room than conventional ones.

ABOVE: A laundry hidden behind louvre doors does not impinge on space in the bathroom and it is close to plumbing connections.

ABOVE: With the sturdy drying rack extended, damp washing can be conveniently air-dried in the laundry.

ABOVE RIGHT: The drying rack folds away leaving a handy storage shelf.

FAR RIGHT: Drying rack patterns.

Do-it-yourself — Make a wooden clothes drying rack

This compact clothes dryer is a useful addition to any laundry. It features a sturdy pull-out rack for hanging clothes and a storage shelf. Choose a timber which best suits your laundry. Radiata pine would be suitable for most situations but Tasmanian oak is an alternative. If you want a painted finish, you can use medium-density fibre (MDF) board for the shelf. Use the diagrams on the following pages to make and assemble the rack.

Making the shelf

Cut the two pieces for the back (A) from 19-mm-thick pine to 180 x 625 mm. Glue the two pieces edge to edge with PVA glue and cramp lightly. Remove any excess glue with a damp rag. When it is dry, trim the panel to the finished length of 615 mm. If using 18 mm MDF board cut out the finished shape 360 x 615 mm.

On a piece of 19 mm pine or 18 mm MDF plane an edge straight and square an end. From the edge and end draw a 200 x 375 mm grid of 25 mm squares using a soft pencil. On this, draw the shape of the end panel (B) shown on the gridded pattern. Mark the centre point for the 3 mm pilot hole shown on the gridded pattern and drill the holes to a depth of 10 mm. Cut the end panel to length with a tenon saw and cut on the waste side of the curved line with a jigsaw. Sand the edges smooth with 120 grit sandpaper.

Plane an edge and square an end for the second end panel (B). Using the first end panel as a template, mark out the shape of the second end panel. Cut the second panel to length and shape then sand the edges smooth as before.

From 19 mm pine or 18 mm MDF cut out the top of the shelf (C) to 200 x 700 mm. Round over the front edge and both ends with an 8 mm radius round-over bit in a router to the edge as a guide, and plane the round using a block plane. Round over the front curved edges of the end panels (B) using a router as before on the shelf, or spokeshave, or surforming tool.

Draw on scrap pieces of 19 mm pine or 18 mm MDF the shape of the rack rests (D) and both parts of the latch (E and F) using the full-sized latch pattern, carbon paper

You will need:

Part	Thickness (mm)	Width (mm)	Length (mm)	Material	Qty
	Finished size*				
A	360	615	19*	Pine or MDF	2 or 1*
B	175	370	19*	Pine or MDF	2
C	200	700	19*	Pine or MDF	2
D	19	75	19*	Pine	2
E	19	45	12	Pine	1
F	25	65	19	Pine	1
G	19	395	12	Pine	2
H	19	305	12	Pine	2
I	19	305	12	Pine	4
J	19	305	12	Pine	4
K	19	164	12	Pine	2
L	19	164	12	Pine	2

Supplies: 7 m of 10 mm diameter dowel; 30 x 1.5 mm bullet-head nails; 15 mm panel pins; three 25 mm x 8 gauge round-head wood screws; two 50 mm x 8 gauge round-head wood screws; Wattyl Woodstop (Pine): PVA glue; 120, 150, 180, 220 sandpaper; Satin Cabothane.

and a pencil. Cut these parts to shape using a jigsaw and sand curved edges using 120 grit sandpaper. Drill the holes in (E) and (F) as shown in the latch pattern.

Sand the surfaces of all the parts of the shelf using 150, 180 and 220 grit sandpaper.

Glue and nail the end panels (B) to the back (A) using 30 x 1.5 mm bullet nails and PVA glue. Punch the nail heads below the surface and stop with Wattyl Woodstop (Pine). (A small pilot hole should be drilled when nailing into the MDF.) Align the top (C) with the back and centre it. Glue and nail it to both the back and the end panels. Glue and nail the back rest (D) inside the cabinet 240 mm beneath the underside of the top (A) as shown in the diagram.

Making the folding drying rack

Using 12 x 19 mm pine battens, cut 16 rack slats (G, H, I, J, K and L) to lengths listed previously. (Label and sort the different slats as they are cut.)

Carefully mark the centre points for the holes on the rack slats (G, H, I, J, K and L) from the dimensions given on the rack slats diagram. Note there are three different hole sizes. The smallest fits the mounting screws, and the largest 10 mm diameter hole gives a clearance hole for the 10 mm diameter dowel. These holes are determined by the size of the dowel used. If you use a 10 mm drill it may be necessary to increase slightly the size of the clearance holes, with a round file to give clearance for the 10 mm dowel. Ensure that the holes are drilled square with the face of the rack slat.

Remove the sharp edges on the ends of each rack slat with 120 grit sandpaper. Sand all rack slats to a final smooth finish.

Cut the 10 mm dowel into 11 x 610 mm lengths using a tenon saw. Ensure that all dowels are identical in length. Fine sand each dowel.

Assemble the drying rack following the three steps shown on the rack assembly diagrams. Start with slats G and H, which are screwed to the inside of the shelf, and insert the centre dowel to make the first cross. Next insert the top and bottom dowels in part H. Then add slats I and J and the dowels needed for the second and the identical third crosses. Finally, form the last

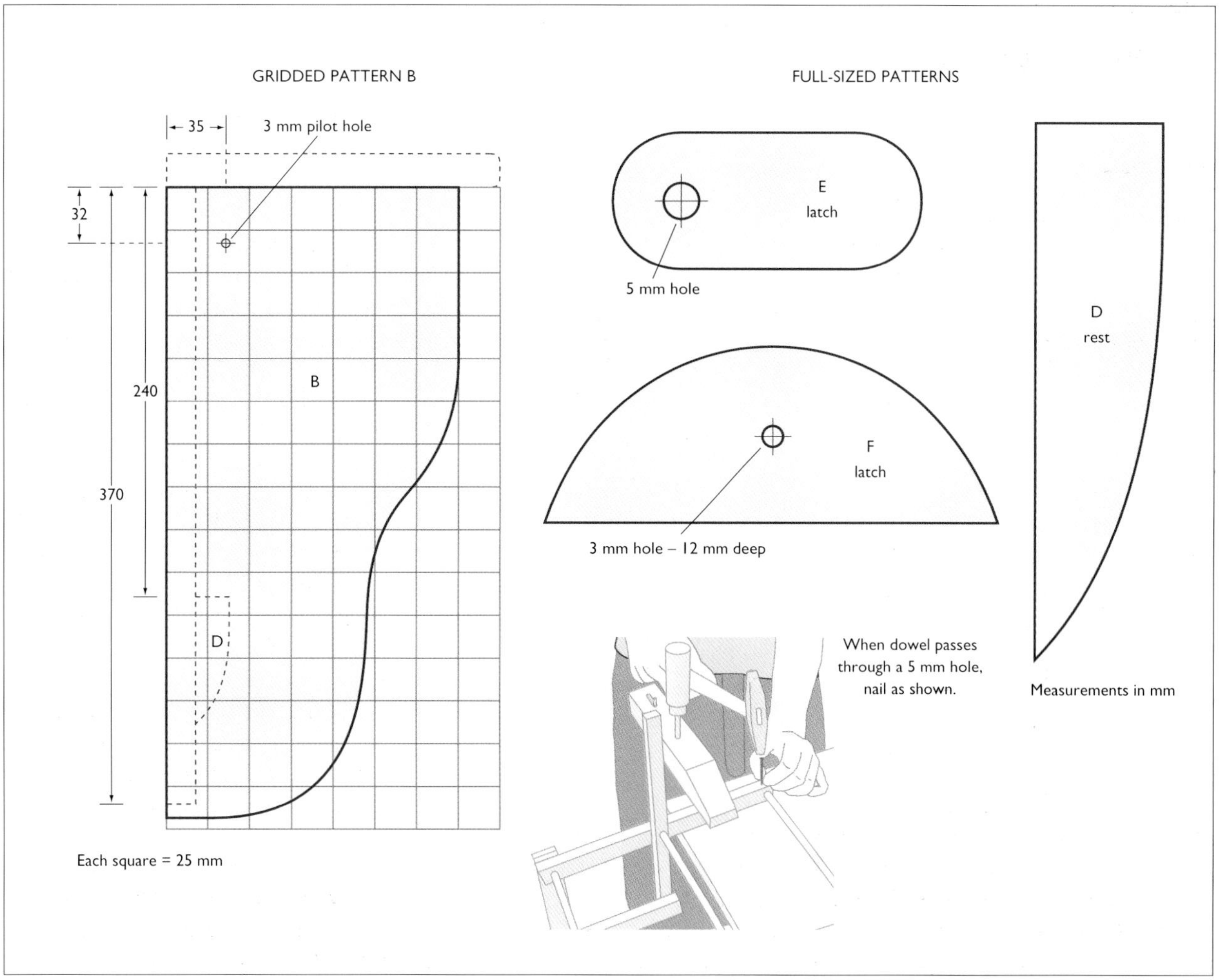

RIGHT: Drying rack assembly.

FAR RIGHT: Rack and shelf components.

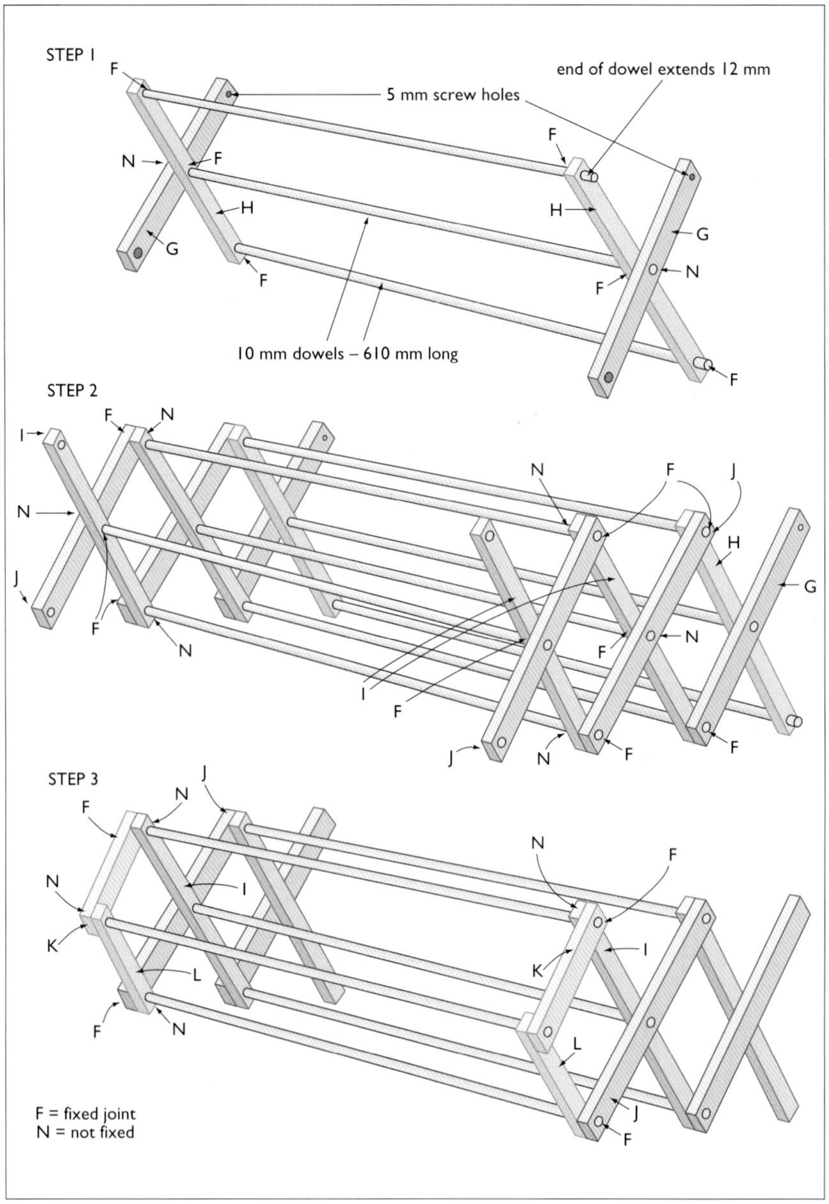

rack section with slats K and L and the dowel. When a dowel passes through a 10 mm hole, fix the dowel in place by driving a 15 mm panel pin through the slat and the dowel as shown. (It is helpful to remember that on the outside slats, the dowels are free-turning at the centre and fixed at the ends, but are the reverse on the inside slats.)

Assembly and finishing

Using 25 mm x 8 gauge round-head screws, attach the assembled rack to the inside of the shelf (the screws fit into the pilot hole previously drilled in the inside face of the end panels). Fold the rack into the space beneath the shelf and mark the position for the half-round latch (F). Nail and glue the latch to the underside of the shelf. Screw the toggle (E) to the half-round latch.

Two coats of Satin Cabothane would give a simple and satisfactory finish (rubbing down with worn 240 grit sandpaper between coats).

Simply secure the shelf to the wall using two 50 mm x 8 gauge round-head screws.

Tip

- Dismantle a project before applying a finish. With the drying rack, unscrew the rack from the shelf and expand it before applying finish.

RACK SLAT DRAWING

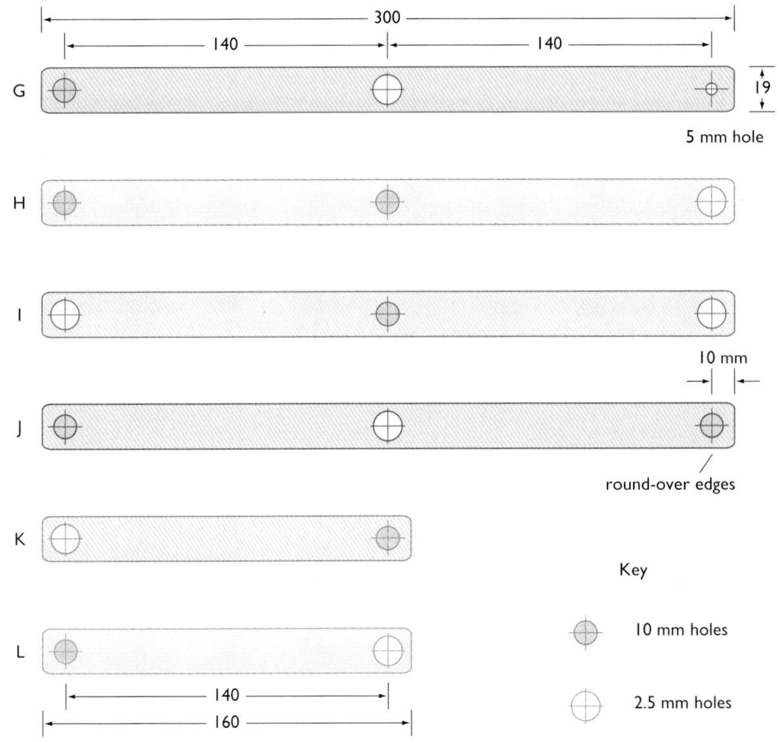
300
140
140
G
19
5 mm hole
H
I
10 mm
J
round-over edges
K
Key
10 mm holes
L
2.5 mm holes
140
160

CLOTHES DRYER

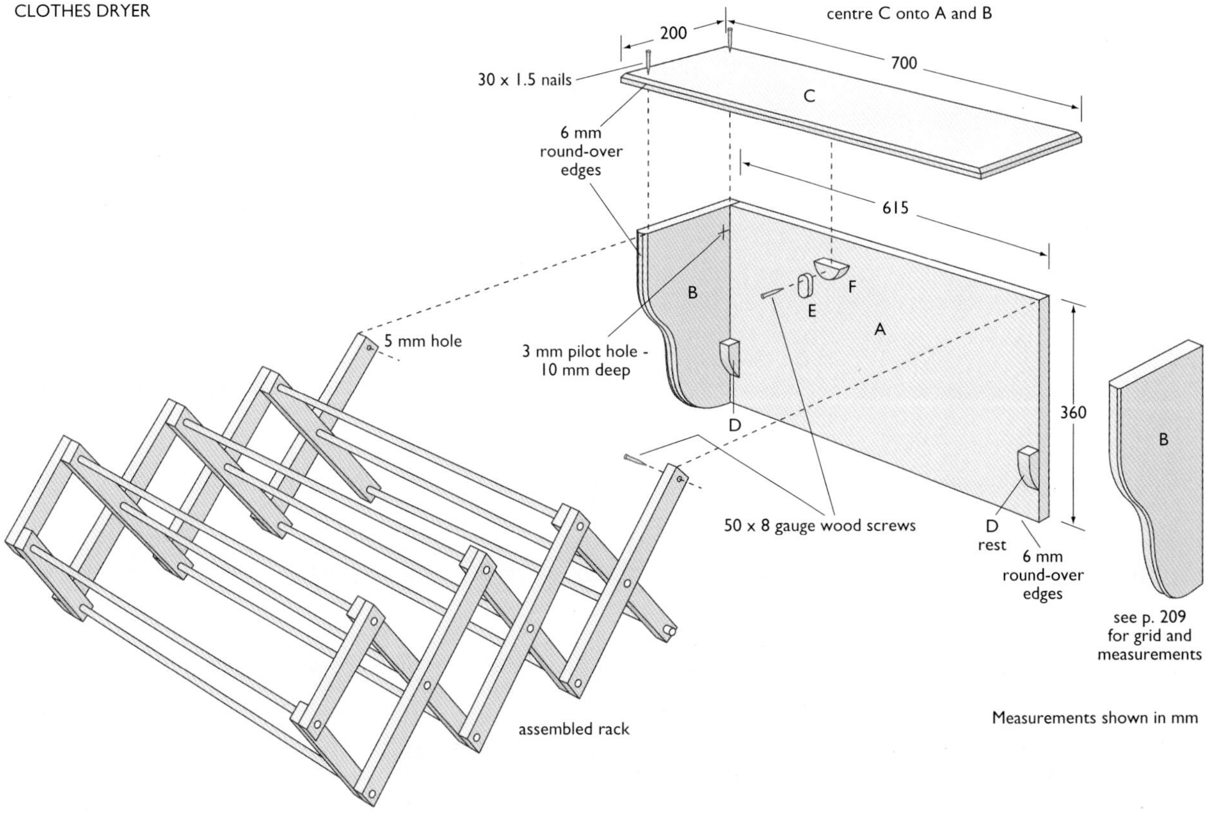
centre C onto A and B
200
700
30 x 1.5 nails
C
6 mm
round-over
edges
615
B
E
F
A
5 mm hole
3 mm pilot hole -
10 mm deep
360
B
D
50 x 8 gauge wood screws
D
rest
6 mm
round-over
edges
see p. 209
for grid and
measurements
assembled rack
Measurements shown in mm

Like Water for Chocolate Laura Esquivel
EARLY SORROW
Ten Stories of Youth
SELECTED BY
Charlotte Zolotow
ANNIE ERNAUX
A MAN'S PLACE

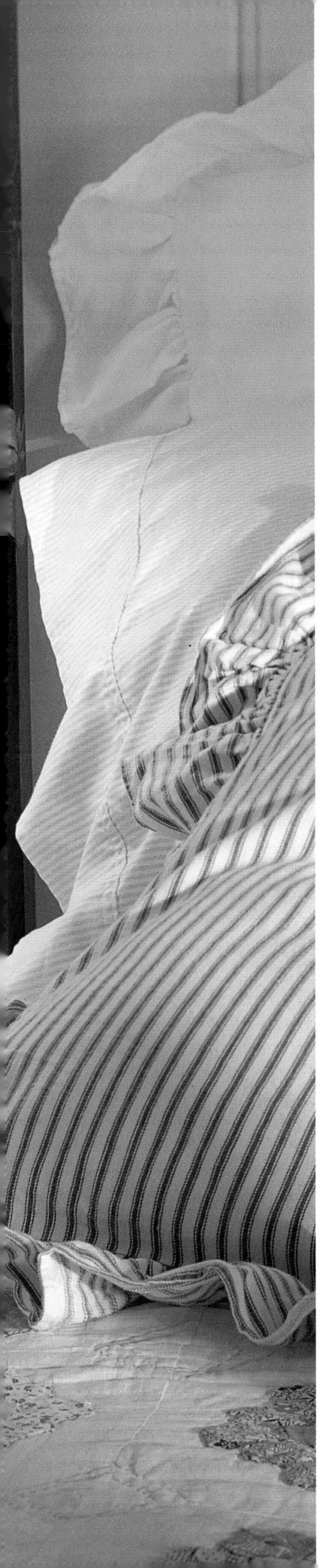

Paint, Painting and Wallpaper

Choosing the colour scheme for your home is potentially the most exciting and rewarding aspect of home improvement and renovation. Painting is often the most inexpensive way to achieve the total transformation of an interior. The wrong colour scheme badly applied, however, can destroy the proportions of a room.

Colour affects our moods, and personal preferences are highly individual, but don't let your emotions rule when you are choosing your colour scheme. Consider the colours (and the neutrals) not only in terms of the paint, but also in collaboration with the other textures in the rooms before you decide on a forest green kitchen or a bright red dining room. It may seem obvious, but a small, dark room will become smaller and darker when painted in a dark tone. The same room will be unrecognisable if you choose neutral creams and white and restrict the darker colours to the trim instead.

Apart from standard paints there is a variety of colour washes, lime washes, stains and milk paints available today that will give interesting painted finishes such as rag rolling, stippling and combing.

Wallpaper can also create an amazing transformation, especially when complemented by the right colours in the surroundings. Modern wallpapers are pre-pasted, easy to apply and come in a vast range of designs.

Yellow tones generally have an uplifting effect on our moods. They are bright during daylight hours and give a warm glow in artificial light, as shown here. Handpainted furniture is an easy do-it-yourself project and can give a facelift to old pieces to harmonise with refurbished surroundings.

How colour works

Knowing how to use colour effectively can make all the difference when you come to put the finishing touches to your renovation. If you are unsure, you can seek professional advice.

Colour has three factors:

1 hue, which gives the colour its name (e.g. red, yellow, blue);
2 chroma or intensity, which relates to its brightness or dullness. If all the colours in a room are low-intensity or dulled, they will create a comfortable, back-to-nature mood ideal for family rooms; and
3 tone, which relates to its lightness or darkness, such as pale pink or maroon.

Colour schemes

You will find that most decorating colour schemes fall into the following broad categories:

- Monochromatic. This is when one hue is used throughout a room, but in varying tone and intensity. There should be deep-coloured areas, mid-tones and highlights. This scheme works well in small rooms because it doesn't break up the space.
- Harmonious. Most rooms are styled in a harmonious colour scheme; that is, colours close to each other on the colour wheel. Some of the colours have a low intensity (some are quite dull) which actually makes the bright colours seem brighter in comparison. All the colours have a common thread, rather like a family where all the children have varying degrees of their parents' traits. This is a good scheme even for beginner decorators because it's logical and easy to apply — a particularly restful scheme for any room.
- Primary. Only primary colours (i.e. red, yellow and blue) are used. This scheme makes a great impact and is particularly effective in modern houses and children's rooms.
- Complementary. This scheme is based on pairs of opposites on the colour wheel (e.g. red and green, yellow and purple, and orange and blue). This is an unusual scheme and works well when one colour totally dominates the other with the second colour being used only in small details, such as for flowers, cushions or crockery.

All colours can be used in different ways; for example, bright and clear, pastel and soft, dark and moody. Reds vary from fire-engine bright to pastel-like pink to dark maroon. These variations are achieved by mixing them with black and white.

ABOVE: The stencilled design lifts the russet coloured walls.

BELOW: Orange-striped walls are contrasted with a blue-and-white checked cloth.

Tints are colours that have white added. By adding more white, you create pastels; for example, red and white make pink, orange and white make peach.

Shades are colours with black added. Blue and black make navy, red and black make maroon, blue, yellow and red make olive.

Different colours in different rooms

If you can see from one room to another, it's more restful to work with colours which are in harmony with each other.

Primary colours

Red, yellow and blue are the primary colours. They cannot be made by mixing other colours together. They energise a room. If you use them together, one of them will have to dominate the others. All other colours are mixtures of the primary colours.

Secondary colours

These are made by mixing equal quantities of two primary colours together. Red and yellow make orange, yellow and blue make green, and blue and red make purple.

Tertiary colours

Tertiary colours are made by adding all the primary colours together in different proportions. Russet is mostly red with a touch of blue and yellow. Olive is mostly blue with a touch of yellow and red. Citrine is mostly yellow with a touch of red and blue.

The more colours you mix together, the duller a colour becomes. When teamed with primary or secondary colours, tertiary colours intensify the bright colour.

Colour psychology

You may choose colours to reflect your personality or to enhance the mood of a room. Even small touches of colour in fabrics, furniture and accessories can give a lift:

- yellow — cheerful, supports intellect, optimistic;
- blue — serene, nurturing, rejuvenating, peaceful;
- red — passionate, enhances appetite, energetic, powerful;
- green — relates to renewal and rebirth, cooling, calming;
- purple — a spiritual colour, ethereal, fantasy;
- white — purity, cleanliness, romantic.

ABOVE: The patterned wallpaper to dado height complements the more intense colour above it.

Take the pain out of painting

Painting can be a messy, time-consuming job, but you can make quicker work of it with these clever tips.

Before you start to paint

Glue a large, flat paper or plastic plate to the base of the can to catch any drips and to prevent the can sticking to newspaper or the drop cloth.

Before pouring paint into a paint tray, line the tray with a plastic bag and then discard the plastic when cleaning.

Painting special areas

- Doors. When painting doors, place several layers of folded newspaper on top of the door before closing it, so that the paint won't 'lock' the door.
- Furniture. Place plastic meat trays under each leg to protect the floor from the paint.
- Stairs. Paint every second step one day. The next day, or when the paint is dry enough to walk on, paint the other steps. This will enable continued use of the staircase.

Paintbrushes and rollers

To paint an area that requires accuracy, place a rubber band around

ABOVE: The right colour can be selected from a swatch or mixed to your requirements.

RIGHT: Detail adds interest to a pastel colour scheme.

ABOVE: Here, wallpaper is used effectively above the picture rail, but paint is more practical on the area below it.

the bristles of your paintbrush just above the line of paint. This prevents the bristles from spreading.

Pat the brush against the inside of the tin before lifting it out to ease off excess paint.

If you're called away from painting, place your brush or roller in a plastic bag. This prevents it from drying out.

Protection from paint

To protect yourself, wear old clothes and cover your face, neck and hands with a thin layer of petroleum jelly. Use tissues to wipe it off later.

Place a canvas tarpaulin or heavy cloth fabric over floors. This will absorb the paint better than plastic.

Cover furniture with old shower curtains or old sheets.

To protect windows and window frames, lay strips of wet newspaper or masking tape on the glass and simply lift it off when the job is complete. Remove masking tape before the paint dries to avoid peeling off new paint.

Cleaning brushes and rollers

Clean paintbrushes easily without staining your hands by placing them inside two strong plastic bags with water or turps and squeezing the brushes through the plastic to remove paint.

When water-based paint has hardened on the brush or roller, soak it for about 15 minutes in a solution of equal parts water and white vinegar, then wash it in a strong detergent solution.

Storing paint

Place a large rubber band around the tin at the level of the remaining paint, so you can tell at a glance how much you have left for the next time you need it.

Dip a wooden ice-block stick in the paint and attach it to the outside of the can with a rubber band. The stick can be used to colour coordinate fabric, borders, cushions and so on.

Lay a sheet of aluminium foil or plastic wrap on top of the paint before replacing the lid to prevent a 'skin' forming.

Storing brushes

Wrap brushes in heavy brown paper to protect the bristles. If you store brushes in a paper bag secure it at the top with sticky tape or a rubber band.

You will damage brushes if they sit bristles-down in cans or jars. Lay brushes flat or drill a hole in each handle and hang them up.

Banish paint odours

Leave a small bowl of sliced onions in the room to absorb odours.

Leave a large bowl of water, to which one tablespoon of ammonia has been added, in the room for about 10 hours.

Add one teaspoon of vanilla essence to each 600 ml of paint that you use.

1
2
3
7
8
9
10
11
12
13
14
15
16
18

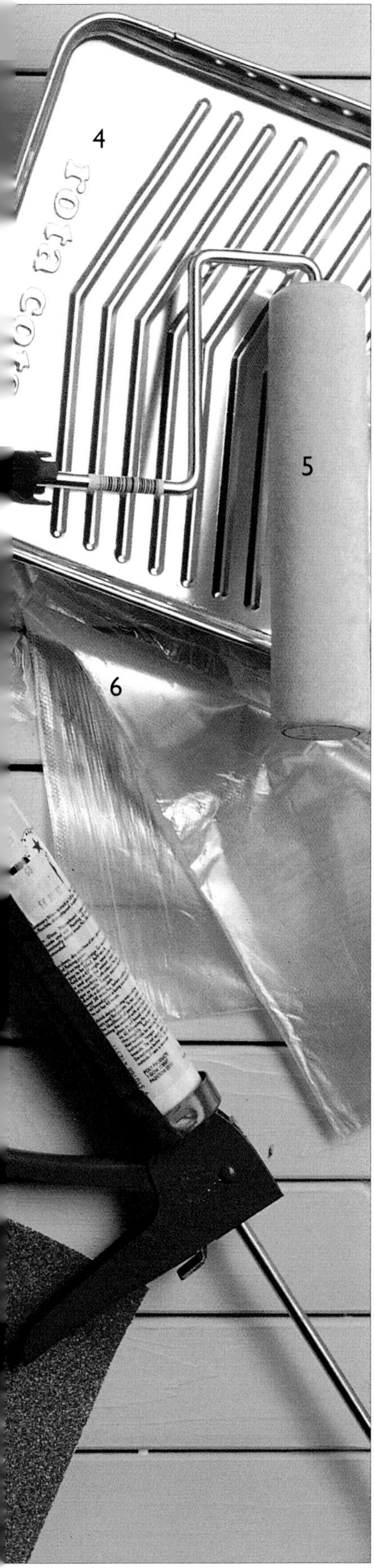

Preparation and painting

Painting is the most popular and instantly rewarding form of decorating. After all, in the whole world of homemaking, what can be more exciting than seeing a room transformed by a new colour? Just as importantly, painting is about making your house look fresh and being able to maintain it in a pristine condition. Anyone who is involved in 'the trade', however, will tell you that painting is about 90 per cent preparation and 10 per cent painting. Your carefully and creatively selected colours are only as good as the surfaces to which they are applied.

LEFT: Some of the tools of the trade

1 Wallpaper steamer
2 Detachable blade scraper
3 Assorted brushes
4 230 mm roller tray
5 10 mm wool roller sleeve (230 mm)
6 Drop sheet
7 Dust masks
8 Point scraper
9 60 mm scraper
10 Flexible paint scraper
11 Combination shave hook
12 Triangular shave hook
13 Wire brush
14 Safety glasses
15 Masking tape
16 Sanding block
17 Caulking gun
18 Wet-and-dry sandpaper

Tips

- Paint pads are an alternative to rollers and brushes and are composed of a large square of fluff with a foam reservoir behind. They are recommended for acrylic paint only and are good for covering large areas and getting into corners.
- Mix paint with a flat stick, preferably one with holes drilled in it.
- Sprays, whether in aerosol cans or the new airless spray guns, are only warranted when you have intricate work such as cane furniture and louvre doors, or if it is new work. Over-spray is always a problem.
- Hire wallpaper steamers from paint and paper centres.
- A Skarsten scraper is good for ripping off paint with a downwards motion.
- Heat guns are a useful investment if you are planning large-scale paint removal.

KEY: BRUSH ROLLER SPRAY

What paint to use where

Imagine going to all that trouble and having the paint start peeling about a year after you've applied it. That would mean going back to the heavy-duty preparation stage. For a lasting job, study this chart carefully.

Estimate the amount of paint you will need by calculating the wall area to be covered and checking it against the coverage column on the chart.

Windows require the same amount of paint as if they were solid wall. Moulded doors need one and a quarter times the amount.

If you're trying to cover a dark colour you'll need two undercoats.

Product	Use on	Application	Coverage	Wash up	Touch dry	Re-coat	Benefits
Interior							
Wash and wear flat acrylic	Interior walls and ceiling	Brush, Roller, Spray	Approx. 16 sq m per litre	Water	20 min.	2 hr	Excellent resistance to wear; very good washability; ideal for hiding surface imperfections
Wash and wear low-sheen acrylic	Interior walls and ceilings	Brush, Roller, Spray	Approx. 16 sq m per litre	Water	30 min.	4 hr	Unbeatable stain resistance; outstanding scrubbability
Wash and wear semi-gloss acrylic	Interior walls, ceilings and woodwork	Brush, Roller, Spray	Approx. 16 sq m per litre	Water	30 min.	4 hr	Suited to all wet areas such as laundries, bathrooms and kitchens; excellent steam and stain resistance
Wash and wear gloss acrylic	Interior walls and trim work	Brush, Roller, Spray	Approx. 16 sq m per litre	Water	1 hr	6 hr	Low colour: non-yellowing; tough resilient film; gloss enamel replacement
One-coat ceiling paint	Interior ceilings	Brush, Roller, Spray	Approx. 12 sq m per litre	Water	20 min.	Not necessary	Ideal for hiding surface imperfections; one-coat coverage saves time and effort; low spatter formula means less mess
Super enamel interior semi-gloss	Interior walls and woodwork	Brush, Roller, Spray	Approx. 16 sq m per litre	Turps	4 hr	16 hr	Is non-toxic; suited to hard-use areas; walls in steamy areas, doors, architraves and all timber trims
Super high-gloss enamel finish	All interior and exterior surfaces	Brush, Roller, Spray	Approx. 16 sq m per litre	Turps	6 hr	16 hr	Suitable for children's toys, cots etc.; hard wearing; long life
Anti-mould low-sheen and semi-gloss acrylic	Interior walls and ceilings	Brush, Roller, Spray	Approx. 16 sq m per litre	Water	30 min.	4 hr	Designed to prevent mould on all interior surfaces; hard wearing; two-year guarantee; non-toxic, contains no fungicides; scrubbable finish for areas where frequent cleaning may be required
Preparation							
Acrylic sealer undercoat	Interior surfaces	Brush, Roller	Approx. 16 sq m per litre	Water	20 min.	2 hr	Seals and undercoats interior surfaces in one coat prior to finishing with either water- or oil-based top coat
Acrylic primer undercoat	All bare timber surfaces (excluding tannin-rich, e.g. cedar, oregon, merbau)	Brush	Approx. 14 sq m per litre	Water	20 min.	2 hr	Convenient primer/undercoat for timber; fills grain; easily sanded
Oil-based undercoat	Interior and primed exterior timber, plaster and masonry	Brush, Roller, Spray	Approx. 16 sq m per litre	Turps	4 hr	16 hr	Suitable for all interior and properly primed exterior surfaces; excellent hiding power with good sanding properties
Sealer Binder	Porous interior and exterior masonry, plaster, cement sheet	Brush, Roller	Approx. 12 sq m per litre	Turps	6 hr	16 hr	Seals porous surfaces and binds kalsomine or thin powdery paint films; provides a sound foundation on which to apply subsequent coats
Stain sealer	Interior and exterior surfaces	Brush, Roller, Spray	Approx. 14 sq m per litre	Water	30 min.	2 hr	Sealer which helps prevent staining from substances such as smoke, oils, tar, bitumen and creosote bleeding through subsequent coats
All-metal primer	All common metals except zinc and galvanised metals	Brush, Roller, Spray	Approx. 12 sq m per litre	Turps	5 hr	16 hr	Anti-corrosive primer for all common metals; ideally suited as a primer for clean scale-free steel
Oil-based primer	All bare timber	Brush	Approx. 16 sq m per litre	Turps	6 hr	16 hr	Suitable for all bare timber and tannin-rich timber; available in pink or white

Note. Coverage rates are approximate only and will vary according to the method of application and the porosity of the surface. Touch-dry and re-coat times are based on a day of around 25°C. Temperature must be above 10°C during application drying times.

Interior preparation

When you can't wait to see the final effect, preparation will seem like the boring part. Everything you do in the preparation stage, however, will help to create a solid basis onto which you can lay any decorating scheme.

Vital preparation

1 Wash old painted walls with sugar soap to remove any grease and dirt.
2 Rinse well with water and allow to dry.
3 Fill any cracks with a non-shrinking, pre-mixed filler and allow to dry.
4 Sand walls smooth, removing any dust with a brush or a dry cloth.
5 If the surface was previously painted with high-gloss paint, sand it lightly before filling to provide a key.
6 If you need to apply a glaze on your chosen surface, make it by mixing paint with a scumble medium (available from art and craft shops). This extends drying time and makes paint more translucent.

Unfortunately, surfaces cannot always be prepared so easily. Shown here on the following pages are the main trouble spots — the potential crisis areas to look out for.

Tips

- Don't press too hard on the roller or you'll get ridges in the paint work.
- Extra-long nap rollers are for heavily textured surfaces. For smooth surfaces, use medium to short nap rollers.

BELOW: Peeling paint on chalky surfaces

This occurs when layers of old paint beneath the surface break down, as in the case of kalsomine.

1 Scrape surface back. Sand thoroughly.
2 Wash with sugar-soap solution and then wash again to provide a clean surface.
3 Seal with Sealer Binder, then fill.
4 Sand before undercoating with an acrylic sealer.

1

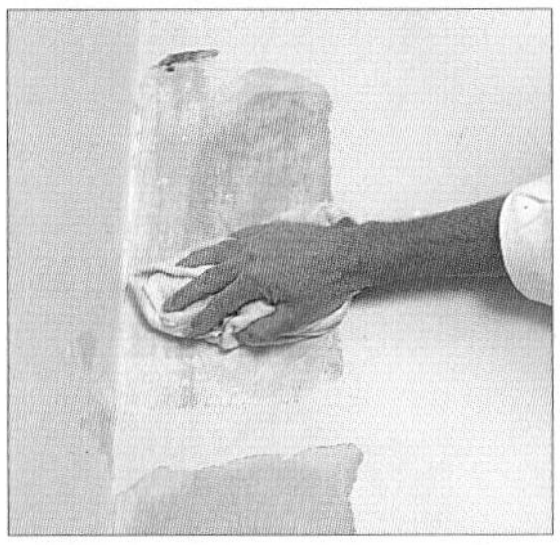

2

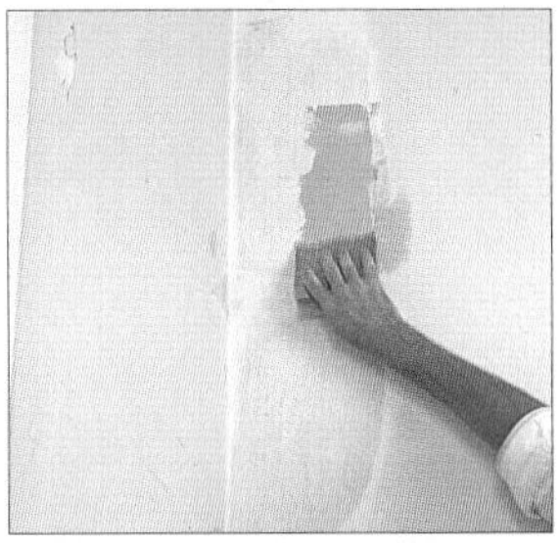

3

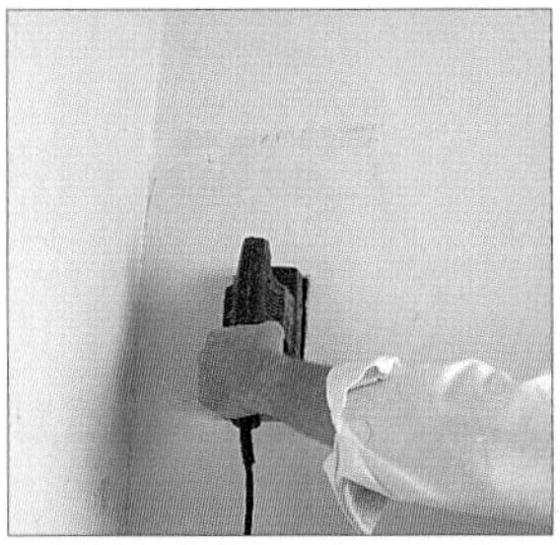

4

BELOW: Cracks in ceilings

These might appear to be just hairline — they need to be investigated with the point of your blade knife.

1 Open up cracks. Brush dust from cracks.
2 Fill with good quality plaster-based filler.
3 Sand before sealing with an acrylic sealer undercoat and painting.

1

2

3

1

2

3

4

ABOVE: Lifting plaster on ceiling or walls

Tap for a hollow sound. Behind a small bubble may be an avalanche of falling plaster.

1 Open up the bubble as far as is necessary.
2 Remove all loose plaster with a scraper to establish solid edges.
3 Dust away all loose particles to give you a stable surface. Fill.
4 Sand then paint with a binder. Undercoat with an acrylic sealer.

1

2

3

4

ABOVE: Cracked cornice

A feature in any house, cornices deserve to be treated with kid gloves. To make the most of them, go over them with an eye for detail.

1 Scrape out the crack with a scraper point.
2 Fill the gap at the bottom of the cornice using a cartridge of flexible caulking filler.
3 Sand cornice grooves with sandpaper rolled into a cylinder.
4 Seal with an acrylic undercoat before finishing with ceiling paint.

1

ABOVE LEFT: Detailed plaster work

Because the grooves get clogged up with successive layers of paint, you have to try to re-establish the plaster's crisp lines.

1 Pick out loose paint with a pointed tool before sealing with a sealer.

1

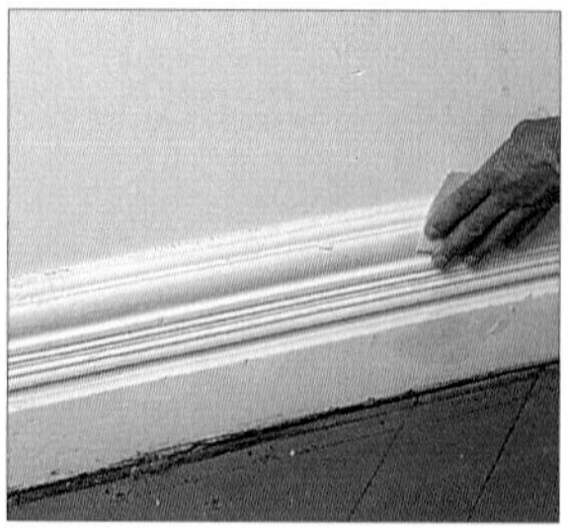

2

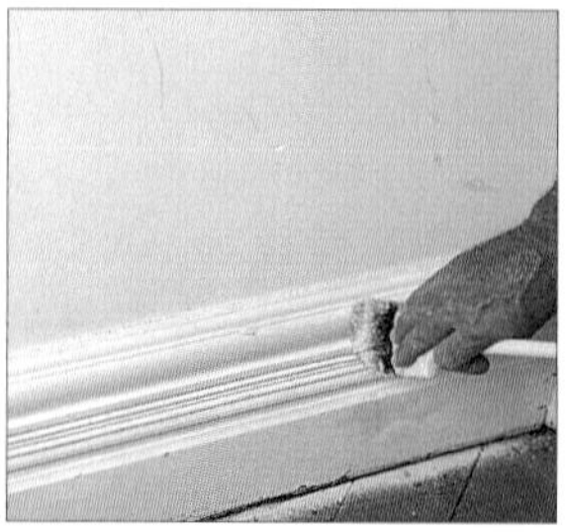

3

ABOVE: Chipped joinery

Nothing looks worse than paint slapped over a chipped surface. Camouflage is the name of the game. Make it even with two-part epoxy filler.

1 Scrape and feather the edges of the chip then fill.
2 Sand filler and painted joinery to an even finish.
3 Seal with an acrylic primer undercoat.

1

2

3

1

2

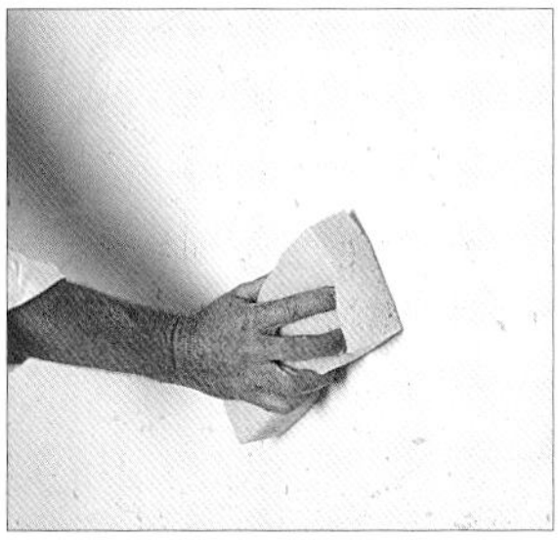
3

1

2

3

4

5

6

ABOVE LEFT: Painted door furniture

Whether it requires stripping or not, don't try to paint around it. Remove it.

1 Break paint seal with a razor and remove hardware.
2 Apply stripper in coats and wash off in between with steel wool and hot soapy water.
3 Replace polished hardware after you have painted the door.

ABOVE RIGHT: Wallpaper

Strip plain papers with a sponge, water and cellulose paste. Painted and impervious papers are more difficult.

1 Scratch paper at regular intervals with a blade or scraper.
2 Fill steamer with water. Apply it and scrape. Proceed slowly and methodically.
3 Wash down thoroughly before sealing with Sealer Binder.

ABOVE: Battered windows

Depending on the seriousness of the condition, consider using a hot air gun. Windows have to look immaculate. All attention focuses on them because they are a major architectural feature.

1 Sand off loose particles. Wipe down to remove dust and chips.
2 Remove paint build-up (likely to occur on the outside) with a hot air gun.
3 Seal with an oil-based primer or acrylic primer undercoat.
4 Fill, sand and brush down to make clean before proceeding.
5 Seal a second time to lock in the fillers.
6 Fill crevices with a flexible filler using a caulking gun.

See pp. 225–26 for advice on preparing specific surfaces for painting.

Pointers for painters

Preparation, the choice of the right tools and how to use them are important, especially if you are inexperienced at painting. This section shows in detail how to choose the tools, how to maintain and store them, how to apply paint and how to fix problems.

Choosing a brush

A well-made natural-bristle brush has some distinct advantages over a nylon-bristle brush. A natural bristle — usually from a pig or boar — has minute indentations all the way along its length; these indentations actually catch the paint and hold it on the brush. Early nylon bristles were smooth so the paint virtually slipped off the brush. However, newer and more expensive nylon-bristle brushes have small indentations manufactured into the strand, making the finish they give more acceptable.

In general, nylon brushes are fine for use with acrylic paints on rough surfaces such as brickwork or cement, but on finer surfaces such as an interior wall, they may leave brush strokes. It is worth investing in a quality natural-bristle brush for interior work.

The next factor in brush choice is the length of the bristles: too short and the paint will simply fall off the brush; too long and you'll get a flip-flop effect, which can waste paint and cause undue tiredness in your hands and wrists.

The third and final important part of brush selection is the thickness of the bristles. A very thinly packed brush will not hold paint well and just makes for more hard work.

Watch out for brushes with bristles set in vulcanised rubber; this setting mixture can dissolve and cause the bristles to loosen and drop out. Epoxy resin is the best setting mixture.

Choosing a roller

When it comes to selecting a paint roller, the same rules apply as those for choosing a paintbrush; natural material covers such as mohair offer a finer finish and a longer life span than synthetic covers. Of course, you have to pay more for the advantages of using a natural fibre.

Roller covers are available in different pile lengths to suit the texture of the surface to be painted. Deeper piles are suitable for coarser surfaces such as cement render, besser blocks or stucco work, while finer piles are best for interior walls and ceilings.

Always wash new utensils in a mild detergent before use. A new roller should be 'de-fluffed' by rubbing it between the palms of your hands to remove excess fibres. A new paintbrush should be flicked back and forth a few times to remove any loose bristles.

The best way to apply paint

The technique you use when painting is an important element in the final finish. Haphazard strokes up

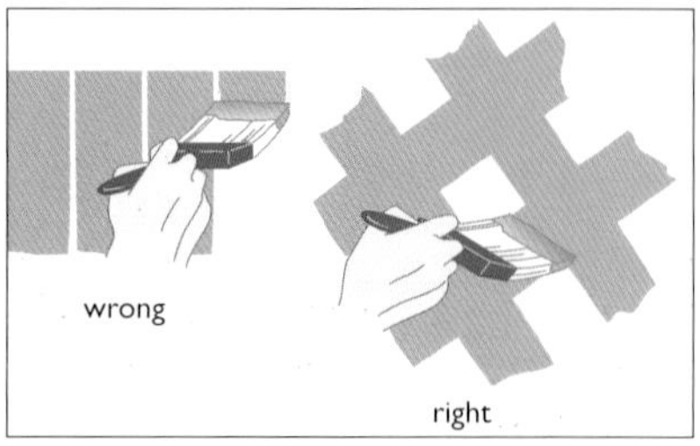

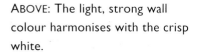

ABOVE: The light, strong wall colour harmonises with the crisp white.

RIGHT: The best way to apply paint.

and down, back and forth across the surface will produce an uneven finish of dense and sparse paintwork. The best technique to use for both roller and brush painting is the lattice pattern, which forms a criss-cross framework over about one metre square. The gaps are filled by lightly feathering in the edges of the frame without applying more paint. This is a good way to make your paint go a lot further, too.

How to hold your paintbrush

To hold a brush correctly, you should grasp the handle completely in your palm. To do this, hold out your hand as if to shake another, place the handle in your palm running parallel to your thumb (which should be pointing skywards), fold the fingers then the thumb over the handle and operate the brush by wrist action only. According to the experts, arm tiredness when painting is directly related to incorrect brush grasp; by using your wrist you should be able to paint more effectively for a longer time, and with much less strain.

Storage tips

The best way to store brushes and rollers after washing is by hanging them from a hook or line in the garage or workshop. Brushes may be stored flat in a drawer, but rollers should always be hung to avoid a flat spot in the cover pile. Wrap roller covers and brush bristles in plastic wrap to shield them from dust after they are completely dry; any trace of dampness may promote fungal growth within the fibre.

Loading up

When loading a paintbrush, dip the bristles up to one-third of their length only into the tin; any further and the unused paint tends to slide back into the handle and clog the bristle base.

When loading a roller, ensure that the entire surface of the roller is covered in paint; however, do not overload the roller as this may lead to spattering.

How to prepare paint surfaces

A quick cosmetic cover-up won't do; proper preparation is vital. Incorrect preparation can lead to new paint peeling, blistering and wrinkling. Here's how to prepare your surface to ensure a professional finish.

New woodwork

Softwoods such as pine need a primer with a high oil content. Hardwoods are often greasy when new, so the primer should be thinned with mineral turpentine before application. Too much oil and the paint may not coat or dry very well. Before priming, ensure that the timber is completely dry, as new timber is often damp. Ask your supplier for advice. Sand lightly, dust off debris and fill knots or veins with a suitable filler.

Previously painted woodwork

If the surface is in reasonable condition, with no peeling, blistering or wrinkling, it will require only light sanding and washing. If it is badly damaged, the affected areas must be sanded smooth and spot-primed. Large portions of paint damage require complete removal by chemical stripping or gas burning. Once the old surface has been thoroughly removed, sand, dust and prime.

New concrete

Wait a minimum of three months to allow thorough curing and settling. After this time, wash the surface with a solution of zinc sulphate (1 kg to every 4 L of water), then seal with a concrete

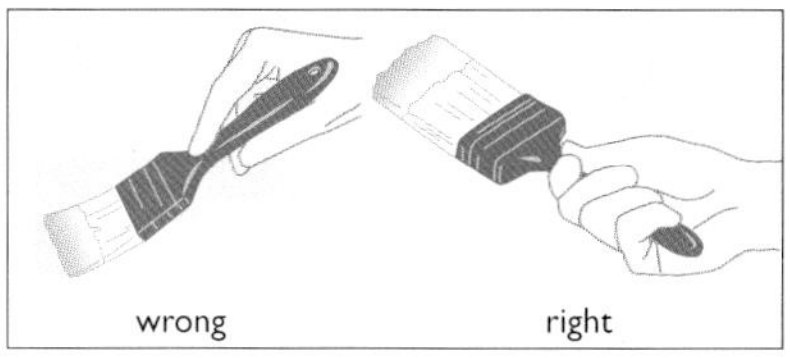

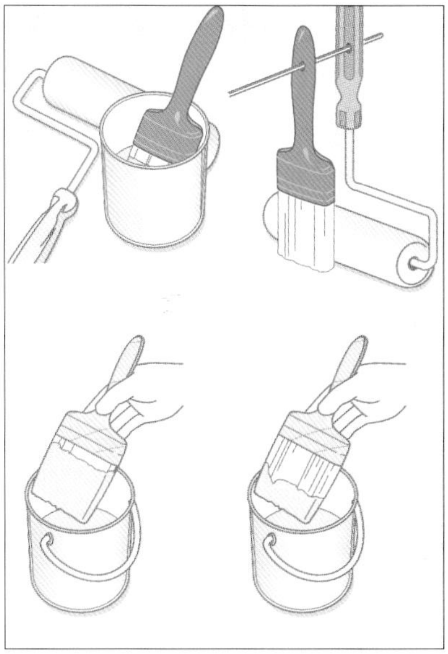

TOP: How to hold your brush.

ABOVE: Storing brushes and rollers. Loading up.

Tips

- Keep an old egg-beater for stirring paint. It's efficient and easy to clean.
- To strain lumpy paint without removing it from the can, cut a circle just smaller than the can from an old wire flyscreen. Stir the paint well and drop the piece of screen into the can. Any remaining lumps will be trapped beneath it.
- If you're a messy painter, wear an old shower cap when painting the ceiling. If you're really the pits, a cheap plastic raincoat complete with hood is the greatest thing since sliced bread!
- It's best to use acrylic paints if oil-based paint and mineral turpentine affect your skin with an allergic reaction.

sealer. This prevents oil-based paints from seeping into the concrete. Acrylic paint may be applied immediately after the curing period without a sealer base.

Previously painted concrete

Remove peeling and flaking paint with zinc-sulphate solution (see as for new concrete) and a stiff wire brush. If the surface is powdery, apply Sealer Binder.

New plaster and fibrous plaster

Newly set plaster surfaces should be allowed a drying-out period; check with the manufacturer or installer. Lime can be a problem in a new plaster, so a coat of zinc-sulphate solution (see as for new concrete) should be applied. If painting with an oil-based paint, a base coat with pigmented sealer will be required. Acrylic paint needs no sealer base.

Previously painted set and fibrous plaster

Sand the surface and coat with cement sealer before attempting to paint with either oil-based or enamel paint. Flaking paint must be removed by sanding and patches should be filled with a suitable plaster filler. No sealer is required for acrylic paint.

ABOVE: The use of a stencil provides an effective border.

BELOW: These timber kitchen cupboards are painted in a mat finish. The russet colour against papered walls is unusual and effective.

New iron and steel

Apply a rust-inhibitive priming paint to new iron and steel surfaces. Remove all dirt and grease before priming to ensure paint adhesion.

Previously painted iron and steel

If the paint is cracking and flaking, remove the old surface by sandblasting or flame cleaning. You can use a paint stripper to help you along. Remove rust with a wire brush; treat affected areas with a rust-proofing agent and metal primer.

Stripping paint from timber

Very often a battered but worthy piece of furniture can be transformed by stripping off old paint, sanding, sealing or waxing.

If you can, apply chemical stripper outdoors and always wear protective gloves and goggles. Don't breathe in the fumes and, if the stripper comes in contact with your skin, wash immediately.

A well-prepared job when painting or varnishing will always deliver better, longer-lasting results. This is particularly true of the removal of paint from furniture or woodwork. Stripping it off with a chemical stripper is one of the best ways to achieve a top result.

1 Read the manufacturer's instructions on the container carefully and apply the stripper strictly as directed.
2 Leave the stripper on for the recommended time, then remove the loosened, old paint with a scraper. Scrub with a stiff brush and water.
3 Wash down with a hose before the surface dries to be sure you've removed all traces of stripper. If necessary, repeat the process until all paint is removed. Let the surface dry thoroughly, then sand.

Applying paint

Even coats of paint and smooth surfaces are only obtained with practice. In this section we discuss types of paint and stain, care of brushes and offer solutions to common problems.

ABOVE: The green colour of a Granny Smith apple makes a strong contrast to the walls of soft daffodil yellow.

Using acrylic paint

Acrylic paint is great for interior walls because it's so hard wearing and easy to clean. It's thicker than oil-based paint and dries more quickly, so it's best not to cover too large an area at once. You can avoid brush marks if you apply it correctly.

1 Apply a long stroke of paint horizontally, then brush it up and down and from side to side, beginning at the top.

2 When you've covered the surface, smooth it with light, vertical brush strokes, lifting the brush at the end of each stroke to avoid overlap marks.

Using oil-based paint

Oil-based paint is perfect if you want to achieve a glossy country-coloured finish for timber panelling. Don't be frightened off by bold colour — enjoy it!

Even coats and smooth surfaces are only obtained with practice! You should always use an undercoat on wood and take the trouble to apply two thin coats of gloss, rather than one thick one. Don't allow the paint to dry on the brush, but clean it at once with turps or the hard residue will ruin it.

1 First, spread a drop sheet. Then, starting at the top, paint three or four vertical strokes about 500–600 mm long, leaving a gap between strokes.
2 When the paint on the brush is used up, don't re-load, but make horizontal strokes to spread the paint you've already applied.
3 After five minutes, gently stroke the near-dry brush over the covered surface, lifting it at the end of each stroke.

Staining timber

Read the instructions on the container carefully, as each type of stain is applied in a slightly different way. Take time to sand all the surfaces to a fine finish before applying the stain. You'll find that blue and green give good results on radiata pine.

1 Begin sanding with 120 grit sandpaper, move to 180 and finish with 240 grit. Use a cork block and sand with the grain.
2 Wear rubber gloves when applying the stain with a 50 mm paintbrush, using long parallel strokes. Feel free to apply the stain liberally but keep the depth of colour even.
3 The stain will leave a slightly roughened surface which should then be smoothed with 600 grit wet-and-dry sandpaper that has been dipped in the stain.
4 Wipe over the surface with a soft, dry cloth using long parallel strokes.

Colourful wood stains allow the grains of different timbers to show through. Furniture looks particularly good treated this way.

Cleaning brushes

Be sure to clean your paintbrushes thoroughly every time you use them, and especially before the paint dries in the bristles. If you have used acrylic paint, wash the brush thoroughly in clean water and detergent or soap. Oil-based paints can be removed with turpentine or brush cleanser and then the bristles should be washed in warm soapy water and carefully dried. Mould the clean, damp bristles to their original shape and then wrap them in paper held with an elastic band. Hang them bristle downwards or lie them horizontally.

ABOVE: You can achieve wonderful effects by using a combination of opaque paint and the lovely softness of a stain in a similar way. Here it's 'solid' paint on the door and stain on the cupboards.

How to fix what goes wrong

It can be disheartening to find, even after you have carefully followed instructions, that you still have problems with paint application and finish. Identify the problem and follow the chart to find a solution.

Name	Symptoms	Cause	Remedy
Bitty surface	Bristles, grit or fluff under the new paint	Lack of cleaning of surface or painting in a dusty environment	Allow to dry, rub down with fine wet-and-dry sandpaper; re-coat with clean equipment
Bleeding	Staining and discolouration of paint	Tannin stains from tannin-rich timber or residues such as bitumen in surface	Remove as much as possible of residue and stained paint then seal or prime
Thickening	Paint increases in consistency and becomes hard to work	Addition of inappropriate thinners or evaporation due to room temperature; lid left unsealed	With old paint or inappropriate seal, discard paint; alternatively, add small amount of thinner and stir with flat stick
Soft surface	Paint is dry but remains soft	Applied too thickly; presence of wax or oils on surface; mixing of different types of paint	Remove and start again
Receding (or cissing)	Paint separates from surface leaving bare patches	Presence of grease, wax or silicon; water-based paints have been applied over new oil-based paints	Allow receded paint to harden before sanding back. To prevent, clean surface thoroughly before painting; sand oil-based paints
Curtaining (or running)	Unsightly drifts of thick paint	Paint applied unevenly and too heavily	Allow to set then sand smooth and re-coat
Discolouration	Dark and light patches or streaks of the same colour, or yellowing	Atmospheric pollutants or moulds and fungus; yellowing due to too much or not enough sunlight	Wash with peroxide solution; repaint with acrylic which will not yellow or paint which resists mould growth
Lack of drying	Sticky surface	Lack of ventilation, low temperature, excessive humidity; lack of allowed time between coats	Improve atmospheric conditions; if surface has been impaired add an additional thin coat
Efflorescence	White crystalline deposit	Moisture continuing to pass through masonry and plaster surfaces	Wash with calcium-chlorine solution and leave for 14 days to check for recurrence; solve the moisture problem
Fat edge	A thick crust of paint adjacent to an edge or corner	Brush deposits extra paint as bristles run over corner	Re-check and spread paint if still wet; allow to harden, rub down, sand smooth and re-coat
Gloss loss	Patches of less shiny finish	Application over an unevenly porous undercoat; unsuitable weather conditions; over-thinning of paint	Rub down and re-coat with full-strength paint
Grinning (showing) through	Underlying coats show through	Too few coats or over-spreading	Use an additional undercoat when making a marked colour change; use recommended undercoat

Tip

- When you are painting all day with oil-based paint, you will frequently need to put your brush aside. To prevent the brush drying out, drill a hole in the handle, push a piece of wire through and suspend the bristles in a jar of mineral turpentine.

Tip

- If you love bright, vibrant colours but don't want to overdo it, remember that decorative stains will give you all the subtle colour you desire, but without the heaviness of a painted finish.

Name	Symptoms	Cause	Remedy
Holidays (misses)	Gaps in the paint coat	Poor lighting conditions while working; undercoat too similar to the finishing colour; careless application	Apply additional coats
Lifting	One coat is softened or disturbed by a subsequent coat	Re-coating under recommended drying time	If in doubt, do a small-scale test before proceeding; if it is too late, cease further work, allow to dry and sand back before re-coating
Foaming	Tiny bubbles that have burst leaving pin holes	Too vigorous brushing or rolling; applying paint to hot surfaces	If it occurs through several layers of paint, the lot has to be stripped off; otherwise, rub back dried top coat and re-coat
Coarse finish	Unsightly texture that can but does not always look like brush marks	Over-working of paint after drying has already commenced	Allow to dry, rub down and re-coat
Saponification	Softened and discoloured paint	Oil-based paints coming in contact with alkalis in the presence of moisture	Alkalis exist in cement, lime, plaster and compressed cement sheet. Make sure they are cured and not damp. Strip and dry the surface before re-coating — preferably in acrylic
Seeding of the paint	Small particles of dried paint rather than pieces of grit	Old paint; wrong thinners	Re-coat with new clean paint
Patchiness	Uneven sheen in low-gloss paint that shows up as roughness	Variations in porosity of surface; brushing of semi-dry paint	Light sanding and re-coat
Wrinkling	Outer surface dries in a series of fine ridges	Occurs most frequently with heavily applied exterior gloss finishes	Drying can take weeks but this is essential before you can rub it down with fine wet-and-dry paper. Otherwise, scrape and wipe with turps

ABOVE: A terracotta colourwash was used to decorate this dining room. Through the doorway the faux effect of stone blocking makes a dramatic and imposing hallway.

RIGHT: The stencilled frieze in this traditional room works well as an alternative to wallpaper.

Paint finishes

These easy paint finishes give you a maximum reward of exciting effects for minimum effort. The combination of different colours, the particular finishes you choose and the patterns you create with them can be applied to so many things. Walls, of course, are natural candidates, but so are furniture and kitchen and bathroom fittings — you're really only limited by your imagination.

Rag-rolling

Wonderful, decorative effects are achieved by dabbing or rolling cloth over wet glaze. You can experiment with lace, hessian or towelling. First, apply your base-coat colour and allow to dry. Then apply the glaze over it in sections and roll your cloth across it, changing direction as you go. It's best to work in pairs before the glaze is too dry. Change cloths as soon as they are paint saturated.

Combing

Cut even notches in the edge of a squeegee blade to use as your combing tool. Paint your base colour and allow to dry. Then paint the coloured glaze over the top, one manageable strip at a time. Draw the squeegee through the glaze in a wavy, straight or random direction. Continue to work your way across the wall in this fashion, in strips. If there are two of you, one can apply the glaze while the other combs through it.

Sponging

This is achieved by dabbing coloured glaze over a dry base-coat colour. Dip a sea sponge lightly into glaze and dab on the entire surface. If more than one colour is desired, apply second or third colours, drying after each application. Concentrate the various colours on blank spots, overlapping them occasionally.

Crackle

In this process, the top paint layer is made to separate into a fine crazed or crackled pattern. Apply two coats of the base colour, allowing to dry after each coat. When dry, apply an even coat of crackle medium (from art and craft shops). Allow to dry thoroughly. Apply the

ABOVE: A mixture of techniques. The wall was painted in wide stripes with a roller, then each colour was lightly sponged with the other. Basic combing has been used on the corner cupboard in a bold but contrasting colour to make a vivid focal point.

LEFT: Rag-rolling.

BELOW LEFT: Combing.

BELOW CENTRE: Sponging.

BELOW: Crackle.

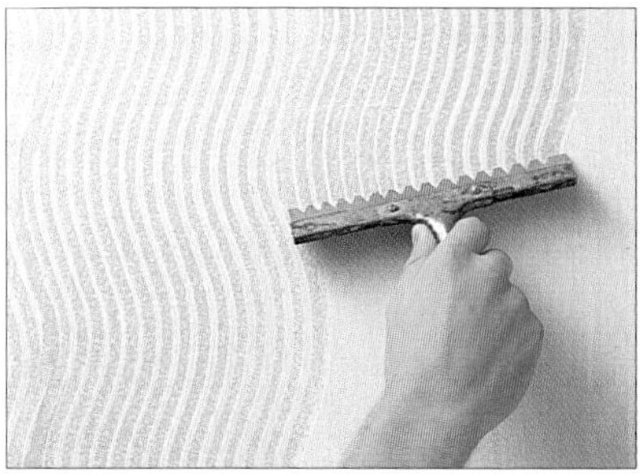

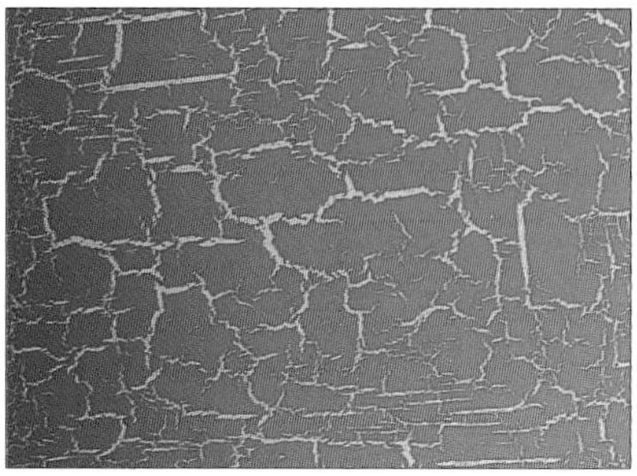

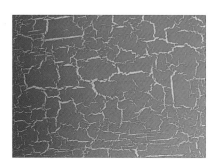

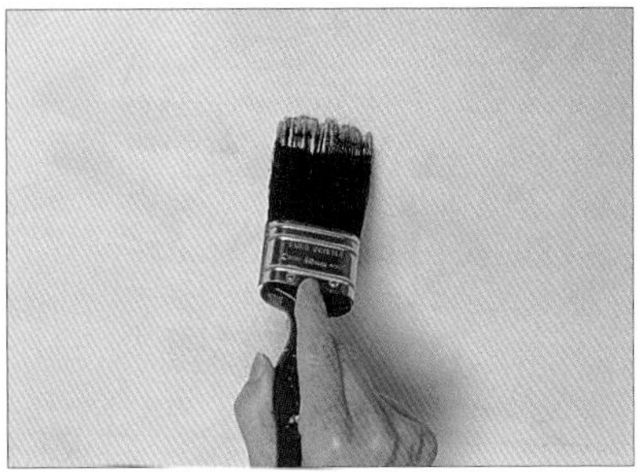

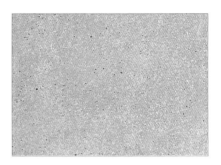

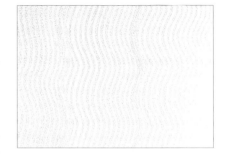

second colour with a sea sponge for overall crackle effect, or brush for a linear-type crackle effect. As the crackle coat reacts with the top coat it shrinks, taking the top coat with it and thus forming cracks.

Colourwashing

For this elegant finish, two colours are washed over a dry base coat, one at a time. Apply the first colour with loose, irregular strokes across the wall, leaving patches of the original base coat exposed. Let this dry, then apply the second colour using the same technique. Concentrate on covering the exposed patches, but leave glimpses of the base coat to show through. This finish looks best in pastels.

Dragging

This finish is formed by dragging a dry, soft-bristled brush through fresh glaze, painted a section at a time over a dry base-coat colour. For best results over large areas of wall, work with a partner. While one person applies the glaze, the other drags the dry brush down or across. Use two strokes to drag a vertical strip, one in a single motion from the top to the centre, the other from the base to the centre. Stagger the junction of the two up-and-down strokes as you move across the wall to avoid a horizontal marking.

Stippling

To achieve this orange-peel-like finish, apply glaze over a dry base coat. Working in pairs, one partner applies it in vertical strips while the other pats the fresh surface evenly with a stiff-bristled brush held at right angles to the surface. Stippling with a rough-textured roller is the quickest method you can use, though this produces a much softer texture. You must first run a clean roller over the wet surface to remove some of the paint.

Stripes

Cut uneven notches along the edge of a squeegee blade. Paint the wall in a base colour and let it dry. Next, paint the coloured glaze onto the

ABOVE LEFT: Colourwashing.

ABOVE CENTRE: Dragging.

ABOVE TOP: Stippling.

ABOVE: Stripes.

FAR LEFT: Darker stripes are hand painted roughly down the wall and the whole wall has been dabbed and streaked with a rag and brush at random in other muted colours.

Tips

- Don't be restricted by the 'tools' suggested here. Hair combs or fingers, for instance, can substitute for a notched squeegee blade for vastly different effects. And for rag-rolling, try scrunched-up lace, plastic or crackly paper.
- Always experiment and perfect a technique on cardboard or another temporary surface before you tackle your walls.

wall with a brush working in vertical strips so it doesn't dry before you can work with it. Draw the squeegee through the glaze with a straight, wavy or random stroke to the bottom of the wall. Continue to work across the wall. Have a partner apply the glaze while you use the squeegee.

For best results

For all finishes except crackle and colourwashing, make a glaze by diluting the top coat with a scumble medium (from art and craft shops or specialist paint shops). This extends the drying time, especially if you're painting large areas such as walls. It also helps the paint hold the brush-stroke patterns and creates a translucent finish.

Give walls the look of aged plaster

To give walls the look of aged plaster, try this technique. Purchase matte-finish, water-based paint in cream, taupe and gold. Paint the walls with a base coat of cream. Thin the taupe and gold paints half and half with acrylic matte medium. Colours will stay vibrant if you thin paint with acrylic matte medium (available at art shops). When used to thin interior paints, it lends depth and sheen to the finished product.

To apply the thinned taupe and gold paints to the walls, use rags and brushes. A little paint goes a long way. Working in 1 x 1 m sections, alternate patting and dabbing the paints on the wall.

Use a soft touch and run the paint out to the edges. Don't worry if you don't like the way it looks. You can go right over it again. If it's too dark, bring in the light colour.

To complete the finish, create a border using taupe paint, a spray-on granite-look paint and cream paint. Mask off the ceiling and create a level line along the walls. Then paint the border with taupe paint. After the paint dries, spray on a light coat of the granite-look paint. (Protect walls and ceiling from spray.) Complete the look by painting thin feathery lines randomly across the border. Detailing takes a couple of hours.

Do-it-yourself—Stripes

Have you ever wondered how to create fresco finishes in your home? They look great and it's easy! To recreate this living room, all you'll need is some time, paint and sponges. Be adventurous and experiment with other colours—dusky pinks, powder blues and greens all look terrific.

You will need: a suitable undercoat for the walls—Dulux Flat Acrylic paint in Riviera Sand (quantity of undercoat and base colour will depend on the size of the room and the extent of woodwork—

ABOVE: The end result, softly contrasting stripes.

ABOVE: Paint and a wallpaper frieze set off rag-rolled walls.

Tips

- Narrower stripes will make the ceiling appear higher; wider stripes will make the walls appear wider.
- Mask off the edges of the cornices and skirting boards before starting the painting.
- If you're approaching a corner and it's only possible to paint part of a stripe, paint the other part of the stripe around the corner.
- The beeswax finish gives the room a delicious scent and removes the smell of paint.

seek advice at a paint store); Colour Solutions Sample Pots Low Sheen Acrylic paint in Scotch Mist (ochre), Bechamel (yellow) and Tibetan Hills (bluish green); suitable undercoat tinted Tibetan Hills for the woodwork; craftwood template (see note below); a pencil; low-tack tape; kitchen sponges; containers for mixing paint; an old t-shirt or lint-free cloth; a rubber; paintbrushes; some white wax candles; 320 grade sandpaper; beeswax; and a soft cloth.

Fresco walls

Note. The template used here was 120 mm wide and the length was just short of the measurement between the bottom of the cornice and the top of the skirting. We used smaller lengths made of cardboard for areas such as under and above windows, doors, fireplaces and so on.

1. Undercoat the walls and apply two coats of Riviera Sand. Let each coat dry.
2. Hold the template against the wall and make light pencil marks on either side of it. Proceed to mark the stripes around the entire room.
3. Using the pencil lines as a guide, mask the stripes with the low-tack tape, smoothing the tape down along the paint edge. Cover the pencil lines with the tape — you will erase them later.
4. Add 10 per cent water to the Scotch Mist and mix well. Dip the corner of the sponge into the diluted paint and randomly dab the paint onto the wall, within the stripe. Spread the paint by wiping the sponge in a circular motion, side to side and up and down. Using the t-shirt, dab off some of the paint. Work every second stripe in this way.
5. When dry, remove the tape by pulling it off diagonally towards the paint stripe. This will help prevent smudging and paint peeling off the wall. Erase the pencil marks.
6. Add 10 per cent water to the Bechamel and mix well. Dip the corner of the sponge into the paint and apply by wiping the sponge backwards and forwards over the entire surface of the walls. Allow to dry. The lighter colour, applied over the walls, softens and reduces the contrast between the stripes.

Woodwork and skirting

1. Using the tinted undercoat, paint the woodwork; let dry.
2. Randomly rub the candle over the woodwork.
3. Having combined a small quantity of equal parts of Bechamel and Tibetan Hills, add five per cent water and mix well.
4. Dry brush over the woodwork with the diluted paint. To dry brush, dip the tip of the brush into the paint, dab it onto a lint-free cloth to remove the excess paint, then apply it to the woodwork. Allow to dry.
5. Lightly sand the woodwork. Where the candle has been rubbed over the surface, the paint will not adhere. This completes the ageing effect and will allow the base colour to show through.
6. Rub beeswax over the woodwork. When touch dry, polish with a soft cloth.

Notes

For the ceiling and cornice, we applied Riviera Sand that was tinted half strength.

For a more subdued appearance, finish with a wash of the base colour over the entire surface. For example, in this case our base colour was Riviera Sand and the stripes were Scotch Mist. For a lighter, less bright look we would have used diluted Riviera Sand over the walls to finish.

Wallpaper

BELOW: Before — Drab brown walls and ceiling created a cave-like appearance in this room.

BOTTOM: After — Green wallpaper with a pattern resembling a painted finish has turned the room into a serene place to sleep. The wallpaper border adds a little 'architectural' interest and links the light and dark greens of the papers.

Most of us associate wallpaper with grandma's dingy living room or wild 1970s designs. It hasn't played a big part in home decorating in recent years, but today's wallpapers offer an exciting and vast range of options when you want something different from a painted finish. As well, they are much easier to apply than before.

Wallpaper can transform a room with little interest into a charming, inviting place. It envelopes you. It can hide uneven walls, create architectural emphasis or add surface interest. Many fabric designs also have related wallpapers, which allows you to create mix-and-match rooms with confidence.

Modern wallpaper comes in vinyl, flock relief or embossed finishes and is ready pasted to allow easy application.

Stripping wallpaper

Most wallpapers can be softened simply with water, but adding wallpaper stripper to it will make the job much easier. Vinyl and foil-faced paper are water resistant, so you must peel these surfaces before applying the diluted stripper. Washable paper should be scored with a wire brush.

1 Protect the floor while you work and wear rubber gloves. Using a large sponge, wet the wallpaper with the diluted stripper, working in sections from the top.
2 Make a cut into a join with a paint scraper and lift the paper. If you have difficulty, simply apply more stripper mix with the sponge.
3 Holding the scraper at a low angle to the wall, push away from you beneath the wallpaper. Take care not to dig into the surface of the wall.

How to wallpaper

Decide how much wallpaper you'll need. This will depend on the size of the room. Your wallpaper stockist can work out how many rolls you need from the height of the walls and perimeter of the room.

Read the instructions on the wallpaper roll carefully. Clear the room of furniture.

Prepare the walls. Remove old wallpaper (see illustration 1 on p. 236). Most old papers are easy to peel, but you may need to hire a steamer to remove more difficult papers. If you use a steamer, wear protective goggles and gloves. Remove excess glue with a sponge and water, then fill any cracks or dents with filler so they won't show through the new paper.

When the walls are smooth and dry, apply a liberal coat of latex or acrylic size and leave for 24 hours to ensure it is dry.

Before hanging the paper, measure the walls and use a plumb line and pencil to mark a straight line 48 cm from the corner (see illustration 2). Start hanging here to ensure the first drop is absolutely vertical and the rest of the wallpaper lines up perfectly.

Unroll the wallpaper and cut the first strip according to the height of your wall, adding 10 cm top and bottom. If your paper is self-adhesive, place the roll in a water trough and slowly draw the length of wallpaper through the water (see illustration 3). Gently place the upper part of the wallpaper against the wall. (Note: After wetting, some papers must be folded and left to stand for a minute or two. Check the instructions.)

Align the edge of the paper with the plumbed pencil line and smooth down with a sponge. Work down, centre to edge, removing air bubbles and wrinkles as you go (see illustration 4). Press paper into corners, cornices and skirtings and cut excess with a blade knife against a broad knife (see illustration 5).

Fixing lifting wallpaper

If glue has been spread unevenly when a wall is being papered, you may find the paper starts to lift and form bubbles. All you need to do is apply some more glue beneath the paper.

1 Using the point of a very sharp Stanley knife or razor blade, make a cut big enough to slide a knife in at the centre of the bubble or lifted area.
2 Lift the edges of the cut carefully, using a flat knife blade. Work some wallpaper glue into the slit using the flat knife blade.
3 Wipe the surface with a damp sponge to remove any excess glue, pressing the wallpaper down as you do so.
4 Cover a block of wood with plastic wrap, place it over the slit and apply firm pressure for several minutes.

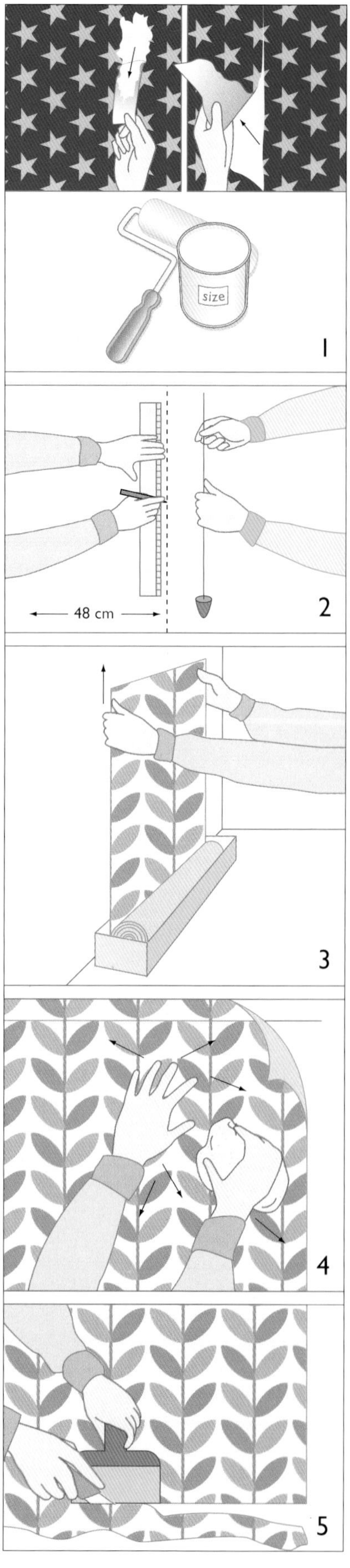

TOP: Emphasise interesting details by wallpapering between the skirting boards and picture rails. You can take the wallpaper all the way up to the ceiling to add height to your walls.

ABOVE: Many wallpapers come with related borders. Use them to frame your windows or doors, around your skirtings and ceilings or to create panels.

Tips

- Never remove power points when wallpapering — water and electricity don't mix. Instead, hang wallpaper over the point and make diagonal cuts which form flaps that can be trimmed off.
- Change trough water regularly, and keep your sponge clean.
- Pay careful attention to special soaking times.
- Manufacturers usually specify the correct paste to use.
- If you haven't wallpapered before, don't start in the toilet. The room needs a lot of fiddly cutting in and there's not much room to move.
- Beginners should practise with a small piece of paper — not a three metre drop.
- If left until the following day, trimming excess paper is much easier.
- Paint all window frames, architraves, cornices, skirtings and ceilings before hanging wallpaper.
- Walls in less-than-perfect condition look best with textured papers to hide faults.
- Solid vinyl wallpaper will outlast paint, so use this in high-traffic areas.
- Vinyl papers should always be hung with fungicidal paste.
- Clean washable vinyl paper with a mild detergent and water solution.
- Remove grease spots with moist fuller's earth. Stubborn stains may respond to rubbing with stale white bread or a soft rubber. If not, try a proprietary cleaner. Patch-test first.
- If possible, buy an extra roll of paper for future repairs.
- Save left-over scraps of wallpaper for spot patching. To spot patch patterned paper, tear roughly into shape. Plain paper will need a full replacement drop.
- Reverse hang textured papers at each drop for the best finish at seams.

ABOVE: The country blue-and-white check wallpaper gives an informal look to this dining area adjacent to the kitchen.

LEFT: This sunroom takes on the air of a conservatory with a lattice wallpaper.

Tip

- Save the ends of wallpaper rolls after a renovating stint, and look out for cheap rolls on sale. Wallpaper makes pretty wrapping paper for birthdays and at Christmas, and is perfect for lining kitchen and bathroom drawers.

CAVEAT
ISTORY OF ART BY H.W. JANSON
RENOIR A RETROSPECTIVE

Storage and Furniture

Solving all of a family's storage problems is a bit like painting the Harbour Bridge — by the time it's finished, it's time to start again. With proper planning, though, you can clear most of your existing clutter and anticipate any future bottlenecks as well.

Begin by asking yourself whether you really need more places to put things, or just better organisation of what you have. Often, the simple space-engineering techniques shown in this chapter can do wonders for a cupboard's capacity. And remember that you can rotate seasonable items. Try letting things such as the sun umbrella swap places with the raincoats as the seasons change. Decide where to locate any new units. Keep everyday items at or near their points of use, and once-a-year specials such as Christmas decorations in more remote spots.

It might help to survey your entire home, noting and measuring all sites with potential for development, then indicating them on a graph-paper floorplan. If you have several options, concentrate on ground-floor storage first— it's handier and will probably add more to your home's value. Finally, select the type of storage you need. Open shelves are relatively inexpensive and easy to install; they also attract dust. Cabinets provide more protection for stored items, and are available in sizes to fit almost any space you have. New built-in cupboards offer the most permanent and least obtrusive storage. Also available is an impressive array of ready-made storage units.

Plan spaces carefully, note the sizes of your household items and be sure to allow for the thickness of shelves and dividers. Don't over-plan and don't forget to allow a few centimetres of space for getting contents in and out, and enough flexibility to accommodate changes later on.

Storage and furniture are often one and the same thing. Most households require space to display decorative pieces as well as storage for everyday items. The shelving unit pictured here serves multiple functions as a display unit, a bookcase and a room divider.

Storage

If you cannot tailor storage to suit your needs, a reassessment of your existing storage capacity may be the solution. Cleaning out unwanted items can create a surprising amount of space.

Organising existing storage

Tailored storage not only makes everything easier to get at, it also increases the capacity of a cupboard or cabinet by as much as a third. This means that modifying three cupboards could give you a fourth — without the trouble of building it.

The diagram below can assist you in room by room planning of your storage. Study the layout, make an inventory of the things you want to make places for, then adapt it to suit your particular needs.

Plan spacings carefully. Tables later in the chapter give typical sizes for many household items. Be sure to allow for the thickness of shelves and dividers when you are using them.

Make sure you don't over-engineer. It's better to be flexible as you may change your mind later on about layout and the items you want to store.

The Ten Commandments of better storage

1 Don't be a hoarder. Discard unwanted items or those you haven't used for years.

2 Consider built-ins whenever possible for maximum and most efficient use of space.

3 Exploit odd spaces such as corners, next to fireplaces and so on to build or place furniture.

4 Don't waste under-stair space. Enclose it for extra storage or turn it into a small home office.

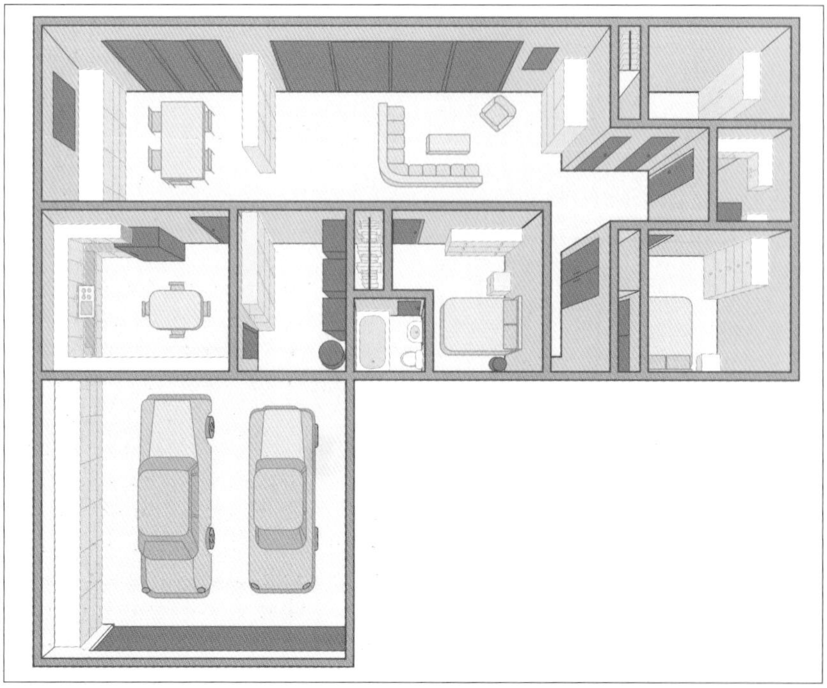

TOP: Space under stairs is ideal for storage.

ABOVE: Shelving across one wall maximises space.

RIGHT: Organise your storage space.

5 Take built-ins right to the ceiling. Finish with cornices.

6 Save floor space with sliding, rather than swinging, doors.

7 Boost wardrobe space by creating a walk-in wardrobe, fitted out with both hanging space and shelving.

8 Make extra room for inactive storage in your roof with attic sections or by placing planks across ceiling joists near the access hole.

9 Make an extra storage room or even a wine cellar by going down. An area that is just one metre deep beneath your floor can be made into a small storage room.

10 Use open shelving — adjustable and/or fixed wherever possible.

Why built-ins?

Upgrading the level of comfort of your house improves both its value and your lifestyle. A good built-in not only enhances a room by rationalising and organising its contents, it also improves the look of that room. But whatever a built-in achieves, it will have to be made specifically for its purpose and for the space it occupies. Unlike anything you can buy from a shop, a built-in takes its form from your precise needs and aesthetic requirements. That's why you can adapt the ideas pictured here to suit your home.

ABOVE: The space either side of a fireplace is useful for built-in storage which can be both functional and attractive.

ABOVE LEFT: Sewing can be a messy job, but if the sewing machine and all its associated bits and pieces can be stored where the work is carried out it will be easier to set up and put away each time. Cupboards with shelves are the key. These can be prefabricated in white plastic-laminated board or custom-built in the colour of your choice.

LEFT: Shelves built into the end of the kitchen wall in this small apartment are a clever and practical idea.

Where will we put it?

Finding places to store things is a constant battle for most of us. Even if you're not a hoarder, you will still need a place for all the essentials you can't live without. And, as you can see, function and beauty can go hand in hand.

With open storage, place important objects at eye level and less attractive items near the floor.

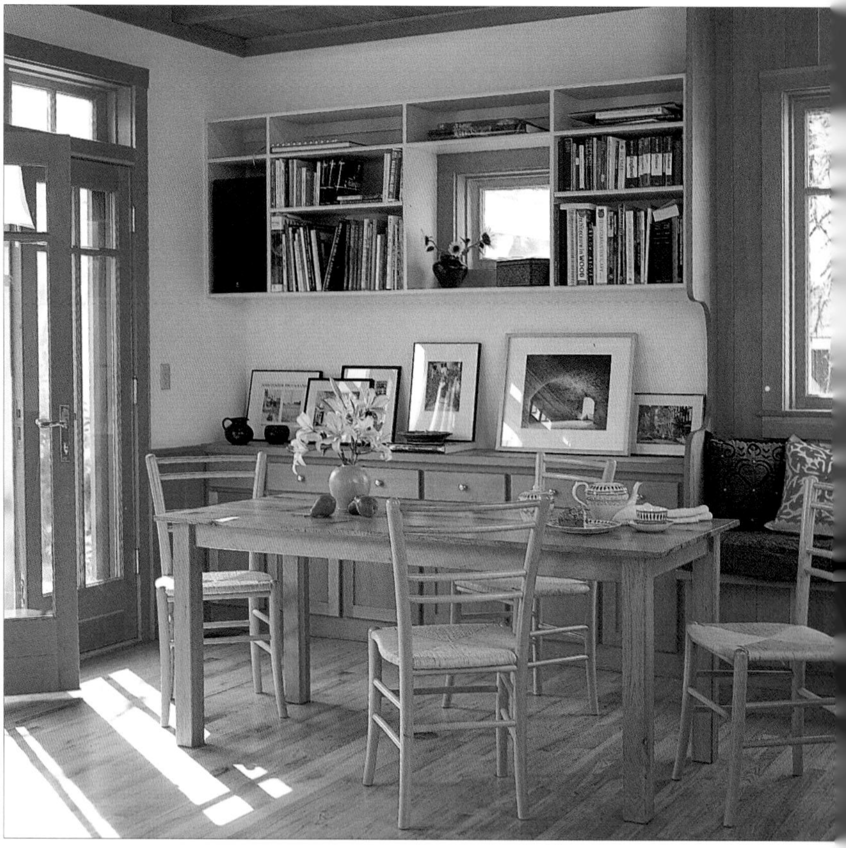

ABOVE: Insets on a staircase make an effective display space.

LEFT: An office combined with the sewing room must have well organised storage.

ABOVE: Follow the lines of the roof and take shelving right to the ceiling, to create a whole wall of books and ornaments.

ABOVE: Television in a built-in unit is unobtrusive yet accessible.

TOP LEFT: A built-in sideboard with bookshelves above combines beauty and function.

RIGHT: A double bookcase, up to the ceiling, is perfect for a traditional room with high ceilings.

DIAGRAMS THIS PAGE: Furniture combining.

Furniture combining

If space is at a premium, you can stack furniture. Whitewood stores offer lots of options.

1 Place a hat rack under a narrow shelf. This is great in a bathroom for towels and bottles and jars.
2 Use a little cupboard, such as one used for a video, on top of a chest of drawers.
3 Place a long narrow cupboard on top of a bedside chest. Don't forget to screw the pieces together for stability.
4 With a chipboard circle and a cloth on top, a little chest can serve as a table and storage.
5 A blanket or toy box on top of a coffee table of similar size makes great storage for the hall, and saves bending.
6 Two tops of a wardrobe, one of them turned upside down, could make a new, interesting piece of furniture.

Room-by-room storage tricks

When you're planning storage or trying to boost what you've got, consider the general storage commandments. However, you can also use the following clever storage tricks for specific rooms.

Kitchen

Kitchens need to be stacked to the rafters with storage facilities. This means you have to exploit every storage possibility. Because there are so many different sorts of kitchen things to be stored, there has to be an equivalent range in storage methods: drawers of all shapes and sizes, shelves to fit the situations, racks and rails, trays that rotate and glide.

Consider a pot rack overhead to hang cookware and create more space in cupboards and drawers.

Install an appliance cupboard to keep appliances within easy reach on your bench top.

Build overhead cupboards to the ceiling for maximum space.

If you have room, install a kitchen island to give you more bench and under-bench space.

Install open shelving on spare wall space to stock recipe books, tea canisters or other attractive kitchen items.

Investigate the vast range of modular racks, baskets, lazy Susans, hooks, waste tidies and so on to increase storage in existing and new kitchens.

ABOVE: Specialist storage means having the right type of storage for the job. Here are three types in one cupboard. The wire baskets (on the right) are hooked onto a vertical hanger and slide easily. Plastic bins (on the left) with a lip around the top are available from hardware stores. You will need to build rebates into the sides of your cupboards for them to slide along. In the centre are slide out shelves.

TOP LEFT: Building an island across the corner makes your kitchen much more multi-faceted and gives you more under-bench storage space as well. The work space, a couple of open shelves and narrow but deep side drawers will always be handy.

TOP RIGHT: Finding space for small items may mean building a large shallow shelving unit. All you need is some 90 x 19 mm timber for the sides, 70 x 19 mm shelves and shelf fronts, a 3 mm plywood back and a good-sized door with clearance from the shelves to hang it on.

ABOVE: Now you can fold away your most space-consuming kitchen appliance as it remains sitting on its own shelf. As this fold-away fitting disappears out of sight beneath your bench top, its parallel-arm system keeps whatever sits upon it perfectly level.

ABOVE RIGHT: Standing plates on their edges means you don't have to stack. Placing your plate rack in an above-bench cupboard is the best possible siting for it. These racks are home made. The slats between plates are 19 x 10 mm, front and side rails are 32 x 19 mm and the main framing timbers are 42 x 19 mm. Butt joints are simply glued and stapled together.

RIGHT: Open up your above-bench storage with exposed shelves. Make shelves, sides and shaped brackets from 190 x 19 mm pine. Use 70 x 19 mm timber for the supporting wall battens.

RIGHT: Closing up a doorway provided the opportunity to build in recessed shelving behind the newly installed sink. Shelving tracks and clips make shelf adjustment easy and bottleneck-sized notches keep an even distance between the wine bottles on the upper shelves.

RIGHT: Suspending saucepans above your work bench makes sense. A shelf mounted on decorative brass shelving brackets, commonly available in hardware stores, gives you a wide horizontal surface. This allows your saucepan/towel rail to be far enough out from the wall to accommodate large utensils.

CENTRE LEFT: Revolving corners make maximum use of corner cavities which inevitably have limited access. Not having a corner door shape cut out of it, this model is completely circular. The central shaft is fixed at top and bottom and comes with two plastic shelves which can be set at any height.

CENTRE RIGHT: Rounding edges of benches and cupboards with quarter or half-circle open shelving gives you accessible incidental shelving for a few everyday essentials or prized possessions, and curved work benches make for easy movement about the work area.

RIGHT: Having rolling shutters down across the back of your bench top allows you to leave your appliances plugged in and ready to use. It also means you can tidy up at short notice. Plastic rolling shutters come in brown and white. Their maximum width is 1200 mm, but you can cut the shutter down with a hacksaw for a perfect fit.

ABOVE: Decorative items and bathing accessories are displayed in this bathroom, but a cupboard under the bath provides storage space for more everyday items.

RIGHT: This small country-style bathroom has utilised a small space for the built-in shelves to store rolled up towels. Above the basin is a handy rack for toiletries.

Bathroom

Place open shelving on walls to store towels, shampoos, soaps, oils and bathing accessories.

You should make the most of ready-made hooks, rails and shampoo caddies to boost storage in your bathroom.

If you have little storage space for medicines and bottles, you can construct a shallow, recessed cabinet into the wall.

Build a cabinet with shelves beneath a freestanding basin for extra space.

Bedroom

Parents

Consider taking extra space from an adjoining room to construct a walk-in wardrobe.

Whether you have a walk-in or built-in wardrobe, you can make the best use of space with a combination of double-hanging, single-hanging, adjustable shelving and a few modular pieces to store smaller clothing items.

Consider using a professional wardrobe company to organise best your existing space. When planning wardrobes, it's vital to allow more space than you'll need and make wardrobes at least 86 cm deep.

Children

Consider bunk beds to save space or install a mezzanine level in the room if you have the space and budget for it.

Use divan beds with drawers beneath for extra storage.

Buy or build modular furniture that can be constructed in space-efficient configurations to include a wardrobe, shelves and a desk for children's study.

Make use of small boxes, trunks and baskets to stock children's toys, books, drawing items, sports equipment and so on.

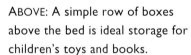

ABOVE: A simple row of boxes above the bed is ideal storage for children's toys and books.

ABOVE LEFT: An open shelving unit in a bedroom can add colour but will only look attractive if it is kept tidy. The wall rack for jewellery and belts keeps the items tangle-free.

BELOW LEFT: This bedroom storage space literally has a place for everything. You do need a big bedroom and a large empty wall space to attempt this level of organisation, however.

LEFT: These tiny built-in shelves will save you from having to rummage for small items in large drawers. Jewellery, watches, hair accessories and scarves can be easily retrieved simply by sliding the shelf out.

TOP FAR RIGHT: A ladder on castors gives easy access to high shelves. The long, shallow shelves are perfect for storing smaller items.

RIGHT: The ideal place for ties and belts is on the inside of the wardrobe door. On their own hooks they save space and are easy to find.

CENTRE FAR RIGHT: Mirrored doors serve as dressing mirrors and help make a small room look larger. The hanging rail is useful.

LEFT: Everything can have its own space in a walk-in wardrobe. Vertical dividers create order and the ladder provides access to high shelves.

Getting more into wardrobes

Typically, a shallow wardrobe of 600 mm deep by 1500–2400 mm wide offers lots of room for improvement. With most, you get a single pole, plus a shelf above it, and a pair of sliding bypass doors.

Start your analysis of a wardrobe's efficiency with the doors. Do you find yourself opening one, then rolling them both to the other side (and maybe back again) every morning? If so, consider replacing these awkward panels with a set of bi-folding units.

Next, study how space is utilised inside. Chances are, you'll notice that a few dresses and coats fill most of the vertical space between the rod and floor, while the bulk of your clothing hangs down only a little more than halfway. Group items by size and you'll 'discover' a sizeable empty space under the shorter items.

Shallow cupboard designs, with either sliding or bi-folding doors that include a shelf unit, take the pressure off freestanding storage elsewhere. A walk-in wardrobe is the ultimate luxury — the one illustrated on page 252 features two rods on one side to accommodate shorter clothes, creating more hanging space for longer items. You can adapt your built-in wardrobe by using this design, but keep in mind that the spaces allowed for hanging clothes are the minimums.

ABOVE: Narrow cupboard doors are easier to handle than full-sized ones. Paint them to suit the room and choose knobs to match.

Getting more into a walk-in wardrobe

Walk-in wardrobes, though usually larger than their shallow cousins, actually provide less storage per square metre. Subtract the minimal 600 mm-wide corridor needed for access and you can see why. If a walk-in measures just 1200–1500 mm deep and access isn't a problem, you might gain by converting it into two shallow cupboards located back to back.

Otherwise, you can install poles along the longer wall or walls, as illustrated. Double-tier poles for suits, skirts and other shorter items can give you half as much again hanging space.

Shelves—either at the back or along one wall—often will hold all of your folded clothes. It's best to space them about 180 mm apart to minimise rummaging.

And don't neglect shelf possibilities above the poles. Though you may have to stretch to reach them, boxes stored here can hold seasonal or seldom-worn clothing. Install a second shelf approximately 300 mm above the existing one and you won't have to stack the boxes on top of each other.

Dimensions you need to know

You'll be wise to familiarise yourself with a few basic measurements before you take on a cupboard re-organisation. A wooden coat hanger with a heavily padded jacket on it occupies a space about 500 mm deep. Poles are normally hung 300–350 mm from the wall, but in a tight situation you could cut this distance to 250 mm. The table lists other typical dimensions. Use them as an aid in allocating space in your remodelled wardrobe.

Living room

Install built-in furniture and shelving right to the ceiling for TV/stereo equipment.

Use a chest or trunk as a coffee table-cum-storage box.

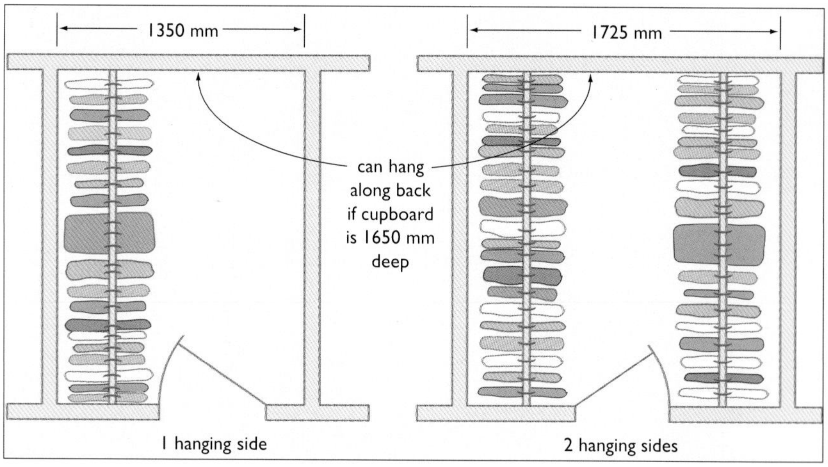

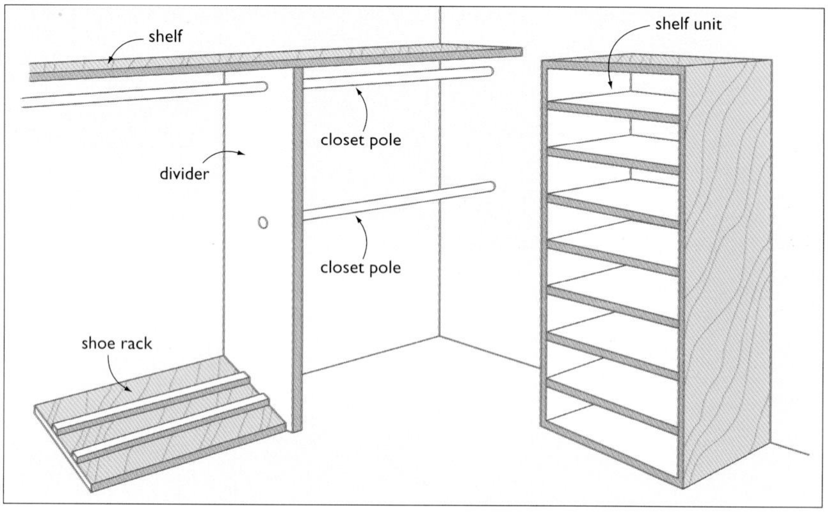

Use wasted under-window space for a short block of bookshelves.

Entertaining storage

We all know how out of control our sound and viewing equipment can become. A large part of making a sitting room work is in organising

ABOVE: Getting more into a walk-in wardrobe.

Wardrobe contents (all measurements are in mm)

Women's items		Men's items		Accessories	
Long dresses	1750	Top coats	1270	Garment bags	1450
Dressing gowns	1320	Suits	960	Hanging shoe bags	900
Skirts	900	Travel bags	1050	Umbrellas	900
Dresses	1150	Trousers (cuff hung)	1120		
Dress bags	1220	Trousers (double hung)	500		
Blouses	700	Ties	700		
Coats	1320	Shirts	700		
Suits	750				
Suit bags	1050				

the storage of television, video and sound systems. To begin solving your storage problems, work out the best furniture arrangement; from there, establish the appropriate location for your home entertainment centre. Now decide how best to use the space that you have available.

ABOVE LEFT: Clearly different-sized items require shelves and cupboards of different depths. A pivoting stand is an excellent extra for the television set.

ABOVE: Extending television turntables which run on heavy-load bearing runners allow the television to be shut away when not in use. These mechanisms are available through specialist hardware manufacturers.

CENTRE LEFT: Grouping different activities into one storage unit is an efficient use of space. This corner unit incorporates an unobtrusive sitting room bar, as well as books, ornaments and sound equipment.

LEFT: Be guided by your site. Here, the below-stairs area is perfect for a triangular format. Even the lowest, least accessible cavities can be used for storage.

ABOVE: Storage units are just boxes, after all. Think about a separate 'box' for each storage category — this one is purpose built for the sound system.

RIGHT: If you can tailor your storage unit to suit your room's style, you will create a finished look that's perfect. Here, it's fine polished timber throughout.

Laundry

Fix the dryer to the wall above the washing machine.

Attach a fold-out ironing board cupboard to the wall. The ironing board can then fold away when it is not needed.

Make more room in an existing laundry for sorting with a small table, then add a few overhead cupboards or shelves for more storage.

Fix hooks behind the door to hang brooms, mops and so on or install a tall cupboard for them.

Linen cupboard contents (all measurements are in mm)	
Pillowcases	180 x 380
Blankets	690 x 570
Sheets	
Flat	460 x 380
Fitted	340 x 270
Washers	180 x 180
Hand towels	150 x 250
Bath towels	350 x 330
Bath mats	250 x 230
Dish towels	250 x 410
(Maximum space requirements — folded)	

Getting more into a linen cupboard

The trouble with tall stacks of folded sheets or towels is that you have to be a magician to get out the lower ones without rumpling the rest ... and maybe toppling adjacent stacks as well. The solution — compartmentalise.

Look at the diagram to see one scheme for putting foldables in their places. Bulky blankets go on the top, then bath towels, sheets, hand towels and so on. Drawers and a cabinet also add concealed storage below.

Plan your dimensions according to the things you have, leaving a few centimetres of clearance for getting them in and out.

And keep your arrangement flexible: home fashions change.

Tips

- Deep cupboards below bench height allow you to store your television and other equipment neatly. Use shallow shelves above for CDs, cassettes, videos and books. This is the most popular storage format.
- Line up storage units with the heights of the window sills, doors and cornices.

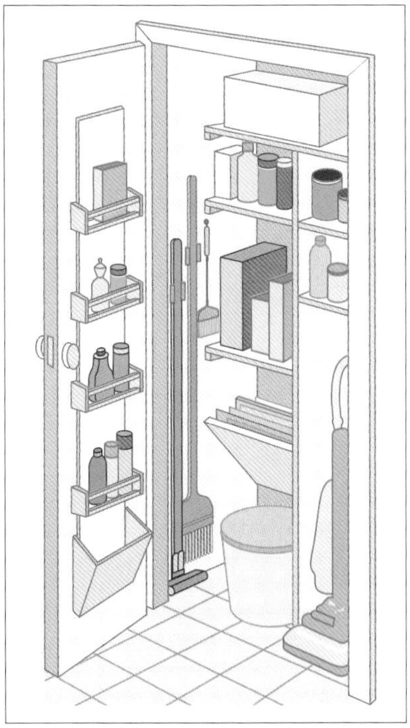

TOP: Getting more into a linen cupboard.

ABOVE: Getting more into a cleaning cupboard.

Getting more into a cleaning cupboard

Compartments can help organise the jumble of awkward shapes that utility storage must handle. The cupboard here stores an upright vacuum, provides shelves for an assortment of cleaning products and secures a mop and broom so they won't fall out every time you open the door. Note, too, how a slanting compartment near the bottom of the cupboard reduces the clutter of stored paper bags.

For even more storage, look to the inside of the cupboard door. Lipped shelves and/or a cloth caddy for vacuum attachments put this bonus space to good use. And if space in a cleaning cupboard is really right, consider outfitting it with perforated metal shelving rather than wood shelving. You'll gain storage space and improve air circulation as well.

Cleaning equipment (all measurements are in mm)	
Canister vacuum	350 x 430
Floor polisher	300 x 1140
Upright vacuum	350 x 1220
Carpet sweeper	410 x 1370
Broom	250 x up to 1520
Whisk broom	150 x 250
Dust pan	280 x 230
Push broom	350 x up to 1370
Dry mop	340 x 1680
Wet mop	300 x 1220
Bucket	270 x 30
Cleansers	200–250 x 150–350

Adding new storage

The answer to a storage shortage may be as simple as a few coat hooks at the front entry or as complex as an entire wall of custom-made living room built-ins. Most solutions fall somewhere in between, with open shelving leading the list. If you select the right hardware and master a few basics, you'll never again be floored by a shelf project. Available in a wide variety of styles and finishes, they make sense of almost any room.

You also could consider building a new cupboard or cupboards. Before you begin, though, consider the almost-instant alternative offered by storage you can buy.

Choosing shelf hardware

The success of any shelving project rests quite literally upon its support system. So you should ask yourself these questions before making your choice. What weights and space must the hardware hold? Can shelves be supported at the ends or must they be rear-mounted? Do you want fixed or adjustable brackets? How will you attach the shelves to the wall? Do you really need hardware at all? Cleats and dadoing offer two alternatives.

Once you've answered the mechanical questions, consider appearance. Styling ranges from strictly utilitarian to hardwood wall furniture. You'll discover that price is a relevant factor, too — the hardware sometimes costs more than the lumber for the shelves.

The box on the next page discusses the eight most commonly used support systems, but there are dozens of variations. With standards and brackets, for instance, you can choose painted or plated finishes, different bracket shapes and locking mechanisms, and even specialties such as angled supports that serve as magazine racks.

And while you're selecting hardware, you should give some thought to buying pre-finished shelving as well. Though considerably more expensive than ordinary lumber or plywood, it saves a lot of tedious work.

Putting up shelf strips

Bracket shelving seems to concentrate a lot of weight on the few

Support systems

- Rigid pressed-steel angle brackets hold medium-weight loads. Always mount them with the longer leg against the wall. For heavier duty, choose types reinforced with triangular gussets between the legs.
- Brackets clip into slotted standards, allowing you to adjust the spacing between shelves. Choose 200, 250 or 300 mm brackets. Properly installed, this system supports surprisingly heavy loads.
- The simplest (and least expensive) way to hold shelves inside cupboards, bookcases or cabinets is to install cleats at each end. For longer spans, attach a third strip to the unit's back to support the rear of the shelves.
- For a dressier look, mount shelves by popping pin-type clips into pre-drilled holes. Relatively inexpensive, they'll support heavy loads on 20 mm-inch-thick boards up to about 750 mm long.
- Alternatively, you can make end-mounted shelves adjustable with standards and clips. Again, limit spans to about 750 mm. For a flush installation, you can dado the standards into the cabinet's sides.
- So-called 'tension' poles (actually they work by expansion) wedge between the floor and ceiling in situations where you can't or don't want to make holes in the walls. They're relatively expensive.
- Folding brackets let you drop a shelf out of the way when you're not using it. You can buy a variation of these brackets for spring-loaded typewriter-style installations; the shelf simply pops up when you pull it out from a cabinet.
- Light-duty wire brackets are among the many accessories you can mount on perforated hardboard. Measure the board's thickness before you buy it: 3 and 6 mm sizes require different devices.

ABOVE: This bookcase, with a deeper central section, is a practical way of providing shelves of various dimensions.

small fasteners that secure the strips. But those fasteners don't actually bear the load; they simply clamp the strips to the wall. This means that the strength of a shelving system actually depends more on the fasteners' holding power than it does on their size.

Use plastic anchors only for light-duty installations. Wood screws driven directly into studs hold much better, but with them you must adjust your design according to the way the wall was framed. Hollow-nail fasteners such as toggle and expansion bolts let you put the strips exactly where you want them.

Armed with the proper fasteners and a screwdriver, drill and spirit level, you can hang the strips in an hour or so. Generally, it's best to plumb the strips so they'll be perfectly vertical. However, if you have walls that are out of square, you may have to measure from floor to ceiling to make the shelving aesthetically acceptable.

Before hanging the first strip, note whether it has a definite top and bottom. Mark and drill for the top hole only.

Insert a bolt, but don't tighten it until you've plumbed the strip, drilled remaining holes and installed the lower bolt or bolts.

Draw a level line from the strip's top or bottom to locate the last strip. See above if you have out-of-square walls.

Position the intermediate strips, using the line you've drawn as a guide. Maintain equal spacing between them.

Estimating shelf spacings and spans

Plot any shelf layout carefully, using graph paper and the dimensions supplied here to minimise any 'surprises' later. The span table gives the maximum distance you should allow between supports. It assumes a full load of books, which are the heaviest items you're likely to put on shelves. Don't allow the unsupported ends of shelves to extend more than half the span distance beyond the last support or they may begin to bow on you.

With adjustable shelving, you can save space and cut down dusting by tailoring vertical spacings to accommodate your possessions exactly. Just be sure to leave an extra few centimetres so you can easily tip out a book (allow a little

ABOVE: The kitchen wall dishrack.

Shelving spans	
Material used	Maximum span
17 mm plywood	900 mm
250 x 50 mm or 300 x 50 mm timber	1200–1350 mm
18 mm particle board	700 mm
13 mm acrylic	550 mm
300 x 25 mm timber	600 mm
10 mm glass	450 mm

(Assumes shelves fully loaded with books)

Item	Space required
Paperback books	200
Hardback books	280
CDs	160
Over-sized hardbacks	380
Cassette tapes	130
Catalogue-format books	400
Videos	190

Shelf spacing guide (all measurements are in mm)

more leeway if you decide to have fixed shelves).

Before determining your final shelving layout, consult the lower table for the spacing required between shelves for several often-shelved items.

Do-it-yourself — A kitchen wall dishrack

A dishwasher, a standard inclusion in today's kitchen, uses energy and water as though there's no tomorrow. The wall-hung dishrack, on the other hand, cuts many corners off the hard slog of washing up. If you position it above the sink, your washed and rinsed dishes can drain in situ, doing away with drying and putting away. This sink is 600 mm deep with a 120-mm-wide shelf behind the bowls. This allows plenty of room to work in front of the rack, which is therefore not in the way. Contact your sink manufacturer about having a sink made to your specifications but using standard bowl arrangements.

We made our dishrack from Tasmanian oak, with 13-mm-thick hollow stainless-steel tubing for the rods. It is best to use a hardwood for the framework, as this allows it to support the weight without looking too bulky. (If you don't feel like going to the expense and trouble of cutting steel rods, you can substitute them with timber dowel rods of the same thickness.)

Tip

- Plan your shelving strategy around available space, while keeping in mind the style and function of the room. But don't be afraid to break a few of the conventional rules. You can be ruthless when it comes to maximising space.

You will need for the dishrack:

Item	Material	Length or size (in mm)	No.
End frame front	32 x 19 mm Tasmanian oak	322	2
End frame back	32 x 19 mm Tasmanian oak	830	2
End diagonal	32 x 19 mm Tasmanian oak	425	4
Front rail	32 x 19 mm Tasmanian oak	1200	3
Back rail	32 x 32 mm Tasmanian oak	1200	3
Back spacer	32 x 19 mm Tasmanian oak	1200	3
Top side rail	32 x 19 mm Tasmanian oak	175	2
Middle side rail	32 x 19 mm Tasmanian oak	145	2
Bottom side rail	32 x 19 mm Tasmanian oak	105	2
Top rod	13 mm timber or steel	200	28
Middle rod	13 mm timber or steel	170	28
Bottom rod	13 mm timber or steel	130	28
Back rod	13 mm timber or steel	750	28
Top capping	32 x 19 mm Tasmanian oak	1200	1

Other: 100 mm expanding bolts; 35 and 50 mm countersunk screws; wood filler; nails for pinning.

1

2

3

4

5

6

7

8

ABOVE: Do-it-yourself—A kitchen wall dishrack.

1 Cut and assemble end frames.

2 Drill holes in front and back rails.

3 Fasten end frames to rails.

4 Assemble rails and rods.

5 Drill and pin rods.

6 Fit spacers.

7 Fit back rods.

8 Fix rack to wall.

1 On the bench top, draw the shape of the end frames to the dimensions on the diagram and lay lengths of 32 x 19 mm timber on it to the exact lengths and angles of the two lots of four components. Rebate the back verticals into diagonals and cut half-lap joints at the front obtuse angles. Glue and screw the end frames together.

2 Our shelves are 1200 mm long. Cut the three 32 x 19 mm front and three 32 x 32 mm back rails to this length and drill 28 holes on their inside surface, halfway down the 32 mm depth. Make the holes 10 mm deep and 13 mm in diameter. Use a dowelling jig for the purpose and mark out the position of the holes, using the shelf layout plan as a guide.

3 Cut pairs of side rails to length. The three different shelf widths will allow you to accommodate the standard range of plates but, if you wish to store extra-large items, make your own calculations. Glue and nail the side rails to either the back or front rail of the shelf you are working on.

4 Rods or dowels should measure 130 mm for the bottom shelf, 170 mm for the middle shelf and 200 mm for the upper shelf. Cut these with a hacksaw or tenon saw, depending on the type of rod you are using, and tap them into the holes with a mallet. Tap the other rail onto the open end of the rods. You will have to line up the 28 rod ends with their holes. Work from one end to the other and, if possible, get someone to help.

5 At four points along each of the back and side rails drill fine holes through the rails and the inserted rod ends. Pin the rails by punching nails from which you have removed the heads. This will stop the rails from flexing outwards when the shelves are loaded.

6 Add 32 x 19 mm spacers to the back of each shelf. Drill, glue and screw these in place.

7 The back rods are 750 mm long. Drill vertical holes into the back rails of the shelves to correspond with the horizontal rods, as close to the inserted rear end of horizontals as possible. Slide the shelves down the back rails. The holes will be tight enough to hold the shelves apart to suggested clearance heights. Next, fit the top rail, with holes drilled to correspond.

8 Screw the ends of the frame in place. Countersink screws through the end frames into the ends of the top capping, as well as the front and rear of each shelf. Plane the top front corner off the top capping to match the angle of the top diagonal. The narrow bottom shelf will cantilever by half its depth past the bottom diagonal of the end frame. Fix the rack to masonry walls using expanding bolts in two places along the back rail of each shelf, and diagonally through the top of the end frames. Lime and coat with polyurethane to protect the timber, or you may prefer the traditional patina of water stains.

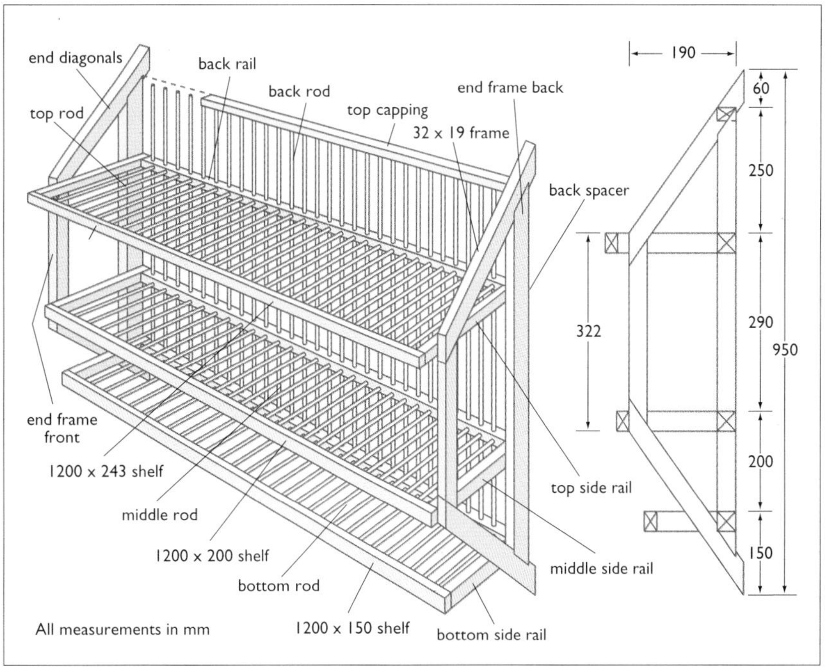

Do-it-yourself — Build a blanket box

Window seats and blanket boxes make fabulous storage. They are deep enough to accommodate the bulkiest goods — doonas, blankets, pillows and big bags, or things you're not ready to part with just yet. We give you the plans for a blanket box which is large enough to be turned into a window seat if you would like.

The blanket box is built from a mixture of hardwoods. They are more difficult to work, and you may choose softwoods such as oregon or even radiata pine. Because all recycled timbers need to be

ABOVE: Take advantage of the space created by a bay window by filling it with extra seating and storage. This seat opens across the front through cupboard doors, instead of having a hinged lid.

ABOVE: If money and space are at a premium, the conventional window seat with a hinged lid is a cheaper style than one with cupboard doors. You have to take everything off it to get into the box, so store only seasonal items there.

ABOVE RIGHT: A blanket box can double as an extra table or seating.

cleaned up with a plane to different degrees, their widths and thicknesses will vary. The sizes we have given are only meant as a guide.

1 Use a router to cut the rebates in the side rails and the lid frame pieces to the depths shown in our diagrams. Mitre the ends.
2 Mitre the ends of the side panels. By gluing and skew screwing (screwing at an angle) through the back of the side panels, fit the rails to the side panels. Form the resultant sides into a box and fix them by nailing through the mitres of the end side rails (hardwoods will need to be pre-drilled to avoid splitting, both with nailing and screwing).
3 After ensuring that the box is square, fit the floor braces. Skew screw them into the side rails, then fit the floorboards into the box and secure them by skew nailing into the bottom side rails and the braces. Complete the box by screwing the brass angle pieces on the corners. (If you are using lining boards for the flooring, you will need to trim the tongue-and-groove edges off the two outside boards so they fit the box.)
4 The lid can be made of plain boards or old tongue-and-groove floorboards. If you are using floorboards, fit them together then clamp them before making the frame for the lid. Similarly, fit the pieces of the lid frame to the side rails. Screw the lid braces to the underside of the lid after ensuring that it is square.
5 Screw and glue the hinge mount to the top rails and fit the hinges and lid. The quality of the final appearance of your blanket box will be in direct proportion to the amount of effort put into the final sanding and finishing of the timber. We used a satin finish polyurethane with plenty of sanding between coats for a hard, smooth finish.

You will need for the blanket box (finished sizes in mm):

Item	Material	No.	Size
Side panels	Iron bark	2 pieces	1456 x 275 x 18
		2	546 x 275 x 18
Side rails	Cypress	2	1500 x 60 x 45
		2	590 x 60 x 45
Lid panels	Stringy bark	4	1448 x 112 x 18
Lid frame	Cypress	2	1500 x 45 x 23
		2	500 x 45 x 23
Lid braces	Iron bark	2	400 x 100 x 18
Hinge mount	Cypress	1	1500 x 90 x 23
Floor	Cypress (t & g boards)	1	1420 x 130 x 20
Floor braces	Cypress	3	500 x 60 x 45

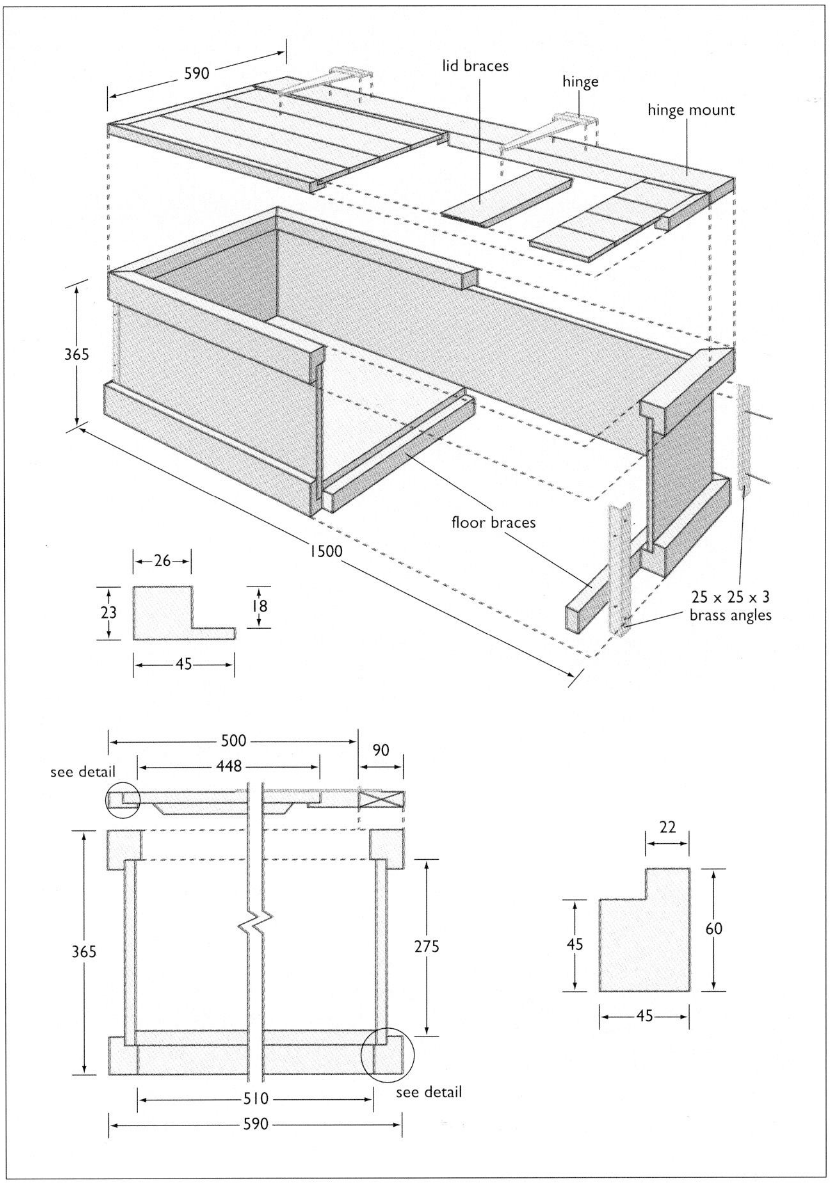

LEFT: Build a blanket box.

BELOW: This back-door arrangement is an effective way to keep the house clean and to stop dirt and clutter from spreading into the house.

Back-door bonus

In any house it is useful to have a place close to the entrance to put coats, boots or shoes and umbrellas. In wet weather this prevents mud and moisture being trailed through the house.

Make the bench as long as you have space for, but you should include a leg and brace support every 1500 mm. Use 40 mm countersunk screws and drill and glue all the joints as you proceed.

Use 50 mm sq timber for all framework. As an alternative to the seat slats pictured, our diagram (on p. 262) indicates 19-mm-thick medium-density fibre board for the seat. Because the leg braces have to be cut from a sheet material, making the seat from the same board will be a substantial cost benefit.

Cut the braces and the decorative braces from the fibre board. Screw through the legs into the back edge of the braces, then screw through the leg back into the wall, using expanding bolts if the wall is built of masonry. In the corner situation you will find it easier to bolt the leg in place through the 38 x 19 mm trims indicated in our diagram.

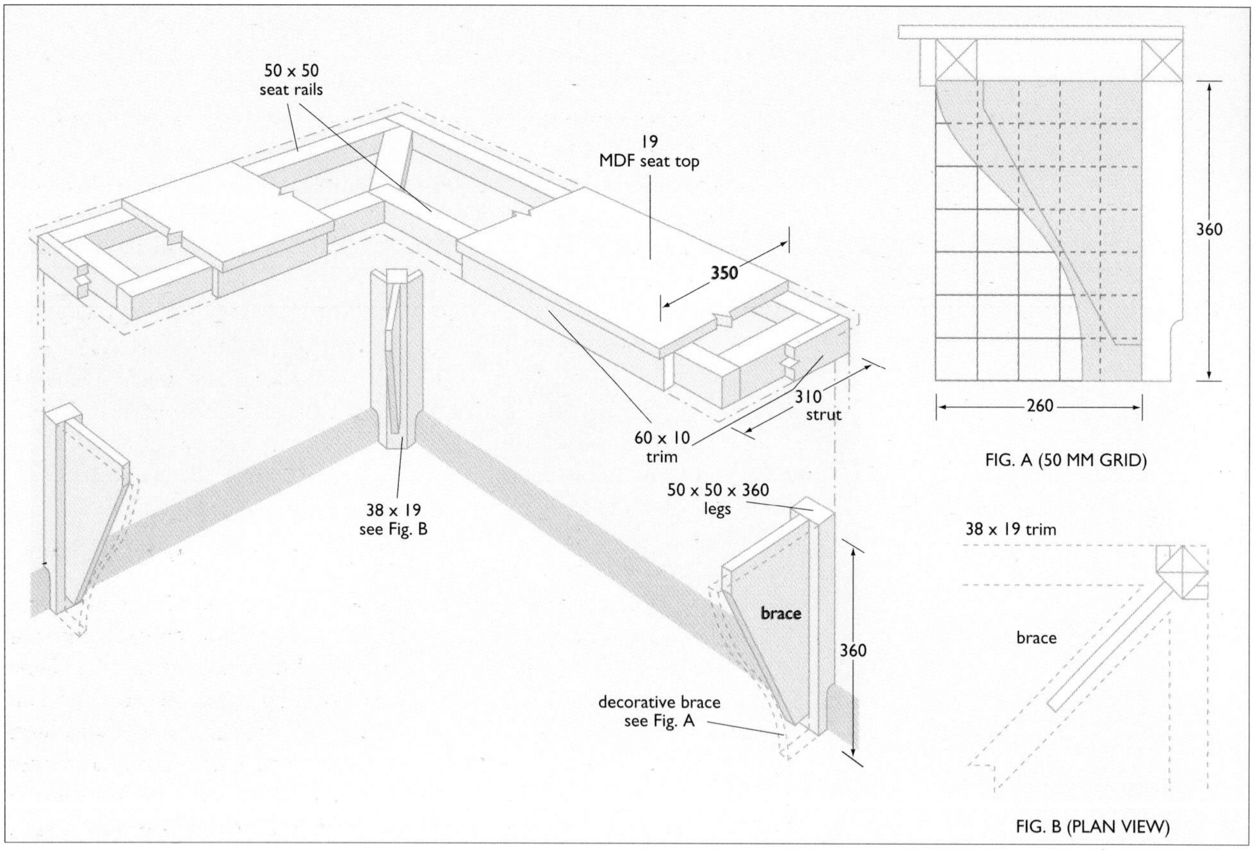

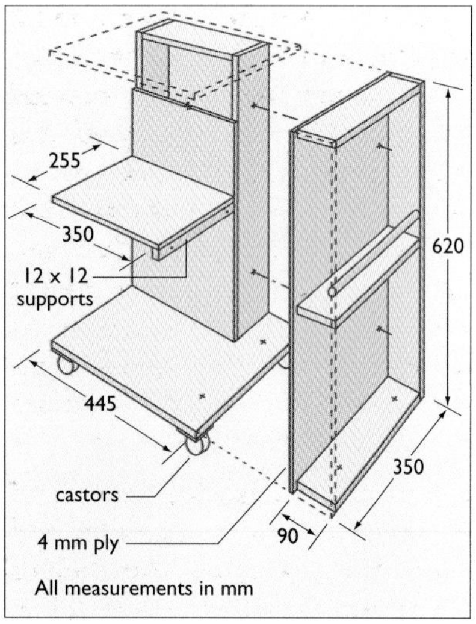

TOP: Back-door bonus.

ABOVE: Mobile storage.

Now fix the 310-mm-wide seat frame to the braces. You should include a transverse strut running the depth of the seat at least every 800 mm.

Complete by adding the seat surface of your choice.

To make the coat and hat rack use 300 x 200 mm prefabricated timber shelving brackets, available from your hardware store. Cut a 325-mm-wide fibre-board back sheet to the length you require, and drill and screw through it into the back of the shelving bracket. Fix through the board into the wall. Drill, glue and inset turned pegs (available from some craft stores) or, alternatively, use timber knobs or small turned legs bought from hardware stores. Glue and screw a 250-mm-wide shelf in place.

Mobile storage

A practical and multi-purpose storage option is a mobile unit. For example, a kitchen and sewing trolley that can be moved where you want, when you want. By adding a pegboard, it can easily become a workshop accessory, or it can be adapted for use in the laundry or study. Mobile units can be stored out of sight in a cupboard when not in use.

Each trolley consists of a base with four castors. The unit comprises two 90-mm-deep shelved boxes with plywood backs, which are mounted on the base in one corner. This forms a right angle which gives rigidity to the trolley. The arrangement of the shelves can be as intricate or as simple as the items to be stored dictate. The best material to use for this unit is 12 mm MDF board or plywood (particle board is also an option, but it requires edging).

Six pieces of 326 x 90 mm MDF or plywood are used for the box shelves (extra if more than one shelf is required). Four pieces of 620 x 90 mm are needed for the

ABOVE: This little mobile storage unit can be at hand when you need the things in it and easily tucked away when it is not in use.

sides. The base (and top, if it is required) measures 445 x 350 mm. If an intermediate shelf is to be included in the back section, it will be 350 x 255 mm and will be supported on 12 x 12 mm timber cleats. The three-ply backing for the boxes needs to be 620 x 350 mm. To stop items falling off the shelves, use dowels, Perspex or whatever you consider suitable.

Alternatively, you could make a tray 90 mm deep, to fit flush behind the boxes. The fastenings include 18 mm countersunk particle-board screws and 38 mm nails. PVA glue and a suitable paint finish complete the requirements.

1 After checking the box components for square and straightness, assemble them using the screws or nails and glue. While the glue is still wet, nail and glue on the backs to square them up. If you're using dowels, bore holes 6 mm deep in the sides and fit them in place as you're assembling the boxes.

2 Fix the boxes to the base and each other as shown, again using glue and screws. Next fix the top, if any, and/or the intermediate shelf (or shelves) once the cleats are screwed into position. The best way to screw them is to come through the plywood into the cleats.

Next fit the castors, but don't secure them in case they get paint on them. Then fill all the holes and apply a suitable gloss or semi-gloss paint, sanding lightly between coats.

3 When finished, fix the castors, Perspex, elastic cords and whatever other refinements you need, and load up the unit. It will provide years of service.

To build your own bookcase you will need:

Components	Material	Length or size in mm	No.
Sides	190 x 20 mm oregon	820	2
Shelves	190 x 20 mm oregon	770	2
Top	230 x 20 mm oregon	850	1
Top rail (back)	70 x 20 mm oregon	770	1
Top rail (front)	45 x 20 mm oregon	770	1
Bottom rail	70 x 20 mm oregon	810	1
Front moulding	25 x 15 mm oregon	810	1
Back	130 x 13 mm pine lining boards	770	6

It's important that the bottom shelf and the two sides are the same width. All the other components can increase a bit in width without interfering with the construction.

Fixings: eight 60 mm countersunk wood screws; 50 mm x 2.5 bullet-head nails; 30 mm x 2 flat-head nails; 30 mm x 1.6 panel pins; PVA wood glue.

Do-it-yourself — Build your own bookcase

Most families contain at least one bookworm, which generally means books all over the place. We show you, step by step, how to build an attractive bookcase and then, with a little more work, make a corner unit. Put a bookcase on each side of the corner unit and you have a special area, to store the books and the bookworm. Another option is to fill an entire wall with simple shelving.

The timber used here is recycled oregon from a demolition yard. It is reasonably easy to work and its beautiful colour gives the finished product real character. You can, however, use new radiata pine if you prefer. The sizes given are as close as possible to standard, but you may find some slight variations in recycled timbers.

1 Cut the sides, top rails and shelves to length, then glue and countersink screw the shelves and top rails to the sides. The simple box section that you are making by doing this must be square and the faces of the rails and shelves should line up with the respective edges of the sides.

2 Nail the lining boards to the back with the flat heads.

3 Glue and screw the top in place, ensuring that the overhangs at each end are equal and that the back edge is flush with the face of the lining boards.

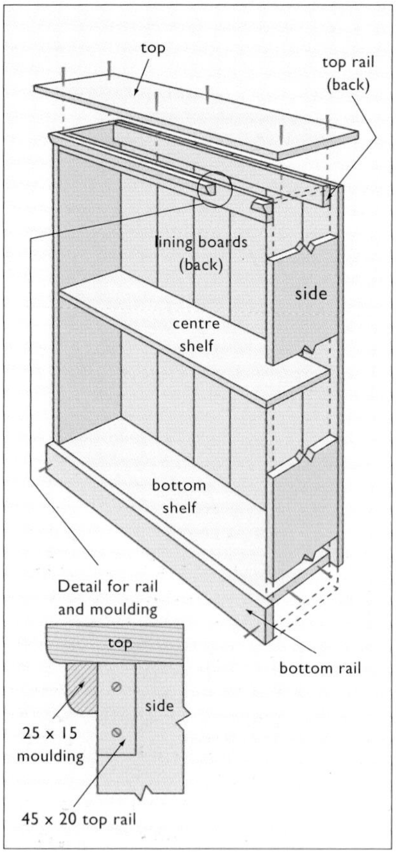

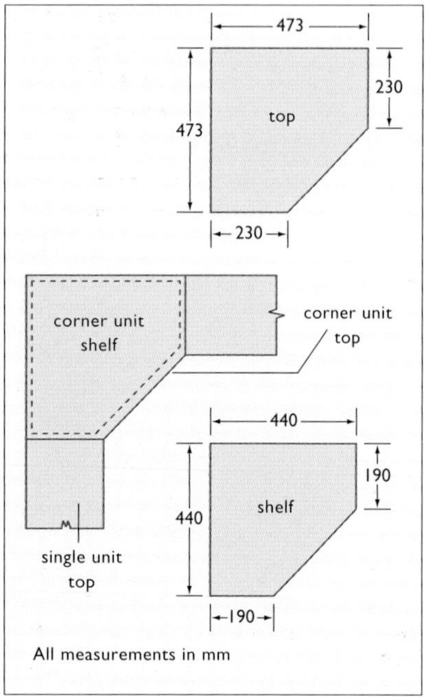

TOP: The bookcase plan.

ABOVE: The corner unit plan.

4 Glue and nail the bottom rail to the bottom shelf and the sides, with the bullet heads, and pin and glue the moulding to the face of the top rail.

5 Either by hand or with an orbital sander, take all the sharp edges off the timber and form the curves to the moulding and the top's edge (see detail). Stain the lining boards to match the oregon and finish the bookcase with a clear varnish or sealer.

Corner unit

This simply consists of two of the bookcases, plus an angled unit for the middle. As the top and shelves for the middle unit are quite wide, they may need to be made from two butt-jointed pieces. When assembling the middle unit, fit the top as part of step 1 before adding the top rails, then the back. The top should not overhang the sides and the two adjoining units should not have an overhang where they abut the middle unit. As the middle unit is a tricky shape, you should take your time when squaring it up and keep comparing its fit with a finished single unit.

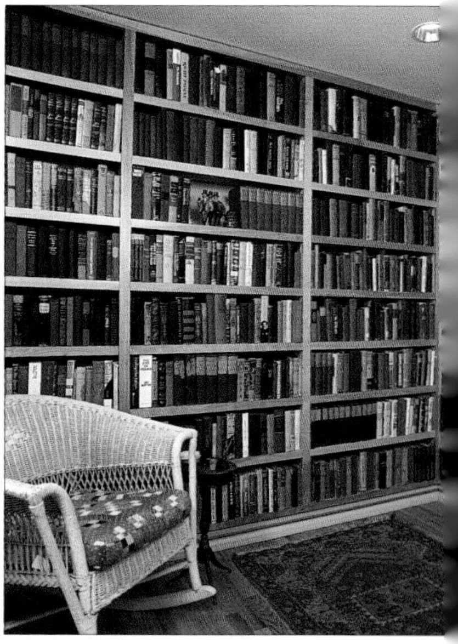

ABOVE: If you have a large collection of books you may find it easier to have a special area for them. These floor-to-ceiling bookshelves occupy two walls without taking up too much space in the room.

BELOW: The corner unit.

Storage you can buy

Sometimes it makes sense for even an ardent do-it-yourselfer to buy storage units rather than build them. Why spend several evenings cutting and joining the timber for a simple bookcase, for example, when you can purchase a similar unfinished piece for just a few dollars more than it would cost to buy the materials?

You don't have to settle for a utilitarian look, either. You can easily dress up unfinished or drab units with paint, stain or even fabric coverings.

The chart below shows some of the more common modular, kit and unfinished units. For additional possibilities, check out paint stores, timber yards, department stores and do-it-yourself centres.

Storage unit	Applications	How to choose
	Unfinished bookcases come in modular sizes ideal for lining up or stacking anywhere you need open-shelf storage. Get steel bookcases from office suppliers. 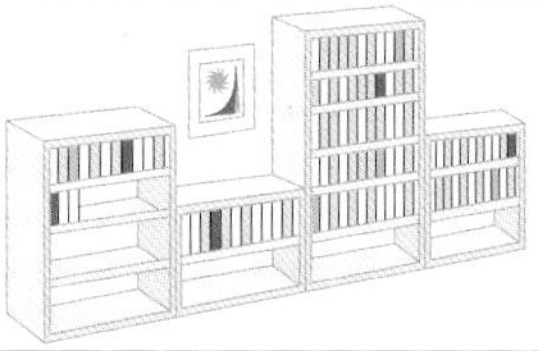	The better quality wood units have rabbeted backs and dadoed shelves; surfaces should need only light sanding.
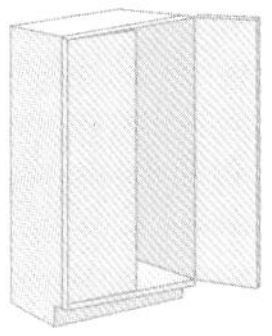	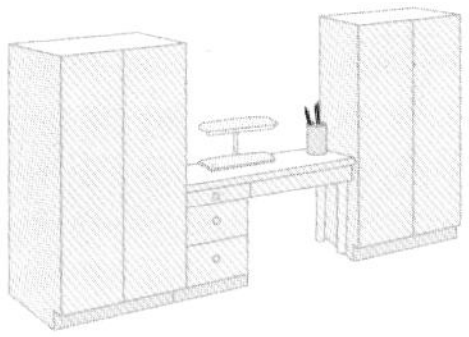 Wardrobes may be wood, metal or hardboard; they come in kit form or assembled. For an entire wall of storage, flank a desk with a pair of them.	Better wood and hardboard versions have hardwood frames. Avoid flimsy construction and metal cabinets with sharp edges.
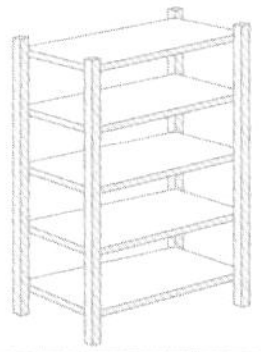	Open-frame steel shelving stands on its own, making it handy for use as a divider as well as against the wall. Shelves run as deep as 60 cm. 	Sturdy posts and nut-and-bolt locking systems minimise swaying. Big units may need cross bracing or fastening to a wall.
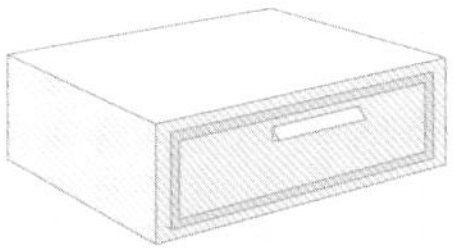	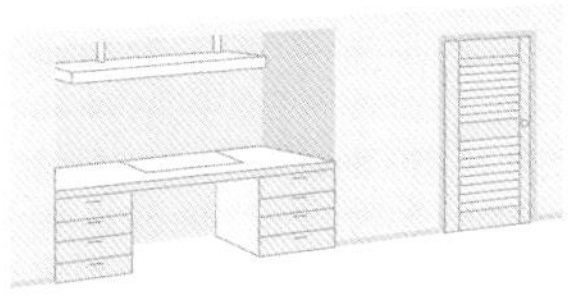 Drawer cases stack to any height. Some have open sides for built-in situations. For a desk, lay a door across two stacks. Note this compact study.	Good ones have rabbeted fronts and move easily on metal or hardwood guides.
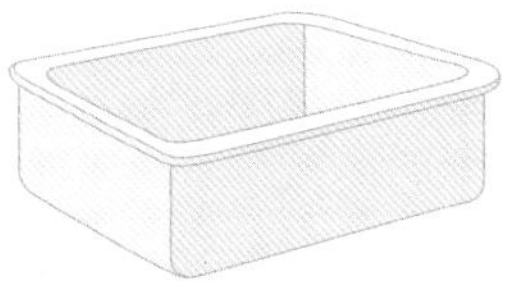	Plastic trays and bins make inexpensive drawers. To construct a case for them, build a large plywood box with cleats inside to support the trays' lips. 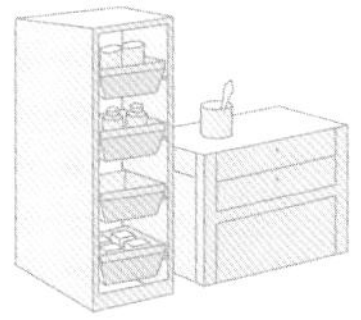	Clear acrylic trays let you see contents at a glance. Rubberised types, available in a variety of colours, hold heavier loads.
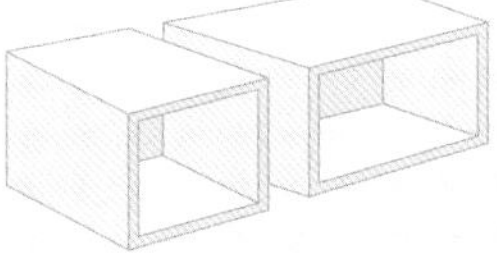	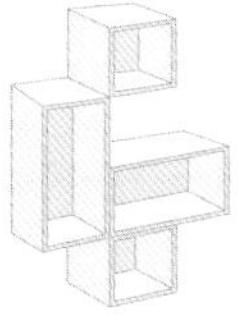 Cubes and boxes stack any which way for modular storage. Choose wood, plastic laminate or solid plastic versions. Some interlock with each other.	Well-made wood cubes have reinforced corners all around. If particle board is used, be sure to surface it with plastic laminate.
	Freestanding cabinets made of wood, metal or hardboard provide storage and a counter. Typically, they're 75–90 cm high and 50–90 cm wide. Keep tools and other bulky gear in file cabinets. Legal-sized drawers measure 28 cm high, 60–70 cm deep, 38 cm wide (inside); letter-sized are 30 cm wide.	For a quick test of a cabinet's quality, try to pick it up; sturdy ones are heavier. Look, too, for tight, well-fitting joints and seams.

LEFT: Odd furniture is no longer a problem with slipcovers. They can unify odd pieces by relating them in colour. In this room all the pieces are slip covered in different fabrics — a solid, a stripe and a floral — with blue as a common link.

ABOVE: Many fabric collections are designed with a choice of patterns, all printed in the same colours so it's easy to match one with another. The frill on these slipcovers is made from a related fabric.

Furniture

The selection and purchase of new furniture adds the finishing touch to your renovations. If new furniture is beyond your budget, consider garage sales and auctions as inexpensive sources. Many old pieces can be transformed with new upholstery or a painted or stained finish.

Covering up

If your furniture needs updating, think slipcovers. They offer a great impact for far less cost than a new suite. They are wonderfully versatile, letting you keep changing your decor, which is very important if you really have the decorating bug.

RIGHT: This setting looks very grand but it's achievable. Open-backed kitchen chairs could be covered like this and used in the dining room. When slip-covers are this short, small ties need to be attached at the corners to fasten them to the chair legs.

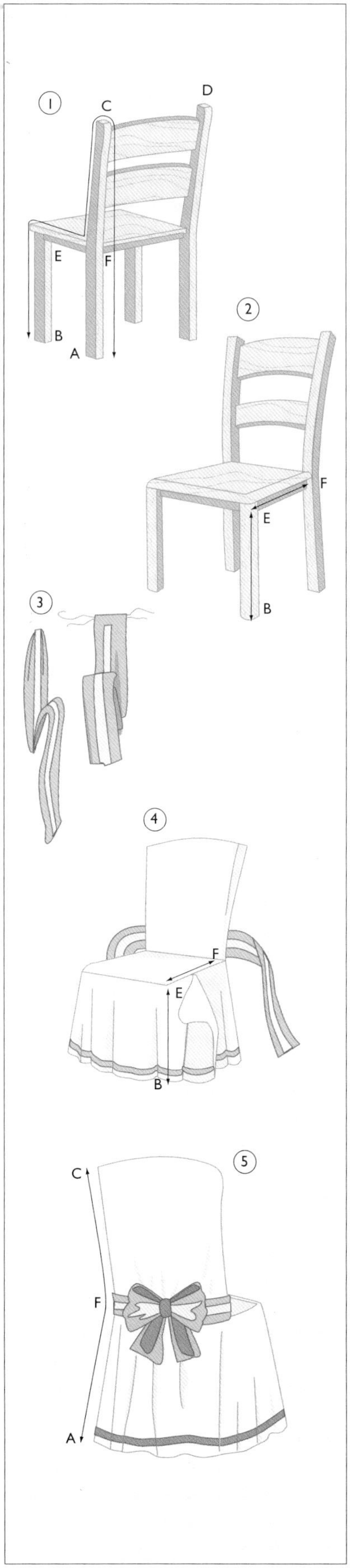

How to make a slipcover

This slipcover is meant to be a loose cover, made from three main pieces — one long piece which covers the front, seat and back, and two side pieces. Ties, joined in at seat level and tied in a bow, take up any fullness. You should choose firm, washable material.

To find the length, measure your chair from the floor at its back A to the top of the chair back C, down to the seat F, across the seat to E and down to the floor at the front B. Add 1.25 cm each end for hems. Now measure the width across the back of the chair C to D, add the thickness of the top of the chair, plus 1.25 cm seam allowance each side. This is the main part of your cover, cut one.

Measure the side of your chair, from the seat E to the floor B, and from the front E to the back of the seat F, add 1.25 cm all around for seams and hem. Cut two. Mark the top with a little notch so you know which way is up.

Cut two long strips of material 1.5 m long by 20 cm wide to use for the ties. Hem around the two long sides and one end. Gather the unhemmed end until it measures 8 cm in width.

With right sides together, attach two sides of the side rectangle to the main piece, B to E and E to F,

ABOVE: Create a classic look in your dining room by making your covers out of cotton canvas. White is not impractical in this case as the fabric is machine washable. Slipcovers will never look as neat as upholstery, but they're not supposed to because the fabric is not pulled tight.

ABOVE LEFT: As dining chairs are usually seen from behind, why not emphasise their backs? Details such as the piping and the fringed hem add interest on this mattress ticking cover and the bows ensure it is easy to fit onto the chair.

LEFT: Make your own slipcover.

You will need for the monk's seat:

Recycled oregon:
Sides and seat/lid from 4000 x 250 x 25 mm
Front and back frame, top and bottom back, rail and hinge support from 6000 x 75 x 25 mm
Braces and battens from 3600 x 50 x 25 mm
Lining boards from 2500 x 140 x 15 mm
Trims from 1000 x 25 x 20 mm and 3000 x 40 x 20 mm
Lattice from 100 x 100 x 38 mm

Plywood:
Front and back panels from 600 x 600 x 3 mm and 10 mm
Bottom 600 x 416 x 10 mm

easing around the corner. Sew the other side of the chair in the same way. With right sides together, centre the gathered end of the tie on point F and tack in place.

With right sides together, sew the side panel to the main piece, from A through F to C; repeat on other side. Finally, hem all around. Turn to right side, press, fit on the chair and tie the bow.

ABOVE RIGHT: The monk's seat.

BELOW: Plan for the monk's seat.

Do-it-yourself—Build a monk's seat

We have called this a monk's seat because it is a little like one of those old church pews but, whether you call it a deacon's bench, a hutch bench or a hall seat, you will find it a useful and attractive piece of furniture. Recycled oregon was used to build this one.

The thicknesses and widths of the timber shown on the plans are those obtained after the recycled material has been cleaned up with an electric planer. As these sizes are determined by the amount of clean-up planing required, you may find them difficult to match, so we give you a buying list as a guide for your visit to the demolition yard rather than a final cutting list. The timbers you buy are then dressed down with the planer to suit the sizes of the plan (70 x 20 mm and 65 x 20 mm, for instance, are both obtained from nominal 75 x 25 mm). You can vary these thicknesses and widths to suit your cleaned-up material. The plans supply all the cutting lengths.

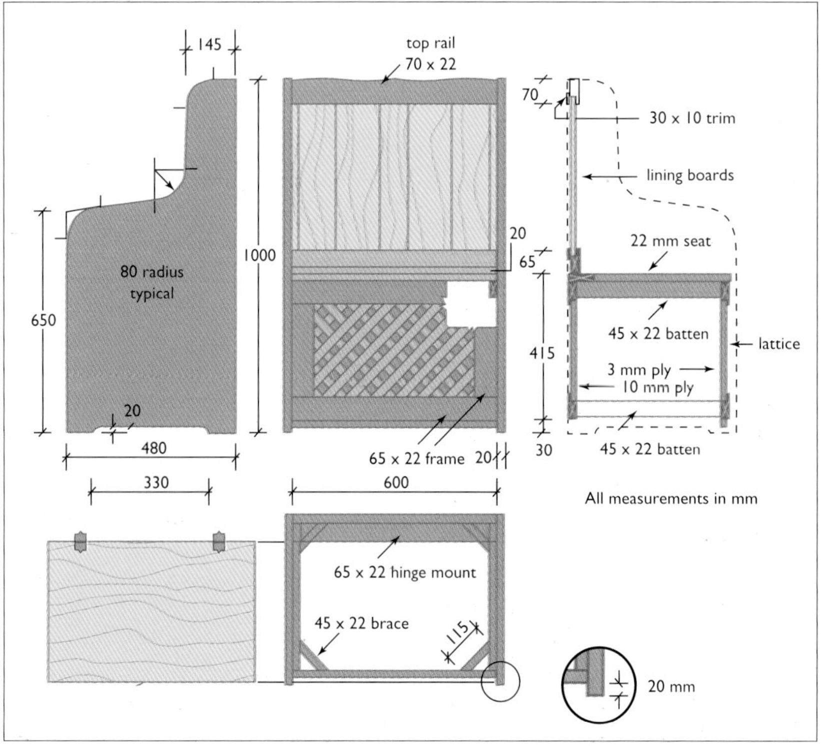

1 Pull out all old nails. With the planer, clean up the timber and take it to thicknesses approximate to those on the plans. Cut to length progressively as you build the unit.
2 Prepare two matching pieces for each side and, using a flat surface, glue and clamp them together at the edges. Put the glued sides aside for 24 hours to dry.
3 Make the front and back frames by gluing and screwing (use one screw at each corner). Add a corrugated nail at each joint. Allow time for the glue to set. Using a router, cut the rebates for the lattice and the plywood in the backs of the frames (10 mm for the back and 8 mm

for the front). Turn the frames over and, with the router, put a decorative edge on the inside of the frames, taking care not to cut into the rebates.

4 The lattice pieces are cut from the 100 x 38 mm timber by setting the cutting guide on a circular saw to a cut of about 6 mm (making strips 1000 x 6 x 38 mm), and finishing them with the planer to 4 x 25 mm. The lattice can be fixed diagonally or square. Using a short piece as a spacer, lay each piece across the rebates and mark and cut until each layer is in place. Each end piece may need to be trimmed to centre the pattern. Fix the lattice pieces with panel pins into the frame and lay the plywood over the back, allowing 15 mm past the rebate to nail it to the frame.

5 Screw the battens to the side pieces, mark out the curves and cut them with a jigsaw. Screwing through the sides, fit the front and back panels, ensure the unit is square, then fit the diagonal braces top and bottom. Finally, drop in the floor and nail it to the bottom battens and braces.

6 Again screwing through the sides, fit the top and bottom back rails and the hinge mount (the back rails will require 15 x 12 mm rebates to take the lining boards). Cut a decorative shape in the top edge of the top rail with a jigsaw.

7 Either use rebated or tongue-and-groove lining boards, or run the edges off plain boards at 45° with the planer and overlap them. Cut four at equal widths and cut the middle one to suit the remaining space. Use panel pins to fix them to the rails and trim them front and back.

8 The seat/lid is constructed in the same way as the sides with two battens underneath. Fix it with a pair of decorative brass hinges. Make sure it bears on the side battens when it closes.

New furniture from old

You may have one of those period wardrobes around the house. They were built in the days when shoulders weren't as wide and jackets weren't as bulky; modern clothes just don't seem to fit in them. But even the cheaper ones maintain an aesthetic appeal and it's a shame to throw them away just because they are a little impractical. A better plan is to turn them into something you can use.

For this project we used a wardrobe with a single door, hanging space at the top and a drawer at the bottom. The top section will become our display cabinet and the bottom section the coffee table. If your wardrobe is the two-piece type (the top separates from the bottom) then your job is much easier; it will already be two freestanding units. Chances are, however, that it will still require a base/skirting for the display cabinet and a couple of pieces of wood on top of the drawer unit, used to fix the top

TOP: Storage you can sit on.

ABOVE CENTRE: Detail showing corner brace.

ABOVE: The hinged seat.

RIGHT: One old wardrobe in two pieces.

ABOVE: A new display cabinet and coffee table made from the old wardrobe.

BELOW: Old tables such as this one can often be found at garage sales.

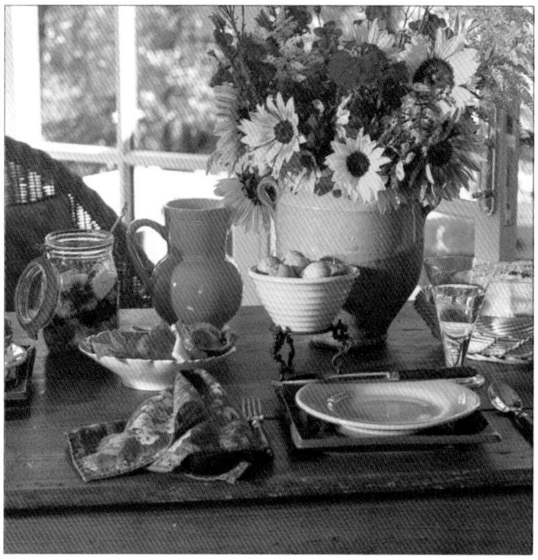

section squarely in place, that will have to be removed before the table top can be fixed.

1 Lay the unit on its back and, using a hand saw, separate the two parts cutting as close to the bottom of the hanging section as possible. Put the drawer unit aside and, with the top section still on its back, remove the door and front panel on either side of it. The door and front panels are usually made from a timber fame with either a plywood insert or, in the case of doors, a mirror.

2 Assuming the frames are in good shape, try not to disturb the joints. Drill a hole through the ply in the panels, close to the edge and, with a jigsaw, cut around the perimeter. This will leave a thin strip of ply wedged in the slot of the frame which can easily be pulled out with pliers. Set a router to cut to the depth of the slot from the back of the panel and turn the slot into a rebate. Use a chisel to square off corners.

3 If the door panel has a plywood centre, repeat step 2. If it has a mirror in a frame of a different shape from the front panels, remove the mirror and, with a jigsaw, cut the frame to the same shape as the other two, adding a rebate with the router.

Note: This may weaken the 'door frame' and require the addition of some battens on the back to strengthen it.

4 Fit 3 mm glass into the rebates (sand first) and secure with glazier points (special flat nails). Before refitting the front panels, install the shelves. Use a timber which will complement the original (you won't be able to match it) — we used recycled oregon — and screw fix through the sides, countersinking the heads. Position the shelves, balancing with the front panel frames. The bottom shelf forms the base of the unit.

5 Replace the front panels and door. You may need to add an extra framing piece across the bottom of the front panels and door to stiffen up the unit, although the shelves could be sufficient. To lift the unit off the floor, add a base/skirting. Use the same timber as used for the shelves and rebate the corners. Skirting only needs to be on the front and two sides. To get a fixing for skirting, you may have to shorten the door. Check before glazing the door.

6 The drawer unit really stays quite intact because it becomes a coffee table. The back may need to be stiffened by adding a batten along the line where it was separated from the top section, but otherwise it is only a case of adding a table top. Make a top by gluing together lengths of timber such as oregon or pine, or even old floorboards. Fit the top with substantial overhang all around (40–50 mm) and then fancy it up with a router.

If you don't own an old wardrobe, look out for one at garage sales and opportunity shops.

Tips

- Never buy anything that wobbles!
- Always carry a tape measure.
- Think 'auction'!
- Become a browser. You'll be surprised how quickly you'll learn to judge prices.
- Add 'cartage' (unless you're a removalist)!
- Use your imagination. It's what's under that ugly fabric that makes it worth re-covering.
- Ignore the stain, look for the grain.
- Plan laterally. A rose may be a rose…but a door can become a table!

ABOVE: Refurbished second-hand furniture can endow your rooms with character. You should remember, though: what you save in dollars you'll spend in energy and enterprise. The table and chairs pictured only needed cleaning up and sanding.

RIGHT: This old chair was originally coated with several coats of varnish and upholstered in dreary, dark fabric. It has been transformed by stripping, sanding and re-upholstering.

Timber and tin pie safe

This is a classic piece of practical and decorative country furniture. Before refrigerators were common household items, most people stored their perishables in a pie safe with either flyscreen or punched tin for ventilation. Use the pie safe in the kitchen or as a bedside feature.

We have chosen to use modern materials rather than solid timber as it makes the construction of the cabinet easier. If you would like a timber-stained finish rather than the coloured enamel paint we have used, radiata pine could be substituted for the medium-density fibre board in the sides and top of the cabinet. A number of edge-glued radiata-pine boards would be needed to obtain the required width for these components.

Authentic 'punched-tin' panels were made from turnplate, a lead and tin coated steel that is no longer readily available. We used 26 gauge galvanised iron, but aluminium of a similar heavier gauge would also be suitable. To punch out the pattern you will need to grind a large nail punch to a 60° conical point. If you'd like to design your own pattern with star, curved or tapered holes, a punch can be ground from any tempered tool steel to produce the mark required. Our pattern has two styles of punch — it is much easier to use a different weight of hammer to produce each sized mark than to try to hit the punch harder and softer with the same hammer.

You will need (measurements are in mm):

Part	Length	Width	Thickness	Material	No.
A Face frame — stile	860	60	19	Radiata pine	2
B Face frame — bottom rail	380	55	19	Radiata pine	1
C Face frame — top rail	380	35	19	Radiata pine	1
D Cabinet side	860	380	18	MDF	2
E Cabinet shelf	464	371	12	MDF	2
F Shelf battens	371	15	15	Radiata pine	4
G Cabinet back	767	484	9	MDF	1
H Cabinet top	560	430	18	MDF	1
J Door — bottom rail	2820	65	19	Radiata pine	1
K Door — middle rail	280	50	19	Radiata pine	1
L Door — top rail	280	50	19	Radiata pine	1
M Door — stile	705	50	19	Radiata pine	2
N Cove mould 19 mm	cut to lengths			Radiata pine	
P Battens	cut to lengths	10	9	Radiata pine	
Q Punched panels	295	285	26 g	Galvanised iron	2

Supplies: 1.6 m x 200 x 19 mm double-dressed radiata pine; 1200 x 900 x 18 mm MDF board; 1200 x 900 x 12 mm MDF; 1200 x 900 x 9 mm MDF; 8 mm dowel joining kit; 40 x 1.5 mm bullet-headed nails; 25 x 1 mm panel pins; PVA glue; Timbermate stopping putty; two 50 mm butt hinges; eight 8 mm x 4 g countersunk screws; 25 mm x 8 g round-head screws; 9 mm washer; 180, 220 and 360 grit sandpaper; 400 grit wet-and-dry sandpaper; spray cans of auto primer and auto touch-up lacquer; sanding sealer; oil-based all-purpose undercoat; oil-based semi-gloss enamel (we used Dulux Semi Super Enamel Blue River UD 307).

Begin with the face frame

1 Using 19-mm-thick radiata pine, cut the two stiles (A), top rail (C) and bottom rail (B) to the sizes listed at left.

2 Mark out the feet as shown in figure 2 (on p. 274) on the bottom inside edge of each stile (A). Use a jigsaw or coping saw to cut the curved shape, then sand the edges smooth.

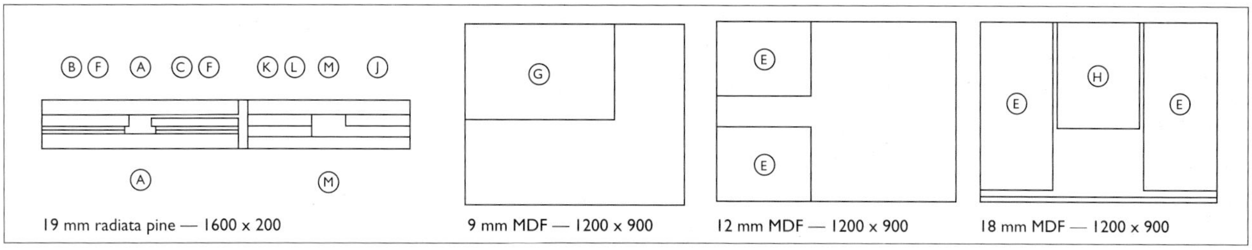

3 Lightly dry clamp the frame together with the rails in their correct position against the stiles. Use a try square and pencil to mark the position of the dowels on the frame. Remove the cramps.

4 Square the pencil lines across the edge of the stiles and mark the centre for the dowels. Then, using the drill from the 8 mm dowel joining kit, drill the holes for the dowels to a depth of 20 mm. Fit the dowel marker pins in the holes and reassemble the frame to mark the position of the dowel holes on the ends of the rails. Drill these holes 20 mm deep.

5 Glue, dowel and cramp the rails between the stiles. Check for square and make sure that the assembly lies flat. Wipe off the excess glue with a damp cloth.

Make the rest of the cabinet

6 Cut the two side panels (D) from the 18 mm MDF board to the size listed on p. 272. Mark out the shape of the feet and cut with a jigsaw. Sand the edges smooth. Using a 10 mm rebate bit in a router cut a 10 x 9 mm rebate in the back edge of each side panel to take the back panel (figure 3). Remember that the sides are not identical but are matching pairs.

7 Cut the shelf battens (F) to size. Mark with a pencil the position of the battens on the inside faces of the side panels (D), then nail and glue the battens in position as shown in figure 4.

8 Cut the two shelves (E) from 12 mm MDF board to the size given on p. 272.

9 Cut the cabinet back (G) from 9 mm MDF board to the size given on p. 272.

10 Cut the cabinet top (H) from 18 mm MDF board, plane a slight round on the front and the side edges, then sand smooth.

11 Glue and nail the face frame to the side panels (D) using 40 x 1.5 mm nails. Make sure the outside surfaces are flush. Close the joint by applying light pressure with sash cramps.

12 Glue and nail the bottom and the middle shelves (E) to the battens (F) using 25 x 1 mm panel pins. Make sure the back edges of the shelves are flush with the bottom of the rebate of the side panels.

13 Glue and nail the back panel (G) in the rebate on the side panels (D) using 25 x 1 mm panel pins, making sure the top edges of the back panel and side panels are aligned.

14 Locate the cabinet top (H) in position (the back edge flush with the cabinet back and an even overhang on both sides). Mark the position with a pencil. Glue and nail the top to the sides and face frame using 40 x 1.5 mm nails.

15 Cut the 19 mm cove moulding (N) to fit under the top of the cabinet with a mitre joint on the front corners, then nail and glue in position with 25 x 1 mm panel pins (figure 5). Punch all nails below the surface and stop with Timbermate stopping putty. Sand smooth when dry.

ABOVE: Cutting diagrams.

FAR LEFT: Timber and tin pie safe.

Making the door

16 Cut the bottom, middle and top rails (J, K, L) and the door stiles (M) to sizes given.

17 Using the method just described for the face frame, mark the position of the dowels, drill the holes, then glue dowels and cramp the door frame. Wipe off excess glue with a damp cloth and make sure the frame lies flat.

18 Using a 10 mm rebate bit in a router, cut a 10 x 10 mm rebate on the back inside edge of the door frame.

19 Use a sharp chisel to square the round routed corners of the rebate.

20 Cut the door battens to size and, using a mitre box and tenon saw, cut lengths to fit the rebate in the door, shown in figure 1.

21 Fit the door to the cabinet, planing the edges to leave a 1 mm gap all around.

22 Mark the position of recesses for the butt hinges 100 mm from the top and bottom of the door. Chisel the recesses and screw the hinges to the door stile and the cabinet.

23 Shape the small swivel catch from a scrap of radiata pine (figure 6). Drill a hole for the 25 mm round-head screw and sand all faces smooth.

Making the punched 'tin' panels

24 Prepare the sheets of galvanised iron by rubbing the faces with 400 grit wet-and-dry sandpaper and dishwashing liquid in water. Rinse the panels well under a running tap.

25 When dry, place a panel on a sheet of 19 mm MDF board. (Avoid touching the face of the panel with your fingers.) Secure the panel to the board with strips of scrap timber and screws, or use large drawing pins. (The panel will buckle when punched unless held securely to the board.) Centre the photocopy (see page 275) of the design and hold in place with masking tape.

26 Start punching at any point on the panel. Check that all the holes have been punched and remove the panel from its mounting. Use a new surface of MDF board and repeat the process for the second panel.

27 Drill a small hole in the corner of each panel and hang the panels on a length of thin craft wire. Spray the faces of the panels with a coat of grey auto primer followed by two coats of deep grey auto touch-up lacquer, following the instructions on the side of the can.

28 When the panels are dry, place them in the door frame. Using 25 mm panel pins, nail the door battens in place to secure the panels in the frame (see figure 1).

RIGHT: The template for making the punched 'tin' panels.

BELOW: The plan for making the pie safe.

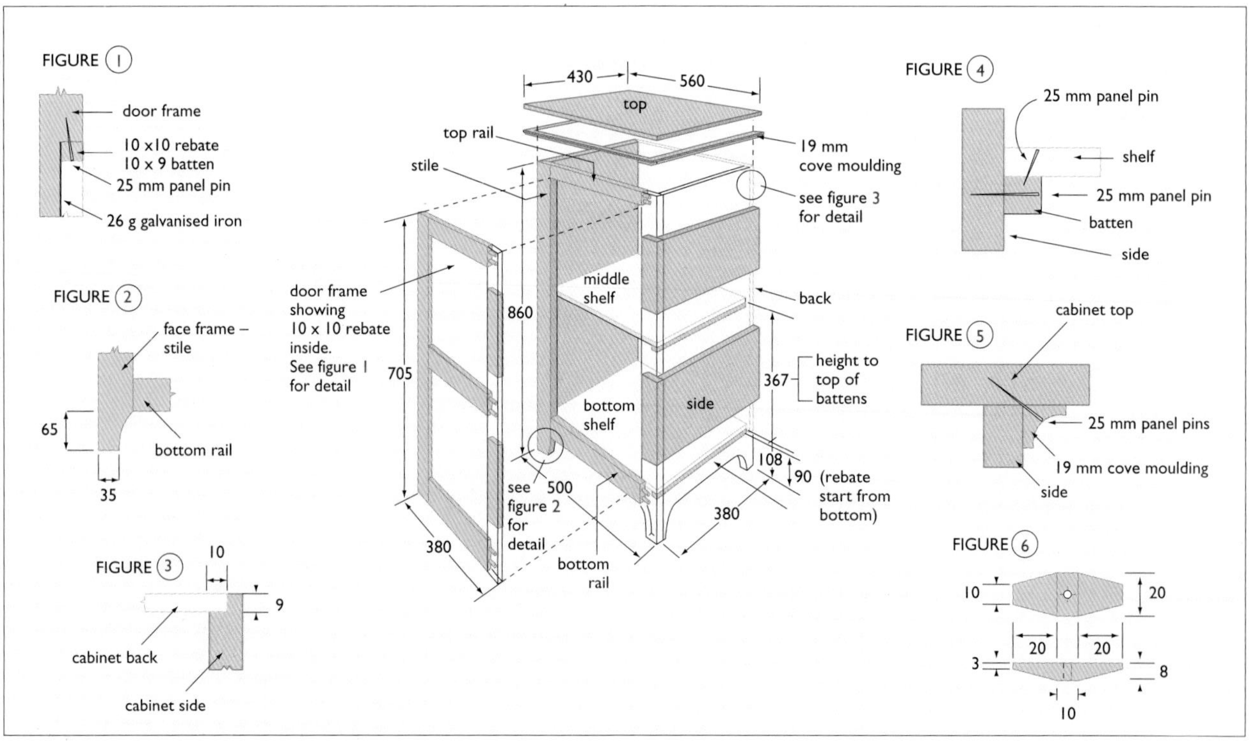

- ● Heavy punch hole
- ● Light punch indent

Photocopy the design twice (at the same size) to match the pattern. Use a different weight of hammer for heavy and light punches.

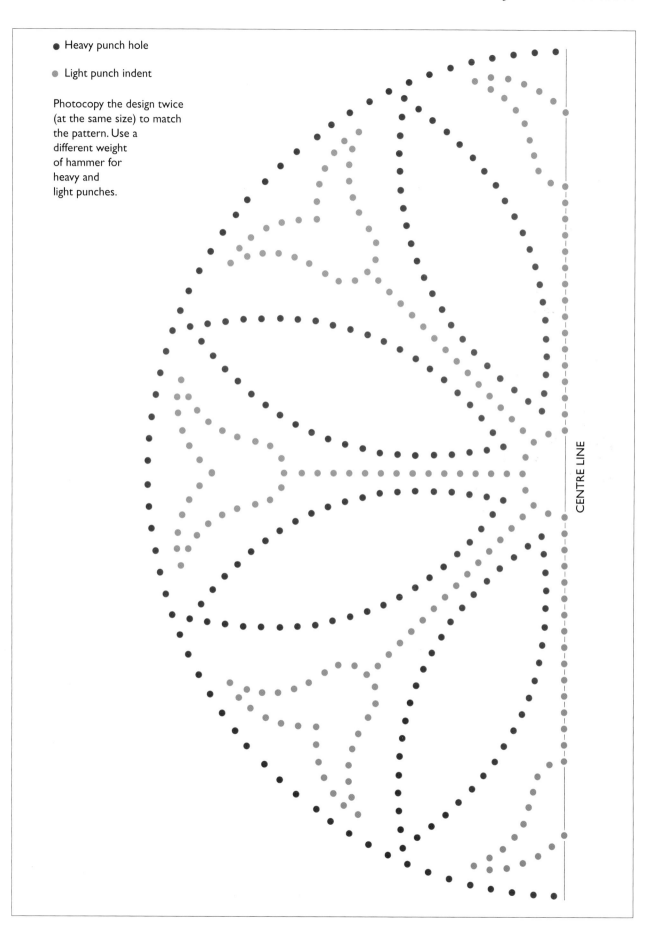

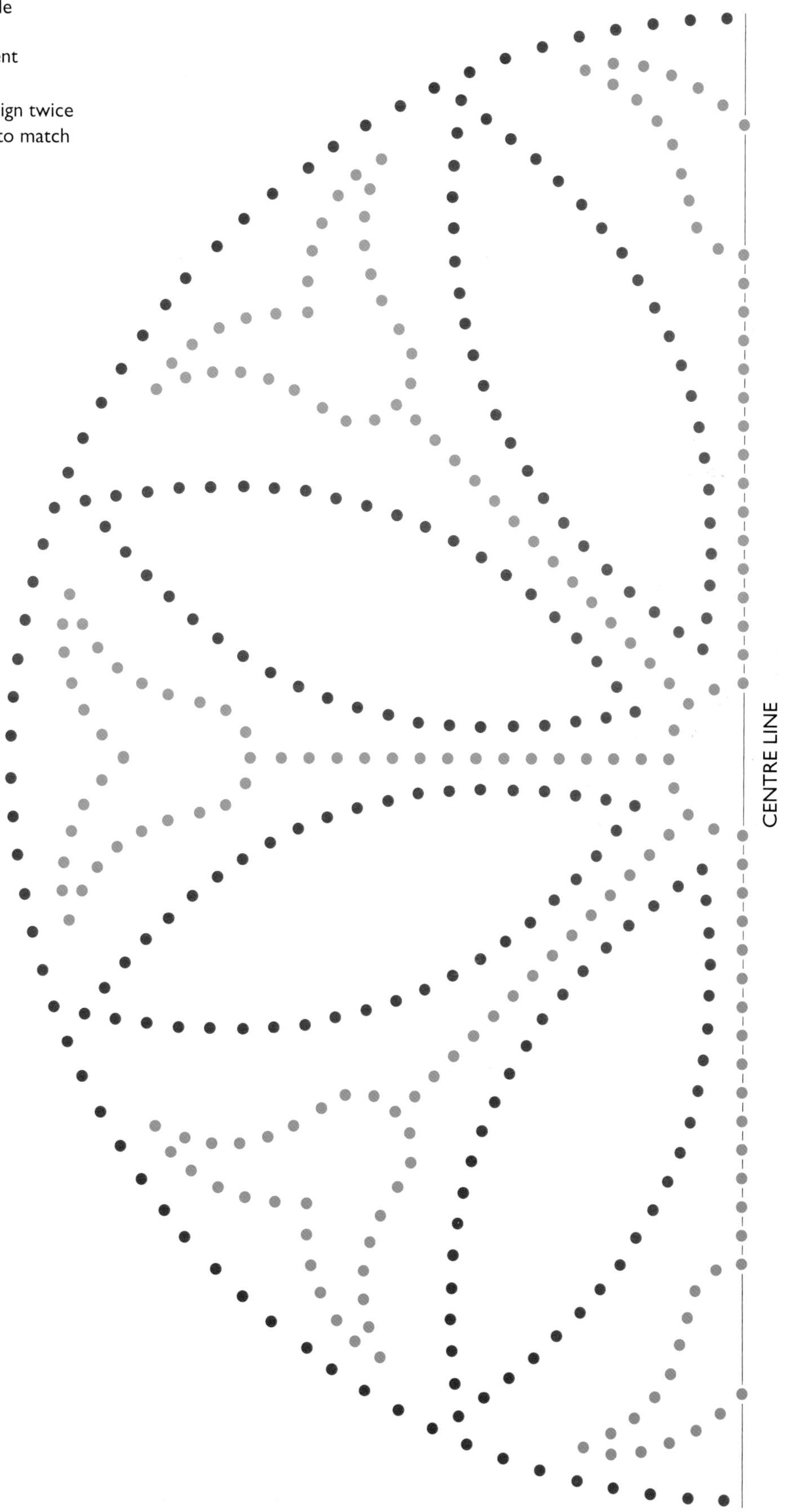

Painting and finishing the cabinet

29 Sand edges and faces with 180 and 220 grit sandpaper. (Unless marked, do not sand the faces of the MDF board.)

30 Mask any edges you do not want to be painted over with masking tape.

31 Apply a coat of sanding sealer to all surfaces and when dry sand lightly with 360 grit sandpaper.

32 Apply a coat of oil-based all-purpose undercoat and, when thoroughly dry, sand lightly with worn 360 grit sandpaper.

33 Apply two coats of oil-based semi-gloss enamel, sanding lightly between coats.

34 Screw the hinges to the door and screw the door in position. Screw the catch to the face of the cabinet with a thin washer between the rubbing surfaces.

Multi Purpose Cupboard

You never seem to have enough of the right storage, so we're going to show you how to build a simple unit which you can adapt to your own requirements. It will serve as a bookcase, linen cupboard, or even a china cabinet.

Follow these simple step-by-step instructions — you can vary the size, and choose to add doors and drawers if you like.

The ideal material for the unit is medium-density fibre board, but you can use particle board. The advantage of MDF is that you can sand the edges to take a paint finish, whereas particle board requires either filling or the fitting of edge strips. As an option you can make the fronts of the drawers, or storage boxes, out of plywood, then let the grain show through the finish. The frames of the doors can be made either from radiata pine or oregon (both dressed).

As you can see from the diagram, we have given you the option of a 300-mm- or 500-mm-wide unit. You can, of course, vary these widths to suit a specific opening, but we don't recommend that you increase the width of the doors. Those described are only suited to the 300-mm-wide unit.

The basic unit

1 Screw and glue the two C panels to the two B panels.

2 By screwing through the outside face of the A panels, glue and screw the B panels to the A panels (countersink all screws for filling later). Make sure you keep the panels square when fixing.

3 Screw and glue in place the back panel D to the A panels and the top and bottom B panels.

Drawer/storage box

1 By screwing from the outside face of the B panels, glue and screw the C panel to the B panels.

2 By screwing through the outside face of the A panels, glue and screw the A panels to the B and C panels.

3 Drill three 20 mm holes in the face of the front A panel to act as finger grips.

Doors

1 Using a plane or a router, cut a 10-mm-wide, 2-mm-deep rebate on one long face of each E, F and G piece.

2 Working on a flat surface, fit two E pieces between two F pieces and two G pieces, and glue and clamp (ensure they are square). The rebates should be on the rear inside face of the frame you are making, to receive the glass.

3 Drill two 20-mm-deep holes as countersinks at each joint of the F and G and the E pieces, through the outside edges of the F and G pieces. Then, using 60 mm screws, screw them to the E pieces. Leave the joints clamped until you are sure that the glue has set.

4 When the doors have been painted, fit the glass, the furniture knobs and the hinges.

You can fix two or more units together by screwing through the adjacent sides or by making a common back (D panel) and forming them into one unit rather like a room divider or wall unit. Don't be afraid to paint them bright colours — perhaps even a different one for each unit. If you intend to place your unit in the kitchen or bathroom, you should add at least one good coat of a hard washable varnish for extra protection.

For one 250-mm-high drawer or storage box to suit the 500-mm-wide unit:

(you can vary the height to suit your needs but don't forget also to vary the height of the opening accordingly)

Item	No.	Size
A Panel	2 pieces	462 x 250 mm
B	2	371 x 250 mm
(All 12 mm MDF board)		
C Panel	1 piece	438 x 371 mm
(18 mm MDF board)		

Eight 40 mm screws for MDF board and eight 60 mm screws for doors.

For the 300-mm-wide door:

Item	No.	Size
E Timber	4 pieces	200 x 50 x 20 mm
F	2	1069 x 50 x 20 mm
G	2	987 x 50 x 20 mm
H Glass	1 piece	987 x 218 x 3 mm
J	1	905 x 218 x 3 mm

Accessories: 2 furniture knobs; 4 hinges (there are several hinge types to choose from, depending on whether you want them to be concealed or exposed. Talk to your local hardware store or cabinet shop); 16 glass clips or mirror clips (again, ask your hardware store about its range).

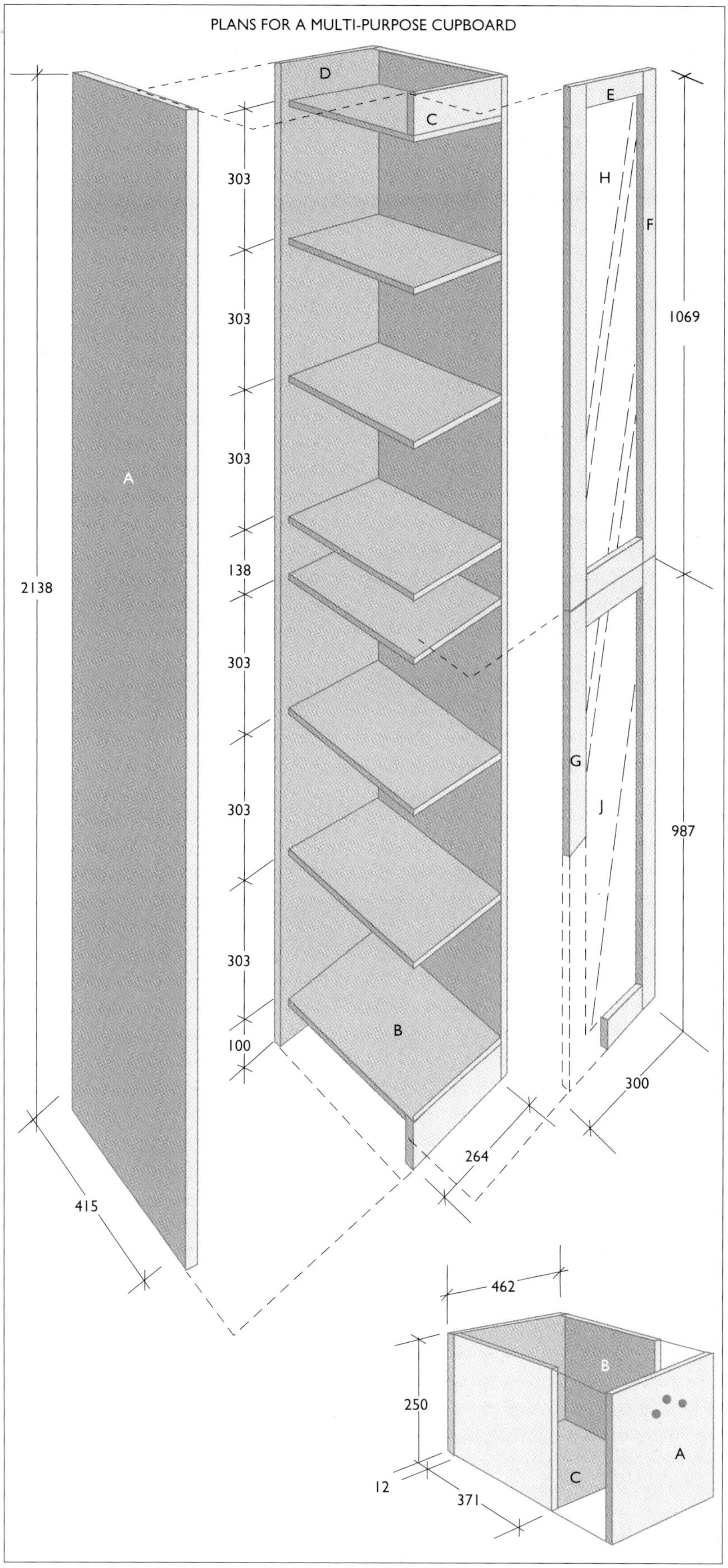

You will need for the 300-mm-wide unit:		
Item	**No.**	**Size**
A Panel	2 pieces	2138 x 415 mm
B	8	415 x 264 mm
C	2	264 x 82 mm
D	1	300 x 2138 mm
(All 18 mm MDF board)		

For the 500-mm-wide unit:		
Item	**No.**	**Size**
A Panel	2 pieces	2138 x 415 mm
B	8	464 x 415 mm
C	2	464 x 82 mm
D	1	500 x 2138 mm
(All 18 mm MDF board)		

BELOW: If you don't want to build your own, you may like to transform an existing cupboard. The louvre doors, painted finish and decorative mouldings on this one show what a little imagination can do.

ABOVE: The newly upholstered chair.

Upholstered chair

New padding, a buttoned seat and fresh fabric will turn a plain, old wrought-iron telephone chair into somewhere that is comfortable enough to sit while you enjoy the fruits of your labours.

You will need: 60 cm each of two co-ordinating print fabrics; 60 cm calico; medium-density seat foam 50 mm thick; electric knife; craft glue; contact adhesive; thick polyester wadding (batting); brown paper; twine; seven 15-mm-diameter self-cover buttons; eight 13-mm-diameter self-cover buttons; fusible interfacing; matching sewing thread; scissors; power drill with 13 mm bit; upholstery needle 10 cm long; staple gun; tape measure; disappearing fabric marker.

Covering the chair back

1 Place one layer of wadding on the inside of the back of the chair and one layer on the outside back. Pin them together, following the outline of the frame. Trim excess the wadding. Glue the wadding together at the outer edges.
2 To make the pattern for the chair back: pin paper to the inside back of the chair. Fold it smoothly over wadding and around the outer edge to the outside back, pleating excess out at corners. Trace around the outline of the chair. Add 1 cm to all the edges for seams and 2 cm to the lower edge for the hem. Pin paper to the outside back and trace the same outer edge of the chair frame. Add seam and hem allowances as for the inside back, then cut out. Cut outside back pattern in half lengthwise; add a 2 cm seam allowance to this centre back edge.
3 From one co-ordinating print, cut an inside back (if you are using a motif print, remember to consider design placement) and two outside backs. Cut a back placket the length of the chair's outside back (plus 1 cm for seam and 2 cm for hem allowance) by 10 cm wide.
4 Apply fusible interfacing to the wrong side of the two outside backs and the placket.
5 To sew chair back cover: press the 2 cm centre back facings to the wrong side. Stitch four evenly spaced buttonholes on either side (to suit the smaller covered buttons).

6 Press and stitch a 1 cm single hem on either side of the placket. Machine edge stitch a 1 cm double folded hem at the lower edge of the placket.

7 Place the two back sections face down, side by side. Place the placket, face down, centrally over them, aligning top and bottom edges. Baste the placket in place at the upper edge.

8 With right sides together, pin the inside and outside backs together, positioning the pleats evenly at the corners of the inside back. Stitch and press seam allowances towards the outside back. Machine stitch close to the seam allowance through all thicknesses.

9 Press and stitch a 1 cm double folded hem at the lower edge.

10 Cover the 13 mm buttons following the manufacturer's instructions. Fit the cover over the wadding, and position and sew the buttons to the placket to correspond with the buttonholes (see photograph).

Covering the chair seat

11 Using the wooden base as a template, cut the foam with an electric knife.

12 Drill one hole in the centre, surrounded by six evenly spaced holes in the timber for buttoning. Mark corresponding points on the foam and cut small slits with scissors. Cut a circle of wadding, a circle of calico and a circle of the second co-ordinating print, at least 30 cm larger overall than the base.

13 Run a line of contact adhesive around the edges of the seat and foam. When tacky, place the foam over the seat, aligning marks on the foam with the drilled holes. Press together. Place the circle of wadding, then the circle of calico over the foam. Thread an upholstery needle with 50 cm of twine and insert from the underside through to the top side. Bring the needle through to one side of the centre hole drilled in the seat, through all layers, leaving at least 15 cm of twine trailing. Take the needle to the other side of the centre hole, catching a little square of calico on top, in the loop of the stitch. Remove the needle from the twine and pull the calico and padding down to form a hollow. While holding the twine ends firmly, staple twice (the second time folding the twine back on itself) beside the drilled holes. Stitch and staple each of the remaining drilled holes in the same way, making sure all the hollows are the same depth.

14 Smooth the wadding and calico to the underside of the seat. Staple the wadding to the timber in at least eight equidistant points. Arrange the calico evenly on the underside, making pleats radiating from the depressions in the padding where necessary. Staple the calico to the timber. Start on opposite sides first, at four equidistant points, and firmly pull the calico before stapling to ensure a smooth result. Trim the excess calico.

15 Cover the seven larger buttons, following the manufacturer's instructions. Apply the cover fabric to the seat and attach as before with twine and needle, using buttons instead of fabric squares on top. Staple the twine as before. Smooth the fabric to the underside, pulling firmly. Before stapling to the timber, pleat the excess from the buttons where necessary. Trim away the surplus fabric.

16 Using the base as a pattern, cut a circle of calico. Press under a 1 cm seam allowance around the circumference. Staple this circle to the base to conceal seams and staples.

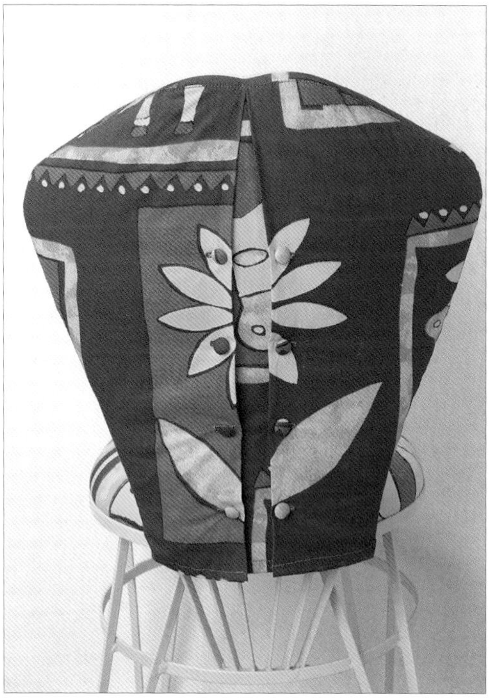

ABOVE: Back view of the upholstered chair.

Tip

- Foam suppliers will usually cut the foam to size and shape for you when you buy it.

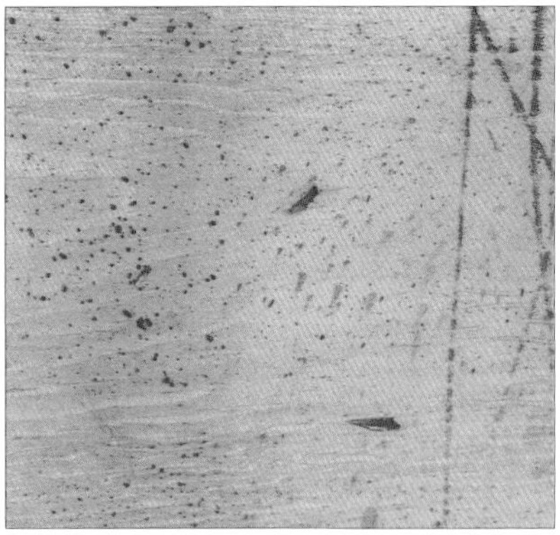

1a

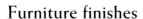

1b

2

Furniture finishes

If you have some items of furniture with a country-style feel that you would like to age with an authentic-looking finish, follow these easy steps. You could also use these techniques to give character to plain whitewood furniture. We show you how to apply a brush finish that simulates the look that normally takes decades to form. You will also learn how to produce the popular crackled and limed features, as well as a simple method of gracefully ageing a natural wood surface under a clear finish. Fine sand all surfaces (using 240 grit sandpaper) before beginning any of these processes.

How to build up a painted country finish

1 Bare wood
2 Dark interior stain
3 Polyurethane finish (two coats)
4 Oil-based primer
5 Colour coat (paint)
6 Interior stain antiquing
7 Spatter

Five easy steps to a painted antique finish

1 Distress the unpainted surface. Antiques usually have a number of nicks and scratches. Before you start simulating a blemished surface for your new project, think where it would have received the greatest degree of wear over the years. Use a round-faced hammer to simulate

ABOVE: Painting an antique finish.

1a Dents, scratches and surface wear age a natural wood surface.

1b Wrap 100 grit sandpaper around a 25 mm dowel to make a tool for rounding edges.

2 The perfect aged look is only achieved by sticking to the steps.

3

4

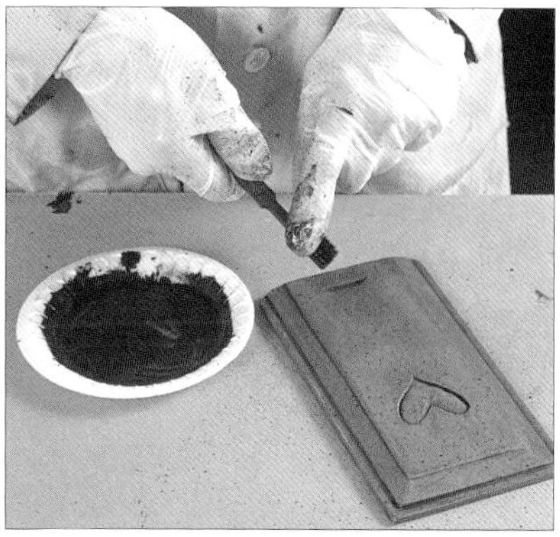

5

3 Remove some of the colour coat with 320 grit sandpaper without sanding through the primer.

4 To simulate patina, leave traces of dark stain in crevices and areas prone to build up of grime.

5 After practising the spattering technique, give the project a uniform coat of fine speckles.

BELOW: Lime washing is another technique used to create an antique finish.

dents, a screwdriver to make scratches and a surforming tool to scuff surfaces. Gently round the edges and corners using 100 grit sandpaper wrapped around a 25 mm dowel. For a natural, worn look, sand the edges unevenly. Don't overdo it. If a surface would have received little wear over the years, leave it alone. You want to distress the piece, not destroy it.

2 Apply the finish in layers. Be patient. This process requires seven layers. If you want to achieve the perfect, aged look, don't be tempted to cut corners by omitting any one of the layers.

Wipe on a dark stain (Cabot's Interior Stain Antique Walnut) and remove excess with a soft cloth. Allow to dry. Apply two coats of clear, satin-finish polyurethane (Cabothane or Estapol). Sand lightly after the second coat with 220 grit sandpaper. Apply one coat of a red, oil-based, paint primer. Once the primer is dry, sand lightly and apply paint of your chosen colour. (The Dulux earthy hues illustrated on p. 280 look good on country projects.) Satin-finish or semi-gloss-finish acrylic or oil-based paints can be used.

3 Now roll back the years. Using 320 grit sandpaper, remove parts of the colour coat along the edges, corners and other areas where the paint would naturally have worn off through use. Change the abrasive paper often as it will tend to clog. First, lightly sand the whole surface, then sand down to the primer coat around the heavy-duty areas, as shown. If you should accidentally sand through the primer, the two coats of polyurethane should protect the stained wood. Because old wood is darker than new, try not to reveal the bare wood as you sand.

4 Patina in a few minutes. Apply a coat of Cabot's Interior Stain (Country Baltic) over the surface, then wipe off with a soft

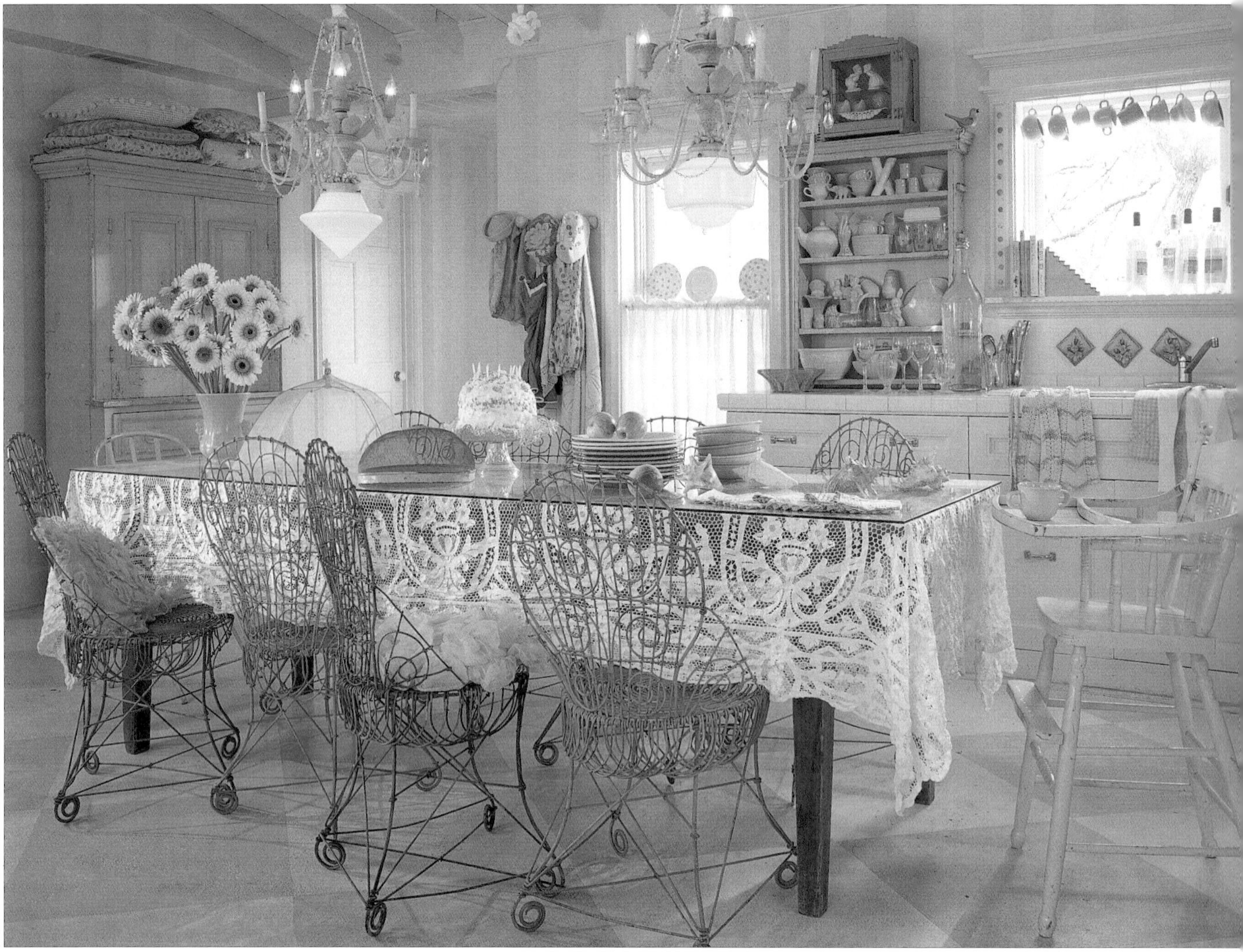

ABOVE: Lime washing need not be limited to items of furniture. In this kitchen it has been used effectively on the floor to complement the pastel shades of the cupboard and shelves.

cloth as shown. Leave deposits in the crevices and other areas — those spots that would seldom have been cleaned over the years had this been a genuine antique or old piece of furniture. This residue simulates the sheen created by long use called 'patina'.

5 Add a bit more character by spattering the surface (called fly specks by some). Dip an old toothbrush into a shallow container of Antique Walnut stain. Practise spattering the stain in a fine shower by holding the toothbrush 150 mm above a sheet of paper and running your finger through the bristles. When you have mastered this technique, add a uniform spattering of fine specks to the project as shown. Don't overdo it. You will find a little spattering goes a long way.

The crackled look

A crackled finish can be made by using acrylic paint over hide glue, or by covering the acrylic paint with an oil-based paint.

A crackled look can take decades to occur naturally, but this method needs only a few days.

Apply a base coat of paint to your project if you don't want the wood to show through the cracks. After this dries, brush on a thin coat of hide glue (animal glue similar to gelatine). Hide glue pellets

Tip

- Use a quality paintbrush as wide as you can easily manage (50 or 75 mm) and apply the paint with long smooth strokes.

must be soaked in water overnight and heated in the top part of a double saucepan over hot water to prevent burning. The glue must dry thoroughly. This may take one or more days. Apply an acrylic paint in long, even strokes. In 20 – 30 seconds, the paint will begin to crack. To achieve the effect shown, skip the first coat of paint and apply hide glue to bare wood, followed with coats of white and green paint.

It pays to experiment to achieve the result you want. If you prefer a more subtle crackled finish, use the above procedure, but cover the acrylic paint with oil-based paint.

The limed look

Furniture was once often limed to prevent darkening with age. As well, old furniture that has been chemically stripped has a limed appearance. The result is most attractive. There are several types of limed interior stain available. You can simulate antique liming by using tinted white paint as shown in the side-by-side comparison of a pine door (above left). Open-grained timbers such as oak soak up more paint, making them appear whiter than others.

Use a shade of white in an oil-based paint which suits your taste. Experiment by mixing small amounts of black, green, yellow and/or other colours into the pure white base. Practise on scrap timber, sanded to a fine finish, before liming the piece you've selected. To start, brush tinted white paint all over a surface and wipe it off before it dries, leaving paint in the crevices and corners. If you want to age the piece more, score around the knots and defects with an X-acto knife. Extra paint will accumulate in the crevices. Allow the limed surface to dry thoroughly before applying coats of satin-finish polyurethane.

Materials list

Sandpaper, 100, 150, 220, 240, 320 grit; Interior Stain (Antique Walnut, Country Baltic); satin or semi-gloss-finish acrylic or oil-based paints; hide glue.

TOP LEFT: A crackle finish made with acrylic paint over hide glue.

TOP RIGHT: A crackled surface that is covered with an oil-based paint.

ABOVE LEFT: Liming, on the left, gives a partially stripped look. The right half is finished without liming.

ABOVE RIGHT: Accentuate knots by cutting paint-retaining crevices around them with an X-acto knife or similar tool.

STAIN

Practical Matters

When you have made your plans, whether they are for a major house renovation or just a simple do-it-yourself project, it is time to address the practicalities. To make a piece of furniture or undertake a renovation you will need a well-organised work space, usually in a shed or garage, where you can work without disturbing the rest of the household. As well as having a suitable work space, appropriate and well-maintained tools for the job are most important. This chapter itemises and illustrates the most commonly used tools and materials and gives practical suggestions for organising them in your workroom.

Another important consideration is safety. While this is always seriously addressed on a commercial building site, it is sometimes overlooked by the home handyperson. Safety is generally a matter of commonsense, but it is worthwhile considering the useful pointers given here concerning the dangers of renovating, wearing protective clothing, and the correct storage and maintenance of tools and equipment.

Finally, don't forget environmental considerations. It is not always necessary to use toxic chemicals for cleaning, painting and finishing — consult the 'green' tips section for some useful pointers to help make your renovating project both a safe and enjoyable experience.

This well-equipped, well laid-out work space for the home handyperson occupies a section of the garage. Having a specific area such as this means you don't have to worry about creating a mess and you can work undisturbed.

The workroom

Whether you are undertaking major renovation work or a small do-it-yourself project, a designated work area will ensure the smooth running of the project.

Organising the perfect workplace

Smooth the path to successful, enjoyable and rewarding weekend projects by plotting and planning a well-equipped workroom. Even if the space for such a room is not much bigger than a tool box, organisation is the key word. Establish a proper place for every piece of equipment and remember that little items are more likely to go astray than big ones. Always keep the chuck key for changing the drill bit tied on to the cord or body of your power drill or it will disappear. Tape measures and needle-nosed pliers also have well-earned reputations for being elusive. In fact, any tool which is used regularly by different members of the family is likely to be misplaced. Have back-up supplies of popular tools and try to buy them in bright, even fluorescent, colours. With the work bench, the pivotal point of the workroom, never skimp on size and weight. It needs to be solid and very stable.

Make way for a workroom or utility area in the house where tools and materials can be stored. Floor-plans of average homes rarely allow

ABOVE AND RIGHT: Tools are within easy reach when hung on the wall.

for such a space, so it is usually up to the resident home-maintenance and carpentry expert to find one. A workroom could be built under a pitched roof, attic style, or placed between the piers beneath the house, or perhaps there is a basement, laundry or even a space under the stairs which could be replanned as a work area.

Ideally, a workroom should be dry, cool and reasonably soundproof, especially if it is located close to the living quarters of the house or the neighbouring property. It should also have excellent natural and artificial light, good cross ventilation (fumes of paints, finishes and various preparations can be not only unpleasant, but dangerous as well), power points (preferably at bench height), a sturdy work bench at hip height for maximum efficiency, a practical floor finish which won't be spoiled by inevitable spills, and suitable storage for all hardware paraphernalia. If the floor is concrete, have a rubber mat over an off-cut of underfelt in front of the work bench for comfort underfoot. Although the workroom is not meant to be luxuriously appointed or a gathering place for wits and scholars, a simple chair or stool (or two) is a good idea for solo tea breaks or when a visitor drops in.

Commonsense and safety in the workroom

- Develop the habit of wearing safety glasses in the workroom.
- Clean up at the end of every workroom session.
- Wear a face mask when sweeping and vacuuming to get rid of sawdust and dirt.
- Read labels on preparations carefully. Some tasks involving potentially dangerous substances are best performed outside.
- Keep instruction books for equipment close at hand on a shelf or in a drawer.
- Have power tools serviced.
- Sharpen cutting edges of hand tools; blunt blades are inefficient and dangerous.
- Keep sharp tools and poisonous preparations out of the reach of children.
- When using tools, keep calm. Haste and bad temper are disastrous in the workroom.
- Unplug tools before leaving the workroom. Fit the door to the room with a lock.
- Clear the floor of obstacles. Carelessly placed extension cords can be tripwires in the workroom.
- Have a fire extinguisher close at hand.

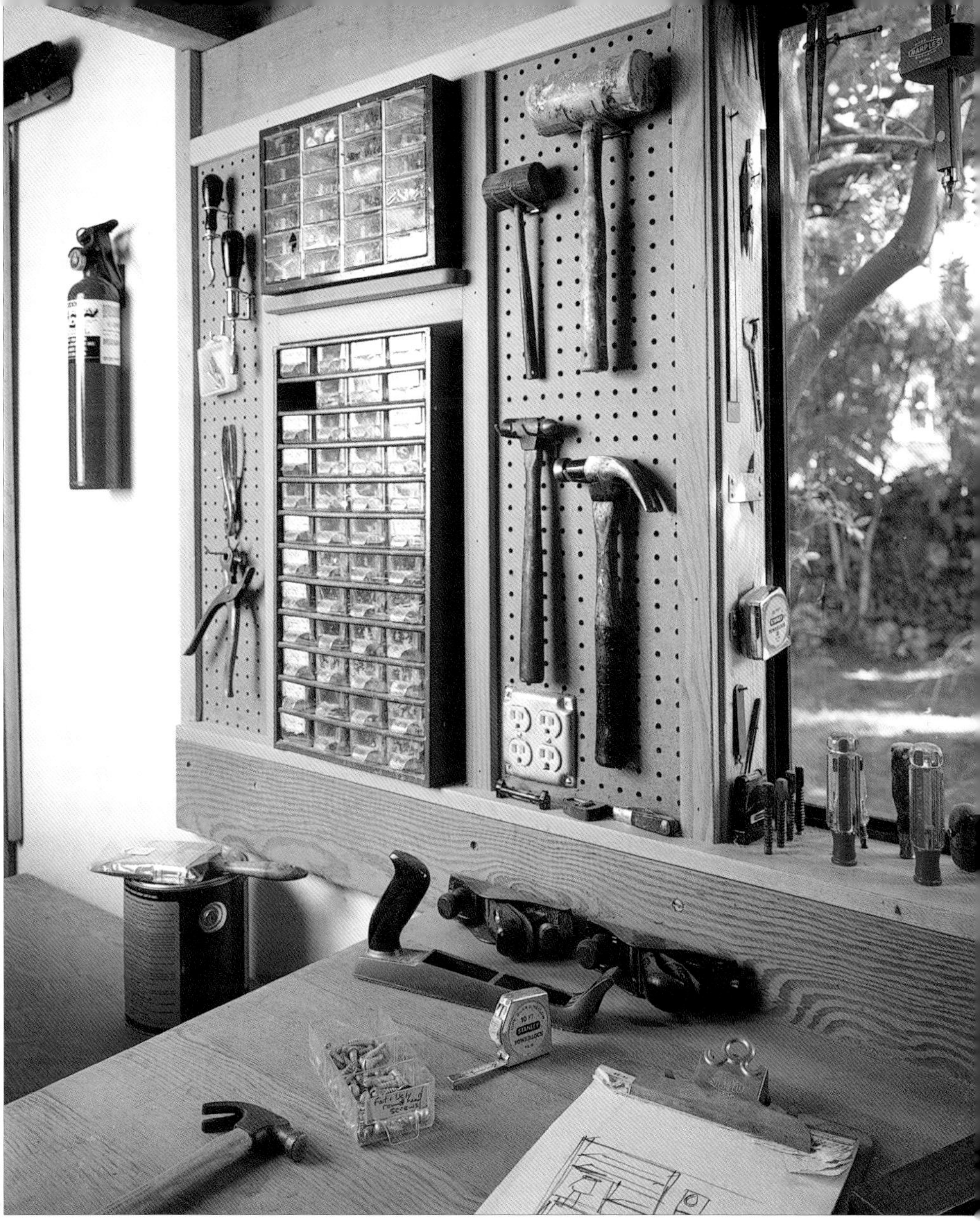

ABOVE: The fire extinguisher should be close at hand.

BELOW: Screwdrivers and files are best stored on a hanging rail.

Workroom essentials

A work bench, a sawhorse, a basic set of hand tools and some powertools are considered the absolute essentials for the workroom. These can be added to as your budget allows and your needs change.

Work bench

No work bench? Use the dimensional drawing below as a guide to making one. Adjust the height to suit your own stature and make the top flush with the front if a vice is to be installed.

Sawhorses

Essential to the serious handyperson, this pair (right) of sturdy sawhorses is made from inexpensive pine. They'll make the job of cutting timber much easier because their height allows the body to bend over the work so maximum strength can be put into the job.

To saw the angles accurately you will need a power saw that is set into its bench. If you have this facility, cut all the angles at 15° outside the right angle. If you are not able to do this, cut the housing recesses in the top at 90° and allow the angled braces to set the legs at the correct slope.

Cut the housings with a saw, hammer and chisel into the top piece in the positions indicated in the diagram. Cut the legs about 25 mm longer than necessary and set them in the housings, protruding above the top surface.

Saw them off level with the top last of all. Screw through the braces into the edges of the legs and through the legs into the housing, using 55 mm screws in the positions that are indicated in the diagram. The splayed legs will stop the sawhorses from toppling over, no matter how much weight may be applied to them.

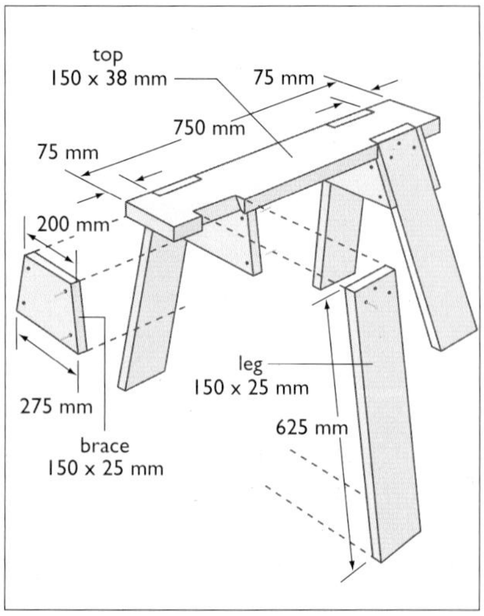

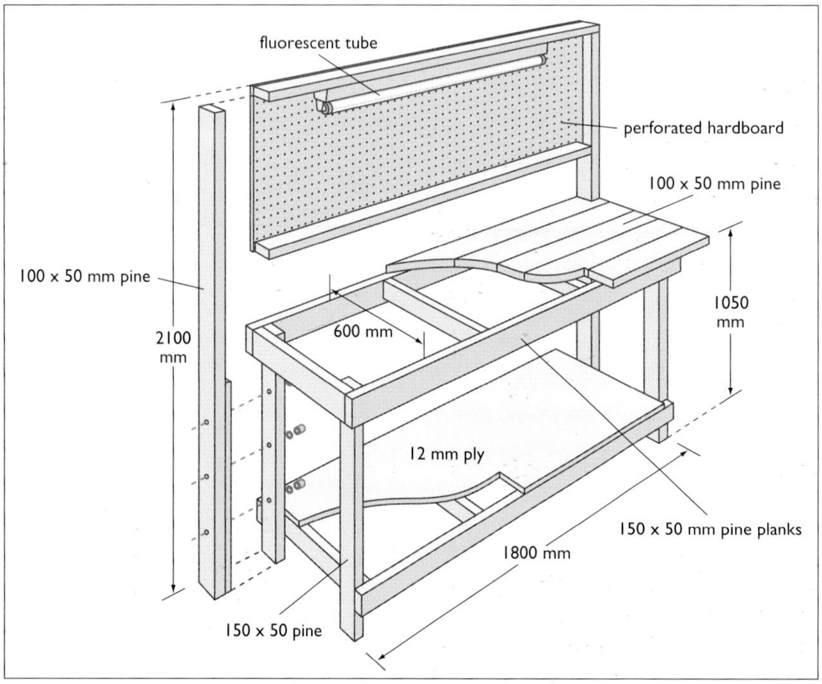

TOP: Pine sawhorses.

ABOVE: Sawhorse plan.

LEFT: Work bench plan.

FAR RIGHT: Power tools.

1 Drill
2 Circular saw
3 Orbital sander
4 Jigsaw
5 Router

Power tools

Although building tasks can be performed with hand tools, using electrical energy rather than the human variety will allow you to get the job done more quickly and, in most cases, more accurately.

These days, power tools are available in different capacities. Most manufacturers produce a light-capacity range which is adequate for weekend projects. The tools are listed in order of priority.

A drill is essential. It is almost impossible to undertake any building project without drilling holes.

A circular saw is a must for work with any wood except small-dimensioned timber.

An orbital sander is invaluable for giving work a professional finish. Most drills have a disc attachment to take circular sheets of sandpaper and act as a power sander, but this tends to leave curved marks in softer surfaces.

The jigsaw allows you to perform a wider range of building activities, and in some cases it can also perform the work of the circular or disc saw.

The router, used to cut rebates in timber for stronger joints, should be your last purchase. Make do with simple timber joints until you become more experienced.

Drill

Most jobs call for holes to be drilled. Everything, from inserting screws to starting saw cuts that do not extend to the edge of the timber, is made much easier with a power drill and a good selection of drill bits. One recommended optional extra is a variable speed control, which enables drilling into materials of different densities.

Circular saw

Though most saw cuts can be made with a hand saw, a power saw will save a lot of time and energy, especially when using hardwoods. A saw with a 185-mm-diameter blade (approximately) will be sufficient for the amateur. Though power saws are noisy and sometimes forbidding, their blade guards ensure that the cutting edge is covered when not in use.

Orbital sander

This is a wonderful companion when it comes to finishing any work. Any job is only as good as the finished surface, and using a sander is the quickest way to achieve a smooth appearance. It allows the filling and smoothing off of any blemishes in timber and plaster surfaces alike, and conceals inaccuracies in building projects.

Jigsaw

This relatively modern invention opens up a whole new world to the home handyperson. It allows the making of curved cuts in just about any material. Also, because its blade is narrow and short, saw cuts can be made in places that would otherwise be too confined. Being able to saw circles and irregular curves allows a greater range of design options.

Router

The strongest joints incorporate rebates (recesses in one piece of timber into which the abutting component fits). The router provides the only quick and accurate method of cutting a rebate. It has a guide at the side which you set on the edge of the timber to keep the cutting tip evenly positioned.

Hand tools — A basic set

With the right tools, any job can be tackled. Basic hand tools haven't changed all that much through the generations, although plastic handles, retractable tape measures and planes indicate some signs of

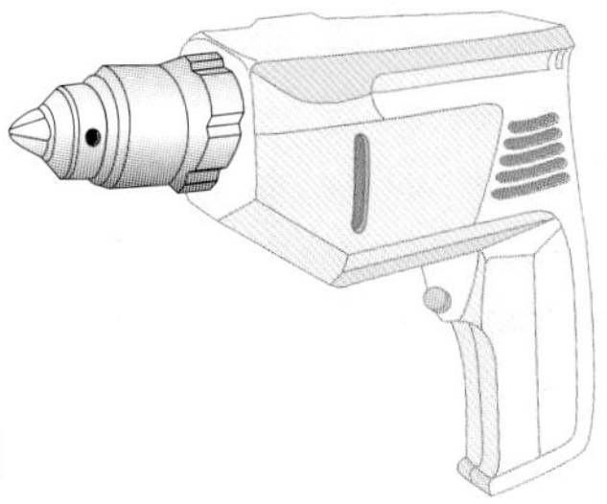

1

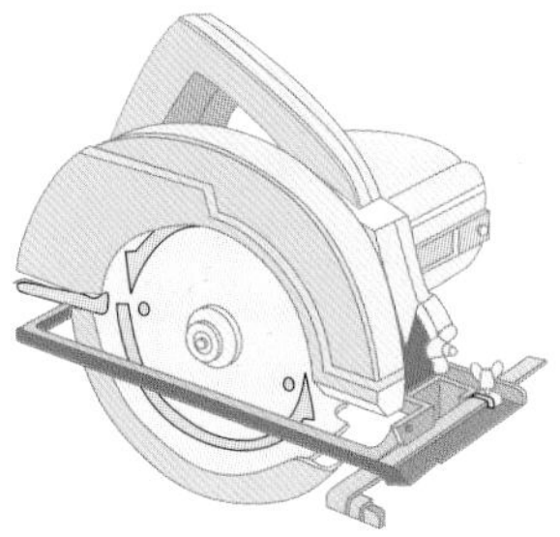

2

3

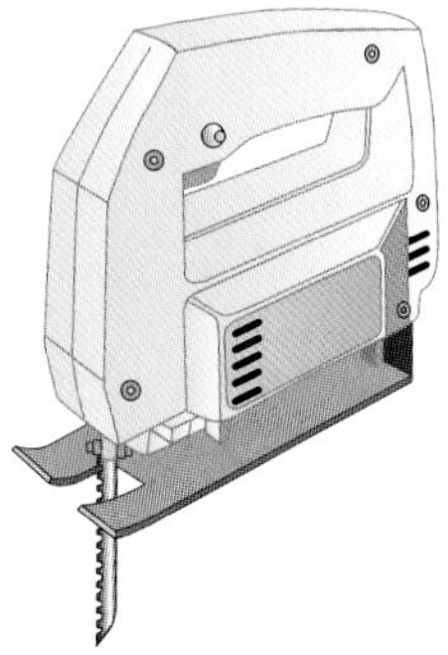

4

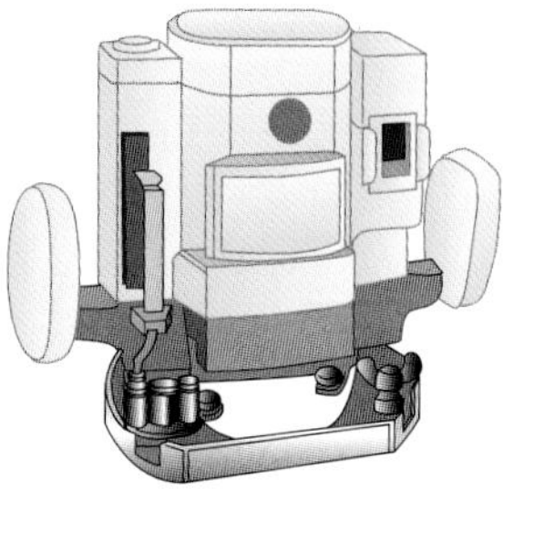

5

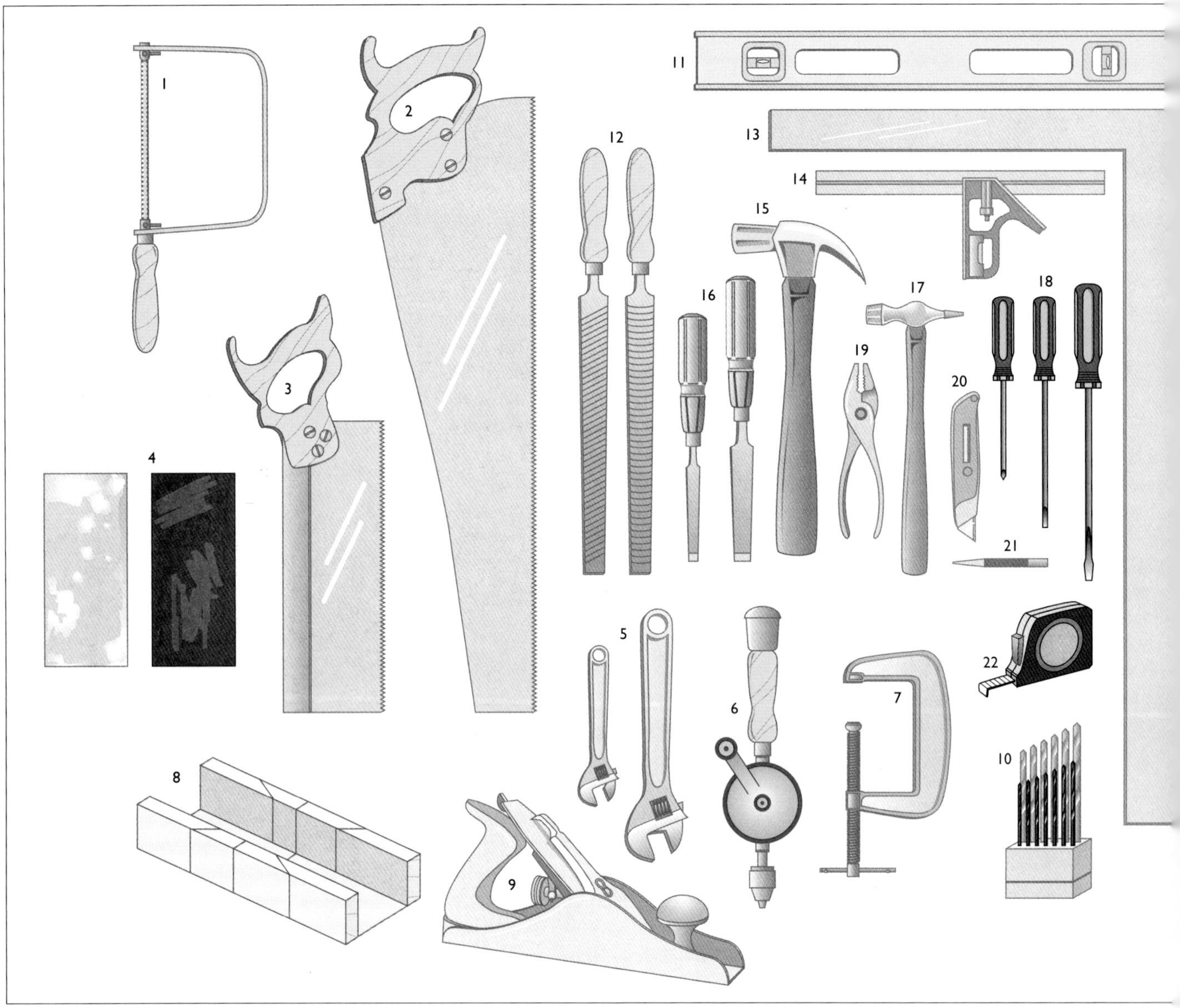

technological advance. Any old tools that are discovered in the course of cleaning out the work-room should be treasured. They are highly prized by collectors and are sometimes of better quality than today's equivalents.

ABOVE: Hand tools.

1 Coping saw. Ideal for cutting curves and intricate joints. Blades are replaceable.
2 Panel saw. For cutting larger pieces of timber to size. Use a small file to sharpen individual teeth.
3 Tenon saw. For cutting joints, such as mitres.
4 Oilstone. For sharpening chisels and blade knives.
5 Adjustable spanners. These ensure that you will always have a tight fit on a nut. Use bolts and nuts for connecting large timber pieces.
6 Hand drill. Handy for small jobs such as making screw holes.
7 G-clamps. For anchoring your timber to the work bench while it is being sawed. You can also clamp timber together during construction.
8 Mitre box. Sets the saw blade at the exact 45° or 90° angle.
9 Plane. Finishes timber to any dimension. You can adjust the blade to alter the depth of the cut.
10 Twist bits. Allow you to drill up to 15 mm with your hand drill. Flat bits will drill larger holes.

11 Spirit level. For checking that all surfaces are exactly horizontal or vertical.

12 Files. Handy for smoothing off corners and edges. Have at least one long, flat, fine-cut file in your tool kit.

13 Framing square. For marking out shapes on large sheets and checking large-scale right angles.

14 Combination square. Makes quick work of marking out 45° and 90° angles and checking for accuracy with the in-built spirit level at the same time.

15 Curved claw hammer. For hammering in and levering out nails in most situations.

16 Chisels. Have one small and one large, for hammering out cavities and grooves in timber.

17 Tack hammer. For small nails and pins in tight situations where a claw hammer is too large.

18 Screwdrivers. Buy these in different sizes as you need them, making sure that the tool fits the screw head exactly.

19 Pliers. For tightening bolts, cutting wires and gripping and removing nails.

20 Trimming knife. Useful for cutting all materials as well as adjusting cuts in your timber components.

21 Nail punch. It may be necessary for you to buy more than one of these to allow you to recess different-sized nail heads into your timber.

22 Tape measure. Simply indispensable.

Tips

- Don't be tempted to buy cheap tools on special in hardware stores — tips may break off screwdrivers, hammer heads could chip and chisels blunt quickly. Invest a bit extra and buy reliable brand names.
- To stop a new saw rusting, wipe it over with an oily rag after use, and avoid cutting wet timber. Lubricate saws with candle wax and remove any rust with turpentine and steel wool.

LEFT: This neat idea safely stores paint, hazardous materials and other workroom items behind roller doors in the garage while still allowing easy access to them.

Some simple how tos

Learning how to assemble things properly will make any do-it-yourself job easier and, with the right finishing touch, you can achieve a professional look.

ABOVE: The finishing touch is important if you are to achieve a professional look.

BELOW: Joint techniques.

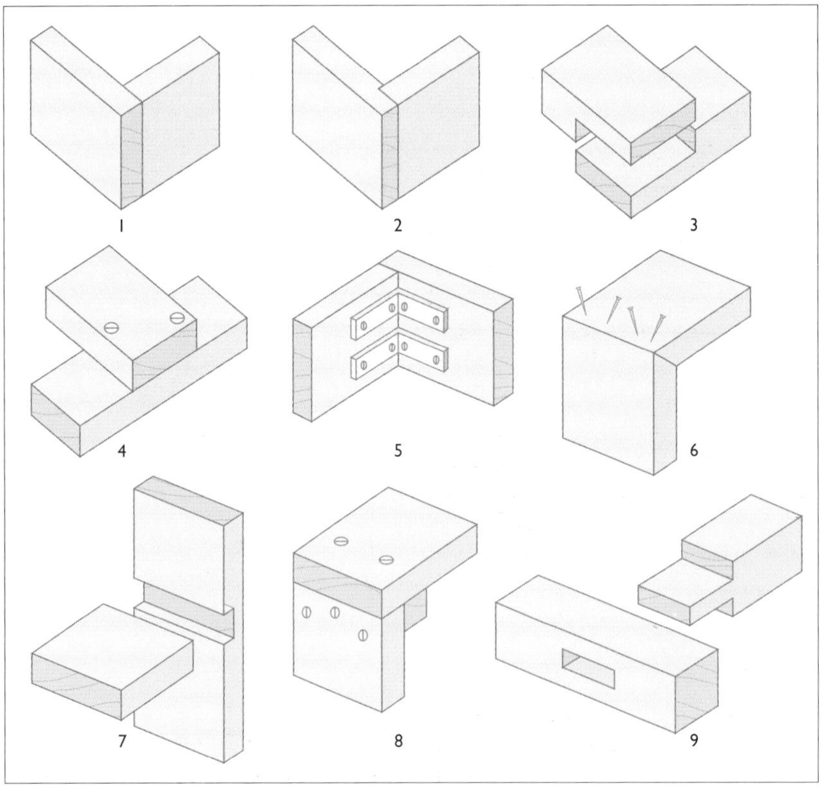

Joint techniques

Joining two pieces of timber together is the basis of most of the projects illustrated in this book. Here are some of the simplest joints, clearly drawn and explained. Try them out with scrap timber, using off-cuts of the same thickness for each one. All joints should be glued and nailed or screwed.

1 Butt. This is the most basic of timber joints and the most frequently used. Execute it simply by butting the two timber surfaces together and fixing one component onto the end of the other. Glue and screws or nails give the joint its only strength.

2 Rebated. You will achieve more strength if you cut a rebate into one piece of timber and position the adjoining piece in it. Cut vertically across the timber grain with a coping or tenon saw (these are more rigid saws that give you greater control) to the depth of the rebate, and use a hammer and chisel to remove the waste timber.

3 Half lap. Use your saw, hammer and chisel for this method also. By cutting recesses into both components to a depth of half the thickness of the timber, you will make a very strong joint. This type is most often used for timber that is joined over its horizontal dimension.

4 Lap. Where the two timbers do not have to finish flush with one another, this basic lap joint will suffice. It is vital that you locate screws or nails diagonally across the joint as this gives the joint its strength.

5 Brackets. Concealed steel brackets of different sizes and shapes may be used to reinforce any timber joint. You should also nail or screw through the joint as for any butt joint.

6 Mitre. When you require a perfect finish and the joint is to be left exposed, you should use a mitre joint. You will need a mitre box and tenon saw to ensure the two cuts are at exactly 45°. A mitre cramp is useful to hold the two components in place while you glue and nail them together. Insert the nails at alternating angles to stop the joint from pulling apart.

7 Housed. When making a T-joint (stronger than the butt), saw and chisel a groove or housing into one component and allow the adjoining timber to sit into it. Start the groove by sawing downwards across the grain, making two parallel cuts through half the thickness of the timber. Chisel out the recess between the cuts.

8 Butt with block. If your basic butt joint is not going to be strong enough for the job, reinforce it with a cleat on the inside of the corner. This makes a very practical joint which you should use whenever appearance is not the main consideration. Screw through both the components into the corner block.

9 Mortice and tenon. This is the strongest way to make a T-joint. Saw the tenon or tongue to fit into the mortice or slot of the other component. Both mortice and tenon should be one-third the thickness of timber. You will have to use a sharp chisel to cut the mortice accurately.

The finishing touch

A professional standard of finish depends on preparing the surface properly before varnishing, waxing or painting.

Filling

Fillers vary from acrylic compounds (purely cosmetic cover-up fillers) to epoxy resins which bond with timber and take screws and nails.

Punch nails and countersink screws with a countersunk drill bit; then use filler to disguise the heads. Smooth furry end grain by filling and sanding. Also conceal knots, splits and grain blemishes with filler. Despite claims to the contrary, all fillers shrink to some extent when drying. For deep cavities, build up layers, allowing each one to dry before proceeding. Sand the top flush with the timber surface.

Colouring may be difficult as fillers often take in more stain than timber. Although there are fillers already tinted to match most common timber types, naturally there are variations. You should test coloured filler on the underside of a project before proceeding.

Plugging

A plug gives an ultra-flush finish over a countersunk screw. After drilling the hole for the screw, use an ordinary drill bit the width of the screw head and drill to a depth of 10 mm below the surface. (A countersunk drill bit cannot make a hole as deep as this.) Cut a same-width dowel plug a little shorter than the depth of the hole, tap it in place and sand flush.

A system comprising a plastic cap with a conical component through which the screw shaft is inserted is another method of concealing screw and bolt heads.

Edging

Timber edging strips conceal the end grains of timber, timber-veneered particle board and plain particle-board sawn edges. Have them the same width as the sheet material, or deeper for a more substantial look. Glue and tack the strips in place and fill and sand the junction. Paint them to match or clear finish them as a feature detail. Pine edging strips combine well with white or coloured plastic-laminated particle board.

Heat-bonded strips in a basic range of timber types and colours for timber-veneered and plastic-laminated particle board give professional quality edges. A household iron provides the necessary heat source.

Sanding

Wrap sandpaper around a cork or timber block and always sand with the grain. To smooth down rough

ABOVE: Stained timber has been given a sheen with polyurethane.

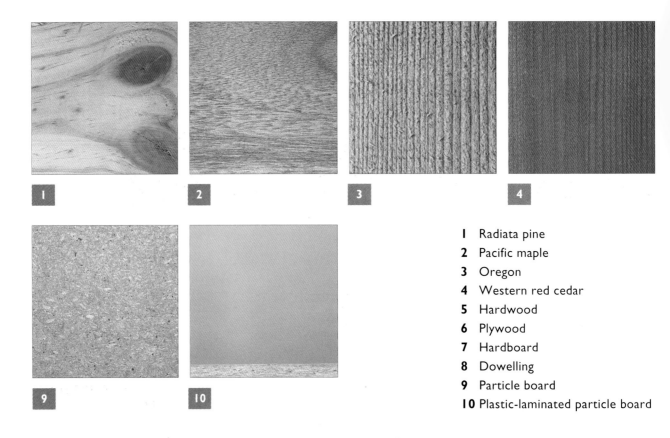

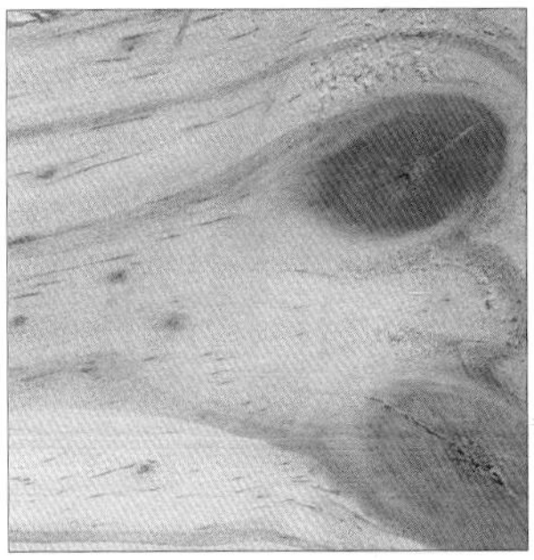
1

2

3

4

9

10

1 Radiata pine
2 Pacific maple
3 Oregon
4 Western red cedar
5 Hardwood
6 Plywood
7 Hardboard
8 Dowelling
9 Particle board
10 Plastic-laminated particle board

timber and end grain, start with a medium-grade sandpaper and work through a couple of lighter grades. Use a light-grade paper between coats of paint and varnish.

An orbital sander makes it easier to achieve a good finish. Keep the sander running along the grain or squiggle marks will occur.

Staining

Work quickly and evenly, covering the entire surface with stain before it dries. Use a soft cloth or brush for application and work in the direction of the grain. Wipe off excess with a clean dry cloth and when dry, wipe again before applying a clear coating. Practise on a scrap of the same timber before you begin.

Choose a stain that is compatible with the finish you have in mind; check with the supplier before purchasing. Most stains produce denser colours than expected.

Timber and boards

Definitions of timber can leave the novice blinking in confusion. Hardwood and softwood seem to be straightforward enough as descriptive terms. However, the botanist and the carpenter or cabinet-maker have different opinions. Tradespeople use these terms literally to describe timber that is either hard or soft to work. In the realms of science, hardwood can include species as different as balsa and iron bark, and also includes Pacific maple — an old 'softie' from way back. In fact, botanists rate the term 'hardwood' as an inaccurate botanical description.

It is possible to buy timber from mills in widths and thicknesses limited only by the size of the tree, but standard sizes available in timber yards and hardware stores are more economical and easier to obtain. In the case of sheet materials, ask your local supplier about sheet sizes available to minimise waste and maximise the purchase.

Although timber is cut and sheet materials produced in an astounding variety of thicknesses, widths and lengths, a retail outlet will only keep those sizes for which there is the most demand. Sometimes it is worth going to a larger timber yard or building supplier to find sizes of materials suited to specific needs. Timber is sold by the linear metre, so estimate the length of each type needed before ordering.

All timber except pine is sold in its nominal undressed dimensions. When it is dressed — that is, planed smooth — its dimensions are considerably reduced. For instance, a piece of timber measuring 100 x 38 mm will be 90 x 30 mm when it is dressed. This is referred to as dressed-all-round or DAR, or sometimes S4S.

The amount by which the timber is reduced when it is planed smooth varies with different timber

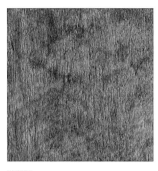

5

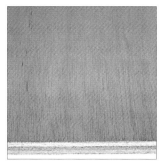

6

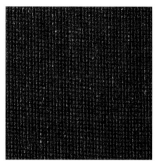

7

8

types and different milling equipment used. Pine is sold in its dressed sizes.

Radiata pine

Radiata pine from New Zealand and slash pine from Queensland are the least expensive natural timbers on the market. The nature of the grain makes them flex as well as splinter when sawn. The grain has very high contrast and in some situations needs to be painted. It is ideal for furnishings and shelving. Unless it has been preservative-treated, radiata pine is not suitable for outside use.

Thickness: 19–20 mm
Widths: 19–290 mm

Pacific maple

Pacific maple is soft to work and commonly used. The closeness of its grain makes it easy to work and sand to a smooth finish. It is strictly an interior timber and is very suitable for furniture and joinery.

Thickness: 13–50 mm
Widths: 25–300 mm

Oregon

Oregon is a high-quality timber which, when properly treated, can be used for exterior applications such as pergolas and other garden structures. It has traditionally been used for house framework, but cheaper materials have now made their way into this area.

Thickness: 25–100 mm
Widths: 50–300 mm

Western red cedar

Western red cedar is one of the most expensive timbers available. It is durable in all exterior conditions. Its natural colour makes it even more appealing and it will weather to a pale grey when it is left untreated. Its softness can be a disadvantage.

Thickness: 19–100 mm
Widths: 25–300 mm

Hardwood

High-density hardwoods are often rated as highly durable in-ground (e.g. tallowwood, iron bark, white mahogany) but others such as Tasmanian oak (really 'ash' type eucalypts) and Pacific maple are ranked as non-durable.

Thickness: 25–150 mm
Widths: 25–250 mm

Plywood

Plywood, which is bonded layers of timber, varies in size, quality and thickness. Because it is composed of layers, plywood comes in sizes wider than 300 mm. The layers give the sheets strength.

Plywood that is 4, 6 and 9 mm thick comes in sheet sizes 1800, 2100 and 2400 mm long. These lengths are available in 900 and 1200 mm widths; 7, 12 and 17 mm thicknesses: 2400 x 1200 mm; 19-mm-thick form ply (exterior grade): 2500 x 1200 mm.

Hardboard

This dark composite board is a relatively dense material. It has no structural capacity and should be used only where it is supported by a frame. Hardboard forms an excellent underlay for floor coverings. One side is smooth, the other rough. Pictured here is the rough back surface.

5.5 mm thicknesses:
1800 x 1200 mm
2400 x 900 mm
2400 x 1200 mm

Dowelling

This material is useful in forming uprights and joining components in building projects. Thicknesses of 6, 8, 10, 12.5, 16, 19, 25, 35 and 44 mm are all available in 1.8 m lengths. The 19–44 mm thicknesses are available in 2.4 m lengths.

Particle board

Particle board is only suitable for interior use. It is composed of timber chips or particles formed with

ABOVE: Parquetry is the most prestigious of floor finishes and can be laid in a variety of designs and types of timber. It is equally suitable for living areas and kitchens.

glues and pressure into a sheet. Only the surfaces of the sheets are smooth and you will usually have to glue and nail timber edging onto the rough sheet edges. Particle board requires special screws with straight-threaded shanks for better gripping power.

Thickness: 13 mm
Sheets: 900 x 450 mm–22700 x 1500 mm
Thickness: 19 mm
Sheets: 900 x 450 mm–3600 x 1800 mm

Plastic-laminated particle board is ideal for situations where a wipe-down surface is an advantage. Its white sheen gives any project executed in it a contemporary appearance. The rough-sawn edges can be covered with iron-on plastic edging strips.

Thickness: 16 mm
Sheets: 1800 x 600 mm and 2400 x 1200 mm
Thickness: 4 mm
Sheets: 1200 x 900 mm and 2400 x 1200 mm
Thickness: 6 mm
Sheets: 2400 x 1200 mm

Medium-density fibre board (MDF board) is a new material with extra density which allows you to screw into its end grain. Sawn edges require no finish other than sanding and painting.

Thicknesses: 13 and 18 mm
Sheets: 2400 x 900 mm
2400 x 1200 mm
1800 x 900 mm
1800 x 1200 mm

Making accurate measurements

Whether you're building a 50-room castle, a dog house or just a section of fencing, there's no such measurement as 'about'. Measurements must be exact. Learning this from the outset will save you a lot of time, money and frustration.

An equally important aspect of making correct measurements is starting square. This isn't automatic, by any means — most materials aren't square, especially on ends of boards and timbers. However, almost all building materials — wood, concrete, metal, plastic and so on — have a 'factory edge'. A factory edge is carpenters' vernacular for the milled edge of the material, which usually is true. Use this edge as a reference point for squaring the rest of the material.

To make truly accurate measurements, you'll need to have several tools, the most important of which is a rule or tape measure. This calibrated instrument is available in many forms, but your best bet is a 3, 5 or 8 m steel tape.

You'll also need a pencil with a sharp point or, better yet, a flat carpenters' pencil (these have flat rather than round lead) to transfer the mark to the material. For even more accuracy, use an awl, which looks like a short ice pick, or a scriber, which resembles a long toothpick. (Many combination squares include a scriber.)

Another important marking device, the chalk line, has many uses. Its chief function, though, is laying down long straight lines. To use a chalk line, first make sure the line has plenty of chalk on it; don't skimp. Then, tie the line to a nail on one end, and stretch it taut. (You must have the line pulled tight to obtain an accurate line.) To make the mark, pinch the line between your thumb and index finger, pull the line out from the surface to be marked, and let the line snap back onto the surface. Snap the line just once.

Using squares and levels

The words 'square', 'level' and 'plumb' are familiar to most people, but deceptively so. Before discussing how to achieve each of these desirables, let's define what they are. Square refers to an exact 90° relationship between two surfaces. When a material is level, it's perfectly horizontal; when it's plumb, it's at true vertical.

Never assume that any existing construction is square, level or plumb. Chances are, it's not. To prove this to yourself, lay a level along any floor in your home, plumb a wall section in a corner, or square a door or window opening. Don't be alarmed at the results.

Variation is normal in most construction, since houses usually settle slightly on their foundations, throwing square, level and plumb out of whack. But when you make repairs or additions, you must compensate for the existing errors.

The three tools needed to establish square, level and plumb are a framing square, a spirit level and a plumb bob.

A framing square has two legs, each at right angles to the other. The blade is longer and wider than the other leg, which is commonly known as the tongue. Usually marked in 1 or 5 mm increments, some squares also have scales so you can align them for rafter and other angle cuts.

A spirit level is used to determine level and plumb. When the work is level (horizontal) or plumb (vertical) the bubbles in liquid-filled glass tubes on the spirit level are centred between the lines drawn on the tubes.

How can you know if a spirit level is accurate? Lay it on a horizontal surface and shim if necessary to get a level reading. Now turn it around. If you don't get the same reading, the spirit level needs to be adjusted and replaced. With some models, you can compensate by rotating the vial.

A plumb bob is used to determine the true vertical position of all upright elements in a building, such as walls and pipes. It is a pointed weight suspended on a line.

Making a tool box

There's about $25 worth of second-hand oregon and a couple of hours of relatively easy work in this tool box. Ours has a drawer in the bottom, which requires either a router or a bit of skill with a power saw.

You will need for the tool box (recycled oregon, all dimensions are in mm):

Components	Measurements	No.
A Ends	450 x 280 x 20	2
B Sides	900 x 225 x 20	1
	900 x 280 x 20	1
C Base rails	900 x 50 x 20	2
	180 x 50 x 20	2
D Floor supports	860 x 20 x 20	2
	200 x 20 x 20	2
E Drawer sides	220 x 52 x 20	2
F Drawer front	857 x 52 x 20	1
G Drawer back	857 x 42 x 20	1
H Handle supports	250 x 70 x 20	2
I Handle	860 x 50 x 40	1
J Drawer base	827 x 245 x 4 plywood	1
K Floor	860 x 240 x 5 masonite	1

BELOW: Detail of tool box handle.

BOTTOM: The finished tool box.

RIGHT: The tool box components.

BELOW: The slide out drawer of the tool box.

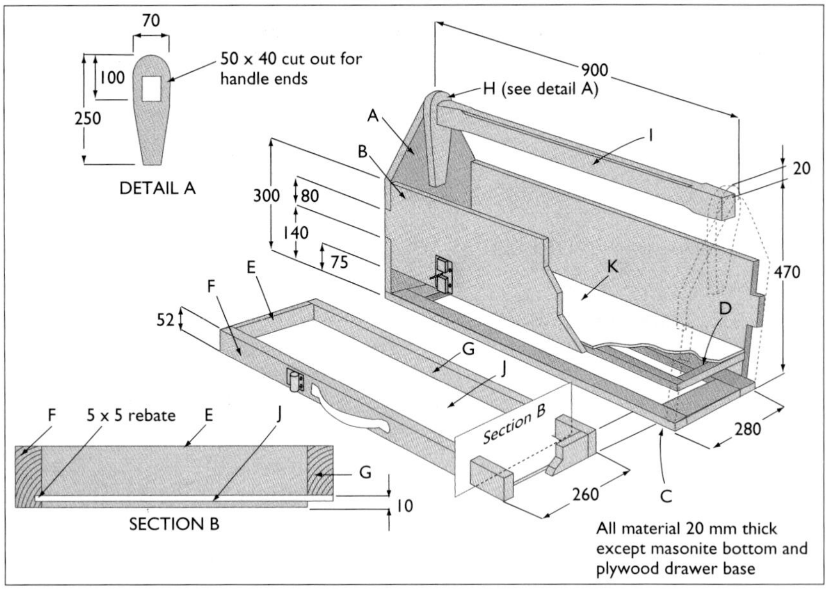

You can leave it out, if you like, and just build the basic box.

1 Cut out the ends. If you have a jigsaw, mark the round piece on the top with the perimeter of a small paint can or jar and cut along the dotted line. Cut out the rebates to receive the tongues from the side with a jigsaw or by making several cuts with a hand saw and knocking out the waste with a chisel.

2 Cut out the sides (making one shorter than the other if you intend to add the drawer) and screw them to the ends.

3 Screw on the base rails and the floor supports. Make the drawer to fit the opening. A drawer front that is 857 x 52 mm should fit, but measure to check. The same applies to the length of the side. Remember, measure twice, cut once.

4 If you don't own a router, two careful cuts with a power saw will do the trick for the drawer bottom rebate. Set the first cut at 5 mm and the second parallel to it at 8 mm. This should give you a groove 5 mm wide.

5 Run a plane down the edges of the handle to knock off the sharp edges, then fit it into the supports and screw them to the two ends. Drop in the masonite bottom, secure it with a couple of panel pins and you're finished.

The tool box can be as big or as small as you care to make it. Just remember, when it's full of tools you need to be able to lift it without the embarrassment of calling for a strong friend's help.

The dangers of renovating

When you renovate, you get up on roofs or down holes, use power tools and come into contact with different chemicals—all of which can present hazards.

The most common injuries on work sites are sprains and strains, back injuries, hand and finger damage, and knee and leg injuries. Many of these are caused by falls which occur on slippery surfaces, ladders, steps, stairs and scaffolding. Set ladders on level ground and secure them firmly at the top. The best angle is with the base one quarter of its height out from the wall. Scaffolding should only be put up by professionals. Keep your site clean and free of rubbish on paths and access ways.

It's vital to keep a well-stocked first-aid kit on site. There are special safety standards for industrial sites, but do-it-yourselfers are rarely aware of these. Find out!

Electrical safety

Keep electrical cables out of reach and away from moisture. Make sure your tools are double insulated and use an earth leakage device or portable safety switch.

If extension cords are frayed or damaged, discard them. Don't use cords that are longer than necessary; coiled cords can cause a build-up of heat in the wires.

Chemical hazards

Renovators have to take special care with chemicals. Corrosive paint stripper, cleaners, gas and fuels, and even paints can be a source of danger. Not only can solvents give off fumes, they're highly flammable, too.

Smell is not always a clue to danger; some gases are colourless and odourless. Remember to protect yourself with a respirator and lots of ventilation. Don't eat, drink or smoke in the midst of renovations, and clean up carefully at the end of the day.

It's worth looking for solvent-free materials wherever available. These include the new water-based timber floor finish called Synteko Supreme. Safe storage—out of children's reach—and proper labelling are also vital with chemicals. And, when it's time for disposal, follow the manufacturer's recommendations or check with your local council.

Care with tools

Obvious care is needed with any sharp tools such as saws. Don't overload tools so that they overheat. If they spark, stop or behave strangely, stop using them and have a qualified electrician inspect them. Let the tool motor stop before putting the tool down because it may kick back. Follow the maker's safety instructions.

Protective clothing

Protective eye wear (goggles), good gloves and tough clothing will protect you from spills and grazes. A dust mask may not be enough if you're using chemicals with harmful fumes; you should also get an approved respirator.

If you're using noisy machinery, ear protectors are vital. And be careful how you dress. Loose clothing or long hair can get caught in tools. Wear solid shoes with good tread. Don't forget the risk of skin cancer, too, if you're working outdoors; cover up from the sun and wear an SPF15+ sunscreen.

Tips

Where do I turn off the water?

All plumbing repairs must be carried out by a licensed plumber, but you may save yourself a lot of damage while you are waiting if you know where to turn off the water.

- Where is your water meter?
- Does it have a tap-type handle on it or do you need a wrench? Do you have the right size wrench available?
- Do you have a stop cock (a separate tap within your property for turning off the water) and where is it?
  (Why not get a plumber to install one which doesn't need a wrench to turn it off in an easy-to-access place?)
- Do you need to turn off the hot water heater if you turn off the water?

You should find out the answers to these questions.

Contacts

- For more advice, contact Worksafe or the Occupational Health and Safety authority in your area. Your local Public Health Unit and State Environment Protection Authority also will be able to offer assistance.

'Green' renovating

For most of us, life gets 'greener' every day. We're composting, recycling, buying products with less packaging, using unleaded petrol and so on. Now the 'green' revolution has even hit building.

'Green' do-it-yourself tips

- Wash brushes used in water-based paint in a bucket of water. Let paint settle and tip water on the garden. Dispose of hardened paint in the bin or in a toxic-waste tip. Do the same with turps, but pour turps back into its jar for re-use.
- When sanding, wear a dust mask and contain the area to limit dust.
- Don't wash filler down the drain. Tip it onto newspaper and leave it to dry. Then dispose of it in the bin or a toxic-waste tip.

Whether you're renovating or building from scratch, 'green' alternatives exist for many products you'll need. They're usually more expensive in the short term, but they can mean a more environmentally healthy home for your family. They can ultimately save you money, too.

Timber tricks

Recycle old timber in building to save money and resources. Once cleaned up, it makes wonderful pieces such as bench tops. If you don't have old timber to use, try plantation-grown varieties. They're good for structural work, can be used in place of many plastic products (such as laminate) and can replace plasterboard for walls. Timber panels can also be removed to allow easy access to electrical work behind. Radially sawn plantation timber can look great as a feature wall, too.

BELOW: In renovating this house the owners have made good use of recycled timber for both furniture and fittings.

Green options

Solvent-based products regularly used in building and cleaning can cause health problems for some people, especially asthmatics.

Paint

Solvent-based paint can be dangerous during application and will continue to emit gases which can affect some people. Use plant-based paint products instead. If removing lead-based paint, use a chemical peel so you don't breath in lead dust.

Polyurethane varnishes

Replace with hard oils made from plant oils and tree resin.

Steam cleaning

Instead of solvent-based cleaning products, try steam cleaning areas of your home. A steam-cleaning machine can remove varnish from rafters and is great for bathrooms, carpet and so on.

Cleaners

There are 'green' alternatives to many solvent-based cleaning products. Some health stores and supermarkets will stock them, and there are stores specialising in environmentally healthy products. Check in the Yellow Pages.

Index

architrave 47, 122
attic 12, 19, 161

balustrade 87, 88, 89, 109
basin 166–7
bath 171–2
  resurfacing 177
  surrounds 181–2
bathroom 18, 135, 157
  assessing needs 158–61
  children friendly 175
  colour schemes 173–4
  expansion 179–80
  facelift 176–7
  floor plans 165
  mirror 174, 196–7
  planning 162
  safety 175
  sizes 163–4
  storage 163, 172–3, 177, 248
  ventilation 162–3
  walls 184–6
  windows 113
battens 46–7, 57
bedroom
  storage 248–52
bench 8, 149, 150
  bathroom 167–9, 177
  granite top 169
  island 146
  jarrah 147
  kitchen 20
  laminate top 154, 167, 168
  marble top 169
  work 288
bidet 170
blanket box 259–61
bookcase 263–4
builders 25, 27, 88
built-ins 241, 243
  toilet 190–1
  vanity unit 190–1, 193–4
butcher's block 154, 155–6

carcasses 148
carpet 70–1
ceiling 31
  insulation 53
  new 55
  replacing 55
  solving problems 53–4
  suspended 58
ceiling tiles 54, 56
chair, upholstered 278–9
chemical hazards 299
circular saw 289
cleaning agents
  "green" alternatives 300
  steam cleaning 300
cleaning cupboard 255
coir matting 66, 69, 81
colour schemes 173, 214–15
  choosing 213
  colour psychology 215
columns 19
condensation 36–7
contract 27, 28–9
contractors, see tradespeople
cosmetic centre 174, 176
cottage 27
cupboard
  cleaning 255
  flexible storage, as 276–7
  linen 254

deck platform 23
dining area 21, 40, 47, 149
dining room 20, 23
dishwasher 136
door 91
  aluminium 93
  construction 97
  double 93
  exterior 92, 149
  flush 97
  flyscreen 109
  folding 92, 94, 100
  French 11, 16, 19, 94, 95, 98, 102, 111, 112
  glass 96
  glazed 92, 93
  hinged 98
  installing new 101–3
  interior 92
  louvre 105
  painting 108
  panel 97
  panelled 92
  patio 110
  pre-hung 103
  problems 98–100
  restoring 107–8
  security 110–11
  sliding 97, 100
  timber 107, 110–11
  weather stripping 105
door hinge 103
door knob 104–5
door seal 105–6
doorway 101, 102
drain, clogged 189
  basin 189–90
  bath 190
  toilet 190
drawing room 18
drill 289

electrical safety 299
environmental considerations 285, 300

family room 13, 22, 23, 65
fanlight 92
fibreglass 182
finishes
  antique 280–2
  edging 293
  filling 293
  laundry 203
  paint see paint finishes
  plugging 293
  sanding 293–4
  staining 294
  walls 48–52
floor 31, 65
  bathroom 182–4
  hard-surface 81–4
    repairing 85
  removing stains 85
  resilient 79–80
    repairing 85–6
  types 68–9, 79–80
  wood 31, 72–4, 149
    repairing 78–9
    sanding 75–7
folding screen 122
fridge 143
furniture
  antique finish 280–2
  combining 244
  crackled look 282–3
  lime-washed 281, 282, 283
  new from old 269–71
  painting 223
  second-hand 271
  storage, as 239

garden 22, 23, 65
glass
  frosted 159
  replacing broken window 128–9
glass brick 165, 186
granny flat 21
"green" renovating 285, 300
Gyprock 55

hand basin 166–7
hand tools 289–91
  tips 291
heating 10

jigsaw 289
joint techniques 292–3

kitchen 22, 23, 24, 37, 47, 135, 136
country style 150–1
customised 145–7
demolition 148
design tips 142
doors 148, 150, 154
drawers 148, 154
galley 24, 139–40
installing 147–8
Mediterranean 151
modern/urban 151
planning 137, 140–6
safety 142
shapes 138
storage 142, 152–3, 244–7
kitchen appliances 136, 143, 150
kitchen cabinet 144–5
kitchen wall dishrack 257–9

ladder, drop down 87
laundry 135
clothes dryer 199, 201, 202
dual-purpose 205
galley layout 201, 206
hide-away style 207
ironing 199, 200
planning 199–204
small 204–5
space-saving ideas 200
storage 199–200, 203, 254
surfaces and finishes 203
tub 199, 202–3, 204
washing machine 199, 201, 202
wooden clothes drying rack 208–11
work flow 202
library 12
light, natural 15, 35, 116, 142, 177–8
light shade 195–6
linen cupboard 254
living room 17, 40
storage 252–4
local councils 19, 20, 21, 25, 163
loft 12

marble 183
faux 184
measurements
accurate 296
squares and levels 296–7
medicine cabinet 191–2
mirrors 118
bathroom 174, 196–7
monk's seat 268–9
moulded cornice 40

Occupational Health and Safety authority 299
open plan living 47
orbital sander 289

paint 10, 176
applying 224–5
acrylic 227
oil-based 228
choosing 220
odours 217
protection from 217
solvent-based 10, 176
storing 217
timber, stripping from 226
paint finishes
aged plaster look 233
colourwashing 232
combing 231
crackle 231
dragging 232
fresco walls 233–4
rag-rolling 231
skirting 234
sponging 231
stippling 232
stripes 232–4
tips 232, 234
woodwork 234
paintbrushes and rollers 216
choosing 224
cleaning 217, 228
how to hold 225
storing 217, 225
painted geometric pattern 86
painting
battered window 223
chalky surfaces 221
chipped joinery 222
cracked cornice 222
cracks in ceiling 221
doors 108
lifting plaster 222
painted door furniture 223
plaster work 222
preparation 219–23
problems 229–30
surfaces, preparation of 225–6
tips 216–7, 219, 221, 225, 229
tools 218–19
windows 108
parquetry floor 73
particleboard 294, 295–6
partitions 47–8
pedestal basin 166–7
pelmet 198
planning 7
45° option 22
defining your hopes 10
layout 8
making plans 21–4
permits 20
priorities list 10
plaster board 41, 44

plaster board ceiling 54, 56
plaster ceiling 54
plumbing
repairs 299
water, turning off 299
polyurethane varnishes 300
power tools 289
privacy 14
protective clothing 299
public health unit 299

rails 89
renovation
adding another storey 11
additional room 59, 161
bathroom 177–80
contractors 25–6, 27–8
dangers 299
do-it-yourself 26–7
enhancing plain houses 15
"green" 285, 300
opening up space 16–17, 19, 47, 177–80
rural 9, 14
suburban 9, 14
urban 8–9, 14
riser 88
roof window 64
router 289
rubbish storage and disposal 148
rug 65, 72, 75

safety 285
chemical hazards 299
electrical 299
floor sanding 77
kitchen 142
protective clothing 299
tools, and 299
workroom, in the 287
sawhorse 288
screening, window 130–2
semi-detached house 9
shelving
choosing hardware 255
shelf strips, putting up 255–6
spacings, estimating 256–7
spans, estimating 256–7
support systems 256
shelving unit 172
kits 265
shower 170–1
surrounds 181–2
showerhead 171
replacing 188–9
shutters 121
skylight 15, 34, 59–60, 177–8
installing 61–4
slipcover 266, 267–8

solvent-based products 300
spa bath 171
space requirements 12–13
splashback 148
staircase 87
stairs 31
  problems 87–9
state environment protection
  authority 299
storage 10, 14, 48
  back door, at 261–2
  bathroom 163, 172–3, 177, 248
  bedroom 248–52
  bookcase 263–4
  corner unit 264
  cupboard 276–7
  kitchen 142, 152–3, 244–7
  kits 265
  laundry 198–9, 203, 254
  living room 252–4
  mobile 262–3
  organising 240–1
  planning 239
  rubbish 148
  stairs 89
  workroom 291
strip-and-plank floor 74
stud 34
sunroom 101

taps 169–70, 201, 203
tiles 8
  bathroom 182
  ceramic 48–9, 81, 84, 85, 182, 186
  fixing fittings 187–8
  floor 21, 81–5, 168, 182
  kitchen 148
  laying 49–50, 82–3
  marble 67
  mosaic 49, 84
  quarry 66, 67, 81, 85
  regluing 186–7
  regrouting 187–8
  slate 84, 85
  terracotta 158
  tips 49
  tools 49–50
timber 294
  door see door
  dowelling 295
  "green" tips 300
  hardboard 295
  hardwood 295
  oregon 295
  pacific maple 295
  plywood 295
  radiata pine 295
  staining 228
  stripping paint from 226
  western red cedar 295
timber and tin pie safe 272–6
timber floorboards see floor – wood
timber panelling 51–2
toilet 165–6, 170
  built-in 190–1
  paper holder 197
  seat 197–198
toilet/powder room layout 162
tool box, making 297–8
tools 288–91
  hand 289–91
  power 289
  safety 299
  tips 291
tradespeople 29
treads 88

vanity basin 167
vanity unit 190–1, 193–4
venetian blinds 117
ventilation 142, 162
verandah 122
Victorian terrace 9, 18

wall-mounted basin 167
wallpaper 46
  applying 235–6
  lifting wallpaper, fixing 236
  stripping 223, 235
  tips 237
walls 31, 184–6
  bearing 32, 34
  cracks and holes 42, 44, 45–6
  cross section 32
  damp 35–7
  finishes 48–52
  finishing and re-texturing 44–5
  glass brick 15, 165
  interior 32
  knocking out 24, 38–9, 41–2, 149
  non-bearing 32, 34
  painted 28
  repairs 38–9, 41–2, 44–6
  shelf 194–5
wardrobe 251
  remodelling 269–70
  walk-in 252
water, turning off 299
weatherboard cottage 27
wet rot 37
window 17, 87, 91, 112
  awning 115, 127–8
  bay 116, 177
  bump-out 132–3, 149
  casement 91, 114, 126–7
  Colonial 112, 117
  conservatory-style 113
  corner 119
  custom-built 115
  dormer 120
  double-hung 113–14
  Federation 117
  floor-to-ceiling 99, 117
  functions 113
  glass, replacing broken 128–9
  louvre 115, 128
  Mediterranean 117
  modern 117
  painting 108
  problems 124–33
  reglazing 128–30
  seat 259–60
  security 122–3
  sliding 114, 127
  vertical 114
  wraparound 118
window lock 122–3
window sash 124–5, 128
window screening 130–2
window spring lift 126
work bench 288
workroom 285
  organising 286–7
  safety 287
  storage 291
Worksafe 299

Published by Murdoch Books®
Cased edition first printed 1998. Reprinted 2000
Limp edition first printed 1998. Reprinted 1999, 2000

National Library of Australia Cataloguing-in-Publication data
The complete home improvement book.
Includes index.
ISBN 1 74045 064 7
ISBN 1 74045 065 5
1. Dwellings – Remodelling – Amateurs' manuals.
2. Dwellings – Maintenance and repair – Amateurs' manuals.
I Better Homes and Gardens. II Title.
643.7

Project Manager: Sally Bird/Calidris Publishing Services
Text/Cover Design and Layout: Trevor Hood/*Anaconda Graphic Design*
Editor: Katie Millar
Diagrams: Di Zign, Sydney

Publishing Manager/Associate Publisher: Kay Scarlett
Production Manager: Liz Fitzgerald

Group General Manager: Mark Smith
Group CEO & Publisher: Anne Wilson

PRINTED IN SINGAPORE
Printed by Tien Wah Press

Published by Murdoch Books® Australia, GPO Box 1203, Sydney NSW 1045. Phone: (612) 9692 2347; Fax: (612) 9692 2559

Acknowledgments:
Additional photography by: Andy Payne pp. 10 (bottom), 27 (top), 87 (top), 123 (1, 2 & 3), 151 (top), 231 (bottom right), 232 (top left, top centre), 235 (top), 242 (bottom left), 291, 296; Rodney Weidland pp. 175 (bottom), 178, 191 (bottom), 286 (bottom), 287 (bottom).

The Publisher wishes to thank RYOBI for the use of the articles on the following pages: 84, 111 & 188.